Leveraging Computer Vision to Biometric Applications

Computer vision is an effective solution in a diverse range of real-life applications. With the advent of machine and deep learning paradigms, this book adopts machine and deep learning algorithms to leverage digital image processing for designing accurate biometric applications. In this aspect, it presents the advancements made in computer vision to biometric application design approaches using emerging technologies. It discusses the challenges of designing efficient and accurate biometric-based systems, which is a key issue that can be tackled via computer-vision-based techniques.

Key Features

- Discusses real-life applications of emerging techniques in computer vision systems
- Offers solutions on real-time computer vision and biometrics applications to cater to the needs of current industry
- Presents case studies to offer ideas for developing new biometrics-based products
- Offers problem-based solutions in the field computer vision and real-time biometric applications for secured human authentication
- Works as a ready resource for professionals and scholars working on emerging topics of computer vision for biometrics

The book is for academic researchers, scholars, and students in Computer Science, Information Technology, Electronics and Electrical Engineering, Mechanical Engineering, management, academicians, researchers, scientists, and industry people working on computer vision and biometrics applications.

Chapman & Hall/Distributed Computing and Intelligent Data Analytics Series

Series Editors: *Niranjanamurthy M and Sudeshna Chakraborty*

Leveraging Computer Vision to Biometric Applications
Arvind Selwal, Deepika Sharma, Mukesh Mann, Sudeshna Chakraborty,
Valentina E. Balas and Ouh Eng Lieh

Machine learning and Optimization Models for Optimization in Cloud
Punit Gupta, Mayank Kumar Goyal, Sudeshna Chakraborty, Ahmed A Elngar

Computer Applications in Engineering and Management
Parveen Berwal, Jagjit Singh Dhatterwal, Kuldeep Singh Kaswan, Shashi Kant

Artificial Intelligence: Applications and Innovations
Rashmi Priyadarshini, R M Mehra, Amit Sehgal, Prabhu Jyot Singh

Artificial Intelligence and Deep Learning for Computer Network: Management and Analysis
Sangita Roy, Rajat Subhra Chakraborty, Jimson Mathew, Arka Prokash Mazumdar
and Sudeshna Chakraborty

Advanced Computing Techniques for Optimization in Cloud
By Madhusudhan HS, Punit Gupta, Pradeep Singh Rawat

Leveraging Computer Vision to Biometric Applications
By Arvind Selwal, Deepika Sharma, Mukesh Mann, Sudeshna Chakraborty,
Valentina E. Balas and Ouh Eng Lieh

For more information about this series please visit: https://www.routledge.com/
Chapman–HallDistributed-Computing-and-Intelligent-Data-Analytics-Series/
book-series/DCID

Leveraging Computer Vision to Biometric Applications

Edited by
Arvind Selwal, Deepika Sharma, Mukesh Mann,
Sudeshna Chakraborty, Valentina E. Balas,
Ouh Eng Lieh

CRC Press
Taylor & Francis Group
Boca Raton London New York

CRC Press is an imprint of the
Taylor & Francis Group, an **informa** business

A CHAPMAN & HALL BOOK

First edition published 2025
by CRC Press
2385 NW Executive Center Drive, Suite 320, Boca Raton FL 33431

and by CRC Press
4 Park Square, Milton Park, Abingdon, Oxon, OX14 4RN

CRC Press is an imprint of Taylor & Francis Group, LLC

ISBN: 9781032614649 (hbk)
ISBN: 9781032614656 (pbk)
ISBN: 9781032614663 (ebk)

DOI: 10.1201/9781032614663

Typeset in Times
by KnowledgeWorks Global Ltd.

Contents

Preface

Computer vision has facilitated to design and develop tools in a diverse range of real-life applications. With the emergence of the machine and deep learning approaches, the task of image and video analysis has become comparatively easy. The various computer vision applications such as biometrics, satellite image analysis, surveillance, object detection, object recognition, image classification, and medical image analysis can be carried out with high accuracy and efficiency via machine learning. The majority of these applications include image or video analysis through distinctive characteristics that include micro-level or deep-level features. Thus, feature extraction and then classification of images are the main goals in computer vision that play a significant role in these applications. The widespread use of biometric recognition technology for identification and verification by government entities is the key driving factor for market growth.

One of the emerging areas of research is biometrics for secured human authentication that widely used in many smart applications. The key examples of biometric traits include fingerprint, iris, face, hand geometry, DNA, gait, palm print, voice, signature, vein pattern, and palm print. The biometrical-based systems are used to offer secured access in real-life applications such as secured surveillance, digital forensics, banking, smart homes, smart cities, border control, attendance monitoring, passport, and e-governance. However, designing efficient and accurate biometric-based systems is a key issue that can be tackled via computer-vision-based techniques.

This book aims to foster machine and deep learning approaches to image processing applications for designing biometrical applications. Original application-based research and review articles with model, build-data-driven applications using computational algorithms are included in different chapters. The reader will learn how different techniques can represent data-driven applications and their behaviors in order to extract key features. The book will enable researchers from academia and industry to share innovative applications and creative solutions to common problems using computer vision applications.

The book provides different approaches for the design perspective of computer vision-based biometric applications in various fields, and it will increase the focus of the research in the industry. It includes fundamental research contributions from the application of design related to secure computing applications to provide sustainable solutions for the future perspective.

The entire book has been organized into 16 chapters contributed by the prominent researchers where first few chapters acquaint the readers about basic concepts of biometrics along with major application areas. Few chapters illustrate a variety of security threats in typical biometric-based recognition systems, whereas another set of chapters focus on deploying computer-vision-enabled algorithms to tackle the security and privacy threats in biometric-based systems.

Editors

Arvind Selwal has been an Assistant Professor in the Department of Computer Science and Information Technology, Central University of Jammu, Jammu & Kashmir, India since 2013. He holds a BTech (CSE), MTech (CSE), and PhD (CSE) degrees as well as being qualified for UGC-NET (Assistant Professor) three times and GATE four times. He has more than 12 years of experience in teaching and research. His research interests include biometric security, cyber security, pattern recognition, digital image processing, lightweight cryptography, machine learning, and soft computing. He has contributed more than 72 research articles in various reputed international journals/conference proceedings/book chapters that are indexed in databases such as Web of Science, Scopus, and DBLP. He has served as a member of the technical program committee (TPC) at many reputed international conferences. He also serves as a reviewer of several international journals that are published by reputed publishers such as *Springer*, *Elsevier*, and *IEEE*. He has supervised 1 PhD and 21 MTech students and currently supervising 4 PhD scholars and 5 MTech students. He has authored a book titled *Fundamentals of Automata Theory and Computation* and co-editor of a book titled *Data Science and Innovations for Intelligent Systems Computational Excellence and Society 5.0* by Taylor & Francis. Besides being a resource person in many reputed workshops/FDPS, he is also a keen learner and enhances his skills by continuously participating in reputed international conferences/workshops. He is an active member of the Computer Society of India (CSI). Presently, he is undertaking two research projects as PI/Co-PI on the topic of computational security from funding agencies like DRDO, Ministry of Defence (Government of India), New Delhi, India.

Google Scholar link: https://scholar.google.com/citations?user=7bDyXWgAAAAJ

Deepika Sharma is an active researcher in the Department of Computer Science and Information Technology, Central University of Jammu, India, in the field of Biometrics Security. She has completed her PhD from the Central University of Jammu, India, in the field of Biometrics Security. She earned her master's degree in Computer Applications (MCA) from the Department of Computer Science and Information Technology, Central University of Jammu, Jammu and Kashmir, India, in 2017. Prior to that, she completed her Bachelor of Computer Applications (BCA) from the University of Jammu in 2014. Her research interests include biometric security, computer vision pattern recognition, machine learning, and deep learning. She has contributed more than 21 research articles in reputed international journals that are indexed in SCI/Scopus databases and conferences. She has cleared UGC-NET exam and SET (J&K) exam once. Recently, she has filed an Indian patent in 2022.

Google Scholar link: https://scholar.google.com/citations?user=TR82gAYAAAAJ&hl=en

Mukesh Mann is an Assistant Professor, Indian Institute of Information Technology (IIIT), Sonipat, India. He earned his PhD (Computer Science and Engineering) from Gautam Budha University. He earned his MTech degree from Gautam Budha University in Computer Science and Engineering. He has completed his BTech from Kurukshetra University in Computer Science and Engineering. His research interests include information security, computer vision blockchain, machine learning, and deep learning. He has contributed more than 30 research articles in reputed international journals that are indexed in SCI/Scopus databases and reputed national/international conferences. He is a recipient of the Direct Senior Research Fellow award in Computer Science and Engineering by the Council of Scientific and Industrial Research, Govt. of India. He was also awarded the Junior Research Fellowship award and the Senior Research Fellow award by the University Grant Commission (UGC), Govt. of India, for research and development.

Google Scholar link: https://scholar.google.com/citations?hl=en&user=GRvo5IkAAAAJ

Sudeshna Chakraborty is a research group leader and professor at the School of Computing Science & Engineering, Galgotias University, Greater Noida, India. She is an experienced academician in the field of Computer Science. She has a PhD in Computer Science & Engineering in Semantic Web Engineering, has versatile experience in industry and academics with the recipient of best IT faculty at INC Hyderabad, and was also a distinguished Academician in 2020–2021 at Sharda University. Dr. Chakraborty has acquired several other awards for the best paper presented, keynote speaker, reviewer's committee, session chairs, highest cited author, and many others. She was the recipient of the Outstanding Academician Award in 2020 and Research Excellence Award and the Academician's Award by the Institute of Scholars in 2021 and Nikhil Bhartiya Parishad Shiksha Parishad in 2022. She has chaired the IEEE conference in Paris ICACCE in 2018 and the Springer conference in Spain. She is the recipient of the Best Speaker Award on Roles & Trends of Engineers on Engineering Day by the Institution of Engineers of India.

She has been instrumental in various industrial interfacing for academic and research at her previous assignments at various organizations (Manav Rachna University, Mumbai University, Lingaya's, and others). She is has 75+ publications in Scopus Indexed/SCI/high-impact journals and international conferences, 18 patents published, and 4 granted. Dr. Chakraborty is guiding various PhD students at the university. She has successfully guided several PG and UG students; nevertheless, she has contributed to various prestigious accreditations like NAAC, NBA, QAA, WASC, UGC, IAU, IET, and others.

Google Scholar link: https://scholar.google.com/citations?hl=en&user=N-S8MMQAAAAJ

Valentina E. Balas is a Professor in the Department of Automatics and Applied Software at the Faculty of Engineering, Aurel Vlaicu University of Arad, Romania. She holds a PhD Cum Laude in Applied Electronics and Telecommunications from Polytechnic University of Timisoara. Dr. Balas is the author of more than 400 research papers. Her research interests are in intelligent systems, fuzzy control, soft computing, smart sensors, information fusion, and modeling and simulation.

She is the Editor-in-Chief to *IJAIP* and IJCSysE journals in Inderscience, a member of the editorial board of several national and international journals, and evaluator expert for national and international projects and PhD thesis. Dr. Balas is the Director of the Intelligent Systems Research Centre and Director of the Department of International Relations at Aurel Vlaicu University of Arad. During the interval 2021–2022, she was a member of the IEEE European Public Policy Committee Working Group on ICT. From May 2023, Dr. Balas is an associate member of the Romanian Academy of Scientists.

She is the recipient of the "Tudor Tanasescu" Prize from the Romanian Academy for contributions to the field of soft computing methods (2019), "Stefan Odobleja" Prize from the Romanian Academy of Scientists (2023), and Diploma – Section Information Technology from The General Association of the Engineers in Romania (AGIR) 2023.

Google Scholar link: https://scholar.google.com/citations?hl=en&user=XaktX0wA AAAJ

Ouh Eng Lieh earned his PhD in Computer Science (Software Engineering) from the National University of Singapore. He is currently involved in undergraduate education as Assistant Professor of Information Systems (Education) at the School of Computing and Information Systems, Singapore Management University. His research interests are in software reuse and education pedagogy. He served as a member of the program committee of several conferences and has numerous publications in the software engineering, computer science, and information systems education conferences. He is involved in several large-scale information technology industry projects for a decade before joining academia as an educator. His research areas are software reuse, software architecture design, design thinking, and analytics with publications in both the information systems and education conferences (e.g. CAiSE, ITiCSE, FIE, TALE, ICCE). He is passionate to deliver quality and innovative systems in his works. His expertise is recognized with engagements to provide an independent expert view in both technical competencies of personnel and curriculum design of technical programs. He has experience delivering courses for postgraduate students, undergraduate students, and industry participants in the software engineering areas including design thinking, practical software architecture design, security engineering, and mobile development. He received multiple teaching excellence awards and industry projects recognition awards throughout his career. He is currently an active member of ACM and ISC2 and a senior member of IEEE.

Google Scholar link: https://scholar.google.com/citations?hl=en&user=ISlJfAEAAAAJ

Contributors

Maroi Agrebi
Université Polytechnique
   Hauts-deFrance
Valenciennes, France

Tsleem Arif
BGSB University,
Rajouri, India

Pavan Kumar B.K
RajaRajeswari College of Engineering
Bengaluru, India

Youakim Badr
Pennsylvania State University,
University Park, Pennsylvania

Rajdeep Bhadra
Jadavpur University, Jadavpur
   University Second Campus
Kolkata, India

Shashi Bhushan
Amity School of Engineering and
   Technology
Amity University
Patna, India

Nandini Chandru
Christ University,
Bengaluru, India

Praveena Chaturvedi
Gurukul Kangri University
Haridwar, India

Pankaj Kumar Dhiman
Jaypee University of Information
   Technology (JUIT)
Solan, India

Vishal Garg
JMIETI,
Radaur, India

Gulshan Goyal
Chandigarh College of Engineering and
   Technology (Degree Wing)
Chandigarh, India

Shaik Jumlesha
Annamacharya Institute of Technology
   and Science
Kadapa, India

Navjot Kaur Kanwal
Dr. Harisingh Gour Vishwavidyalaya
Sagar, India

Shekhar Karanwal
Department of CSE,
Chandigarh Engineering College,
   CGC, Landran
Mohali, India

Kashishpreet Kaur
Chandigarh College of Engineering and
   Technology (Degree Wing)
Chandigarh, India

Kuldeep U. Kawar
Dr. Harisingh Gour Vishwavidyalaya
Sagar, India

Ashok Koujalagi
Godavari Institute Engineering and
   Technology
Rajahmundry, India

Satish Kumar
BGSB University
Rajouri, India

Shivam Kumar
Chandigarh College of Engineering and
    Technology (Degree Wing)
Chandigarh, India

Sunil Kumar
Guru Jambheshwar University of
    Science & Technology
Hisar, India

Tajinder Kumar
JMIETI
Radaur, India

Ambika Nagaraj
St. Francis College
Bangalore, India

Silpa Nair
Dr. Harisingh Gour Vishwavidyalaya
Sagar, India

N. Merrin Prasanna
Annamacharya Institute of Technology
    & Sciences (Autonomous)
Kadapa, India

S. Hrushikesava Raju
Koneru Lakshmalah Education
    Foundation, Green Fields
Guntur, India

Ambreen Sabha
Central University of Jammu
Samba, India

Mridhu Sahu
National Institute of Technology
Raipur, India

Adinarayana Salina
Department of Computer Science and
    Systems Engineering
College of Engineering
Andhra University
Visakhapatnam, India

Arvind Selwal
Central University of Jammu
Samba, India

Uruturu Sesadri
Vardhman College of Engineering
Hyderabad, India

Ankita Sharma
Chandigarh College of Engineering and
    Technology (Degree Wing)
Chandigarh, India

Annu Sharma
RajaRajeswari College of Engineering
Bengaluru, India

Deepika Sharma
Central University of Jammu
Samba, India

Neha Sharma
Jaypee University of Information
    Technology (JUIT)
Solan, India

Pooja Sharma
JMIT
Radaur, India

Pawan Kumar Singh
Jadavpur University, Jadavpur
    University Second Campus
Salt Lake, India

Neha Singhal
Christ University
Bengaluru, India

Chinu Singla
Punjabi University
Patiala, India

Vivek Upadhyaya
Poornima University
Jaipur, India

Zeenat Zahra
Central University of Jammu
Samba, India

1 Biometrics
Introduction and Applications

Deepika Sharma and Arvind Selwal

1.1 INTRODUCTION

The term biometrics has been coined from the combination of two Greek words "Bio" which is related to life and "metrics" denotes measurement. Hence, biometrics is a science where humans are recognized on their distinctive behavioural, physiological, and chemical traits. The extension of secured authorization in the modern era brings with it a foremost apprehension of security risk. Such threats must be handled by establishing robust and extremely efficient pattern recognition algorithms. As a result, biometric authentication is favoured over traditional human recognition systems [1]. As traditional systems are knowledge-driven ("what do you remember?" such as login credentials, PIN codes), or token-enabled ("what do you acquire?" such as smart cards and ID cards), such presentations of identification are susceptible to various attacks, loss, and theft. Modern biometric-based methods, on the other hand, establish an individual's identity and integrity based on "who we are?" rather than memorizing or holding anything [2]. The distinctive biometric traits that have been discovered over the time in human body are depicted in Figure 1.1.

The traits which are typically used in the biometric recognition system are summarized in Table 1.1 along with their characteristic features, strengths and weaknesses.

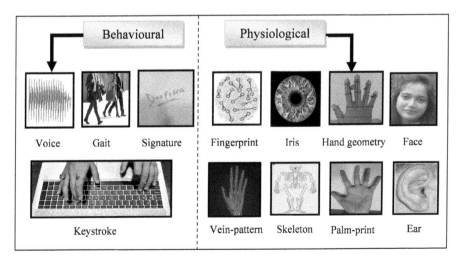

FIGURE 1.1 A depiction of behavioural and physiological biometrical traits.

DOI: 10.1201/9781032614663-1

1

TABLE 1.1

Description of Various Biometric Traits that Can Be Used for Authenticating an Individual

Biometric Trait/Type	Description	Typical Features	Strengths	Weakness
Face Physical	Facial attributes are the most common features used by individuals for recognition process. The most common approaches to face recognition are based on the location and spatial relationships of nose, chin, eyes, lip, and eyebrows.	Relative position and shape of nose, lips, eyes, and position of cheekbones.	• Totally non-intrusive that is no physical contact is involved. • Similar to human process of authentication. • Convenience and matured technology.	• In case of identical twins uniqueness is not guaranteed. • Varying expressions could affect the accuracy. • 2D data contains limited information.
Iris Physical	Iris is the region that is bounded by the pupil and the white portion of the eye. The iris texture carries the distinctive information that is useful for recognition of a person.	Furrows and striations in iris. Arching ligaments, ridges, crypts, rings, corona, freckles, and a zigzag collarets.	• Highly scalable. • No physical contact with the system. • Minimal false acceptance rate.	• Relatively costlier. • Challenging at a long distance. • User cooperation is needed for accurate scanning.
Fingerprint Physical	Fingerprints were used in identification process for many centuries and its matching accuracy is very high. Every individual has unique structure of ridges and valleys on his or her fingers, which is used for identification or verification purpose.	Location and direction of ridge endings and bifurcations on fingerprint.	• Highly reliable and more secure. • Matching process is fast as the size of template is small. • It consumes less memory space.	• Easily deceived through fake fingerprints made of silicon. • Scars or cuts on finger can produce obstruction in the recognition process. • Exposed to noise or distortion due to twists and dirt.

(Continued)

TABLE 1.1 (Continued)
Description of Various Biometric Traits that Can Be Used for Authenticating an Individual

Biometric Trait/Type	Description	Typical Features	Strengths	Weakness
Hand geometry Physical	Hand Geometry follows simple techniques of processing. It is less distinctive hence cannot be used for verification or identification of a person from a large set of population.	Height and width of bones, density of the palm and joints in hands and fingers.	• Durable and user friendly. • Non-intrusive • Failure to enroll (FTE) rate is low.	• Not unique and less accurate. • Wearing of Jewellery may cause problem while scanning. • Fairly expensive
Ear Physical	Ear geometry is used for recognition of individual using shape of the ear. The shapes and characteristic of human ear are usually distinct. A shape verifier similar to handset of telephone contains a lighting unit and a camera to capture the image of an ear also known as Otophone.	Shape of year and the structure of a tissue of pinna.	• Faster identification • Processing time is less. • Most reliable and computational complexity is less.	• Blurred recognition because of the effect of hats, hair and earrings. • Recognition error may come as the images are not perfect always. • Less distinctive.
Voice Behavioural	The voice features of an individual are based on the size and shape of the vocal tracts, nasal cavities, lips, and the mouth that are used for sound synthesis.	Frequency, cadence and duration of vocal Pattern. Vocal tracts, mouth, nasal cavities, and lips that are used in creating a sound.	• No need for any extra new device. • Low cost. • Easy to implement.	• Vulnerable to quality of noise and microphone. • Can be easily forged. • High rate of false non match.

(Continued)

TABLE 1.1 (Continued)
Description of Various Biometric Traits that Can Be Used for Authenticating an Individual

Biometric Trait/Type	Description	Typical Features	Strengths	Weakness
Signature Behavioural	The way an individual signs his or her name is said to be a unique characteristic of that individual.	Speed, order, pressure, and appearance of signature.	• Accuracy rate is reasonable. • Restoration of template is easy if it is stolen. • Public acceptance is wide.	• Individual's signature may change over time. • One individual can have contradictory signature. • Signatures can be forged easily.
Palm print Physical	Palm has also ridges and valleys structure but palm has larger area than finger so it is expected to be more distinctive than fingerprint.	Ridge and valley features, principal lines, and wrinkles.	• More consistent and lasting in nature. • Good recognition even with a low-resolution camera. • More distinctive than fingerprint.	• Recognition problem for less quality images. • Scanners are bulkier and expensive. • Distortions in an unrestrained environment.
Keystroke Behavioural	Keystroke is a way each individual types on keyboard, it is a behavioural biometric, and it offers less distinctive information.	Keyed sequence and duration between characters.	• Identification is secured and fast. • No extra training is required for registering the live samples. • Needs no new sensors or special hardware.	• Less convenient in use. • No discriminating information. • Change of keyboard can change the typing speed or style.
Gait Behavioural	Gait refers to the way in which an individual walks. However, this feature is affected by numerous factors, including the nature of clothing, choice of footwear, shape of the legs, walking area, etc.	Peculiar way in which one walks.	• It is a non-invasive technology. • Convenient in usage. • Simply acquired from distance.	• Less reliable technique • Accuracy is less. • More computations are required.

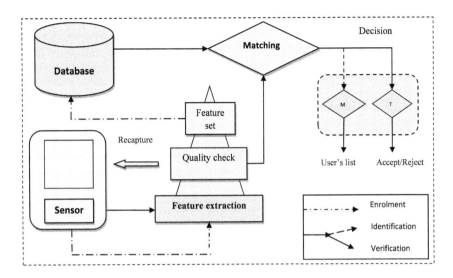

FIGURE 1.2 An architecture of biometric-based recognition system.

The generic architecture of a biometric system is shown in Figure 1.2, which highlights its key sub-modules such as sensor, quality assessment, and feature extractor, matching algorithm and template database. The raw biometrical information from users is acquired through a sensing device (i.e. a fingerprint sensor, iris scanner, and hand scanner). Thereafter, the quality of the captured samples is assessed and appropriate operations are applied to remove any type of undesired signals like noise, blurriness, and inconsistencies. Then, the distinctive characteristics from the samples are extracted by a specific feature extraction algorithm that yields a characteristic template. The resultant templates of registered users are placed in a centralized database module. To authenticate an enrolled user, a matching procedure is used to perform a comparison among query template and the already stored data yielding a matching score that is used for decision-making process. In addition, a biometric-based human recognition system (BHRS) operates in two phases: enrolment and identification or verification as shown in Figure 1.2. A learning phase known as enrolment mode seeks to gather biometric data about individuals in order to identify them. The biometric traits of the prospective users are recorded by a biometric sensor during this phase, rendered digitally (as signatures), and then saved in the template database or learned by a classifier [3, 4]. Once, all the users have been successfully enrolled to use the biometric system for secured authentication then it can be operated in either verification or identification mode. Typically, the verification mode is used in the applications where identity of a user is established by comparing the query templates with the already information of the same person. Thus, the verification mode employs one-to-one comparison by using a unique ID assigned to the user at the time of enrolment, which helps in searching the corresponding template in the database. These modes are generally deployed in simple biometric applications such as attendance, welfare disbursement schemes, and passports; on the other hand, by comparing the provided template with every other template stored, the identity of an individual can be determined in identification mode where the identity of user is revealed by comparing the presented template with all the saved templates stored in the data repository through one to many procedure. Therefore, this mode is most appropriately deployed in, critical biometrical areas such as forensics, parenthood determination, criminal identification, and border control [5].

By comparing the provided template with every template stored, the identity of an individual can be determined in identification mode.

1.2 BIOMETRIC CHARACTERISTICS

A variety of applications use different biometric characteristics. Each of biometric trait has its pros and cons, and therefore, the choice of a biometric trait for any application depends on multiple issues besides its performance (PR). Jain et al. [1] have found seven different factors that determine the suitability of a biometric trait to be used in any biometric application. **Universality (UV):** Each individual who accesses any biometric application should have the biometric characteristic [6]. **Uniqueness (UQ):** Each individual should have distinct feature. **Permanence (PM):** The biometric trait should be constant; it should not be changeable with time. **Measurability (MB):** The biometric trait should be possible to acquire and digitize by using appropriate devices that do not cause inconvenience to an individual. **PR:** The recognition system should meet accuracy, speed, and robustness. **Acceptability (AC):** Individuals utilizing the application should willingly present their biometric trait to the biometric recognizing system [6]. **Circumvention (CV):** The ease with which the trait of an individual can be counterfeit using artefacts. Different biometric traits are compared on the basis of these characteristics as shown in Table 1.2.

1.3 CONVENTIONAL HUMAN IDENTIFICATION MECHANISMS

Human identification has been used in a diverse range of real-life applications and these mechanisms have been in practice since ancient times. One of the significant applications of human centred authentication has been used in forensics where

TABLE 1.2
The Comparison of Various Biometric Traits Based on the above-mentioned Characteristics (Adapted from Ref. [7])

Biometric Trait	Characteristic						
	UV	UQ	PM	MB	PR	AC	CV
Face	High	High	Medium	High	Low	High	High
Fingerprint	Medium	High	High	Medium	High	Medium	Medium
Iris	High	High	High	Medium	High	Low	Low
Signature	Low	Low	Low	High	Low	High	High
Keystroke	Low	Low	Low	Medium	Low	Medium	Medium
Voice	Medium	Low	Low	Medium	Low	High	High
Hand Geometry	High	High	High	Medium	High	High	High

security personals used to identify criminals from the crime sides by gathering manual information. In another case, individuals have been verified by presenting a printed ID card such as voter ID, ration card, student ID, passport, PAN card, and driving licence. Furthermore, various government welfare schemes used to be launched via traditional manual procedures in paper formats to prove the identity of the valid beneficiaries. One of the real-life examples of government public schemes includes ration distribution to individuals below poverty line. Another scenario is human authentication in education sector where various scholarships or fellowships are offered to students through manual submission and validation procedures. To safeguard physical assets such as home, buildings, and vehicles, traditional mechanical lock-key systems were in practice since past several decades. Moreover, for online human identification in Indian banks, the old password or PINs were frequently utilized by the customers or officials. However, these conventional methods suffer from several issues that may lead to inconvenience to public due to different fraudulent attempts. The manual forensics applications are time-consuming and may be sometimes ineffective to identify criminals due to lifting latent fingerprints from the crime sites. Besides, the manual mechanisms of implementing various welfare schemes in a large population of 1.4 billion can be a tedious task to the government departments. In addition, several cases of welfare disbursement scams have been reported in recent past where the actual beneficiaries were not benefitted from the schemes. The verification methods that rely on passwords and PINs may suffer from several drawbacks where the passwords can be hacked by the attacker and PINs may be forgotten that result in several cyber frauds. Likewise, the traditional lock-key mechanism used to secure human assets can be vulnerable as locks can be broken and keys can be duplicated or misplaced.

1.4 PARADIGM SHIFT: TRADITIONAL TO BIOMETRIC-ENABLED AUTHENTICATION

In India, since last decade the traditional human authentication approaches are being frequently replaced with modern biometric-based recognition systems. One of the most significant initiatives taken by Indian Government includes the implementation of unique identification number (AADHAAR) for every citizen of India. In comparison to traditional mechanisms in India, the AADHAAR system helps to identify or verify the validity of an individual via three key modalities of the users. Thus, the modern method of human identification has significantly improved the effective and accurate implementation of various government schemes such as fellowships or scholarships, driving licence, ration distribution, competitive examinations, employees attendance, health insurance under AAYUSHMAN scheme, banking sector, and RSBY (Rashtriya Swasthya Bima Yojna), among others. Moreover, according to expert market research (EMR) report, the size of the Indian biometrics market reached approximately to 2.56 billion USD in 2022. Furthermore, the market share is anticipated to continue expanding between 2023 and 2028 at a compound annual growth rate (CAGR) of 14.5%, reaching a value of around 5.77 billion USD. The increased level of product integration in consumer electronics is the key reason behind the growth of biometrics market in India. Because biometrics is being increasingly adopted by both the public and business sectors, the nation has experienced tremendous growth in recent years. Additionally, the biometrics industry in India is assisting the worldwide biometrics market's expansion, which is being fuelled by banks and other organization's increasing use of biometric technologies to prevent fraud. The growing use of various biometric technologies, including facial, fingerprint, and voice recognition to verify identity and process payments, is the key driver of the Indian biometrics industry. Additionally, various applications areas in India, where biometric-enabled recognition systems are rapidly replacing the conventional knowledge-based approaches, are discussed in detail [8].

1.4.1 AADHAAR

In January 2009, the Unique Identification Authority of India (UIDAI) was created to assign each Indian citizen a "Aadhaar Number" or UID number by utilizing their biometric (face, eye's iris scan and the prints of all the fingers of your hand) and demographic (name, address, contact number, and age) information as shown in Figure 1.3.

These details are recorded at a centralized database which is monitored and maintained by the UIDAI. Besides keeping a record of all the details, UIDAI also allows an individual to update details on AADHAAR cards [9].

1.4.2 VISA APPLICATION PROCESS

Biometric-based recognition plays a vital role in the application process of Visa. All the applicants need to enroll with ten finger prints and face image captured by

FIGURE 1.3 A depiction of capturing biometric modalities for AADHAAR enrolment.

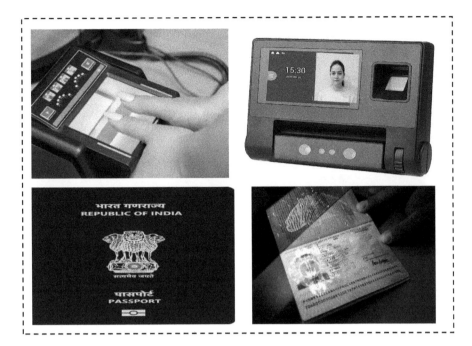

FIGURE 1.4 Biometrics role in I visa and passport processing.

facial cameras as shown in Figure 1.4. Providing biometrics data helps to secure the identity of legitimate applicants and to prevent forged attempts by the intruders. Consequently, it becomes easier for users to prove their identity and helps country to tackle immigration abuse and frauds.

1.4.3 Welfare Disbursement

The infrastructure required to efficiently process and deliver payments to welfare programme participants is typically lacking in the people with low- and middle income. Subsequently, large number of poor people are either financially excluded or only receive a percentage of the resources that have been allocated for them. Hence, Public Distribution System (PDS) that makes use of biometric-enabled identification demonstrates the revolutionary impact on anti-poverty initiatives as shown in Figure 1.5.

Such change may be viewed as an incremental remedy if its policy context is not taken into account, consisting of the introduction of biometric security to address the problem of market diversion. Although it represents a fundamental shift in various program's architecture, the policy intention behind it is to move to a cash transfer system that does away with the distortions and opportunities for leakage caused by subsidies remains to be determined. When seen in this context, the PDS's biometric reconstruction represents a political shift that will have a significant impact on benefits of participants of any government scheme [10].

FIGURE 1.5 Deploying biometric modalities in social welfare disbursement schemes and secure payments.

1.4.4 BIOMETRIC-ENABLED LOCKING SYSTEM

Smart biometric locks are door and safe-locking systems that use biometric technology such as fingerprints, voice, or facial recognition to lock and unlock as depicted in Figure 1.6. Nowadays the traditional locks and security solutions are over and locks are becoming more reliable through the use of biometric-based identification. The growing significance and focus on security and safety have spurred innovation in the security industry, leading to the emergence of smart lock systems. With the advent of these smart locks, the extra level of security they provide has made homes and businesses safer and more secure [11].

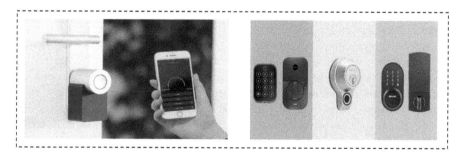

FIGURE 1.6 A depiction of secured biometric-enabled locks.

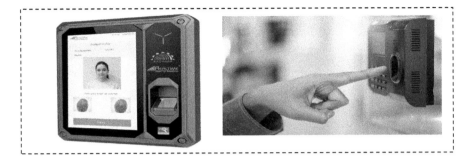

FIGURE 1.7   A representation of biometric modalities in attendance system.

1.4.5 BIOMETRICS IN EDUCATION

Biometrics give a perfect arrangement for school, college, and universities administrators in their endeavours to distinguish understudies, convey exact and auditable understudy records, and guarantee a more secure environment for understudies, instructors, and staff. Finger checking biometric innovation can also give benefits in terms of comfort, security, speed, precision, and security. The innovation is most frequently being utilized for nourishment benefit, participation, library, transportation, connected learning, and security purposes with finger filtering being the essential. Apart from this, biometrics promotes online education by giving students who are unable to attend class a substitute that will allow them to keep up their progress. It offers the option of distance learning for those who are unable to relocate to complete their academic degrees. It is the most economical option that does away with paperwork and drawn-out processes as illustrated in Figure 1.7 [11].

1.4.6 BIOMETRIC IN BANKING SYSTEM

By offering reliable identity verification and security solutions, biometrics plays a crucial part in contemporary banking. It improves authentication procedures by leveraging distinctive physical or behavioural qualities like fingerprints, facial recognition, or speech patterns, strengthening the security of client accounts and transactions. In addition to streamlining customer on boarding and access to digital banking services, biometric technologies reduce the risk of fraud and unauthorized access as portrayed in Figure 1.8. This technology enhances the overall security and ease of banking operations by enabling banks to comply with regulatory standards, ensuring efficient and secure customer experiences, and supporting the evolving remote and mobile banking landscape [11].

1.4.7 BIOMETRIC IN VEHICLE SYSTEM

Particularly in the automotive and transportation sectors, biometrics is becoming a more important component of vehicles. Using biometrics for driver identification in automotive applications enables the car to adapt settings like seat position, mirrors,

FIGURE 1.8   Biometric for secured banking services.

and climate control to the preferences of the recognized driver. To lower the danger of theft and unauthorized usage, biometric authentication can also be integrated into vehicle entry and ignition systems. By guaranteeing that only authorized drivers use cars in commercial transportation, biometrics can improve fleet management and help preserve safety and regulatory compliance. The future of transportation will be shaped by biometric technology as it continues to advance and revolutionize vehicle security, personalization, and safety [11].

1.4.8   Critical Infrastructure and Defence Services

The use of biometrics is essential in the modern period as a mechanism to safeguard military installations, protect a variety of armed forces operations, and control access to physical military locations. The capacity to deny entry to an unauthorized individual or enemy trying to enter a closed facility or a restricted area of troops/militants space is provided by biometric access control systems that use fingerprint, face, or iris scanners. Armed forces, the navy, the air force, or any other military agency can benefit from biometric technology's ability to supply reliable, scalable, high-performance, and off-the-shelf access control solutions. In addition, biometric technology aids governments in restricting the entry of adversaries and, if their biometric information is already saved, even in identifying intruders. Additionally, by maximizing real-time data on the invaders, it can enable border control officials or authorities to enhance border control intelligence as shown in Figure 1.9 [12].

Besides, it has been observed that the popularity and usage of various biometric-based applications are increasing in various sectors across the world. According to a recent report published by Jaemont, the market-wise share of various biometric traits is shown in Figure 1.10 (a). It can be clearly observed that fingerprint recognition systems are the most widely deployed among all followed by face and iris biometric modalities.

Moreover, Figure 1.10 (b) reveals that the global market industry is growing exponentially, which leads to various opportunities for research in this field. It is also predicted that the revenue may grow at a rate of 9.2% from 2021 to 2027 that can be approximately estimated as 3.81 billion dollars. Figure 1.10 (c) illustrates

FIGURE 1.9 Biometrics for secured identification in Indian defence services.

that these systems are frequently used for security in government applications (with a share of 35%) for implementing various schemes such as ADHAAR, welfare disbursement, and passport or driving license issuance. Another area of application includes banking and finance sector where these systems are used for secured transactions or ATM security. The continent-wise deployment of various biometric-based security systems is shown in Figure 1.10 (d) where Asia is the leading

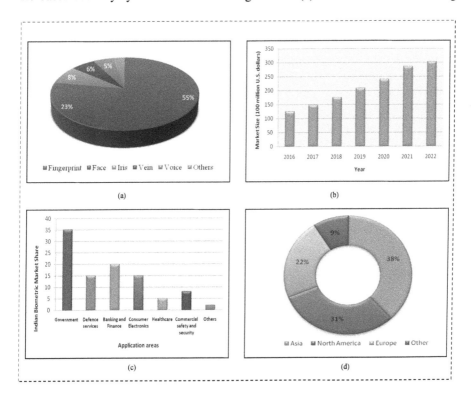

FIGURE 1.10 Statistics of biometrical-based systems (a) percentage share of biometric traits in the market (b) year-wise market growth of biometric technology (c) Indian biometric market share by end users (d) regional market distribution for biometrics.

continent with a share of 38% followed by North America with 31%. In nutshell, the field of biometrics has fascinated the world of secured human authentication in wide range of applications. Hence, the area of biometric offers several opportunities and challenges for designing more accurate as well as efficient BHRSs.

1.5   BIOMETRICS PERFORMANCE METRICS

A variety of biometric systems have been developed during the past decades, which are prone to some intrinsic failure. These failures are mainly due to error which occurs during the testing phase of the biometric system. A biometric system will be considered to perform more accurately if it results in lower error rates. Hence, to comparatively evaluate the biometric system, a variety of performance metrics have been used by the researchers which are explained below [1, 13].

   i. *False Acceptance Rate (FAR):* FAR is the rate at which imposters are successfully accepted as genuine users by the biometric system. FAR may be computed by using Equation 1.1.

$$FAR = \frac{\text{Number of Accepted Imposters}}{\text{Total Imposters trials}} \times 100 \qquad (1.1)$$

   ii. *False Reject Rate (FRR):* FRR is the rate at which genuine users are considered imposter by the biometric system. FRR may be computed by using Equation 1.2.

$$FRR = \frac{\text{Number of Rejected Genuines}}{\text{Total Genuine trials}} \times 100 \qquad (1.2)$$

   iii. *Genuine Accept Rate (GAR):* It is the rate at which the biometric system successfully accepts the genuine user as a genuine. GAR may be computed by using Equation 1.3.

$$GAR = 1 - FRR \qquad (1.3)$$

   iv. *Equal Error Rate (ERR):* ERR is the point at which the imposter score overlaps with the genuine score as shown in Figure 1.11.
   v. *Identification Accuracy:* It is a measure of the overall acceptance rate of all the enrolled users in the biometric system. This may be computed in terms of error rate like FAR and FRR as using Equation 1.4

$$\text{Identification Accuracy} = \left(1 - \frac{FAR + FRR}{2}\right) \times 100 \qquad (1.4)$$

   vi. *Receiver Operating Curve (ROC Curve):* It is a curve between FAR and FRR observed at different levels of threshold as shown in Figure 1.12.

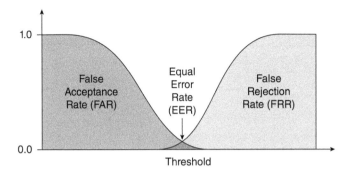

FIGURE 1.11   Equal error rate.

1.6   BIOMETRIC SECURITY ISSUES

The conventional systems that utilize passwords, PINs, tokens, etc. to validate an enrolled user are prone to variety of attacks. Hence, biometric recognition systems can help to mitigate the issues that are linked with the traditional methods of authentication and require more effort from adversaries to breach the security aspects [14–16]. Recently, it has been observed that biometric technologies are replacing conventional recognition systems as these are comparatively efficient, reliable and provide high security but are also susceptible to various attacks [17]. Usually, biometric systems while processing a captured biometrical trait through sub-modules for human authentication purpose are subjected to a variety of assaults or security breaches [18]. According to Ratha et al. [17], there exist eight typical sensitive points

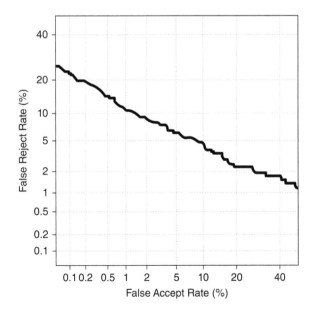

FIGURE 1.12   Receiver operating curve.

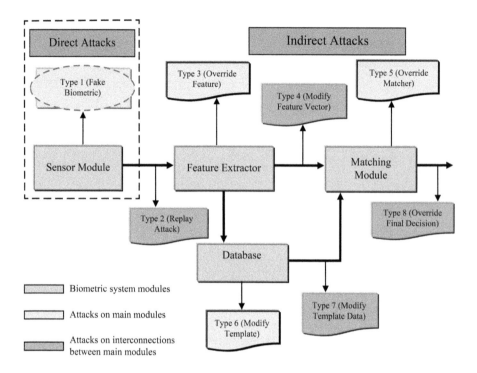

FIGURE 1.13   A biometric recognition system framework illustrating eight probable attack points [17].

in a BHRS where adversaries can host various kinds of attacks. Consequently, these systems are vulnerable to attacks, which may put their security at risk and result in degradation in overall performance or a complete system failure [19]. These vulnerable points may be categorized as direct as well as indirect attacks as shown in Figure 1.13. In direct assaults that include only Type 1 attack, the explicit knowledge regarding the internal functioning of the overall system is not vital to the attacker. On the contrary, in case of indirect attacks (Type 2–Type 8) the adversary somehow manages to gather internal technical information about the BHRS from various sources. The internal information about the feature extraction algorithm, the logic behind the matcher, the threshold for decision process, template information as well as data related to their communication links is used by the attacker to hinder the overall operation of the biometric system [20].

It is evident from the literature, in comparison to indirect attacks; the direct one is the most frequently attempted threats on a biometric authentication system. In Type 1, i.e. spoofing or presentation attack, an attacker creates an exact artificial replica of the bonafide biometric trait and circumvents the sensor device to get illegal access to the authentication system, whereas **Type 2,** which is also termed attack on the communication channel between the scanner and the feature extractor module. The channel is detained to steal the raw data and the intercepted information can be replayed later to feature extractor to circumvent the sensor module. The **Type 3 attack** is on the feature extractor component of a biometric system where the attacker uses a Trojan horse to modify the feature extractor algorithm of the system. In this case an intruder overrides the feature extraction algorithm to yield a feature vector as desired by the imposter instead of extracting feature vectors from a real biometrical source. The **Type 4 attack** point is known as "Attack on the channel between the feature extractor and matcher." The attacker seizes the communication link between the matcher and the feature extractor component for stealing the templates of a real user and playing them back to the matcher module later. The **Type 5** attack point is known as "Attack on the matcher." In this case, the matcher algorithm is replaced with a Trojan horse program in the biometric-enabled system. The attacker can give commands to the Trojan horse program for producing high matching scores regardless of the scores obtained from original template data [21]. The point where an attack is hosted on the centralized template storage database is known as **Type 6**. The attacker gets unauthorized access to the template database and tries to compromise the template data by modifying these using operations such as deletion, updation or cross-linking the templates of enrolled users. In addition, **the Type 7** point is coined as "Attack on the channel between the system database and matcher module." The attacker deflects the communication channel which lies between the database and matcher to either steal or update the data. Finally, in **Type 8** assault, an attacker may nullify the overall decision provided by the matching module and it is a kind of bypass attack [18].

REFERENCES

1. A. K. Jain and A. Ross, *Handbook of Biometrics*, A. K. Jain, P. Flynn and A. A. Ross, Eds. Springer London, 2008, pp. 1–22.
2. A. K. Jain, A. Ross and S. Prabhakar, "An Introduction to Biometric Recognition," *IEEE Trans. Circuits Syst. Video Technol.*, vol. 14, no. 1, pp. 4–20, 2004. doi: 10.1109/TCSVT.2003.818349
3. D. Sharma and A. Selwal, "FinPAD: State-of-the-Art of Fingerprint Presentation Attack Detection Mechanisms, Taxonomy and Future Perspectives," *Pattern Recognit. Lett.*, vol. 152, no. 1, pp. 225–252, 2021.
4. D. Sharma and A. Selwal, "A Survey on Face Presentation Attack Detection Mechanisms: Hitherto and Future Perspectives," *Multimed. Syst.*, vol. 29, no. 3, pp. 1527–1577, 2023. doi: 10.1007/s00530-023-01070-5
5. A. K. Jain and A. Kumar, "Biometrics of Next Generation : An Overview," 2010.
6. Z. Rui and Z. Yan, "A Survey on Biometric Authentication : Towards Secure and Privacy-Preserving," *IEEE Access*, vol. 7, pp. 5994–6009, 2018. doi: 10.1109/ACCESS.2018.2889996
7. A., Jain, R., Bolle, and S. Pankanti (1996). *Introduction to Biometrics*. In A. K. Jain, R., Bolle, S. Pankanti (Eds) *Biometrics*. Springer, Boston, MA. https://doi.org/10.1007/0-306-47044-6_
8. S. Sumner, "Biometrics and the Future," *Syngress*, vol. 2, pp. 183–198, 2016.
9. S. Agarwal, S. Banerjee and S. Sharma, "Privacy and Security of Aadhaar: A Computer Science Perspective," *Econ. Polit. Wkly.*, vol. 52, pp. 93–102, 2017.
10. S. Masiero, "Biometric Infrastructures and the Indian Public Distribution System," *South Asia Multidiscip. Acad. J.*, 2023, doi: 10.4000/samaj.6459
11. "Biometrics: Definition, Use Cases, Latest News," *Thales Building a Future We Can All Trust*, 2023. https://www.thalesgroup.com/en/markets/digital-identity-and-security/government/inspired/biometricshave, regulated legal and technical framework.

12. A. Singh, "How Biometrics Technology Can Be Used in Defence and Intelligence," *Mantra Innovation That Counts*, 2019, https://blog.mantratec.com/how-biometrics-technology-can-be-used-in-defence-and-intelligence#:~:text=Merits%20of%20Biometrics%20in%20Defence&text=Easily%20tracks%20any%20unauthorized%20access,combatant%20commands%20and%20military%20services

13. A. K. Jain, A. Ross, S. Pankanti and S. Member, "Biometrics : A Tool for Information Security," *IEEE Trans. Inf. Forensics Secur.*, vol. 1, no. 2, pp. 125–143, 2006.

14. D. Sharma and A. Selwal, "On Data-Driven Approaches for Presentation Attack Detection in Iris Recognition Systems," 2021.

15. D. Sharma and A. Selwal, "An Intelligent Approach for Fingerprint Presentation Attack Detection Using Ensemble Learning With Improved Local Image Features," *Multimed. Tools Appl.*, no. 0123456789, 2021, doi: 10.1007/s11042-021-11254-8

16. D. Sharma and A. Selwal, "HyFiPAD : A Hybrid Approach for Fingerprint Presentation Attack Detection Using Local and Adaptive Image Features," *Vis. Comput.*, no. 0123456789, 2021, doi: 10.1007/s00371-021-02173-8

17. N. K. Ratha, J. H. Connell and R. M Bolle, "An Analysis of Minutiae Matching Strength," pp. 223–228, 2001.

18. C. Roberts, "Biometric Attack Vectors and Defences," *Comput. Secur.*, vol. 26, no. 1, pp. 14–25, 2007, doi: https://10.1016/j.cose.2006.12.008

19. W. Yang, S. Wang, J. Hu and G. Zheng, "SS symmetry Security and Accuracy of Fingerprint-Based Biometrics : A Review," 2019, doi: 10.3390/sym11020141

20. M. Adámek, M. Matýsek and P. Neumann, "Security of Biometric Systems," *Procedia Eng.*, vol. 100, pp. 169–176, 2015, doi: 10.1016/j.proeng.2015.01.355

21. A. Adler and S. A. C. Schuckers, "Biometric Vulnerabilities : Overview Identity Claim (A) Presentation (B), " pp. 1–11, 2014, doi: 10.1007/978-3-642-27733-7

2 Security and Privacy Issues in Existing Biometric Systems and Solutions

Annu Sharma, Praveena Chaturvedi, Neha Singhal, Nandini C., and Pavan Kumar B.K

2.1 INTRODUCTION

Recent developments in the rapidly evolving field of automatic recognition have raised issues regarding its security and privacy. The past decade has witnessed a rapid increase in biometrics research in addition to the deployment of large-scale biometrics solutions in both civilian and law enforcement applications. The exponential growth of biometric systems and their rapid adaption lead to a concern that these systems may compromise the security and privacy of individuals. For a particular application, it is a challenging task to choose the best recognition system; a number of core research issues are there which still need to be addressed in this field. This chapter is a detailed study of various issues and challenges in existing biometric systems and also techniques involved in providing solutions to these issues. To ensure the safety and security of human recognition systems, it is advised to modify these systems to create concealable templates through transformation.

Traditionally human recognition was based on tokens and passwords; however, since last decade the government and private organizations have adopted automatic human recognition system as biometric systems are more reliable and robust as compared to the existing traditional method of authentication which were based on token and password [1], which can be stolen, forgotten, or lost. In contrast, biometrics offer an alternative solution to the task of personal authentication or identification based on biometric traits as they are hard to forge. Most commonly used traits for human recognition are fingerprints, face, palm, iris, gait, etc.; some others are DNA, EEG, ear, and speech [2]. These systems use permanent pattern of the trait which are unique and intricate to identify an individual. Biometric systems work on trusted mechanism and are gaining popularity in law enforcement, education, healthcare, retail, and manufacturing. Mobile phones, tablets, smartphones, door locks, and many electronic gadgets are using biometric based-authentication tremendously in past few years. These systems are also employed for social benefits such as record tracking, vaccination monitoring, children separated from family, and controlling fraud related to food subsidies, etc. [1, 3]. Biometric system provides nonrepudiable authentication. Outline of chapter: the chapter consists of the following

DOI: 10.1201/9781032614663-2

sections: introduction of biometric systems is in Section 2.1 along with its framework in Section 2.2. Section 2.3 discusses about different biometric modalities and their applications. Section 2.4 focuses on security issues in it and challenges to biometric system; the existing problems are stated and discussed. Section 2.5 details about unimodal biometric systems and its disadvantages. After analysing attacks in biometric recognition, the solution to handle the attack potentials based on multimodal and multispectral biometric is proposed in Section 2.6. The last section summarizes the chapter. It also provides directions to future work in the field of multimodal and multispectral biometrics.

2.2   FRAMEWORK OF BIOMETRIC SYSTEMS

In this section, we explain the framework of general biometric system as shown in Figure 2.1, and it includes the following parts:

a. *Sensor module*: A suitable biometric reader or scanner is required to acquire the raw biometric data of an individual.

b. *Quality assessment and feature extraction module*: The quality of the biometric data acquired by the sensor is first assessed in order to determine its suitability for further processing. The biometric data is then processed and a set of salient discriminatory features extracted to represent the underlying trait.

c. *Matching and decision-making module*: The extracted features are compared against the stored templates to generate match scores.

d. *System database module*: During the enrolment process, the feature set extracted from the raw biometric sample (i.e., the template) is stored in the database (possibly) along with some biographic information (such as name, personal identification number (PIN), and address) characterizing the user [2, 4].

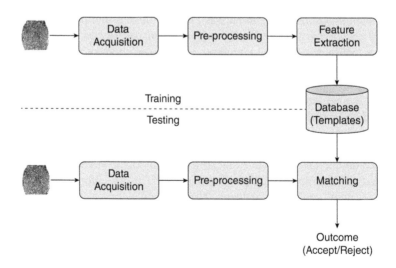

FIGURE 2.1   Diagram of a generic biometric recognition system.

2.3 BIOMETRIC MODALITIES

In this section, we describe various traits present in humans as shown in Figure 2.2, which can be used as biometric modalities. The biometric modalities fall under two types:

1. Physiological biometric
2. Behavioural biometric

2.3.1 PHYSIOLOGICAL BIOMETRIC

Physiological biometrics are based on an individual's physical characteristics. These traits are inherent to a person's physiology and are relatively stable over time [5, 6]. Physiological biometrics are commonly used for identity verification and authentication due to their uniqueness and stability.

A few variants of physiological biometrics are as follows:

Fingerprint: Fingerprint works by scanning and analysing the unique patterns, ridges, and valleys on an individual's fingertip.

Hand geometry: Hand geometry biometrics is a technology that measures and analyses the shape and size of a person's hand for identification purposes. It involves capturing the unique characteristics of an individual's hand, such as the length, width, curvature, and relative location of features.

Iris: This biometric authentication is a highly accurate and fast system that is widely used for identification purposes in various sectors. This technology captures an image of a person's eye and analyses the unique patterns and characteristics of the iris for matching and authentication by governments and businesses in developed countries

Retina: Retina biometrics is a unique and highly accurate biometric modality that analyses the patterns of blood vessels in the back of the eye to identify individuals.

Face: Face biometrics is a technology that uses facial characteristics for identification and authentication purposes. It analyses unique facial features such as the distance between the eyes, the shape of the nose, and the contours of the face to create a biometric template.

2.3.2 BEHAVIOURAL BIOMETRICS

Behavioural biometrics is a fascinating field within the realm of biometric technology, focusing on identifying individuals based on their distinct behavioural patterns and characteristics [1, 7].

A few variants of behavioural biometrics are as follows:

Voice recognition: Speech recognition biometrics is a technology that utilizes the unique characteristics of an individual's voice for identification and verification purposes.

Nature of Biometric Modality	Features	Applications
Fingerprint 	Unique and Permanent High Accuracy Easy to Use Wide Range of Applications Time and Attendance Tracking	Issuing of passports Banking sector Identifying criminals in crime scenes Digital payment applications National identification system Mobile devices
Hand Geometry 	Non-intrusive and user-friendly High accuracy Fast and efficient	Physical access control Employee attendance tracking systems personal verification National identification system
Iris 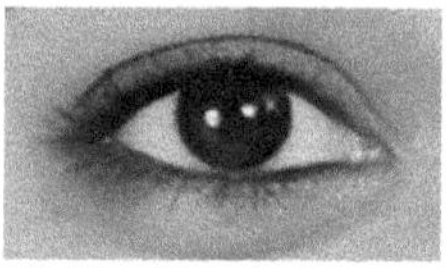	Unique and Stable Non-intrusive Fast and Accurate	Healthcare Immigration and Border Control Law Enforcement Mobile Devices Smart Cities
Retina 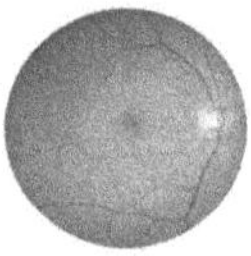	Uniqueness Stability Non-intrusive High accuracy	Secure user authentication Forensic investigations Healthcare Immigration and border control Law enforcement
Face 	Universality Non-intrusive Speed and accuracy Anti-spoofing techniques	Law enforcement Financial services Travel and immigration Mobile devices Time and attendance tracking Social media
Voice 	Unique Voice Characteristics Non-Intrusive Dynamic Aspects	Voice Banking Customer Service Forensic Investigations Healthcare: In healthcare settings Voice Assistants Law Enforcement Fraud Prevention
Gait 	Unique Characteristics Non-Intrusive Dynamic Aspects	Surveillance and Security Access Control Forensic Investigations Health Monitoring Human-Computer Interaction
Signature 	Unique Characteristics Non-intrusive Dynamic Analysis	Dynamic Analysis Financial Services Legal and Forensic Applications Access Control Time and Attendance Tracking E-commerce and Online Services

FIGURE 2.2   Representation of features and applications of biometric modalities.

Signature recognition: Signature biometrics, also known as signature recognition, is a biometric technology that analyses and authenticates an individual's unique signature characteristics.

Gait: Gait biometrics refers to the analysis and recognition of an individual's
walking pattern.

2.4 VARIOUS BIOMETRIC TRAITS AND THEIR ISSUES

Even though the biometric systems have replaced the traditional authentication systems,
there remains an open issue regarding the security of the existing systems. Several
potential attacks have been reported, and these systems are vulnerable to attacks.

This chapter focuses on analysing vulnerabilities, their fraud resistance, and recognition accuracy specific to biometric systems, like fingerprint recognition systems,
face recognition, and iris [3, 8].

2.4.1 FINGERPRINT

Fingerprint recognition is a widely used method of biometric authentication due
to its convenience and reliability. However, like any technology, it is not entirely
immune to attacks. As shown in Table 2.1, various types of attacks [9, 10] on fingerprint recognition systems exist, including the following:

1. *Fake Finger (Spoof) Attacks*: In this type of attack, an attacker creates a replica of a genuine user's fingerprint, commonly using materials like latex, gelatin, or silicone. They then use this fake finger to spoof the fingerprint sensor.
2. *Latent Fingerprint Attacks*: Attackers can exploit latent fingerprints left on
   surfaces to create a replica. These latent prints are typically not visible to
   the naked eye but can be lifted and used for spoofing.

TABLE 2.1
Security Issues with Fingerprint

Attack	Elapsed-Time	Expertise	Knowledge of TOE	Window of Opportunity	Equipment	Required Attack Potential	
						Sum	Rating
Fabricate	1	3	0	0	4	8	Basic
Circumvent liveliness detection	4	6	7	1	4	22	High
Lift a latent fingerprint from a touched surface	0	3	0	10	1	14	Moderate
Use a real finger	13–19	0	0	1	0	14–20	Moderate to high

3. *Gummy Fingers Attack*: Gummy fingers involve using materials like gelatin or silicone to create a mould of a real fingerprint. This mould can then be filled with a material that mimics the properties of human skin.

4. *3D Fingerprint Attacks*: Some fingerprint recognition systems use 2D sensors, making them vulnerable to 3D fingerprint attacks. Attackers create a 3D model of a fingerprint to overcome the 2D sensor's limitations.

5. *Photo-Sketch Attacks*: Attackers can use high-resolution photos or sketches of fingerprints to create replicas. This method is less common but still a potential threat.

6. *Impersonation Attacks*: Rather than creating fake fingerprints, an attacker may attempt to impersonate a genuine user. This could involve coercing the user to provide their fingerprint willingly.

7. *Brute-Force Attacks*: In cases where the fingerprint system allows multiple attempts, attackers may employ brute-force techniques to guess the correct fingerprint. They systematically try various fingerprints until they gain access.

8. *Fingerprint Database Attacks*: In situations where fingerprint templates are stored in a database, attackers may target the database to steal or manipulate the templates.

9. *Sensor Spoofing*: Attackers may attempt to deceive the fingerprint sensor itself by using various methods, such as applying pressure, temperature changes, or other techniques to manipulate the sensor's readings [11].

10. *Data Interception Attacks*: When fingerprint data is transmitted over a network, attackers may intercept and manipulate the data packets to gain unauthorized access or impersonate a legitimate user.

It's important to note that modern fingerprint recognition systems often incorporate advanced security measures to counteract these types of attacks [12, 13]. These measures include liveness detection (to differentiate between live fingers and fake ones), multi-factor authentication (combining fingerprint recognition with other methods), and secure storage of fingerprint templates [8]. Additionally, continuous research and development are ongoing to enhance the security of biometric authentication methods.

2.4.2 FACE BIOMETRIC

Face biometric recognition systems have become increasingly popular for authentication and identification purposes due to their convenience. However, like any biometric technology, they are not entirely immune to attacks [14]. Here are some types of attacks that can target face biometric systems:

1. *Spoofing Attacks*: In a spoofing attack, an attacker attempts to deceive the face recognition system by presenting a counterfeit image or video of the genuine user's face. This can involve printed photos, videos, masks, or other techniques to mimic the appearance of the authorized user.

2. *3D Mask Attacks*: Attackers may create high-quality 3D masks or models of a user's face to bypass 2D face recognition systems. These masks can

be crafted using materials like silicone or latex to replicate facial features accurately.

3. *Video Replay Attacks*: **In** video replay attacks, attackers capture a video of the authorized user's face and then replay that video in front of the camera to trick the system. This is similar to spoofing but involves moving images.

4. *Deepfake Attacks*: Deepfake technology leverages artificial intelligence (AI) to create highly convincing video or audio recordings that impersonate someone else. Attackers can use deepfake technology to create lifelike videos of authorized users.

5. *Photo Attacks*: Attackers may use a high-resolution photo of the authorized user's face to impersonate them. This type of attack is effective against some less sophisticated face recognition systems.

6. *Mimicry Attacks*: In mimicry attacks, attackers attempt to mimic the facial expressions and movements of the authorized user. This can be more challenging to detect as it involves live action.

7. *Composite Attacks*: Composite attacks involve combining different techniques, such as using a 3D mask along with voice imitation to bypass both facial and voice recognition systems.

8. *Impersonation Attacks*: Instead of attempting to spoof the system, an attacker may impersonate the genuine user and try to deceive human operators or social engineering.

9. *Environmental Attacks*: Changes in environmental conditions, such as varying lighting, may affect the performance of face recognition systems. Attackers can exploit these conditions to gain unauthorized access [4].

10. *Data Poisoning Attacks*: Attackers may attempt to manipulate the training data used by machine learning-based face recognition systems. By injecting poisoned data, they can degrade the system's accuracy.

It's important to note that the security of face recognition systems can be enhanced by implementing liveness detection mechanisms, which aim to distinguish between a live person and a static image or mask. Additionally, combining face recognition with other authentication factors, such as PINs or passwords, can provide an extra layer of security. Ongoing research and development are continually improving the resilience of face biometric systems against various attacks.

2.4.3 IRIS BIOMETRIC

Iris recognition is considered one of the most secure biometric technologies, but it is not entirely immune to attacks. Here are some types of attacks that can target iris biometric systems [7, 15]:

1. *Presentation Attacks (Spoofing)*: Attackers may attempt to present a high-quality photograph or printed image of an authorized user's iris to the biometric system. This is known as a spoofing attack and is one of the primary concerns for iris recognition systems.

2. *Contact Lens Attacks*: Some attackers use coloured or patterned contact lenses to mimic the appearance of an authorized user's iris. While this attack can be effective against some iris recognition systems, it is challenging to execute successfully.

3. *Video Replay Attacks*: Attackers may record a video of the authorized user's iris and then replay it in front of the iris recognition camera. This can deceive some systems that do not have robust anti-spoofing measures.

4. *3D Model Attacks*: In 3D model attacks, attackers create a physical or digital 3D model of an authorized user's iris to present to the system. This approach is more complex but can be effective against certain systems [16].

5. *Mathematical Attacks*: Mathematical attacks involve manipulating the iris template or biometric data to create false matches or gain unauthorized access. This can include data tampering and template manipulation.

6. *Camera Manipulation Attacks*: Attackers may tamper with the iris recognition camera, such as by adjusting focus or lighting conditions, to disrupt the system's ability to capture an accurate iris image.

7. *Template Database Attacks*: If an attacker gains access to the iris templates stored in a database, they can use them for identity theft or to impersonate authorized users.

8. *Cross-Modal Attacks*: Cross-modal attacks involve using a different biometric trait, such as a photograph of the face, to impersonate the authorized user to the iris recognition system.

9. *False Acceptance and False Rejection Attacks*: These attacks aim to manipulate the system's false acceptance rate (allowing unauthorized access) or false rejection rate (denying legitimate users). Attackers may try to adjust system settings to favour one type of error over the other.

10. *Brute-Force Attacks*: Attackers may attempt to guess or test multiple iris patterns to gain access. This is challenging due to the complexity of iris patterns, but it is still a possibility.

It's important to note that modern iris recognition systems incorporate various anti-spoofing measures, such as liveness detection, to detect and prevent presentation attacks [17, 18]. Additionally, iris recognition technology has a high level of accuracy and is considered one of the most secure biometric modalities. As with any security system, the overall effectiveness depends on the specific implementation and the countermeasures in place. A comparative analysis of various biometric traits is illustrated in Table 2.2.

2.4.4   Retina Biometric

Retina biometric systems, which use the unique patterns of blood vessels in the retina to identify individuals, are generally considered highly secure [1, 16]. However,

TABLE 2.2
Comparative Analysis of Existing Biometric Systems

Modality	User's Participation	Spoof Vulnerability	Accuracy	Cost	Ease of Use
Fingerprint	Required	Medium	High	Very economical	Simple
Face	Not necessary	High	High	Costlier	Complex
Iris	Required	Low	Very high	Costlier	Very complex
Hand Geometry	Required	High	Low	Economical	Simple
Gait	Not necessary	Low	Low	Costlier	Complex
Voice	Required	High	Moderate	Costlier	Complex
Signature	Required	High	Moderate	Costlier	Complex
DNA	Required	Very low	Very high	Very expensive	Very complex

like any biometric system, they are not immune to attacks. Here are some types of attacks that can be directed at retina biometric systems:

1. *Presentation Attacks (Spoofing)*: Retina Image Forgery: Attackers may attempt to present a photograph or a fake image of a retina to the biometric system in an attempt to gain unauthorized access.
2. *Video Replay Attacks*: Attackers may record a video of an individual's eye while they are authenticating themselves and then replay this video to trick the system into granting access.
3. *Biometric Data Theft*: If an attacker gains access to the stored retina images or templates in the biometric database, they could use this information to impersonate a legitimate user.
4. *Machine Learning Attacks*:
   a. *Adversarial attacks*: Attackers might use adversarial machine learning techniques to create subtle alterations in retina images that are imperceptible to humans but can fool the biometric system.
   b. *Transfer learning*: Attackers might train a deep learning model on a different dataset of retina images to develop an algorithm that can mimic legitimate users.
5. *Environmental Attacks*:
   a. *Changes in lighting conditions*: Altering the lighting conditions during the retina scan might make it difficult for the system to capture accurate images.
   b. *Use of infrared light*: Some retina scanners use infrared light, and attackers might attempt to manipulate or block this light source.
6. *Physical Attacks*: Tampering with the scanner: Attackers could physically tamper with the retina scanner to disrupt its operation or collect unauthorized data.
7. *Data Interception*: Intercepting communication between the scanner and the system's database could allow attackers to obtain sensitive biometric data.
8. *Biometric Coercion*: In some cases, attackers may attempt to force a person to authenticate themselves using their retina, either through physical coercion or other means.

It's important to note that retina biometric systems often incorporate anti-spoofing measures and liveness detection techniques to counter presentation attacks. Additionally, encryption and secure storage methods are used to protect the biometric data in the database [19]. Regular updates and security audits are essential to minimize vulnerabilities and ensure the system's integrity.

2.4.5   HAND GEOMETRY BIOMETRIC

Hand geometry biometric systems, which use the physical measurements of an individual's hand as a means of identification, are generally considered to be relatively secure. However, like any biometric system, they are not entirely immune to attacks. Here are some types of attacks that can be directed at hand geometry biometric systems:

1. *Impersonation or Forgery Attacks*: Fake Handprints: Attackers may attempt to present a fake handprint or an imitation of a hand to the biometric system. This can be done using materials like silicone moulds, gelatin, or even a high-resolution photograph.
2. *Biometric Data Theft*: Database Breach: If an attacker gains unauthorized access to the stored hand geometry templates or images in the biometric database, they could use this information to impersonate legitimate users.
3. *Liveness Attacks*:
   a. *Static Images*: Attackers might present a static image of a hand to the system instead of a live, three-dimensional hand, thereby attempting to trick the system.
   b. *Video Playback*: Similar to static images, attackers could use recorded videos of a hand to mimic a live hand presentation.
4. *Machine Learning Attacks*:
   a. *Adversarial Attacks*: Attackers might use adversarial machine learning techniques to manipulate the features of hand images in a way that the changes are not perceptible to humans but can fool the biometric system.
   b. *Transfer Learning*: Attackers may train a machine learning model on a dataset of hand images to create an algorithm that can mimic legitimate hand presentations.
5. *Environmental Attacks*:
   a. *Changes in Lighting*: Altering the lighting conditions during hand scanning might make it difficult for the system to accurately capture hand geometry.
   b. *Obstructing the Scanner*: Attackers might physically obstruct or tamper with the hand scanner to disrupt its operation.
6. *Data Interception*: Intercepting the communication between the scanner and the system's database could allow attackers to obtain sensitive biometric data.

7. *Biometric Coercion*: In some cases, attackers may attempt to force an individual to place their hand on the scanner for authentication, either through physical coercion or other means.
8. *Template Attacks*: Attackers may try to reverse engineer or manipulate the stored hand geometry templates to create fake templates for authentication [18].

Hand geometry systems often incorporate anti-spoofing measures and liveness detection techniques to counter presentation attacks. Moreover, secure encryption and storage methods are used to protect the biometric data in the database [20]. Regular system updates and security audits are essential to minimize vulnerabilities and ensure the system's integrity.

2.4.6 SIGNATURE BIOMETRIC

Signature biometric systems, which rely on capturing and verifying an individual's unique signature as a form of authentication, are susceptible to several security attacks. It's important to be aware of these potential vulnerabilities and take appropriate measures to mitigate them:

1. *Forgery*: Attackers may attempt to forge a signature to gain unauthorized access. This can be done using various methods, including tracing, imitation, or copying a signature from a legitimate source.
2. *Spoofing*: Attackers may use high-quality replicas of a genuine signature to trick the biometric system. This can involve printing or reproducing a signature with high fidelity.
3. *Skimming*: In cases where the signature is captured using a digital stylus or pen, attackers might compromise the device to intercept or manipulate signature data.
4. *Database Breaches*: If signature templates or data are stored in a database, a breach of that database could expose sensitive signature information to attackers.
5. *Replay Attacks*: Attackers may record a legitimate signature during an authorized transaction and attempt to replay it at a later time to gain unauthorized access.
6. *Man-in-the-Middle Attacks*: Attackers could intercept the communication between the signature capture device and the verification system to manipulate or substitute the signature data.
7. *Insider Threats*: Employees or insiders with access to the biometric system may misuse or abuse their privileges to manipulate or bypass the signature verification process.
8. *Denial of Service (DoS)*: Attackers may attempt to overwhelm the biometric system with a flood of signature verification requests, causing it to become unresponsive.

To enhance the security of signature biometric systems, it's important to employ a multi-layered security approach that combines signature analysis with other security measures such as encryption, access controls, and intrusion detection [21, 22]. Regularly updating and patching software and hardware components is also crucial to address known vulnerabilities.

2.4.7 GAIT BIOMETRIC

Gait biometrics, which involves analysing an individual's unique walking pattern for authentication, is a relatively new and emerging field in biometrics. While it offers potential advantages, it is not immune to security attacks and vulnerabilities. Here are some potential security attacks and mitigation measures for gait biometrics [22]:

1. *Impersonation*: Attackers may attempt to mimic or impersonate the gait pattern of an authorized user to gain access.
2. *Spoofing*: Attackers might use devices or techniques to spoof gait data by manipulating sensors or input signals.
3. *Privacy Concerns*: Gait biometric data can reveal sensitive personal information, and the storage or transmission of this data must be protected to prevent privacy breaches.
4. *Database Breaches*: If gait templates or raw gait data are stored in a database, they could be vulnerable to breaches, exposing users' gait patterns.
5. *Replay Attacks*: Attackers may record an authorized user's gait pattern during a legitimate session and replay it at a later time.
6. *Man-in-the-Middle Attacks*: Intercepting and tampering with gait data during transmission could compromise the integrity of the authentication process.
7. *Insider Threats*: Employees or insiders with access to the gait biometric system may misuse their privileges or manipulate the data.
8. *Environmental Factors*: Gait biometrics can be affected by environmental conditions, such as lighting, terrain, or footwear, which may result in false negatives.

To enhance the security of gait biometric systems, it's essential to follow best practices in biometric security, including data protection, access controls, encryption, and continuous monitoring [23]. Regularly updating and patching software and hardware components is also crucial to address known vulnerabilities and stay ahead of emerging threats.

2.5 UNIMODAL BIOMETRIC

"Unimodal" is a term, to describe something that has a single mode or predominant characteristic within a particular context. The term "mode" in this context refers to the most frequently occurring value or category within a set of data. In general, "unimodal" simply means "single mode" or "pertaining to one mode", when a person is identified on the basis of only one trait which can be either fingerprint or some other biometric trait but only single modality is used to identify a person.

2.5.1 LIMITATIONS OF UNIMODAL BIOMETRIC

1. *Inherent Variability*: Biometric traits can change over time due to various factors such as ageing, injury, or illness. For example, a person's fingerprint may change due to skin conditions or ageing, making it less reliable for long-term use.
2. *Security Concerns*: Biometric data can be sensitive, and if it is compromised, it cannot be changed like a password. Therefore, securing biometric data is crucial to prevent unauthorized access and identity theft.
3. *Privacy Concerns*: The collection and storage of biometric data raise privacy concerns. People may be hesitant to provide their biometric information if they fear it could be misused or accessed without their consent.
4. *Accuracy and Reliability*: The accuracy of biometric systems can vary depending on the modality and the quality of the equipment used. Factors such as lighting conditions, sensor quality, and the individual's cooperation can affect accuracy.
5. *Cost*: Implementing biometric systems can be expensive, especially for large-scale deployments. This includes the cost of hardware, software, and maintenance.
6. *Cross-Device Compatibility*: Biometric data collected on one device may not be easily transferable to another, which can limit the convenience of using biometrics for authentication across different platforms and services.
7. *Spoofing and Forgery*: Some biometric systems can be vulnerable to spoofing or forgery attempts. For example, fingerprint sensors can be fooled by high-quality fake fingerprints or images.
8. *Ethical and Legal Issues*: The use of biometric data is subject to legal regulations and ethical considerations, and these can vary from one jurisdiction to another [24]. Compliance with these regulations can be complex.
9. *Single Point of Failure*: Relying solely on one biometric modality can be risky. If the chosen modality fails or is compromised, there may be no backup method for authentication.

2.6 CONCLUSION

The chapter presents overall introduction of biometric systems, and the framework of biometric system is explained with its working. The applications of the system have been discussed. It covers various modalities of biometric system their applications in various sectors and the issues related to the security of the different traits. It also focuses on unimodal biometric system performance and its drawbacks. The solutions to the problems in unimodal system have been proposed. The use of multimodal, multispectral, and thermal biometric system can be a replacement for unimodal biometric system. We use deep learning for authentication of various traits in biometric systems. It is observed that deep learning techniques have outperformed the traditional state-of-the-art methods due to their capability of learning features efficiently. While authentication is the main focus of biometric systems, various vulnerabilities such as attacks on enrolled templates and attacks using forged identities are some of the biggest challenges faced. The chapter reviews the studies that employ the use of robust deep learning frameworks to deal with these challenges. We summarize the strengths and drawbacks of various frameworks which explore the role of deep learning.

REFERENCES

1. K. Nandakumar and A. K. Jain, "Biometric Template Security," EURASIP Journal on Advances in Signal Processing Volume 2008, Article ID 579416, 17 pages doi:10.1155/2008/579416, no. September, 2007.
2. A. K. Jain, L. Hong and S. Pankanti, "An Identity-Authentication System Using Fingerprints," *Proceedings of the IEEE,* vol. 85, no. 9, pp. 1365–1388, 1997.
3. H. Xu and R. N. J. J. Veldhuis, "Binary Spectral Minutiae Representation With Multi-Sample Fusion For Fingerprint Recognition," Mm&Sec, vol. 1, no. 1, pp. 73–79, 2010.
4. U. Uludag, B. Günsel and M. Ballan, "A Spatial Method for Watermarking of Fingerprint Images," Pris, 2001.
5. D. Maltoni, "A Tutorial on Fingerprint Recognition," *Advanced Studies in Biometrics: Summer School on Biometrics, Revised Selected Lectures and Papers,* pp. 43–68, 2005.
6. V. S. Reddy, "Fingerprint Recognition Using Minutiae Based and Discrete Wavelet Transform," Int. J. Innov. Res. Adv. Eng., vol. 3, no. 05, pp. 2014–2017, 2016.
7. R. K. Rowe, K. A. Nixon and P. W Butler, "Multispectral Fingerprint Image Acquisition," *Advances in Biometrics: Sensors, Algorithms and Systems.* London: Springer London, 2008, pp. 3–23.
8. A. Sharma, S. Arya and P. Chaturvedi, "A Novel Image Compression Based Method for Multispectral Fingerprint Biometric System", Procedia Comput. Sci., vol. 171, 2020, pp. 1698–1707, ISSN 1877-0509, https://doi.org/10.1016/j.procs.2020.04.182.
9. A. Selwal, A. Sharma, S. Arya, and P. Chaturvedi, "Multispectral Image Fusion System Based on Wavelet Transformation for Secure Human Recognition," Int. J. Adv. Sci. Technol., vol. 28, no. 19, pp. 811–820, 2019. Retrieved from http://sersc.org/journals/index.php/IJAST/article/view/2667
10. A. Sharma, J. Shankar M, "Speech Emotion Feelings Recognition Biometric Using Machine Learning ", Dogo Rangsang Res. J. ISSN: 2347-7180, vol. 13, no. 7, July 2023, p. 15.
11. J. Th, "Orientation scanning to improve lossless compression of fingerprint images," *Audio-and Video-Based Biometric Person Authentication: 4th International Conference, AVBPA 2003 Guildford, UK, June 9–11, 2003 Proceedings 4.* Springer Berlin Heidelberg, 2003.
12. Ruud M. Bolle, et al. *Guide to Biometrics.* Springer Science & Business Media, 2013
13. S. Kumar and S Arya. "Change Detection Techniques for Land Cover Change Analysis Using Spatial Datasets: A Review," Remote Sens. Earth Syst. Sci. 4, 172–185 (2021). https://doi.org/10.1007/s41976-021-00056-z
14. J. A. Montoya Zegarra, N. J. Leite and R. da Silva Torres, "Wavelet-Based Fingerprint Image Retrieval," J. Comput. Appl. Math, vol. 227, no. 2, pp. 294–307, 2009.
15. A. Sharma, S. Arya, and P. Chaturvedi, "On Performance Analysis of Biometric Methods for Secure Human Recognition", Recent Innovations in Computing: *Proceedings of ICRIC 2020.* Singapore: Springer. 2021.
16. A. Sharma, P. Chaturvedi and S. Arya, "Article: Human Recognition Methods Based on Biometric Technologies," Int. J. Comput. Appl., vol. 120, no. 17, pp. 1–7, June 2015.

17. B. S. Manjunath and W. Y. Ma, "Texture Features for Browsing and Retrieval of Large Image Data," *IEEE Transactions on Pattern Analysis and Machine Intelligence,* vol. 18, no. 8, pp. 837–842, 1996.
18. S. Kumar, S. Arya and K Jain. A SWIR-Based Vegetation index for Change Detection in Land Cover Using Multi-Temporal Landsat Satellite Dataset. Int. J. Inf. Technol. 14, 2035–2048 (2022). https://doi.org/10.1007/s41870-021-00797-6
19. H. S. Hadi, M. Rosbi and U. U Sheikh, "A Review of Infrared Spectrum in Human Detection for Surveillance Systems," Int. J. Interact. Digit. Media, vol. 1, no. 3, pp. 13–20, 2013.
20. A. T. B. Jin, D. N. C. Ling and A. Goh, "Biohashing: Two Factor Authentication Featuring Fingerprint Data and Tokenised Random Number," Pattern Recognit, vol. 37, no. 11, pp. 2245–2255, 2004.
21. Y. Qin, B. Tang and J. Wang, "Higher-Density Dyadic Wavelet Transform and Its Application," Mech. Syst. Signal Process., vol. 24, no. 3, pp. 823–834, 2010.
22. D. Gafurov, "A Survey of Biometric Gait Recognition: Approaches, Security and Challenges", In *Annual Norwegian Computer Science Conference* (pp. 19–21). Norway: Annual Norwegian Computer Science Conference, November 2007.
23. R. Nagdir and A. Ross. A Calibration Model for Fingerprint Sensor Interoperability. In SPIE Conference on Biometric Technology for Human Identification III, Orlando USA, 2006.
24. S. Arora and M. P. S Bhatia, "Fingerprint Spoofing Detection to Improve Customer Security in Mobile Financial Applications Using Deep Learning," Arabian J. Sci. Eng., vol. 45, no. 10, pp. 2847–2863, 2020. https://doi.org/10.1007/s13369-019-04190-1

3 Examining the Vulnerabilities of Biometric Systems
Privacy and Security Perspectives

Tajinder Kumar, Shashi Bhushan, Pooja Sharma, and Vishal Garg

3.1 INTRODUCTION

As a ground-breaking technique for identification and authentication, biometric systems have emerged. Biometric systems use distinctive physiological or behavioral traits of people, including fingerprints, iris patterns, or facial features, to authenticate identity, in contrast to conventional password-based techniques. Numerous benefits of this technology include convenience, accuracy, and better security. The increased demand for adequate security measures across various industries, including access control, government, banking, and healthcare, can be ascribed to the expanding deployment of biometric systems. Due to the inherent difficulty of duplicating or faking certain qualities, biometrics offers a more trustworthy method of confirming identity. Biometric technologies considerably lower the danger of unauthorized access and fraudulent actions by utilizing individual-specific features [1].

The value of biometric systems rests in their capacity to improve security and simplify procedures in private and professional contexts. Biometric authentication offers a simple and effective user experience by doing away with the need to carry physical tokens or memorize complicated passwords. Additionally, biometric solutions can increase general security measures, enable secure transactions, and stop identity theft. However, as the use of biometric devices increases, worries about security and privacy have surfaced. Biometric data collection, storage, and use raise concerns about protecting sensitive personal data. To keep the public's trust in biometric systems, severe issues like unauthorized access to biometric data, potential data breaches, and the threat of identity theft must be resolved. Therefore, it's critical to comprehend the flaws in biometric systems and look at security and privacy issues. Stakeholders can ensure the responsible and secure application of biometric technologies, allowing for continuous usage across various areas while protecting people's right to privacy by recognizing and resolving these challenges [2].

DOI: 10.1201/9781032614663-3

3.1.1 OVERVIEW OF THE INCREASING ADOPTION OF BIOMETRIC TECHNOLOGIES

Many different companies and sectors have adopted biometric technologies quickly and widely. These technologies' distinct advantages in authentication, identification, and security augmentation can be blamed for the rising reliance on them. An overview of the expanding use of biometric technologies in many fields is given below [3]:

- *Government Sector*: Governments worldwide know how biometric technology may improve identity management, border control, and security. Using biometrics in national ID schemes, passports, and visa systems has become widespread. These technologies make it possible to identify people quickly and precisely, supporting efforts to increase national security.
- *Financial Services*: In the financial industry, biometrics have been widely used, primarily for safe access control and fraud prevention. Facial or fingerprint recognition for biometric verification has been included in ATMs, payment systems, and mobile banking applications. These technologies offer a practical and safe approach to confirming user identities, preventing unauthorized transactions, and lessening the dangers related to lost or stolen cards or passwords.
- *Healthcare*: In the healthcare industry, biometric solutions are used more frequently to guarantee precise patient identification, lower medical errors, and improve data security. To ensure the proper patient receives the right care, biometric identifiers like fingerprints or palm prints are used to link patients to their electronic health data—additionally, biometric technologies aid in thwarting insurance fraud, pharmaceutical fraud, and identity theft.
- *Access Control and Surveillance*: In physical and digital domains, biometric technologies are frequently used for access control. Biometrics offers a reliable and unique way of authentication for everything from unlocking cellphones or computers to securing access to restricted business areas. Biometric solutions in surveillance systems help identify and follow persons of interest, advancing efforts to improve public safety and deter crime.
- *Consumer Electronics*: Consumer electronics gadgets now frequently include biometric authentication. Smartphones, tablets, and laptops have fingerprint scanners, facial recognition, and voice recognition technologies for simple and secure user authentication. The demand for smooth and adequate security protections in commonplace devices is reflected in this widespread adoption.
- *Transportation and Travel*: Biometrics are essential to increase security and effectiveness in transportation and travel systems. Airports use biometric-based technologies for passenger authentication, speeding check-ins, streamlining boarding, and improving border control. Smart cards for transport also have biometric IDs to guarantee safe and convenient travel.

The expanding usage of biometric technologies in these fields demonstrates the rising acceptance of their efficiency in enhancing security, optimizing workflows, and improving user experiences. The widespread use of biometric technologies is anticipated to increase as they develop and become more sophisticated, revolutionizing how people and organizations identify and verify identities.

3.1.2 IMPORTANCE OF ADDRESSING PRIVACY AND SECURITY CONCERNS

It is critical to address the privacy and security issues raised by biometric systems as they become more prevalent and pervasive in many facets of our lives. The following details emphasize how critical it is to address these issues [4,5]:

- *Protection of Personal Information*: Individuals' distinctive physiological or behavioral traits, which are fundamentally private and delicate, are collected and stored through biometric systems. It is crucial to guarantee the privacy and security of this biometric data to safeguard people's identities and stop unauthorized access or usage. By addressing privacy issues, we can protect people's fundamental right to privacy and keep them confident in technology.
- *Mitigation of Identity Theft and Fraud*: Biometric systems are made to offer precise and trustworthy identification. Biometric information, however, can be used for fraud and identity theft if it is compromised. Strong security measures must be implemented to stop spoofing attacks, data breaches, and unauthorized access to biometric data. Fraudulent actions can be reduced by resolving security issues and shielding people and organizations from monetary losses and reputational harm.
- *Preservation of Individual Autonomy*: Biometric systems can protect people's autonomy if adequately regulated and safeguarded. People should be able to make decisions about using their biometric data and have control over it. By addressing privacy issues, it is possible to respect people's rights and freedoms and allow them to choose how their biometric data is gathered, saved, and utilized.
- *Compliance with Data Protection Regulations*: The collection, storage, and use of personal data, including biometric data, is governed by data protection laws and regulations that numerous jurisdictions have adopted. In addition to being necessary for compliance with the law, following these rules is crucial for maintaining organizational credibility and avoiding fines. A culture of responsible data management is promoted, and compliance with applicable data protection standards is ensured through addressing privacy concerns.
- *Trust in Biometric Systems*: For biometric technology to be widely used and accepted, trust must be established. Addressing privacy and security issues reveals a dedication to safeguarding people's interests and data. Organizations and service providers can foster confidence in the dependability and integrity of biometric systems and promote their widespread use and acceptance by prioritizing privacy and adopting strong security measures.
- *Ethical Considerations*: Concerns about accountability, transparency, and consent are raised by biometric technologies. Organizations can respect

moral values by addressing privacy and security issues, ensuring informed consent is gained from people, transparent procedures are followed, and accountability systems are in place. This encourages the ethical and responsible use of biometric technologies while upholding the rights of individuals and reducing the likelihood of exploitation or abuse.

Addressing the privacy and security issues raised by biometric technology is crucial. It defends people's right to privacy, fights against fraud and identity theft, assures adherence to data protection laws, promotes trust, and respects moral principles. Stakeholders may maximize the benefits of biometric technologies while retaining the appropriate security and privacy protections by proactively addressing these issues.

3.1.3 BIOMETRIC SYSTEMS: PRINCIPLES AND FUNCTIONING

Discussion of various biometric identifiers, such as face traits, iris patterns, and fingerprints, to authenticate and identify people; biometric systems use a variety of biometric identifiers. The following list of frequently used biometric markers is followed by a brief explanation of the hardware required to collect them [6]:

- *Fingerprint*: One of the earliest and most extensively used biometric technologies is fingerprint recognition. It depicts the distinctive ridges and patterns found on each person's fingertips. The ridges and valleys of a person's fingerprints are recorded using fingerprint scanners, frequently based on optical or capacitive technology. These scanners provide high-resolution images or minute details for matching and verification using light or electrical fields.
- *Iris*: Utilizing the distinctive patterns in the colored area of the eye known as the iris, iris recognition is a very accurate biometric identification technique. Systems for iris recognition use speed cameras to take in-depth pictures of the iris' anatomy. High-resolution sensors are used to record the iris pattern, and near-infrared illuminators that generate light to improve iris visibility are part, for example, the hardware. The arrangement of points, for instance, is one of the characteristic aspects that sophisticated computers analyze to develop a recognizable pattern for identification.
- *Facial Features*: One of the facial traits that facial recognition studies and utilizes to identify persons is the shape, curves, and proportions of the face. Facial recognition systems use cameras, typically equipped with high-resolution sensors, to collect facial images. Algorithms are employed to analyze these photographs and find important visual indications like the distance between the eyes, the nose shape, and the lips. 3D facial recognition systems may incorporate depth sensors or infrared cameras to gather depth information and increase accuracy.
- *Voice*: To identify a person, speech recognition technology examines the distinctive features of their voice. Mics are generally part of voice recognition gear to record the user's spoken words or phrases. Pitch, tone, speech

patterns, and vocal tract resonances are a few voice parameters analyzed by sophisticated algorithms. These characteristics produce a voiceprint that may be compared to those already stored for identification or verification.

- **Palm Prints**: Recognizing a person's palmprints involves photographing the unique creases on each person's palm. Specialized palm scanners take high-resolution pictures of the palm surface using the recorded palm print feature, and the hardware may use optical or thermal to precisely record palm print features or multispectral imaging techniques.
- **DNA**: A highly accurate method of identification that looks at a person's genetic code is DNA (deoxyribonucleic acid) analysis. Equipment and procedures specific to laboratories are needed for DNA-based biometrics. Individual samples, such as saliva or blood, are taken, and DNA sequencing techniques are used to eDNA analysis is frequently performed in mine and compare the genetic data. In forensic investigations, identification precision DNA analysis is commonly performed.

3.1.4 OVERVIEW OF THE AUTHENTICATION AND IDENTIFICATION PROCESSES IN BIOMETRIC SYSTEMS

Biometric systems use particular procedures for identification and authentication that take advantage of each person's distinctive biometric traits. An outline of these procedures is given below [7].

Authentication: The process of using biometric information to confirm a person's claimed identification is known as authentication. It encompasses the biometric sample added to the reference template previously stored and connected to the alleged identity. Typically, the steps of the authentication process are as follows:

- *Enrollment*: A person's biometric information, such as fingerprints, iris patterns, or facial features, is recorded using specialized hardware during the enrolment step. The processed data is used to construct a special reference template that depicts the person's biometric traits.
- *Presentation*: When authentication is required, the individual presents their biometric sample, such as placing a finger on a fingerprint scanner or looking into an iris recognition camera.
- *Feature Extraction*: To extract pertinent traits or distinctive data points, the submitted biometric sample was processed. These characteristics produce a condensed version of the biometric sample, often known as a biometric template.
- *Template Comparison*: The stored reference template linked to the claimed identification is compared to the extracted biometric template. Different matching algorithms are used to assess the templates' similarity or similarity.
- *Decision*: The claimed identification is accepted or rejected based on the comparison results. The claimed identity is verified, and verification is successful if there is a significant similarity between the given and

reference templates. Otherwise, access is prohibited, and authentication is unsuccessful.

- *Identification*: A choice is made regarding whether to accept or reject the claimed identity based on the comparison results. Authentication is booming, and the claimed identity is validated if there is a significant similarity between the given and reference templates. If authentication is unsuccessful, access is prohibited.
- *Enrollment*: The first part of the process entails enrolling biometric data of individuals and producing reference templates, much like the authentication process.
- *Presentation*: The system extracts features from the supplied sample when the person gives their biometric data.
- *Template Comparison*: The extracted template is compared to various templates kept in a database, which might comprise templates belonging to multiple people.
- *Matching Algorithm*: The provided template is compared to the database templates using sophisticated matching algorithms. The algorithm ranks the templates according to their similarity to the provided template or computes similarity scores for each template.
- *Decision*: The algorithm finds the best matching template, or it chooses the top-ranked templates that are more over a particular threshold. The system returns the identity of the identified person if a match is made. The person's identity is unknown when no match is made.

To improve accuracy and lower the danger of false matches or unauthorized access, biometric systems may integrate extra security features like multi-factor authentication (MFA). These procedures allow biometric systems to precisely validate asserted identities or identify unknown people based on their particular biometric traits, offering secure and trustworthy access control and identification solutions.

3.2 PRIOR WORK

User authentication and identity are crucial in the IoT (Internet of Things) age for ensuring the security of linked devices and the personalization of passive services. Traditional techniques of identification, however, have glaring drawbacks such as being covert, obtrusive, and vulnerable. The continuous authentication method based on behavioral biometrics is a revolutionary strategy that is introduced in this chapter. It highlights continuous authentication's salient features, such as its defense against intrusion, seamlessness, and user-friendliness. The essay also offers an overview of current sensing and computing-based continuous authentication technologies. The talk then digs into the difficulties and unanswered concerns surrounding continuous authentication, looking at them from the perspective of artificial intelligence (AI) [8].

This chapter aimed to understand deploying biometric tech at land borders and the impact of legal frameworks like General Data Protection Regulation (GDPR) on border control tech. Biometric tech is central to border check development, as European States launch more projects. It's crucial for traveler ID and data storage in

EU systems like VIS, SIS II, and EES. Border authorities use biometrics for efficient, secure, and reliable self-service clearance [9].

The purpose of the research was to investigate how a biometric system could be used to authenticate retail payments, digital banking, and financial technologies while maintaining security and ease of use. It also looked at the merits, disadvantages, and potential solutions of using biometric authentication in payment systems. The study's conclusions prompted a thorough debate on biometric solutions that can enable financial institutions and merchants to support innovative and secure methods of managing money, including access, transfers, and sharing. Conclusion: Banking institutions can use biometric technology as a cutting-edge tool to strengthen security and protect consumer funds from scammers, fraudsters, hackers, and other risks. Future research may take into account how closely interwoven biometrics, digital banking, and financial technology are [10].

In this research, authors expand on earlier evaluations by analyzing the usability and effects of touch-dynamic behavioral biometrics on authentication performance. With a thorough list of usability and ergonomic elements influencing user interaction and performance outcomes, we emphasize the significance of prioritizing usability in performance evaluations. Our main focus is on usability evaluations for the three distinct touch-dynamics modalities of signature, keystroke, and swipe, including user acceptability and performance studies. We also compare the accuracy and mistake rates across different research investigations. Additionally, we compile open-source datasets and talk about new attack vectors, weaknesses, and the viability of touch-dynamic behavioral biometrics [11].

This chapter investigated access control recovery techniques for blockchain-based Electronic Health Records (EHRs) shared among scattered healthcare providers. We surveyed blockchain research in healthcare first before concentrating on EHR systems. We identified prerequisites for efficient access control recovery and examined issues with blockchain-based electronic health records. We suggested Biometric-Based Electronic Health Records (BBEHR), a multi-layered approach allocating roles to healthcare providers, blockchain, and cloud storage to provide EHR recovery access over the blockchain network. Additionally, by interacting with traditional healthcare settings through external UIs, this strategy could hasten the transfer of healthcare providers to blockchain platforms [12].

3.3   PRIVACY AND SECURITY RISKS IN BIOMETRIC SYSTEMS

3.3.1   PHYSICAL BREACHES AND THEFT OF BIOMETRIC IDENTIFIERS

Although compared to conventional identification techniques, biometric systems provide increased security, there have been cases of physical violations and theft of biometric identifiers. Here are some noteworthy examples [13]:

- *Office of Personnel Management (OPM) Data Breach*: A significant data breach at the US OPM in 2015 led to the loss of private data, including the fingerprints of more than 5.6 million federal government employees. The hack exposed the weakness of biometric information and sparked worries about the potential abuse of stolen fingerprints.

- *Aadhaar Data Breaches*: One of the world's most extensive biometric identity systems, Aadhaar in India, has experienced numerous data breaches. It was revealed in 2018 that the Aadhaar database had been compromised, exposing millions of people's biometric data and personal information. These incidents also raised the security of biometric databases and the possibility of identity theft.
- *Biostar 2 Data Leak*: A data breach involving Biostar 2, a well-known biometric security platform, exposed more than 1 million fingerprint prints, face recognition data, and other private data in 2019. The hack illustrated the potential dangers of centralized biometric databases and the significance of strong security controls to safeguard biometric information.
- *Ongoing Security Vulnerabilities*: It has been discovered that biometric systems are vulnerable by nature. Researchers have proven successful attacks, including spoofing fingerprints using synthetic prints or high-resolution photographs and getting around facial recognition systems with masks or edited photos. These flaws underscore the requirement for ongoing investigation and development of defenses to strengthen the security of biometric systems.

It is essential to address these thefts and breaches to make biometric systems more secure. Strong access controls, frequent security audits, employee awareness, and training, as well as the encryption and secure storage of biometric data, can all help reduce risks and safeguard people's biometric identifiers. A further layer of security against unauthorized access and identity theft can be added by deploying MFA, which combines biometrics with other authentication factors.

3.3.2 CYBERATTACKS TARGETING STORAGE AND TRANSMISSION OF BIOMETRIC DATA

Cyber attackers may target important points of vulnerability, such as the transmission and storage of biometric data. Some prominent instances of cyberattacks that targeted biometric data are listed below [14].

Table 3.1 highlights various cyberattack examples, while Table 3.2 offers concise mitigation measures to counteract these cyber threats. Organizations can improve the security of biometric data and lessen the possibility of successful cyberattacks targeting its transmission and storage by implementing these procedures.

3.3.3 THREATS AND RISKS ASSOCIATED WITH DATA BREACHES

Biometric data breaches can present serious dangers, threats, and repercussions for people and organizations. The following are some typical hazards and threats connected to data breaches involving biometric information as shown in Figure 3.1.

By using these steps, organizations can more effectively protect biometric data, reduce the risks of data breaches, and preserve people's security and privacy. Table 3.3 delineates threats and risks related to data breaches [16], while Table 3.4 presents succinct mitigation measures to mitigate these risks [17].

TABLE 3.1
Cyberattack Examples

S. No.	Cyberattack Examples	Description
1.	OPM Data Breach	In 2015, the OPM (US Office of Personnel Management) data breach resulted in the theft of personal information, including biometric data, of millions of individuals.
2.	WannaCry Ransomware Attack	The 2017 WannaCry attack affected healthcare facilities, like the United Kingdom's NHS, highlighting the risk to biometric data stored in healthcare systems.
3.	Biometric Database Hacks	In 2019, an unsecured database exposed over 27.8 million biometric records, including fingerprints and facial recognition data, posing identity theft risks.
4.	Insider Threats	In 2020, a Chinese biometrics company employee stole millions of people's facial recognition data for illegal purposes.

3.4   SPOOFING ATTACKS AND IDENTITY THEFT IN BIOMETRIC SYSTEMS

Biometric systems are significantly in danger from spoofing attacks and identity theft. Adversaries may use several strategies to get around biometric authentication, compromise sensitive systems, or pass themselves off as someone else. Here are some typical forms of identity theft and spoofing attacks in biometric systems [18].

TABLE 3.2
Cyberattack Mitigation Measures [15]

Mitigation Measures	Description
Encryption	Implement robust encryption algorithms to protect stored and transmitted biometric data. Encryption ensures that even if data is intercepted or compromised, it remains unreadable and unusable by unauthorized parties.
Secure Transmission Protocols	Use secure transmission protocols like HTTPS or VPNs to encrypt biometric data while transferring over networks. This prevents eavesdropping and tampering during transmission.
Access Controls and Authentication	Implement robust access controls to restrict unauthorized access to biometric data storage systems. Adopt multi-factor authentication to enhance security by combining biometrics with other authentication factors, such as passwords or tokens.
Regular Security Audits	Conduct regular security audits and vulnerability assessments to identify and address potential biometric data storage and transmission system weaknesses.
Employee Training and Awareness	Provide comprehensive training to employees regarding the importance of data security, the risks associated with cyberattacks, and best practices for safeguarding biometric data. Employee awareness is crucial in preventing insider threats and other security breaches.

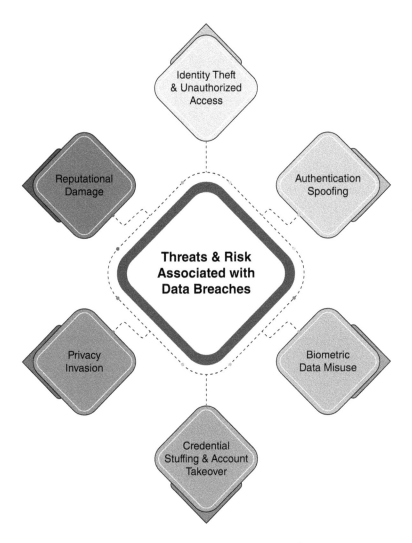

FIGURE 3.1 Threats and risks associated with data breaches [15].

Table 3.5 outlines spoofing attacks and identity theft in biometric systems, and Table 3.6 provides mitigation measures to address these threats.

3.5 IMPLICATIONS OF BIOMETRIC DATA RETENTION AND SHARING

3.5.1 CENTRALIZED BIOMETRIC DATABASES AND THEIR VULNERABILITIES

Centralized biometric databases, which keep a person's biometric information in one place, can be subject to several dangers and weaknesses. Here are a few typical defects related to centralized biometric databases [12]:

TABLE 3.3

Threats and Risks Associated with Data Breaches

S. No.	Threats and Risks	Description
1	Identity Theft	Biometric data breaches can lead to identity theft, where stolen biometric identifiers are exploited to impersonate individuals. Cybercriminals can use compromised biometric data, such as fingerprints or iris scans, to gain unauthorized access to systems, accounts, or facilities and conduct fraudulent activities.
2	Unauthorized Access	Breached biometric data may grant unauthorized individuals access to sensitive systems, secure areas, or confidential information. Compromised biometric identifiers could bypass authentication and gain unauthorized entry to restricted areas or accounts.
3	Authentication Spoofing	Breached biometric data can lead to spoofing attacks, where adversaries attempt to mimic an individual's biometric characteristics to deceive biometric systems. For example, fingerprint or facial recognition spoofing techniques can be used to gain unauthorized access.
4	Privacy Invasion	Biometric data breaches can invade individuals' privacy by exposing their unique physiological or behavioral traits to unauthorized entities, causing distress and loss of trust in biometric systems.
5	Credential Stuffing and Account Takeover	Compromised biometric data and other stolen credentials can facilitate credential-stuffing attacks, leading to account takeovers and unauthorized control of individuals' online profiles, financial accounts, or sensitive data.
6	Biometric Data Misuse	Breached biometric data can be misused for various purposes, such as creating fraudulent identities, committing financial fraud, or engaging in social engineering attacks. Criminals may attempt to sell or trade stolen biometric information on the dark web.
7	Reputational Damage	Organizations that experience data breaches involving biometric data can suffer significant reputational damage due to loss of customer trust, negative media coverage, and potential legal repercussions.

TABLE 3.4

Threats and Risks Associated with Data Breaches Mitigation Measures

Mitigation Measures	Description
Strong Encryption	Ensure that biometric data is stored and transmitted using robust encryption algorithms to protect it from unauthorized access.
Multi-Factor Authentication	Implement multi-factor authentication mechanisms that combine biometric data with other authentication factors, such as passwords or tokens, to enhance security and prevent unauthorized access.
Regular Monitoring and Auditing	Monitor systems for suspicious activities, perform regular security audits, and promptly investigate potential breaches or unauthorized access attempts.
Data Minimization	Employ data minimization practices by collecting and storing only necessary biometric information, reducing the overall risk of exposure in a breach.
Employee Training	Educate employees on the importance of data security, safe handling of biometric information, and awareness of potential threats such as phishing or social engineering attacks.

TABLE 3.5
Spoofing Attacks and Identity Theft in Biometric Systems [18]

S. No.	Mitigation Measures	Description
1	Fingerprint Spoofing	To trick fingerprint identification systems, adversaries fabricate fake fingerprints using molds, lifted prints, or high-resolution photographs. Creating counterfeit fingerprints and getting around fingerprint scanners using substances like silicone, gelatin, or conductive ink is possible.
2	Face Mask Attacks	To fool facial recognition systems into identifying them as authorized users, adversaries don masks or employ printed images/3D shows. Attacks using masks take advantage of the system's inability to tell a live person from a static image, giving them access.
3	Iris Forgery	To trick iris recognition systems, adversaries fabricate false iris patterns utilizing high-resolution pictures or printed contact lenses with altered iris patterns.
4	Voice Replication	To trick voice recognition systems, adversaries replicate a person's voice using recorded samples and cutting-edge voice synthesis or conversion techniques.
5	Presentation Attacks	Adversaries trick the system into believing that modified or fake biometric samples (such as printed images or video recordings) are real by presenting them with it.
6	Identity Theft	Identity theft caused by exploiting stolen biometric data to impersonate somebody to access systems or accounts results from biometric data breaches. Theft of biometric information may be used with other personally identifiable information by adversaries to construct false identities, perpetrate financial fraud, or launch social engineering assaults.

Table 3.7 summarizes centralized biometric databases and their vulnerabilities, while Table 3.8 presents mitigation measures.

3.5.2 RISKS OF COMBINING BIOMETRIC DATA WITH OTHER PERSONAL INFORMATION

Combining biometric data with other personally identifiable information can increase risks and cause privacy, security, and potential abuse issues. The following are some dangers connected with combining biometric information with additional personal information as shown in Tables 3.9 and 3.10. [19].

Organizations can reduce privacy and security concerns, create trust, and ensure responsible and ethical management of individual data by carefully evaluating the risks of merging biometric data with other personal information and implementing suitable measures. Consequences that could result from unauthorized access to and exploitation of biometric data. Biometric data exploitation and unauthorized access can severely affect both persons and organizations. The following are some possible effects that could result from such unauthorized access and abuse (Table 3.11).

TABLE 3.6
Spoofing Attacks and Identity Theft in Biometric Systems Mitigation Measures

Mitigation Measures	Description
Anti-Spoofing Techniques	Use robust anti-spoofing techniques like liveness detection to identify and stop presentation attacks. Liveness detection algorithms can examine facial movement, eye blinking, or texture analysis to distinguish between actual samples and imitations.
Multi-modal Biometrics	Use numerous biometric modalities to increase security and make it more difficult for adversaries to concurrently fake multiple biometric attributes (for example, facial recognition with fingerprint or iris recognition).
Continuous Monitoring	Use real-time monitoring and analysis of biometric system data to look for and respond to suspicious patterns or abnormalities that could be signs of identity theft or spoofing attempts.
Regular System Updates	Regularly update firmware and security patches on biometric systems to fix known flaws and guard against new spoofing methods.
User Education	Users should be made aware of the dangers of spoofing attacks and identity theft, and they should be urged to keep their biometric data private and to report any suspicious activity or unauthorized access attempts.

TABLE 3.7
Centralized Biometric Databases and Their Vulnerabilities

S. No.	Vulnerabilities	Description
1	Single Point of Failure	A single point of failure is created by centralized databases when a security breach or database hack exposes all stored biometric data to unauthorized access or theft.
2	Data Breaches	Cybercriminals are drawn to centralized biometric databases, and weak security can result in data breaches from outside hacking or insider threats. Biometric data may be stolen, sold, or misused due to violations, which could result in fraud, identity theft, or other bad behavior.
3	Privacy Concerns	Privacy issues arise when sensitive biometric data from several people is gathered in one place. People may be concerned about unauthorized access to or use of their biometric data.
4	Inadequate Security Measures	The centralized database may be susceptible to unauthorized access due to lax security measures, such as inadequate access controls or poor encryption, weak authentication, or inadequate access controls.
5	Potential for Mass Surveillance	Concerns regarding widespread surveillance and possible power abuse can arise when centralized biometric databases are connected to massive surveillance technologies. The potential for extensive surveillance and data misuse rises with the collection of biometric data.
6	Difficulty in Revoking Biometric Data	Due to the immutability of biometric data, it is difficult to cancel or alter compromised biometric identifiers. Long-term concerns can result from a compromise in the centralized database because people cannot quickly change or update their biometric traits.

TABLE 3.8
Centralized Biometric Databases and Their Vulnerabilities Mitigation Measures

Mitigation Measures	Description
Strong Security Controls	Establish strong security measures, such as encryption, access controls, and authentication procedures, to guard the centralized biometric database against hacking and other unauthorized access.
Regular Security Audits	To find and fix vulnerabilities or weaknesses in the centralized biometric database system, conduct routine security audits and assessments.
Data Minimization	By gathering and retaining only a minimal amount of biometric data, you can reduce your overall risk exposure in the case of a breach.
Decentralized or Distributed Systems	Alternative strategies should be considered, including decentralized or distributed systems, where biometric information is kept across numerous places or devices, minimizing the impact of a single point of failure and lowering the potential harm from a security breach.
Privacy-by-Design	Develop and run the centralized biometric database system using privacy-by-design principles. Implement privacy-enhancing technology and measures to preserve people's rights to privacy and assure compliance with applicable privacy rules.
Transparency and Accountability	Encourage openness and responsibility in the operation and maintenance of centralized biometric databases. Establish procedures to exercise their rights and seek redress if their privacy has been violated or their biometric data has been improperly acquired, stored, or exploited.

Businesses and individuals must prioritize the security and protection of biometric data to reduce these potential adverse effects. Strong security measures, encryption, access limits, frequent security audits, and adherence to privacy best practices are some examples of what should be done. Additionally, people should exercise vigilance, immediately report suspicious activity, and take all required security measures to protect their biometric data and personal information (Figure 3.2).

3.6 LEGAL AND ETHICAL CONSIDERATIONS

Typically, the individuals whose data is being gathered must give their express and informed consent before any biometric data may be collected or used. Approval ensures people have control over their personal information and is a core concept of privacy and data protection. Obtaining explicit and informed consent is crucial for biometric data, which is extremely sensitive and particular to each person. To obtain permission for the collection and use of biometric data, the following points must be taken into account [15]:

- *Informed Consent*: The intent, nature, and scope of the collection and use of biometric data should all be made clear to the public by organizations. This includes outlining the precise biometric identifiers or traits that will be

TABLE 3.9

Risks of Combining Biometric Data with Other Personal Information

S. No.	Risks of Combining Biometric Data with Other Personal Information	Description
1	Increased Identifiability	A person's ability to be identified is improved when biometric data is combined with other personal information, which raises the possibility of privacy violations and unauthorized surveillance or profiling. By integrating biometric data with additional personally identifying information, adversaries can DE anonymize a person, presenting the case of identity theft or intrusive surveillance.
2	Expanding Attack Surface	The attack surface for cybercriminals is increased when biometric data is combined with other personal information. A breach of the combined dataset might give potential attackers access to a richer and more valuable data set that could be exploited for identity theft, fraud, or targeted assaults by taking advantage of biometric and personal data flaws.
3	Aggregated Profile Creation	Using biometric data and other personal information, comprehensive profiles of people can be created. These profiles may be used for manipulation, profiling, or targeted advertising. Advertisers, data brokers, or malevolent actors may use this aggregated profile to learn about a person's preferences, behaviors, or weak points, potentially resulting in privacy violations or discriminatory practices.
4	Data Breach Impact	When biometric data is joined with other pieces of personal information, the effects of a data breach are exacerbated. Since biometric traits cannot be changed, compromising biometric data may expose individuals to long-term hazards. When paired with additional personal information, hacked biometric data makes mitigating the effects difficult for those impacted.
5	Informed Consent Challenges	Obtaining informed consent from people is more complicated by combining biometric data with additional personal information. Due to the sensitive nature of biometric data, obtaining approval for its collection, storage, and usage is already tricky. Individuals could have more difficulty understanding the scope and potential hazards of using their combined data when paired with additional personal information.
6	Discriminatory Practices	The possibility of discriminatory practices is increased when biometric data is combined with other personal information. When used with different individual characteristics, biometric identifiers can reinforce prejudices or result in unfair treatment based on ethnicity, gender, or outward appearance. This can have significant ethical and social repercussions, underscoring the importance of managing and protecting pooled databases wisely.

TABLE 3.10

Risks of Combining Biometric Data with Other Personal Information Mitigation Measures

Mitigation Measures	Description
Privacy Impact Assessments	Conduct privacy effect analyses when integrating biometric data with other personal information to detect and resolve potential privacy issues and ensure compliance with relevant privacy rules.
Data Minimization	Adopt data minimization principles and only gather and store the minimum personal data required to fulfill the intended purpose. Only combine biometric data with other personal information for a compelling reason.
Strong Security Practices	Establish robust security mechanisms, such as encryption, access limits, and monitoring, to shield the merged databases from hacking or other unauthorized access.
Privacy-enhancing Technologies	Investigate using privacy-enhancing technology to enable data analysis while protecting individual privacy, such as differential privacy or safe multi-party computation.
Transparent Data Practices	Maintaining transparency in data practices is essential, as is giving people clear information about the combination, storage, and use of their biometric data. Give people the power to manage their data and decide how to utilize it in an educated manner.

TABLE 3.11

Potential Consequences of Unauthorized Access and Misuse of Biometric Data [20]

S. No.	Potential Consequences of Unauthorized Access and Misuse of Biometric Data	Description
1	Identity Theft	Identity theft can result from unauthorized access to and misuse of biometric data because criminals can use stolen data to assume victims' identities, access accounts or systems without authorization, and commit fraud in their names. Financial hardship, harm to one's reputation, and severe emotional pain may follow for the victims.
2	Fraudulent Transactions	Biometric information that is misused can be exploited by criminals to conduct fraudulent activities. For instance, if financial transactions rely on biometric authentication, unauthorized access to biometric data may allow adversaries to carry out financial operations—such as payments and transfers—on behalf of the victims, resulting in losses.
3	Unauthorized Access to Systems or Facilities	Biometric data is frequently used to control access to secure locations or systems. Personal safety, intellectual property, and national security risks may result from unauthorized individuals accessing sensitive areas, classified information, or restricted regions.

(Continued)

TABLE 3.11 *(Continued)*
Potential Consequences of Unauthorized Access and Misuse of Biometric Data [20]

S. No.	Potential Consequences of Unauthorized Access and Misuse of Biometric Data	Description
4	Privacy Infringement	Biometric information reveals individuals' distinctive physiological or behavioral traits and is highly private and sensitive. Biometric data misuse and unauthorized access can lead to serious privacy violations against people's rights to privacy and individuality. Without the subject's knowledge or permission, adversaries might track, monitor, or profile them using the hacked data.
5	Social Engineering Attacks	Biometric information can create convincing social engineering attacks when paired with other personal data. Through their hacked biometric data, adversaries can trick people into divulging critical information or taking actions they wouldn't usually take. This may result in additional private or financial information theft, extortion, or other harmful effects.
6	Loss of Trust and Reputation	Businesses that fail to safeguard biometric data and suffer from unauthorized access or exploitation risk damaging their brand and confidence. Customers' loyalty, business alliances, or the organization's reputation may suffer if people lose faith in protecting their private information.
7	Legal and Regulatory Consequences	Biometric data misuse and unauthorized access may have legal and regulatory repercussions. Companies disregarding privacy and data protection regulations risk fines, penalties, or legal consequences. Legal action against those accountable may also be taken by those impacted by unauthorized access.
8	Psychological Impact	Individuals may experience psychological effects due to unauthorized access to and exploitation of biometric data. Knowing that their distinctive biometric characteristics have been compromised and can be used against them can make people feel violated, anxious, or as though their security has been lost.

recorded, how they will be utilized, how long the data will be stored, and any dangers or repercussions resulting from gathering and using biometric information.

• *Voluntary Consent*: Freely given consent must be granted without compulsion or improper influence. The decision to give or withhold permission for collecting and using biometric data should be up to the individual. Organizations should only require approval if there are valid and vital justifications for doing so to receive essential services or benefits.

FIGURE 3.2 Potential consequences of unauthorized access and misuse of biometric data [20].

- *Explicit Consent*: The individual's clear and positive action is required to get express consent for collecting and using biometric data. The unambiguous consent of the person to the collection and use of their biometric data may be expressed in writing, electronically, or in any other manner.
- *Granular Consent*: Organizations should obtain separate consent when collecting and using biometric data for a specific purpose. As a result, people can provide their permission for particular uses while still having control over how their biometric data is used. For use in access control, authentication, or other specific objectives, extra consent would be needed.
- *Revocable Consent*: People should be free to revoke their consent at any moment for collecting and using their biometric data. Unless there are legal obligations or valid grounds for storing the data, organizations should offer individuals explicit ways to withdraw consent and guarantee that their data is immediately and securely erased or anonymized upon withdrawal.

- *Age and Capacity Considerations*: Obtaining consent from minors with reduced decision-making capacity requires extra care. To ensure that the consent procedure is acceptable and that the person or their legal guardian fully understands the implications of giving consent for collecting and using biometric data, additional security measures could be required.
- *Privacy Policies and Notices*: Organizations should have precise data collection and use practices, including acquiring and using biometric data, communicated in their transparent privacy policies and notifications. These rules should be simple to find, presented in plain language, and give people a thorough understanding of how their biometric data will be used.

As consent requirements may change depending on the jurisdiction, organizations must abide by applicable privacy and data protection laws and regulations that regulate the collection and use of biometric data. It is possible to ensure that organizations adhere to the required consent standards and best practices while handling biometric data by consulting legal or privacy professionals.

3.6.1 Transparency and Accountability in Biometric Systems

For biometric technology to be used responsibly and ethically, transparency and accountability are essential. The following are some critical facets of accountability and transparency in biometric systems [21,22]:

- *Clear Communication*: When communicating with people about gathering, storing, and using their biometric data, organizations should be open and honest. This includes disclosing specific biometric identifiers that are being collected, why they are being gathered, how they will be stored and safeguarded, and the purposes for which the data will be used in a clear and understood manner.
- *Privacy Policies and Notices*: Organizations should have transparent data practices, including handling biometric data and transparent privacy policies and notices. It is essential that people can easily access and understand these rules so that they are fully aware of how their biometric data will be used, shared, and safeguarded.
- *Consent and Opt-Out Mechanisms*: Organizations should get informed consent before collecting and using biometric data from individuals. People should be able to make an informed choice about submitting their biometric data since the consent process should be straightforward. Additionally, businesses should offer unambiguous opt-out options that permit people to revoke their consent and prevent the gathering or use of their biometric information.
- *Data Protection Measures*: To guarantee biometric data security and privacy, biometric systems should integrate robust data protection mechanisms. This includes putting access controls, encryption, and other suitable security measures in place to avoid unauthorized access or breaches. Organizations should be open and honest about the security precautions

they have taken to safeguard biometric data and regularly review and update those precautions as needed.

- *Data Retention and Deletion*: Organizations should set up explicit policies and procedures for storing and erasing biometric data. Communication about the length for which the data will be retained and the conditions under which it will be destroyed must be transparent. Organizations should abide by these guidelines and ensure that when biometric data is no longer required, it is safely and permanently removed.
- *Accountability for Data Handling*: For organizations to comply with privacy rules and regulations, clear accountability procedures should be in place. This involves choosing a privacy officer or other responsible person to oversee the company's data handling procedures, monitor compliance, and respond to customer complaints or questions about biometric data.
- *Auditing and Oversight*: To maintain compliance with privacy and security standards, biometric systems should undergo routine audits and evaluations. Independent oversight or third-party audits might provide additional assurances of openness and responsibility in handling biometric data.
- *Compliance with Regulations*: Organizations should be aware of pertinent laws and rules governing the use of biometric data, such as data protection legislation, industry-specific rules, and regional rules. Respecting people's private rights requires accountability, as observed by these rules.

Organizations may increase customer trust, display responsible data handling procedures, and guarantee that the usage of biometric data complies with ethical and legal norms by adopting openness and accountability in biometric systems.

3.6.2   COMPLIANCE WITH DATA PROTECTION REGULATIONS AND PRIVACY LAWS

Compliance with data protection laws and regulations is crucial for gathering, storing, and utilizing biometric data. The following are some essential factors to ensure compliance [23,24]:

- *Understanding Applicable Regulations*: The data protection rules and privacy legislation that apply to the collection and use of biometric data in a given country must be understood by organizations. This involves becoming familiar with relevant national and regional regulations, such as the California Consumer Privacy Act (CCPA) in the United States and the GDPR in the European Union.
- *Lawful Basis for Processing:* As needed by applicable rules, organizations should determine and create a legitimate basis for processing biometric data. Standard legal bases that may be used include consent, contractual necessity, adherence to legal requirements, legitimate interests, or accomplishing a task in the public interest. Finding the proper foundation and adequately documenting it is crucial.
- *Individual Rights*: Under data protection legislation, individuals are given specific rights about their data, including biometric data. These rights, such

as the right to access, rectification, erasure, or restriction of the processing of biometric data, must be respected by organizations and made possible. Policies and controls should be in place to meet specific demands and uphold these rights.

- *Data Minimization and Purpose Limitation*: Using only the biometric data required for the intended use, organizations should practice data reduction. Additionally, they should ensure that people are informed of and understand the explicit purpose of processing biometric data. Obtaining extra consent or demonstrating a different legal basis may be necessary for using biometric data beyond the stated purpose.
- *Security Safeguards*: To prevent unauthorized access, disclosure, or misuse of biometric data, organizations need to implement the proper organizational and technical safeguards. These precautions should align with how sensitive the biometric data is and any potential risks involved in processing it. Security measures that can be used include encryption, access limits, frequent security assessments, and employee training.
- *Cross-Border Data Transfers*: Organizations must ensure that laws governing cross-border data transfers are followed if biometric data is sent to people or servers abroad. This may entail putting in place suitable measures like Standard Contractual Clauses or Binding Corporate Rules or ensuring the receiving nation provides adequate data protection as determined by competent authorities.
- *Data Breach Notification*: In the event of a biometric data breach, organizations should have procedures to identify it, respond to it, and notify the affected parties and the appropriate authorities. Prompt and open communication about the breach is crucial to comply with data breach notification regulations and minimize harm to impacted individuals.
- *Privacy Impact Assessments (PIAs)*: It is advised to conduct privacy impact analyses before implementing new biometric systems or processing techniques. PIAs enable organizations to establish suitable procedures to manage the privacy risks associated with collecting and using biometric data by assisting in identifying and assessing those risks.
- *Documentation and Record-keeping*: Ensure that all policies, processes, consent forms, data processing agreements, and records of processing operations are adequately documented. These records can be used to show compliance efforts and to support responses to regulatory questions or audits.
- *Data Protection Officer (DPO)*: Where a DPO has been designated, continuing compliance with data protection laws can be helped. The DPO is a point of contact for people, organizations, and internal stakeholders on data protection issues and offers compliance advice.

Organizations must regularly evaluate and update their data protection procedures to stay current with changing laws and best practices. Obtaining legal advice or consulting privacy experts can help you through the complicated web of data protection rules and privacy legislation that apply specifically to biometric data (Table 3.12).

TABLE 3.12

Detection and Removal of Vulnerabilities in Biometric Systems [25,26]

Technique Name	Year	Outcomes	Usage
Threat Modeling	2017	Identification of potential system vulnerabilities and their impacts	Biometric system design and development
Penetration Testing	2019	Identification of system weaknesses and vulnerabilities through simulated attacks	Assessing system security and improving defenses
Security Patch Management	2020	Timely application of patches and updates to address known vulnerabilities	Mitigating risks and maintaining system integrity
Risk Assessment and Mitigation	2018	Evaluation of potential risks and implementation of measures to reduce their impact	Identifying and managing security risks
Secure Development Lifecycle	2016	Integration of security measures throughout the development process	Building secure biometric systems from the ground up
Continuous Monitoring	2021	Ongoing monitoring for system vulnerabilities and potential threats	Real-time threat detection and response
Biometric Template Protection	2022	Secure storage and encryption of biometric templates to prevent unauthorized access	Protecting sensitive biometric data
Anti-Spoofing Techniques	2019	Detection and prevention of spoofing attacks to ensure the authenticity of biometric samples	Enhancing system security against presentation attacks
Secure Communication Protocols	2023	Encryption and secure transmission of biometric data during communication	Protecting the privacy and integrity of biometric information
User Awareness and Education	2021	Educating users about security best practices and potential risks associated with biometric systems	Enhancing user security awareness and reducing vulnerabilities
Compliance with Privacy Regulations	2020	Ensuring adherence to data protection laws and regulations to safeguard user privacy	Meeting legal and regulatory requirements

3.6.3 Mitigating Vulnerabilities and Enhancing Security

3.6.4 Encryption of Biometric Data

Encryption is a vital security precaution for storing and transmitting biometric data. To prevent unauthorized parties from accessing or deciphering the data, encryption ensures that the data is changed into a safe and unreadable state. Here is an illustration of how biometric data is currently being encrypted [27,28]:

- *Biometric Database Encryption*: Encryption is frequently used to protect data while storing biometric data in a centralized data instance, a database. A financial organization using fingerprint biometrics for customer authentication might encrypt the fingerprint templates kept by this encryption process. They use algorithms to convert the raw biometric data into an encrypted version. The original biometric data can only be accessed or retrieved by anybody with the correct decryption keys.

- *Secure Transmission of Biometric Data*: A biometric sensor might send data to a central server for verification, whereas biometric data is frequently exchanged between devices or systems. This message uses encryption to shield the data from eavesdropping and unauthorized access. For instance, iris recognition data can be encrypted and transmitted from an iris scanner to a central authentication server using secure protocols (such as Secure Socket Layer [SSL]/Transport Layer Security [TLS]) to create a safe communication channel. This ensures that the biometric information is protected and bad actors cannot readily intercept or alter it.

- *Mobile Device Encryption*: Encryption is essential for safeguarding biometric information stored on mobile devices, which is increasingly used for biometric authentication. For instance, the biometric templates and associated data saved in the device's secure enclave or a trusted hardware module are frequently encrypted in smartphones that unlock the device using a fingerprint or facial recognition system. Even if the device is lost or stolen, the biometric data will be safe thanks to its encryption.

- *Cloud Storage Encryption*: Businesses can use encryption to protect biometric data stored in the cloud. Before being uploaded to the cloud storage provider, biometric data might be encrypted. Only those with the necessary decryption keys and authorization can access the cloud storage of the encrypted data. In the case of a data breach or unauthorized access to the cloud storage infrastructure, this shields the biometric data from unauthorized access or exposure.

A vital part of protecting biometric data throughout its lifecycle is encryption. Organizations can significantly lower the danger of unauthorized access and safeguard the privacy of people whose biometric information is being kept or transmitted by encrypting the data in transit and at rest.

3.6.5 MULTI-FACTOR AUTHENTICATION TECHNIQUES

To increase the security and dependability of the authentication process, MFA techniques in biometrics combine multiple biometric elements or combine biometrics with other authentication methods. Here are some popular strategies for MFA in biometrics [29]:

- *Biometric Fusion*: To authenticate a person, biometric fusion combines different biometric factors from that person. Combining fingerprints, iris patterns, face traits, voiceprints, and other biometric identifiers can be one way to do this. The technology lowers the possibility of false positives or false negatives by using numerous biometric factors, increasing authentication accuracy and dependability.

- *Biometric and Personal Identification Number (PIN)/Password*: This method combines a password or PIN with biometric authentication. The user enters a PIN or password combined with a biometric sample (such as a fingerprint or iris scan) to prove their identity. Both factors are validated to maintain a better level of security because, even if one is compromised, the attacker would still require the other element for successful authentication.
- *Biometric and Token-based Authentication*: This method combines a physical or digital token with biometric authentication. The user displays a token, such as a smart card, USB token, or mobile device, along with their biometric sample. The authentication process's overall security may be improved by the token's inclusion of extra security measures or cryptographic keys.
- *Biometric and One-Time Password (OTP)*: This method combines the OTP produced for each authentication attempt with biometrics. The user submits their biometric sample along with the OTP, which is often made by a different device or application. Given that the OTP is time-limited and different for each authentication attempt, this adds extra protection.
- *Biometric and Behavioral Biometrics*: Analyzing user behavior patterns, such as typing patterns, mouse movements, or gait analyses, is a component of behavioral biometrics. The system may confirm a user's identification based on both physical and behavioral traits by fusing biometric authentication (such as fingerprint or facial recognition) with behavioral biometrics.
- *Multi-modal Biometrics*: Multiple biometric characteristics from various modalities are combined in multi-modal biometrics for authentication. A system could combine speech recognition, iris scanning, and fingerprint scanning to authenticate a user. Utilizing the advantages of many biometric modalities improves the authentication process's accuracy and dependability.

By requiring the presentation and verification of multiple elements, using MFA procedures in biometrics offers an extra layer of security. It lowers the danger of unauthorized access or impersonation. By strengthening their general resilience and reliability, biometric systems become less susceptible to spoofing assaults or false identifications.

3.6.6 Secure Storage and Transmission Protocols

Secure storage and transmission procedures are crucial to prevent unauthorized access to or interception of biometric data. Here are some current protocols that are frequently used for the safe transmission and storage of biometric data [30]:

- *SSL/TLS*: Many networks employ SSL/TLS protocols to protect the transmission of biometric data. These protocols create an encrypted communication channel between a client (a biometric device) and a server, guaranteeing the security of the data being exchanged between them. Cryptographic techniques are used by SSL/TLS protocols to encrypt data during transmission, ensuring secrecy and integrity.

- *Internet Protocol Security (IPsec)*: A set of network protocols called IPsec offers security features for communications using IP addresses. It may be applied to protect the transfer of biometric information across IP networks. IPsec protocols verify the communication parties and create an encrypted tunnel between them to guarantee the confidentiality and integrity of transmitted data.
- *Secure File Transfer Protocol (SFTP)*: The secure file transfer protocol known as SFTP is frequently used to transmit and store biometric data safely. It creates a secure connection between the client and server using SSH (Secure Shell). For the confidentiality and integrity of files, including biometric data, during storage and transfer, SFTP offers encryption and authentication techniques.
- *Pretty Good Privacy (PGP)*: PGP is a program that encrypts data and offers cryptographic privacy and authentication. Before being stored or transmitted, biometric data can be encrypted using this method. Using the recipient's public key to encrypt the data, PGP uses public-key cryptography to ensure that only the recipient holding the appropriate private key can decrypt and read the data.
- *Trusted Platform Module (TPM)*: TPM is a hardware-based security module that performs cryptographic operations and safe storage. It can safely store cryptographic keys or biometric data encryption templates. TPM guarantees the integrity and security of the data saved, preventing it from being accessed or altered by unauthorized parties.
- *Biometric Template Protection Techniques*: Instead of protecting the transmission or storage protocols, biometric template protection solutions concentrate on preserving the biometric templates. These methods include biometric cryptosystems, cancelable biometrics, and fuzzy commitment. These methods give an extra layer of security to stored biometric templates by converting them into a safe format that cannot be reverse-engineered or utilized to recreate the original biometric data.

It is crucial to remember that the particular needs and circumstances of the biometric system should guide the choice and implementation of secure storage and transmission methods. To guarantee the confidentiality, integrity, and accessibility of biometric data, organizations should determine the level of security required, consider compliance with pertinent rules, and adhere to industry best practices.

3.6.7 IMPORTANCE OF CONTINUOUS MONITORING, AUDITING, AND SECURITY UPDATES

The integrity, confidentiality, and availability of biometric systems must be maintained by constant monitoring, auditing, and security updates. This is why they are significant [31]:

- *Detection of Anomalies and Suspicious Activities*: Real-time detection of anomalies or suspicious activity within the biometric system is made possible by ongoing monitoring. Organizations can spot security breaches, unauthorized access attempts, or unusual system behavior by monitoring system logs, network traffic, and access patterns. Rapid discovery provides quick reaction and security event mitigation, minimizing the possible impact on the biometric system and the data it stores.

- *Prevention of Unauthorized Access*: Only authorized individuals have access to the biometric system and its sensitive data, thanks in part to regular monitoring and audits. Organizations can detect unauthorized access attempts or unusual user behavior by monitoring user accounts, access limits, and authentication logs. This makes it possible to take proactive measures to stop unauthorized access and safeguard the privacy and confidentiality of biometric data.

- *Compliance with Security Standards and Regulations*: Maintaining compliance with security standards and laws governing biometric systems requires ongoing monitoring and auditing. Industry-specific rules or data protection legislation may apply to organizations requiring constant monitoring, auditing, and security updates. Organizations can reduce legal and regulatory risks and uphold stakeholder trust by showing compliance through efficient monitoring and auditing procedures.

- *Identification of System Vulnerabilities*: Regular security updates and vulnerability analyses are essential for finding and fixing potential flaws in the biometric system. Over time, new flaws or exploits may appear, and to fix them, software or hardware components of the system may need fixes or upgrades. System vulnerabilities are found through continuous monitoring and auditing, which enables organizations to implement the appropriate security updates and preventative actions to safeguard against prospective threats.

- *Incident Response and Recovery*: Continuous monitoring and audits give vital information for incident reaction and recovery activities in the case of a security incident or data breach. Forensic investigation, assessing the extent of the issue, and putting suitable measures in place to contain and remedy the situation can all be helped by detailed logs and audit trails. This entails stopping future occurrences of the same problems, such as restoring lost data, upgrading incident response strategies, and strengthening security controls.

- *Proactive Security Measures*: Organizations can proactively discover and address biometric system flaws or security weaknesses through ongoing monitoring and audits. Organizations can better put the right security measures in place on time by remaining informed about new threats, vulnerabilities, and industry best practices. To ensure the system's resistance to evolving threats, this may entail putting extra security measures in place, improving user awareness and training, or conducting security assessments.

3.6.8 Necessity of Striking a Balance between Privacy and Security Concerns

In biometric systems, balancing privacy and security concerns is crucial to preserve users' data while maintaining the required security measures. Here's why maintaining a balance between security and privacy is essential [32]:

- *Preserving Individual Privacy*: Biometric information is highly private and sensitive, such as fingerprints, iris patterns, or facial traits. It can reveal specific personal information and individually identify persons. Individuals' biometric data will be gathered, stored, and utilized in a way that respects their private rights if privacy and security are balanced appropriately. To avoid unauthorized access to or exploitation of biometric data, privacy considerations include gaining informed consent, setting strict time limits on data keeping, and putting strong security measures in place.

- *Preventing Unauthorized Access and Identity Theft*: Biometric data must be safeguarded against unauthorized access, identity theft, and harmful usage. Strong security measures like encryption, access limits, and secure storage are crucial for biometric data to remain private and prevent easy exploitation by attackers. By striking a balance, security measures are achieved without jeopardizing people's privacy or leading to excessive data collection or surveillance.

- *Compliance with Privacy Regulations*: Biometric data is among the types of personal information protected by privacy laws and regulations in many jurisdictions. Compliance with these laws, such as the CCPA in the United States or the GDPR in Europe, is ensured by striking a balance between privacy and security. To prevent fines, reputational harm, or legal repercussions, organizations must balance privacy obligations while putting in place solid security measures.

- *Maintaining Public Trust*: Public confidence in biometric systems depends on balancing privacy and security. People need to feel confident knowing that their biometric data will be handled securely and with consideration for their privacy. The public's trust may be damaged by overly intrusive or unsafe biometric systems, which may discourage the use of the technology. Building trust and promoting biometric technologies as dependable, safe, and privacy-respecting solutions require a well-balanced strategy.

- *Ethical Considerations*: Ethical considerations are involved in achieving privacy and security balance in biometric systems. Organizations must consider the moral ramifications of collecting, using, and possibly subjecting surveillance to biometric data. Respecting privacy and implementing robust security measures is consistent with moral ideals like data minimization, purpose limitation, and transparency while preventing potential misuse of biometric data.

3.6.9 IMPORTANCE OF USER AWARENESS AND EDUCATION REGARDING BIOMETRIC SYSTEMS

User awareness and education are essential to ensure efficient and appropriate use of biometric systems. Here are some reasons why user awareness and education are crucial [33]:

- *Informed Consent*: Using user awareness and education, people can better grasp the intent, ramifications, and possible risks of biometric systems. Individuals can consent by being informed about collecting, storing, and using their biometric data. This encourages openness and gives people the power to decide whether to use biometric technology.

- *Privacy Protection*: People who are aware of their rights to privacy and the value of securing their biometric data are better able to protect it. Users' comprehension of how their personal information is secured and their motivation to take an active role in protecting their privacy is improved by providing information regarding the security protections put in place, data handling procedures, and privacy safeguards.
- *Responsible Use*: Using biometric technology is encouraged responsibly through user awareness and education. People become aware of biometric technologies' proper and authorized services and the possible repercussions of exploiting or misusing the system. It is possible to reduce security lapses and misuse by educating users about their responsibility for the secure storage of biometric data, the value of employing robust authentication techniques, and the dangers of sharing their biometric information with unauthorized parties.
- *Mitigating Social Engineering Attacks*: Users can identify and counteract social engineering attempts that explicitly target biometric data by increasing their user awareness. Users can be cautious and watchful when giving their biometric information or responding to requests for authentication by being aware of standard social engineering techniques, including impersonation, coercion, or manipulation. Protecting against identity theft and unauthorized access is made more accessible by informing users of these dangers and offering instructions on confirming the legality of requests.
- *Empowering User Control*: Individuals are assigned to take control of their biometric data through user awareness and education. People can participate in biometric systems, manage access to their biometric information, and exercise their rights connected to data protection by being aware of their rights and the options accessible to them. User awareness facilitates active participation in managing their biometric data and fosters a sense of empowerment.
- *Building Trust and Acceptance*: Building user acceptance and fostering user awareness of biometric technologies is crucial. People are more likely to trust and approve of biometric technologies when they know the advantages, hazards, and safety measures involved. In addition to encouraging a good assessment of the value and contribution of biometric systems, this enables their increased adoption and use.

3.6.10 ROLE OF REGULATIONS, STANDARDS, AND BEST PRACTICES IN ENSURING PRIVACY AND SECURITY

Ensuring privacy and security in biometric systems depends on regulations, standards, and best practices. Here is how each of them helps to protect security and confidentiality [34]:

- *Regulations*: Biometric data management is governed by privacy and data protection laws, such as the CCPA in the United States and the GDPR in Europe. Regarding data collecting, storage, processing, and user rights, these regulations set out standards and duties for organizations. They ensure that privacy standards like data reduction, purpose limitation, and user permission are adhered to during the design and operation of biometric systems. Regulations must be followed to safeguard individual privacy and avoid negative legal repercussions for noncompliance.

- *Standards*: Technical requirements and specifications are defined using biometric systems. They offer recommendations for the safe and reliable implementation of biometric technologies. Standards are developed for biometric data formats, encryption methods, security protocols, and testing procedures by organizations like the International Organization for Standardization (ISO) or the National Institute of Standards and Technology (NIST). By adhering to these standards, biometric systems are enhanced in terms of security and privacy and are created, implemented, and evaluated by acknowledged industry best practices.
- *Best Practices*: Best practices are standards and recommendations for developing, using, and maintaining biometric systems established by the industry. They are created using knowledge gained through experience, research, and industry professionals to promote efficient security and privacy safeguards. The numerous facets of biometric systems covered by best practices include data protection, access control, encryption, authentication methods, and incident response. Following best practices enables organizations to develop robust security controls, safeguard people's privacy, and reduce potential hazards related to biometric technology Aspects of privacy.

The following briefly describes the part that laws, standards, and best practices play in maintaining the privacy and security of biometric systems:

- *Providing a framework*: Regulations establish legal requirements and guidelines for handling biometric data, ensuring that privacy rights are respected and individuals' personal information is protected.
- *Defining technical specifications*: By establishing uniform security practices and guaranteeing system compatibility, standards provide the technical specifications and requirements for the secure and interoperable deployment of biometric systems.
- *Guiding implementation*: Best practices provide organizations with helpful advice and suggestions on developing and running biometric systems safely and with respect for user privacy. They aid businesses in identifying potential dangers, picking suitable security safeguards, and setting up efficient privacy protection systems.
- Using biometric technologies responsibly and securely is supported by a complete framework built from laws, regulations, and best practices. Building trust among users and stakeholders while protecting privacy and biometric data is made possible by following rules, adhering to standards, and implementing best practices.

3.7 CONCLUSION

A thorough examination of biometric systems' privacy and security issues is provided in "Examining the Vulnerabilities of Biometric Systems: Privacy and Security Perspectives." The study highlights key findings and insights, including the vulnerabilities of different biometric identifiers, the risks of physical breaches and theft of biometric data, cyberattacks targeting the storage and transmission of biometric data, spoofing attacks and identity theft, vulnerabilities of centralized biometric databases, risks of combining biometric data with other personal information, consequences of unauthorized access and misuse of biometric data, the importance of consent requirements and user awareness, the role of regulations and standards in ensuring privacy and security, the use of encryption and secure storage, MFA techniques, secure transmission protocols, continuous monitoring and security updates, and the necessity of striking a balance between privacy and security concerns. The study emphasizes the importance of user awareness and education to encourage the ethical and safe use of biometric systems. Biometric systems may be created and run in a way that secures personal information, upholds data security, and fosters confidence in their use by addressing these weaknesses and putting in place the necessary protections.

3.7.1 RECOMMENDATIONS FOR ADDRESSING VULNERABILITIES AND IMPROVING BIOMETRIC SYSTEM SECURITY [35]

- *Implement Robust Authentication Mechanisms*: Use MFA methods, which pair biometric identification with other authentication elements like tokens or passwords. Introducing an additional layer of protection lowers the danger of unauthorized access and lessens the effects of potential biometric spoofing attacks.
- *Deploy Anti-Spoofing Measures*: Incorporate cutting-edge anti-spoofing technology and algorithms to identify and stop spoofing attempts. To confirm the validity of the biometric sample, this involves using liveness detection methods that examine physiological or behavioral traits. Update and improve these procedures often to account for developing spoofing strategies.
- *Secure Storage and Transmission*: Use robust encryption techniques to safeguard biometric data in transit and at rest. To avoid unauthorized access and data breaches, ensure that data storage systems have robust access controls, auditing processes, and backup methods. Utilize secure transmission methods, such as SSL/TLS, to protect the data when communicating between the various biometric system components.
- *Regular Security Assessments and Audits*: Conduct routine security audits and assessments to find the biometric system's vulnerabilities and weak points. Hire outside security professionals to conduct penetration tests and vulnerability analyses to find potential security holes. Address problems when discovered and apply patches and security upgrades as needed.
- *Privacy by Design*: Integrate privacy concerns into the planning and creation of biometric systems immediately. Use privacy-enhancing strategies, including purpose limitation, data reduction, and data anonymization.

When privacy practices and rules are made clear, users are given transparency and control over their biometric data.

- *User Education and Awareness*: Inform users on biometric technologies' advantages, drawbacks, and proper application. Encourage user awareness of the need to protect their biometric data, particularly the need to keep it private and avoid disclosing it to unauthorized parties or platforms. Explain how to securely register, utilize, and terminate access to biometric identifiers.
- *Compliance with Data Protection Regulations*: Ensure adherence to pertinent privacy and data protection legislation. Keep abreast of new regulatory frameworks and standards so you may adjust the biometric system's security safeguards as necessary. Establish detailed data protection rules and processes, such as those for responding to and notifying of data breaches.

Organizations may improve the security of biometric systems, reduce vulnerabilities, safeguard user privacy, and promote technological trust by implementing these ideas. Staying ahead of new threats and ensuring the continuous efficacy of the security precautions built into the biometric system need constant monitoring, review, and development of security measures.

3.7.2 FUTURE RESEARCH DIRECTIONS AND POTENTIAL ADVANCEMENTS IN BIOMETRIC TECHNOLOGY

Future work in biometric technology has a big chance to improve usability, security, and privacy. The following are some prospective developments and research paths for biometric technology [36]:

- *Anti-Spoofing Techniques*: To remain ahead of emerging spoofing assaults, anti-spoofing technique research must continue. The development of more advanced liveness detection algorithms that can reliably discriminate between actual and fake biometric features is one example of such advancement.
- *Template Protection and Revocability*: Research might concentrate on creating secure template protection systems to avoid unauthorized reconstruction of biometric templates from stored data. The security of biometric systems can also be improved by researching methods for revocability, which allow compromised biometric templates to be invalidated and replaced.
- *Biometric Fusion*: Researching ways to merge biometric modalities, such as voice recognition, facial recognition, and fingerprints, can improve system reliability and resistance to spoofing assaults. Fusion methods can raise the biometric systems' overall performance and reliability.
- *Deep Learning and Machine Learning*: It may be possible to increase biometric systems' precision, effectiveness, and flexibility by investigating deep learning and machine learning algorithms. These methods may be applied to biometric data for feature extraction, classification, and anomaly detection.
- *Privacy-Preserving Biometrics*: The research topic might be the development of biometric systems that allow authentication without disclosing raw

biometric data. It is possible to investigate methods like differential privacy, secure multi-party computing, and homomorphic encryption to safeguard user privacy while maintaining biometric authentication.

- *Usability and User Experience*: A vital study field is enhancing biometric systems' usability and user experience. To make biometric systems more understandable and user-friendly entails researching user-centric design methodologies, conducting usability tests, and looking at novel interaction modalities.
- *Ethical and Social Implications*: The ethical and societal ramifications of the widespread use of biometric technologies can be investigated through research. Addressing issues with data ownership, permission, discrimination, and possible biases in biometric technologies is part of this.
- *Standardization and Interoperability*: The development of compatible formats and protocols for exchanging biometric data might be the focus of standardization efforts to guarantee seamless integration between various biometric systems and enable cross-platform compatibility.
- *Continual Monitoring and Evaluation*: The main emphasis of research should be the development of reliable methods for ongoing security and performance monitoring, assessment, and enhancement of biometric systems. Evaluating the efficiency and dependability of biometric systems requires creating detailed metrics and assessment procedures.
- *Cryptographic Techniques*: Exploring cryptographic methods might strengthen privacy guarantees and safeguard delicate biometric data throughout registration, storage, and authentication procedures. These methods can include zero-knowledge proofs or secure multi-party computing.

Future studies in these fields will develop biometric technology by fixing its flaws and improving its usability, security, and privacy. To encourage the wide and responsible deployment of biometric systems, it is essential to look for novel solutions that balance security, privacy, and user acceptance.

REFERENCES

1. Arora, S., & Bhatia, M. P. S. (2022). Challenges and opportunities in biometric security: A survey. *Information Security Journal: A Global Perspective*, *31*(1), 28–48.
2. Veeraiah, V., Kumar, K. R., Kumari, P. L., Ahamad, S., Bansal, R., & Gupta, A. (2022, April). Application of biometric system to enhance the security in virtual world. In *2022 2nd international conference on advance computing and innovative technologies in engineering (ICACITE)* (pp. 719–723). IEEE.
3. Alwahaishi, S., & Zdrálek, J. (2020, November). Biometric authentication security: An overview. In *2020 IEEE international conference on cloud computing in emerging markets (CCEM)* (pp. 87–91). IEEE.
4. Skalkos, A., Stylios, I., Karyda, M., & Kokolakis, S. (2021). Users' privacy attitudes towards the use of behavioral biometrics continuous authentication (BBCA) technologies: A protection motivation theory approach. *Journal of Cybersecurity and Privacy*, *1*(4), 743–766.
5. North-Samardzic, A. (2020). Biometric technology and ethics: Beyond security applications. *Journal of Business Ethics*, *167*(3), 433–450.

6. Kumar, T., Bhushan, S., & Jangra, S. (2019). A brief review of image quality enhancement techniques based on multi-modal biometric fusion systems. In *Advanced informatics for computing research: Second international conference, ICAICR* 2018, Shimla, India, July 14–15, 2018, Revised Selected Papers, Part I 2 (pp. 407–423). Springer Singapore.

7. Kumar, T., Bhushan, S., & Jangra, S. (2021). An improved biometric fusion system of fingerprint and face using whale optimization. *International Journal of Advanced Computer Science and Applications*, 12(1), 664–671.

8. Liang, Y., Samtani, S., Guo, B., & Yu, Z. (2020). Behavioral biometrics for continuous authentication in the internet-of-things era: An artificial intelligence perspective. *IEEE Internet of Things Journal*, 7(9), 9128–9143.

9. Abomhara, M., Yayilgan, S. Y., Nweke, L. O., & Székely, Z. (2021). A comparison of primary stakeholders' views on the deployment of biometric technologies in border management: A case study of SMart mobILity at the *European land borders. Technology in Society, 64*, 101484.

10. Morake, A., Khoza, L. T., & Bokaba, T. (2021). Biometric technology in banking institutions customers' perspectives. *South African Journal of Information Management*, 23(1), 1–12.

11. Ellavarason, E., Guest, R., Deravi, F., Sanchez-Riello, R., & Corsetti, B. (2020). Touch-dynamics based behavioral biometrics on mobile devices – A review from a usability and performance perspective. *ACM Computing Surveys (CSUR)*, 53(6), 1–36.

12. Barka, E., Al Baqari, M., Kerrache, C. A., & Herrera-Tapia, J. (2022). Implementation of a biometric-based blockchain system for preserving privacy, security, and access control in healthcare records. *Journal of Sensor and Actuator Networks*, 11(4), 85.

13. Sudar, K. M., Deepalakshmi, P., Ponmozhi, K., & Nagaraj, P. (2019, December). Analysis of security threats and countermeasures for various biometric techniques. In *2019 IEEE international conference on clean energy and energy efficient electronics circuit for sustainable development (INCCES)* (pp. 1–6). IEEE.

14. Obaidat, M. S., Traore, I., & Woungang, I. (Eds.). (2019). *Biometric-based physical and cybersecurity systems* (pp. 1–10). Springer International Publishing.

15. Carmel, V. V., & Akila, D. (2020). A survey on biometric authentication systems in the cloud to combat identity theft. *Journal of Critical Reviews*, 7(03), 540–547.

16. Roy, S., Matloob, S., Seetharam, A., Rameshbabu, A., O'Dell, W. C., & Davis, W. I. (2017). Biometrics data security techniques for portable mobile devices. *Inae Letters*, 2, 123–131.

17. Baichoo, S., Khan, M. H. M., Bissessur, P., Pavaday, N., Boodoo-Jahangeer, N., & Purmah, N. R. (2018). Legal and ethical considerations of biometric identity card: Case for Mauritius. *Computer Law & Security Review*, 34(6), 1333–1341.

18. Uliyan, D. M., Sadeghi, S., & Jalab, H. A. (2020). Anti-spoofing method for fingerprint recognition using patch-based deep learning machine. *Engineering Science and Technology, an International Journal*, 23(2), 264–273.

19. Zafar, M. R., & Shah, M. A. (2016, September). Fingerprint authentication and security risks in smart devices. In *2016 22nd international conference on automation and computing (ICAC)* (pp. 548–553). IEEE.

20. Brown, E. A. (2020). A healthy mistrust: Curbing biometric data misuse in the workplace. *Stanford Technology Law Review, 23*, 252.

21. Kindt, E. J. (2021). *Transparency and accountability mechanisms for facial recognition.* The German Marshall Fund of the United States.

22. Ghafourian, M., Sumer, B., Vera-Rodriguez, R., Fierrez, J., Tolosana, R., Moralez, A., & Kindt, E. (2023). Combining blockchain and biometrics: A survey on technical aspects and a first legal analysis. *arXiv preprint arXiv*:2302.10883.

23. Sanchez-Reillo, R., Ortega-Fernandez, I., Ponce-Hernandez, W., & Quiros-Sandoval, H. C. (2019). How to implement EU data protection regulation for R&D in biometrics. *Computer Standards & Interfaces, 61*, 89–96.
24. Nguyen, F. Q. (2018). The standard for biometric data protection. *Journal of Law & Cyber Warfare, 7*(1), 61–84.
25. Sharma, D., & Selwal, A. (2022). An intelligent approach for fingerprint presentation attack detection using ensemble learning with improved local image features. *Multimedia Tools and Applications, 81*(16), 22129–22161.
26. Khurshid, M., & Selwal, A. (2020). A novel block hashing-based template security scheme for the multimodal biometric system. *Decision Analytics Applications in Industry, 2020*, 173–183.
27. Mehmood, R., & Selwal, A. (2020). Polynomial-based fuzzy vault technique for template security in fingerprint biometrics. *The International Arab Journal of Information Technology, 17*(6), 926–934.
28. Mehmood, R., & Selwal, A. (2020). Fingerprint biometric template security schemes: Attacks and countermeasures. In *Proceedings of ICRIC 2019: Recent innovations in computing* (pp. 455–467). Springer International Publishing.
29. Rafiq, S., & Selwal, A. (2020). Template security in Iris recognition systems: Research challenges and opportunities. In *Proceedings of ICRIC 2019: Recent innovations in computing* (pp. 771–784).
30. Dwivedi, R., Dey, S., Sharma, M. A., & Goel, A. (2020). A fingerprint-based crypto-biometric system for secure communication. *Journal of Ambient Intelligence and Humanized Computing, 11*, 1495–1509.
31. Ali, M. H., Ibrahim, A., Wahbah, H., & Al_Barazanchi, I. (2021). Survey on encoding biometric data for transmission in wireless communication networks. *Periodicals of Engineering and Natural Sciences, 9*(4), 1038–1055.
32. Garcia, A. A. (2021). Socially private: Striking a balance between social media and data privacy. *Iowa Law Review, 107*, 319.
33. Purohit, H., Dadhich, M., & Ajmera, P. K. (2023). Analytical study on users' awareness and acceptability towards adoption of multimodal biometrics (MMB) mechanism in online transactions: A two-stage SEM-ANN approach. *Multimedia Tools and Applications, 82*(9), 14239–14263.
34. Monajemi, M. (2017). Privacy regulation in the age of biometrics deals with a new world order of information. *University of Miami International and Comparative Law Review, 25*, 371.
35. Harvey, J., & Kumar, S. (2020, May). A survey of intelligent transportation systems security: Challenges and solutions. In *2020 IEEE 6th international conference on big data security on cloud (BigDataSecurity), IEEE international conference on high performance and smart computing (HPSC) and IEEE international conference on intelligent data and security (IDS)* (pp. 263–268). IEEE.
36. Shopon, M., Tumpa, S. N., Bhatia, Y., Kumar, K. P., & Gavrilova, M. L. (2021). Biometric systems de-identification: Current advancements and future directions. *Journal of Cybersecurity and Privacy, 1*(3), 470–495.

4 Biometric Systems Security and Privacy Issues

Sunil Kumar

4.1 INTRODUCTION

This chapter discusses the various security and privacy issues in biometric systems. Biometric systems are used to recognize and authenticate individuals based on their special and unique physical or behavioral characteristics. A few common instances of biometrics traits include fingerprints, iris patterns, voice patterns, facial structures, and hand geometry. Every biometric system functioning involves three main steps enrollment, storage, and matching as shown in Figure 4.1.

- *Enrollment*: During this enrollment phase, an individual's biometric features are scanned and collected as a biometric database, such as fingerprint images or voice recordings. For this hardware components are used to capture the biometric traits of an individual. The sensor type could be a fingerprint scanner, a camera for facial recognition, or a microphone for voice recognition. The quality and accuracy of the sensor device play a decisive role in the overall performance of the system.
- *Storage*: The scanned biometric data is transformed into a digital format and stored securely in a database. This system extracts specific features that are distinctive and unique to each individual. For example, in fingerprint recognition, where system may extract ridge patterns, while in facial recognition, it may extract key points or ratios between facial features. It is also significant to confirm the privacy and security of the stored biometric data.
- *Matching:* During the authenticated process of a person, their biometric characteristics are scanned again and compared with the stored biometric data. The system uses algorithms to compare the level of similarity (threshold value) between the new data and the stored templates. If the matching level is satisfactory, then the person may access the resource.

The whole process of a reliable and accurate biometric scheme depends on the quality of the captured data, the robustness of the designed algorithms used for matching, and the overall design and implementation of the system. Biometric systems are extensively used in numerous applications, such as access control, border control, period and attendance tracking, and portable device authentication.

 DOI: 10.1201/9781032614663-4

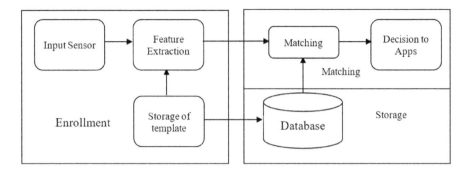

FIGURE 4.1 Major components of biometric system.

Biometric systems have a significant impact on various sectors, like the government, healthcare, and finance.

Government: Biometric systems are extensively used in different government sectors for identification and verification purposes. In this sector, biometrics are used for citizen registration, voter identification, issuance of identity documents like passports and visas, and border control areas. Biometric systems guarantee accurate identification and help authorities in preventing identity theft and fraud, improving overall security.

Healthcare: Biometric authentication systems are increasingly being adopted in healthcare to ensure the safety and confidentiality of patients' data. Biometrics, such as fingerprint or iris recognition, can be used to control access to medical records, secure medication distribution, and prevent unauthorized access to healthcare facilities. Biometric systems also enable efficient patient identification, reducing administrative errors and enhancing patient safety.

Finance: Biometric systems have become prevalent in the financial industry to provide secure and convenient authentication processes. Biometrics, such as fingerprint, facial recognition, or voice recognition, can be used for secure access to bank accounts, ATMs, and mobile payment apps. Biometric authentication adds a layer of security compared to traditional methods (e.g. PINs or passwords) by minimizing the risk of identity theft and unauthorized transactions. In the retail or banking sector, biometric systems may help to prevent fraud by accurately identifying customers during transactions and enabling a secure payment authentication mechanism. This can reduce the chance of identity theft and unauthorized access to credit cards and other relevant documents.

The more and oldest trustworthy identification method than passwords, ID cards, keys, or other conventional systems is provided by biometric authentication, which refers to a variety of physical and behavioral traits that are particular to an individual (Kataria et al., 2013). Automated person authentication systems are used by a wide range of enterprises to increase operational effectiveness, customer satisfaction, and the security of vital resources. Today, an increasing number of countries, together with India, have decided to implement a biometric structure for national security and the prevention of identity holdup. An individual can be recognized using a variability of biometric identification techniques that quantify their voice, hand, face, fingerprints, hands, or any combination of these characteristics. Every year, new biometric algorithms and technologies are put forth, tried out, evaluated, and put into use. Multi-factor authentication using biometric traits and other factors such as passwords or tokens to provide robust security to protect sensitive information is also the most popular approach to keep biometric information safe and secure sensitive data. It might play a significant role in enhancing cybersecurity measures in various fields.

This chapter discusses the introduction of biometric system and their relevant terms: like techniques for secure storage and transmission of biometric data, encryption methods, and authentication mechanisms to prevent impersonation attacks. The latter section addresses an overview of security and privacy risks and also discusses the types of security threats in biometrics, unauthorized access and identity theft, data breach and misuse of biometric data, biometric spoofing and tempering, and security measures in biometric systems. One of the issues is spoofing, in which an attacker tries to deceives the system by presenting fake biometric samples. Countermeasures such as liveness detection techniques are employed to identify and reject spoofed attempts, ensuring security by preventing unauthorized access to sensitive data and shielding individuals' identities.

The section covers the literature survey related to biometric security and privacy of data belonging to various organizations and industries. The last second section talks about the research implications and findings. Finally, the chapter ends with a conclusion and future directions.

4.2   OVERVIEW OF SECURITY AND PRIVACY RISKS

Biometric systems are found increasingly prevalent in various applications like access control, identity verification, and transaction authorization. However, the storage and transmission of biometric data pose several potential risks and vulnerabilities. Security and privacy risks are prevalent in our increasingly digital and interconnected world. With the rapid advancements in technology, individuals and organizations face a wide range of potential threats to their sensitive information. These risks can arise from various sources, including cyberattacks, data breaches, and identity theft.

One major security risk is the threat of cyberattacks. Malicious users may exploit susceptibilities in computers, networks, and software to get an unauthorized right to sensitive data and disrupt operations. Cyberattacks can take many forms, such as malware, ransomware, phishing, and denial-of-service attacks. The significance of these attacks can be severe, foremost to data loss, monetary losses, reputational damage, and even legal liabilities.

Another important concern is the risk of data breaches. The collection of data and storing them at local storage may be a vast amount of personal and confidential information from their customers, employees, and partners. If this data sprays into the incorrect hands, it can be hand-me-down for various malicious purposes, including identity theft, fraud, and blackmail. Data breaches can occur due to security vulnerabilities, human error, or insider threats. The impact of a data breach can extend beyond financial losses, as it can erode trust, damage reputation, and result in regulatory penalties. Privacy breaches can result in the exploitation of personal information, targeted advertising, or even surveillance. Additionally, individuals are at risk of their privacy being violated through unauthorized access to their devices or accounts. This can include camera and microphone hacking, password breaches, and unauthorized sharing of personal photos or videos.

To mitigate these security and privacy risks, individuals and organizations must take proactive measures. For this, they must implement a strong security scheme like firewalls, anti-malware software, and regular data backups. It is also important to keep yourself and your application on the latest security threats and educate yourself about safe online practices. For organizations, investing in secure technology infrastructure and conducting consistent security examinations can support identifying vulnerabilities and addressing them effectively. Individuals should also be cautious about sharing personal information online, use secure passwords, and exercise skepticism toward suspicious emails or messages.

Some other biometric concerns are as follows:

i. *Data Breaches*
Biometric data needs to be securely stored and encrypted to prevent unauthorized access. Any data breach could expose individuals' biometric information which can be later used for malicious activity through data impersonation.

ii. *Insider Threats*
Biometric data is often stored by organizations or service providers (who manage it), which makes it vulnerable to insider threats. Nefarious employees may illegally access and misuse the data for personal gain or sell it to malicious third parties.

iii. *Replay Attacks*
Biometric data transmitted over networks can be intercepted and compromised if appropriate security measures are not followed. This may result in unauthorized access to the data, allowing criminals to exploit it for malicious purposes.

iv. *Inadequate Encryption*
Appropriate encryption techniques are essential to protect biometric data whether it is in rest or transit. However, if there are vulnerabilities in the encryption algorithms, the biometric data can still be at risk of being exposed. It is important to carefully select and implement encryption techniques that have been proven to be secure and resistant to attacks. Regular monitoring and updating of encryption systems are necessary to ensure continued protection of biometric data.

4.2.1 SENSITIVITY AND UNIQUENESS IN BIOMETRIC INFORMATION

Sensitivity in biometric information systems refers to the level of detailed and personal information that can be derived from a biometric trait(s) or characteristic. Some biometric information (fingerprints or DNA profiles) can reveal sensitive information about an individual's identity, health, or genetic structure. Uniqueness, other side refers to the distinctiveness of biometric details within a population. Biometric traits are usually unique to an individual as they can be used to differentiate one person from another. For example, fingerprints are unique to each individual even two fingerprints look the same.

Both sensitivity and uniqueness are important observations when using biometric information for identification or authentication purposes. Sensitivity highlights the need for strong data protection measures to prevent unauthorized access or misuse of biometric data. Uniqueness ensures that biometric traits can be effectively used for reliable identification and verification of individuals. There are several factors to consider when aiming to achieve sensitivity and uniqueness in biometric information:

i. *Type of Biometric*: Choose a biometric modality that is highly sensitive and unique, such as fingerprint, iris, or palm vein recognition. These modalities have inherent characteristics that make them well-suited for every individual identification.

ii. *Feature Extraction:* Develop algorithms and techniques for extracting distinctive features from the biometric sample. These features should capture the unique aspects of the individual's biometric trait while minimizing variations caused by environmental conditions or aging.

iii. *Template Generation*: Create a template or reference model based on the extracted features. The template should encode the essential information necessary for comparison and verification while discarding any non-essential details that may introduce noise or compromise privacy.

iv. *Robustness to Variations:* Design the biometric system to be robust against variations in the biometric trait caused by factors such as changes in appearance, aging, injuries, or diseases. This ensures consistent performance under different environmental conditions and over time.

v. *Accuracy and False Acceptance/Rejection Rates*: Strike a balance between sensitivity and specificity by optimizing the biometric system for accuracy. Minimize the false acceptance rate (incorrectly accepting an imposter) and false rejection rate (incorrectly rejecting an imposter).

4.2.2 IMPORTANCE OF PRIVACY AND SECURITY IN BIOMETRIC SYSTEMS

Biometric systems have become increasingly popular for personal identification and access control in various sectors such as finance, healthcare, education, and law enforcement. These systems offer to use unique behavioral characteristics or physical parts like fingerprints, face recognition, and iris, to verify and authenticate individuals. Their many advantages, security, and privacy are essential aspects that cannot be overlooked in biometric systems.

First, the importance of security in biometric systems lies in protecting sensitive data and preventing unauthorized access. Biometric data, which represents a person's unique physiological or behavioral characteristics, is highly personal and cannot be easily replaced or changed. Therefore, securing this data is crucial to ensure that it cannot be intercepted, tampered with, or used fraudulently. Robust security procedures, such as encoding and securing storage, play a vital role in safe-guarding the integrity and privacy of biometric information. Second, privacy is of utmost importance in biometric systems as it directly relates to the protection of an individual's identity and personal autonomy. Biometric data, combined with other personal information, can provide a comprehensive profile of an individual, raising concerns about potential privacy breaches and misuse. Strict privacy policies and regulations must administer the assembly, storing, and use of biometric information to ensure that persons' privacy rights are respected.

4.2.3 Types of Security Threats Faced by Biometric Systems

Biometric systems have become increasingly popular for enhancing security in vari-ous industries and settings. However, they are also vulnerable to certain types of security threats that can compromise their effectiveness. One common threat is iden-tity theft, where an attacker uses stolen biometric data to gain unauthorized access. For example, if a biometric system uses fingerprints for identification, a hacker could potentially replicate the fingerprint and deceive the system. This poses a significant risk to the confidentiality and integrity of the system. The security threat faced by biometric systems is spoofing attacks. This involves creating a replica or imitation of a biometric trait, such as a fake fingerprint or a voice recording, to trick the sys-tem into granting unauthorized access. Spoofing attacks can be quite sophisticated, often involving advanced technologies and techniques. Biometric systems that rely solely on a single biometric trait are particularly susceptible to this type of attack. Therefore, organizations need to implement measures to counter spoofing attacks, such as liveness detection techniques, which can differentiate between real and fake biometric traits.

Biometric systems can also be vulnerable to threats like insiders or outsiders. Insider threats refer to individuals inside the organization who misappropriate their sanctioned access to the biometric system for personal gain or to carry out mali-cious activities. Figure 4.2 shows the main attack points, and how every connecting

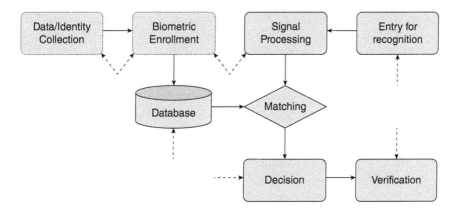

FIGURE 4.2 Various possible attack points for biometric system.

edge and module are points of attack. This could involve an employee manipulating the biometric system to grant access to unauthorized individuals or tampering with biometric data to cover their tracks. The threats that occur at the insider level can be challenging to perceive and mitigate as the individuals involved typically have authentic access to the system. Therefore, organizations must implement strict access controls, monitor system activities, and establish a culture of security awareness to minimize the risk of insider threats.

4.3   UNAUTHORIZED ACCESS AND IDENTITY THEFT

Unauthorized access refers to the act of gaining entry into a system, computer network, or personal accounts without proper authorization. It is an illegal activity that can have severe consequences for the victims and the perpetrators. Unauthorized access can occur through various means, such as hacking, phishing, or exploiting vulnerabilities in software or systems. Once unauthorized access is achieved, it opens the door for potential identity theft. Identity theft is a serious crime that involves stealing someone's data, including their name, credit card details, social security number, or online account credentials, to use it for fraudulent purposes. The stolen data can be cast-off to make illegal transactions, open fresh accounts, or even commit a crime with the name of the victim. Identity theft can cause significant financial loss, reputational damage, and emotional distress for the victims.

Unauthorized access and identity theft go hand in hand as unauthorized access often leads to identity theft. Once a hacker or an attacker gains access to someone's accounts or systems, they can easily access and steal valuable personal information. Individuals or organizations need to apply preventive measures through strong and unique passwords, permitting two-factor authentication, and regularly monitoring their accounts for any suspicious activity. Moreover, both cybersecurity awareness and education are vital to recognize and avoid phishing attempts and other methods used by attackers to gain unauthorized access. It is assumed important for companies and organizations to prioritize cybersecurity measures to protect their customers' personal information and prevent unauthorized access to their systems and networks. Implementing strong security protocols, conducting regular susceptibility assessments, and regularly updating software and systems are essential to prevent unauthorized access and protect against identity theft.

4.4   DATA BREACHES

Data breaches and the misuse of biometric data have become a serious concern in today's digital age. Biometric data is increasingly being used for authentication and identification purposes. However, with the rise in the collection and storage of biometric data, there is an alarming increase in the number of data breaches and the potential for misuse. One of the major challenges with biometric data is its permanence. Unlike passwords or PINs, if biometric data is compromised in a data breach, it cannot be changed or reset. This means that individuals' unique biometric identifiers are at risk of being used by unauthorized individuals for fraudulent activities or identity theft. The impact of such breaches can be severe, as they can result in financial loss, reputational damage, and even physical harm if used for criminal activities.

On the other hand, the misuse of biometric data raises serious privacy worries. As we know biometric data is highly personal and can reveal sensitive information about an individual's identity and physical characteristics. If this data gets into the incorrect hands, they may use it for surveillance, tracking, or profiling individuals without their consent or knowledge. Such misuse of biometric data not only infringes upon individuals' right to privacy but can also have far-reaching societal implications, such as discrimination, bias, or the targeting of specific individuals or groups based on their biometric characteristics. This includes applying encryption and multi-factor authentication protocols, regularly auditing and monitoring systems for vulnerabilities, and ensuring strict access controls and permissions. Furthermore, individuals must also be educated about the risks associated with biometric data and encouraged to take necessary precautions, such as regularly updating their biometric profiles and being vigilant about their data usage.

4.5 BIOMETRIC SPOOFING AND TAMPERING

Biometric spoofing and tampering refer to fraudulent activities aimed at deceiving or manipulating biometric security systems. Biometric systems, such as fingerprint recognition, facial recognition, or iris scanners, are becoming increasingly popular as a means of secure authentication. However, these systems are not foolproof, and hackers are constantly finding ways to bypass or manipulate them. One common form of biometric spoofing is the use of fake fingerprints or faces to fool the system into granting unauthorized access. With advancements in technology, it has become relatively easy for hackers to create synthetic materials that closely mimic an individual's unique biometric features. This can be done by using materials such as silicone or gelatin to create fake fingerprints or masks. By placing these materials onto a scanner or a camera, hackers can gain access to sensitive information or enter restricted areas.

Tampering with biometric systems involves manipulating the data captured by the system to gain unauthorized privileges. This can be achieved by altering the biometric information stored in a database or intercepting and modifying the signals transmitted between the scanner and the system. Hackers can use various techniques, such as overlay attacks or image manipulation, to modify the biometric data to match their own or someone else's identity. By doing so, they can effectively deceive the system and gain unauthorized access or privileges. To combat biometric spoofing and tampering, organizations need to implement robust security measures. This includes continuously updating and improving the biometric systems to detect and prevent spoofing attempts. One best way to attain this is by the use of liveness detection mechanisms, which can assist in determining if a biometric example is from a live person or a fake replica. Organizations should also implement multi-factor authentication systems that combine biometrics with other authentication factors, such as passwords or tokens, to increase security.

Consistent training and awareness schemes should also be conducted to instruct users about the risks of biometric spoofing and tampering. Users should be encouraged to report any suspicious activity and follow best practices when it comes to biometric authentication. Meanwhile, researchers and developers should continually study and improve biometric technologies to stay one step ahead of hackers.

4.6 SECURITY MEASURES IN BIOMETRIC SYSTEMS

Biometric systems have become increasingly popular as a means of enhancing security measures in various industries. However, despite their advantages, biometric systems are not completely foolproof and require additional security measures to safeguard them against potential threats. One of the key security measures in biometric systems is the use of encryption techniques. Encryption ensures that the biometric data captured during the identification or verification process is converted into a code that can only be accessed with the correct decryption key. This protects the privacy and integrity of the biometric information, making it extremely difficult for hackers or unauthorized individuals to access or tamper with the data.

Another vital security measure is the implementation of multi-factor authentication. In addition to biometric identification, multi-factor authentication involves the operator providing one or more additional authentication factors, such as a password or a security token. This significantly enhances the security of the biometric system, as it adds an extra layer of protection. Even if an intruder manages to bypass the biometric identification, they would still need the additional authentication factor(s) to gain access.

The continuous monitoring and auditing of the biometric system are need of hour for security measures. Regular monitoring enables the identification of any unusual or suspicious activities that may indicate a security breach or attempted unauthorized access. Additionally, auditing ensures that the system is functioning as intended and that all security protocols are being followed. This helps in identifying any weaknesses or vulnerabilities in the system and allows for timely remediation to prevent potential security incidents.

4.6.1 AUTHENTICATION PROTOCOLS

These protocols are designed to verify the individuality of users or entities before granting them access to sensitive information or services. One widely used authentication protocol is the Secure Socket Layer protocol, which begins a secure connection between a client and a server. It uses a combination of asymmetric and symmetric cryptography to authenticate both the server and the client, ensuring the integrity and confidentiality of data transmission.

4.6.2 LIGHTWEIGHT DIRECTORY ACCESS PROTOCOL (LDAP)

Another commonly used authentication protocol is the Lightweight Directory Access Protocol (LDAP), which is a directory service-based protocol that offers a means for clients to query and modify directory server information. LDAP authenticates users by checking their credentials against the directory server, which stores user information such as usernames and passwords. It utilizes a challenge-response mechanism to verify the user's identity and ensures that individual authorization can access the directory and its resources.

4.6.3 KERBEROS

Kerberos is another authentication protocol widely used in network environments. It operates based on tickets, where a central authentication server issues a ticket to a client, granting it access to specific resources or services for a limited period. This protocol uses symmetric key cryptography to prevent unauthorized access and replay attacks. Moreover, it provides mutual authentication, ensuring that both the client and the server verify each other's identities before establishing a secure connection.

4.7 ENCRYPTION TECHNIQUES

These approaches are used to translate plain, readable text or information into an indecipherable format, known as ciphertext. These techniques play a crucial role in protecting sensitive information from unauthorized access or interception.

4.7.1 SYMMETRIC KEY ENCRYPTION

One commonly used encryption technique is symmetrical key encryption, wherein the common key is shared by both encryption and decryption processes. This technique is fast and efficient, making it suitable for applications such as secure communications and data storage.

4.7.2 ASYMMETRIC KEY ENCRYPTION

The second type of encryption technique is an asymmetric key, also identified as public-key encryption. Unlike symmetric key encryption, this technique is based on two keys: one is for encryption and the second for decryption purposes. The public key is openly available or distributed to allow anyone to encrypt messages, while the private key is reserved undisclosed by the intended recipient. This technique ensures secure communication and facilitates digital signatures, enabling verification of the sender's identity.

4.7.3 QUANTUM ENCRYPTION

One of the most advanced encryption techniques is quantum encryption, which takes advantage of the principles of quantum mechanics to provide an unprecedented level of security. Quantum encryption uses the properties of quantum particles, such as photons, to generate random keys and guarantee the confidentiality and integrity of the data. As quantum computing advances, the importance of quantum encryption grows, as it offers protection against attacks that classical encryption techniques cannot withstand.

4.8   ACCESS CONTROL MECHANISMS

Access control mechanisms are security measures put in place to regulate and manage the access of individuals or users to a system, network, or resources. These mechanisms are essential for ensuring the confidentiality, integrity, and availability of sensitive information and resources. Access control mechanisms can take various forms, such as physical controls like locks and biometric systems, or logical controls like passwords, user authentication, and authorization protocols.

4.8.1   ROLE-BASED ACCESS CONTROL

Role-based access control (RBAC) is a popular access control mechanism that assigns permissions and privileges based on predefined roles or job functions. RBAC simplifies access management and reduces administrative efforts, as access rights can be assigned to specific roles, rather than to individual users. This mechanism improves security by ensuring that users have access only to the resources they need to perform their roles, minimizing the risk of unauthorized access or accidental exposure of sensitive data.

4.8.2   MANDATORY ACCESS CONTROL

Mandatory access control (MAC) is typically used in environments with high-security requirements, such as government and military facilities. MAC enforces strict access controls based on security labels assigned to users and resources. The labels define the sensitivity and classification of data and determine who can access, modify, or transmit it. MAC ensures that access decisions are determined by security policies and not by individual users or administrators, making it more resilient against insider threats or unauthorized access attempts. This mechanism provides a higher level of control and protection for sensitive information.

4.8.3   DISCRETIONARY ACCESS CONTROL

In addition to RBAC and MAC, access control mechanisms also include discretionary access control (DAC) and attribute-based access control (ABAC). DAC allows users to determine and control access to their resources, not only giving them flexibility but also increasing the risk of unauthorized access if not properly managed. ABAC, on the other hand, uses attributes or characteristics associated with users, resources, and environmental conditions to make access control decisions. ABAC provides a more granular and flexible control mechanism, allowing organizations to implement complex access policies based on multiple attributes.

4.9   PRIVACY CONCERNS IN BIOMETRIC SYSTEMS

Biometric systems have gained significant interaction in different domains such as authentication, access control, and surveillance. However, the increased use and implementation of biometric systems have raised serious privacy concerns. One major concern is the assembly and storage of individual biometric data. Since biometric data is identified uniquely to individuals, it can be particularly sensitive, and the risk of its misuse or unauthorized access is high. If these databases are compromised, individuals may face severe consequences, such as identity theft or fraud.

Biometric systems have one more issue which is the potential for function creep, wherein the original purpose of the system expands to include new applications without individuals' consent or knowledge. For instance, a biometric system used for employee time tracking can be repurposed for monitoring attendance, access control, or even determining engagement levels. This expansion of the system's functionality raises legitimate concerns about individual privacy and autonomy. Individuals should have control over how their biometric information is used and shared, but without appropriate safeguards, it becomes challenging to prevent potential misuse.

These systems raise concerns about the possibility of mass surveillance and the erosion of anonymity. As biometric technologies become increasingly integrated into public spaces, individuals may feel constantly monitored and scrutinized, leading to a decline in personal privacy. Biometric systems, such as facial recognition or gait recognition, can be used to keep an eye on an individual's activities and movements short of their knowledge. To address these privacy concerns, it is vital to launch robust legal and regulatory frameworks for the use of biometric systems. Governments and organizations should implement rich guidelines and standards for the assembly, storage, and use of biometric data. These regulations should ensure transparency, informed consent, and strict limitations on the sharing of biometric information. Safeguards such as encryption and secure storage should also be in place to prevent unauthorized access or data breaches. In Figure 4.3 privacy concern block diagram indicates the parameters that must be kept in mind when using biometrics devices.

Public awareness and education about the risks and challenges of biometric systems are essential. Individuals must be well-informed about the potential privacy implications and their rights regarding biometric data. Privacy advocates, policymakers, and technology developers should work together to foray stability among the profits of biometric systems and the protection of specific privacy, crafting policies and practices that address privacy concerns while allowing for the responsible and ethical use of biometric technologies.

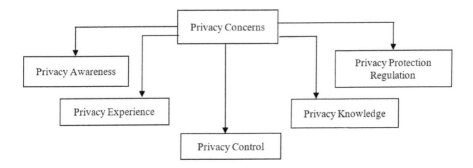

FIGURE 4.3   Block diagram for biometric privacy concerns.

4.10 REGULATIONS AND STANDARDS FOR ENSURING SECURITY AND PRIVACY

Biometric data, such as facial recognition, or iris scans, and fingerprints are highly sensitive and unique to individuals. Therefore, it is important to have regulations in place to protect this data from unauthorized access or misuse. These regulations provide guidelines for the collection, storage, and use of biometric information, ensuring that it is done in a secure and privacy-conscious manner. The standard for data privacy can be represented through a Venn diagram as shown in Figure 4.4.

Regulations for biometric systems also address the possible perils associated with information breaches. They require system operators to implement vigorous security measures, such as encryption and access controls, to safeguard biometric data against cyber threats. Additionally, regulations mandate regular audits and assessments of the security and privacy practices of biometric system providers, ensuring they comply with industry best practices. By complying with these regulations, organizations can create a framework that promotes trust and confidence in biometric systems, ultimately benefiting both individuals and businesses.

4.11 LITERATURE WORKS

The study of literature has increased significant attention and importance in recent periods due to its possible applications in several areas, such as security, surveillance, and access control systems. The foremost benefit of biometric recognition systems is that they offer a high level of accuracy and reliability, as each individual's biometric traits are distinct and difficult to forge or replicate. The basic idea explores the various techniques that discuss challenges such as accuracy, security, and privacy.

There is a long list of surveys on biometric authentication in the literature, including (Crawford, 2010; Duta, 2009; Yampolskiy & Govindaraju, 2008) primarily concentrating on a very narrow biometric domain. For instance, Yampolskiy and Govindaraju (2008) carried out a survey and showed the classification of behavioral biometrics systems. Zhang and Gao (2009) presented an investigation of image-based face recognition, and Duta (Duta, 2009) gave a survey related to the technology utilized a hand geometry-based biometric systems.

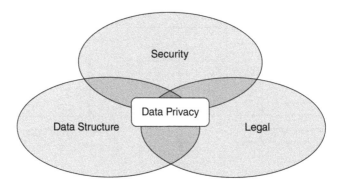

FIGURE 4.4 Venn diagram for data privacy standard.

Ratha et al. explored the challenges and potential solutions for ensuring both security and privacy for authentication systems in biometrics. Biometric authentication, such as fingerprint or facial recognition, has gained popularity due to its convenience and accuracy. However, the authors argue that potential vulnerabilities and privacy concerns need to be addressed to encourage widespread adoption. This research proposed a technique such as template protection, anonymization, and secure matching protocols to improve the privacy and security of biometric data. Ratha et al. (2001) believe that by implementing these techniques, biometrics-based authentication systems can offer a robust and privacy-preserving solution for liveness detection and biometric encryption to protect user privacy. By incorporating these approaches, the authors aim to provide a comprehensive framework that ensures both privacy and security in biometrics-based validation systems.

Li and Jain (2005) proposed a book that offers a wide-ranging guide to the field of facial recognition technology. It shelters a wide range of areas, from the basics of face detection and feature extraction to advanced algorithms for face recognition and identity verification. The book is divided into several sections, each dedicated to a specific aspect of face recognition. Here this section covers only important points. One of the main sections of the book focuses on the different approaches to face detection. The authors have discussed various techniques, such as the Viola-Jones algorithm and local binary patterns, and their advantages and limitations. They also provide a thorough overview of the challenges in face detection, such as variations in lighting conditions, pose, and facial expressions.

This book presents various methods for extracting facial features, such as eigenfaces, local binary patterns, and Gabor filters. They elaborate advantages, limitations, and applications of each area in different scenarios. They also highlight the importance of feature normalization and dimensionality reduction in improving the accuracy of face recognition systems. The book also delves into the field of 3D face recognition. The authors offer an overview of the diverse techniques for capturing and representing 3D face data, such as stereo photography, laser scanning, and structured light. They also discuss the challenges in 3D face recognition, such as occlusions and pose variations, and present various algorithms and approaches to overcome these challenges. It also discusses applications of face recognition technology in various domains.

The research proposed by Ramachandra and Busch (2017) provides a thorough analysis of various methods for detecting presentation attacks in face recognition systems. It addresses the growing concern of security vulnerabilities in face recognition systems, where attackers can use presentation attacks such as photo, video, or 3D masks to deceive the system. This research reviews and evaluates existing techniques and algorithms proposed by researchers to tackle this issue.

The authors begin by categorizing the presentation attack detection methods into four major groups: texture-based analysis methods, motion-based analysis methods, depth-based analysis methods, and component-based analysis methods. They discuss the advantages and limitations of each method, providing insights into their effectiveness in sensing different types of presentation outbreaks. Moreover, the research addresses potential challenges faced by these methods, such as environmental factors, device variations, and attack diversity, which can significantly impact detection accuracy. By providing a comprehensive survey of presentation attack detection methods, this research paper equips researchers and practitioners with valuable information to enhance the security and reliability of face recognition systems.

Biometric sensors, such as fingerprint scanners and facial recognition systems, are widely used in various applications, ranging from unlocking smartphones to personal identification at border control. These sensors play a crucial role in ensuring the security and authenticity of the users. However, recent studies have shown that these sensors can be vulnerable to spoofing attacks, where an attacker manipulates the sensor to falsely recognize their biometric attributes. The commonly used method of spoofing biometric sensors is through the use of artificial replicas or synthetic materials that mimic the appearance and characteristics of the genuine biometric attribute. For example, an attacker may create a replica of a fingerprint using materials such as silicone or gelatin, and then use it to fool a fingerprint scanner. Similarly, they can create a 3D mask or a high-resolution photograph to trick a facial recognition system.

Various procedures have been projected to detect and prevent such spoofing attacks. One approach is to use liveness detection techniques, which aim to distinguish between live and spoofed biometric attributes (Galbally et al., 2014). These techniques can involve analyzing the movement, texture, or thermal properties of the biometric attribute to detect artificial replicas. Another approach is to employ multimodal biometric systems, which combine multiple biometric attributes, such as fingerprints and iris patterns, to enhance the security and accuracy of the system. By comparing multiple biometric attributes, the system can increase the difficulty for an attacker to spoof all of them simultaneously.

In addition to these, researchers have also explored the use of machine learning algorithms to detect spoofing attacks. These algorithms can be trained on a large dataset of genuine and spoofed biometric templates and then used to classify new samples as either genuine or spoofed (Jain et al., 2008). However, it is important to note that these algorithms can also be vulnerable to adversarial attacks, where an attacker manipulates the system to bypass the detection algorithm.

The research paper proposed by Ross and Jain (2004) provides a comprehensive examination of multimodal biometrics technologies, highlighting their importance and applications in the field of authentication and identification. The study explores the concept of combining multiple biometric traits to enhance accuracy, reliability, and security in biometric systems. The findings shed light on the potential benefits of multimodal biometrics, including improved accuracy, robustness against spoofing attacks, and increased system performance. Moreover, the paper emphasizes the significance of multimodal fusion techniques and highlights existing challenges, such as interoperability and privacy concerns, that need to be addressed for the widespread adoption of multimodal biometrics in various real-world applications. Vielhauer et al. discussed about how biometric matching approaches work in the encrypted province (Vielhauer et al., 2013). For the use of face biometrics, the general algorithm strategy, execution, and setup challenges are outlined and explained in an illustrative way.

The usage of biometrics brings up several privacy issues. It may be important to make a wise trade-off between security and privacy, but we can only impose a shared set of standards for acceptability and responsibility through legislation. The use of biometrics to establish responsible logs of system transactions and safeguard people's right to privacy is a positive development in the privacy debate (Prabhakar et al., 2003). The market and the technology will interact more as biometric technology develops. However, biometric recognition will have a significant impact on how we go about our daily lives.

In a general biometric system, Ratha et al. (2001) have identified eight places of weakness and talked about potential assaults. They offered numerous solutions for reducing some of these security risks. Data-hiding methods have been used to covertly implant a telltale mark right in the compressed fingerprint picture to counter replay attacks. This research discussed the sometimes overlooked issues of privacy and biometric revocation. The fact that biometrics do not change over time, which is both their greatest asset and their worst weakness, is somewhat ironic.

A collection of biometric information that has been compromised once is compromised always. Authors have suggested applying repetitive non-invertible distortions to the biometric signal to solve this problem. Simply specifying a new distortion transform is enough to cancel. Because different distortions can be used for various services and the real biometric information is never kept or made available to the authentication server, privacy is improved. Lai et al. (2011) have studied the circumstance when a system attacker has side knowledge and the privacy-security region's inner and outer bounds are taken into account. It is demonstrated that only mutual arbitrariness can be produced from dual biometric measurements with full privacy. Jain et al. have considered into account randomized and nonrandomized key-binding and key-generating biometric cryptosystems, respectively (Jain et al., 2008).

The protection of resources and services from illegal usage is necessary to preserve the security of biometrics inside distributed systems for diverse services. The most popular technique for confirming a distant client's identity is remote authentication. This study examines a methodical procedure for customer authentication using a password, smart card, and biometric data. The transition from two-factor authentication to three-factor authentication is suggested using a general and safe architecture by Huang et al. (2011). In distributed systems, the conversion not only greatly raises information assurance at a minimal cost but also safeguards client privacy.

Designing trustworthy user authentication for mobile devices is a crucial challenge for safeguarding users' confidential data. Subsequently, biometric technologies can provide several advantages over traditional authentication methods, and they have gained attention from both academics and businesses. Using five physiological and six behavioral biometric approaches, Meng et al. (2015) have reviewed the evolution of current biometric verification systems on mobile phones, in particular on touch-enabled hand-held devices. They outline a taxonomy of ongoing projects for mobile biometric authentication and assess their viability for use with touch-enabled devices. They also explored the characterization of a generic biometric verification system through eight possible sites of attack and how to assess actual attacks on mobile devices as well as potential defenses. On touch-enabled hand-held phones, multimodal biometric user authentication that is adequate for security can be used to dramatically lower the false percentage of a sole biometric system.

Since biometric traits are linked to specific individuals, their privacy will be violated, which can lead to major and ongoing issues because a person's unique biometric data cannot be replaced. Several privacy-preservative biometric schemes were developed over the past ten years to safeguard the biometric data carrying privacy data; however, they have several limitations. This research provides a thorough analysis and offers suggestions for future biometric research that protects user privacy. In particular, Natgunanathan et al. (2016) have shown the most advanced biometric approaches based on these principles that protect privacy.

Memon (2017) explained the difficulties that biometric authentication appears in network security and privacy. Biometric information, or a person's quantifiable physical and behavioral traits, has been used for a long time. For instance, Apple's iPhone enables customers to authenticate payments, safeguard mobile bill records, and unlock the device by scanning their fingerprints. Companies like Lenovo and Dell utilize fingerprint technology to let consumers sign into their laptops with only a swipe. As a solution, the usage of biometric data to access our gadgets is growing. An enhanced biometrics-based remote user authentication system with user anonymity was put forth by Khan and Kumari (2013). Wen et al. (2015) have suggested a reliable biometric-based remote user authentication strategy. They have used the BAN logic to simulate their scheme for the formal security verification to make sure it is operating properly by satisfying the mutual authentication objectives.

Patro et al.'s (2022) literature survey delves into the realm of electrocardiogram (ECG) biometric recognition, focusing on the integration of efficient feature selection techniques with machine learning methods. It synthesizes existing research to provide a comprehensive overview of methodologies, algorithms, and datasets used in this domain. The paper assesses the effectiveness of feature selection in enhancing ECG-based biometric recognition systems' accuracy and efficiency. Jahan et al. (2019) present a comprehensive exploration of a robust user authentication model tailored to enhance the security of electronic healthcare systems. Leveraging fingerprint biometrics as a primary means of user identification, the study critically evaluates existing authentication approaches, emphasizing the importance of fortifying electronic healthcare system security. After a thorough examination of the relevant literature, this paper not only elucidates the effectiveness of fingerprint biometrics in bolstering security but also addresses privacy and usability concerns in healthcare contexts, with a focus on striking a balance between robust security and user convenience.

Yoshizawa et al. presented a literature survey (2023) that explores the evolving landscape of security and privacy concerns in vehicle-to-everything (V2X) communication systems. It comprehensively reviews existing research, highlighting vulnerabilities, encryption techniques, and authentication protocols. The chapter also sheds light on emerging threats and promising solutions, offering a holistic perspective on safeguarding the future of connected transportation. The survey provides a concise overview of the field of visual cryptography, summarizing key concepts and recent advancements discussed by Punithavathi and Geetha (2017). It covers fundamental visual cryptography schemes, their applications, and challenges. By presenting a snapshot of the state-of-the-art, this concept serves as a valuable resource for researchers and practitioners interested in this intriguing cryptographic technique.

Another literature survey investigates the intersection of biometrics and mobile user authentication, with a focus on addressing the unique needs of elderly users (Wang et al., 2023). It examines existing research, evaluating the accessibility of biometric methods for older individuals, and assessing their performance in real-world scenarios. It also explores innovative method designs tailored to the aging population, offering valuable insights into enhancing the security and usability of mobile authentication for this demographic. Researchers, developers, and policymakers will find this survey instrumental in advancing inclusive and secure mobile technologies.

Alhomayani and Mahoor (2020) provide a comprehensive review of deep learning methods applied to fingerprint-based indoor positioning systems. Fingerprint-based localization has gained prominence in indoor navigation, and deep learning techniques have shown promising results in enhancing its accuracy and robustness. The study surveys the state-of-the-art deep learning models, their architectures, and their applications in indoor positioning. It also discusses the challenges and future directions in this domain, offering valuable insights to researchers and practitioners interested in advancing indoor positioning technologies using deep learning approaches. This review serves as a vital resource for understanding the evolving landscape of indoor localization through fingerprint-based methods.

Biometric security systems have gained widespread adoption across various domains, offering a convenient and robust means of authentication. This survey paper delves into the multifaceted landscape of biometric security, systematically addressing the myriad challenges and opportunities presented by Arora and Bhatia (2022). It categorizes challenges into technical aspects, encompassing accuracy, spoofing, and interoperability, as well as ethical and legal considerations involving privacy and data protection. In contrast, opportunities encompass emerging modalities, such as behavioral and physiological biometrics, and the integration of biometrics with emerging technologies like blockchain and AI. It also highlights the pivotal role of biometrics in addressing contemporary security needs, including mobile devices, IoT, and healthcare. This research article examines the evolution of biometric technologies, from traditional fingerprint and iris recognition to newer behavioral and multimodal approaches. It explores the fusion of biometrics with cryptography and machine learning techniques, emphasizing the importance of robust security in an increasingly interconnected world. This comprehensive survey aims to guide researchers, practitioners, and policymakers in understanding the current state of biometric security, paving the way for informed decisions and innovative solutions to meet the growing challenges and harness the immense potential of biometric authentication systems.

Rui and Yan provided (2019) biometric authentication which has emerged as a prominent paradigm for secure and user-friendly identification across various applications. This comprehensive survey paper critically examines the state-of-the-art in biometric authentication with a dual focus on security and privacy preservation. It categorizes the challenges faced by biometric systems, including vulnerability to spoofing attacks, privacy concerns, and scalability issues. The survey explores the evolution of biometric modalities, from traditional fingerprints and facial recognition to emerging behavioral and multimodal approaches, with a keen eye on their potential security implications. The paper delves into the latest advancements in biometric template protection techniques, emphasizing the importance of safeguarding biometric data from breaches and ensuring user privacy. It discusses the integration of biometrics with cryptographic protocols, machine learning, and blockchain technologies to bolster security while preserving user privacy. It offers insights into the challenges, emerging trends, and innovative solutions that contribute to the development of secure and privacy-preserving biometric identification systems, promoting the adoption of this technology while addressing ethical and legal considerations.

The literature review provided by Singh et al. (2021) delves into the evolving landscape of biometric technology, emphasizing the intricate interplay between security and privacy. It categorizes security concerns, ranging from vulnerability to spoofing attacks and system breaches, to the ethical use of biometric data. This paper scrutinizes the multifaceted privacy challenges posed by biometric systems, addressing issues such as data protection, consent, and user control. It highlights the importance of designing privacy-preserving biometric solutions through techniques like secure template storage and cryptographic protection. It discusses the ethical considerations surrounding biometric data collection and usage in light of evolving regulatory frameworks.

The next authors Abdul et al. (2017) have highlighted the promising role of visual encryption techniques as a means to enhance the security of biometric information in distributed fog edge environments. Through an in-depth survey of existing research, it categorizes various visual encryption methods and evaluates their applicability in fog edge scenarios. It also discusses the integration of biometric modalities, such as facial recognition and iris scans, into fog edge systems and their implications for security and efficiency. The extensive literature review discussed by Mendel and Toch categorizes the strategies, tools, and communication channels employed by younger generations to assist older relatives with mobile security and privacy (Mendel & Toch, 2020). It also considers the psychological and emotional factors influencing both the helpers and the recipients of assistance in this context. Furthermore, the paper examines the potential impact of intergenerational assistance on the overall digital literacy and security awareness of older adults.

Wang et al. (2023) address a critical aspect of user authentication in mobile devices. It highlights the significance of accommodating the elderly population's unique needs in authentication systems. The literature of this paper explores existing biometric authentication methods and their suitability for elderly users, focusing on accessibility issues and performance metrics. This research contributes to the growing body of knowledge in mobile security and emphasizes the importance of designing user-friendly authentication methods for this vulnerable demographic. Khandekar and Bendale (2023) have discussed about biometric authentication which has gained significant popularity due to its high reliability compared to password-based methods. Biometrics are challenging to forget, steal, or guess, making them a preferred technology for enhancing security. However, this increased reliance on biometrics raises privacy concerns. Biometric data, like fingerprints and iris patterns, can uniquely identify individuals and potentially be used to track their activities across various databases, posing a significant privacy risk. Striking a balance between enhanced security and safeguarding user privacy is crucial as biometrics continue to advance in the realm of authentication technologies.

Bernal-Romero et al. (2023) provide a comprehensive overview of security measures in biometric systems. It explores various protection and cancelable techniques employed to safeguard biometric data. The literature review in this paper discusses the significance of protecting sensitive biometric information, including fingerprints and facial features, against potential breaches. It highlights the evolution of cancelable biometrics as a promising approach to enhance security by transforming biometric templates while preserving recognition accuracy. This research contributes valuable insights into the ongoing efforts to fortify the security of biometric authentication systems. Alsowail and Al-Shehari (2022) present a comprehensive review of strategies aimed at mitigating the risk of insider threats within organizations. It delves into the various techniques employed to detect, monitor, and prevent malicious activities by individuals within the trusted network. The literature review within this paper underscores the evolving nature of insider threats and the importance of proactive measures to safeguard sensitive data and critical assets. It provides an essential foundation for organizations seeking their cybersecurity posture by addressing the often-underestimated threat posed by insiders.

4.12   RESEARCH METHODOLOGY

This chapter on biometric systems involves a systematic approach to studying the basic contents related to security and privacy. It analyzes the various challenges and concerns associated with the use of biometrics for identification and authentication purposes. The section begins with a thorough introduction, various types of threats, and a literature review to understand the current state of knowledge and identify existing gaps in research. This helps in formulating the base of security and privacy that will guide understanding the overall safety measurements. This includes understanding the potential threats and attacks faced by biometric systems, such as spoofing or unauthorized access.

This methodology for biometric systems requires a rigorous and systematic approach to address the complexities and challenges associated with the biometric system. The literature survey has a vast review of the previous research in the field of biometric security and privacy. The researchers can contribute to the development of secure and privacy-preserving biometric systems by ensuring the protection of sensitive personal information while maintaining the integrity and accuracy of the authentication process.

4.13   RESEARCH IMPLICATION OR FINDINGS

Biometric systems play an increasingly vital role in our daily lives, from unlocking smartphones with fingerprints to facilitating international travel with facial recognition. However, as these systems become more pervasive, there are growing concerns about security and privacy. One of the foremost challenges faced by biometric systems is the risk of data breaches. Since biometric traits come for use, if this data is compromised, it can have severe implications for personal security and privacy. Therefore, it is imperative to develop robust encryption and authentication methods to protect biometric data from potential attacks.

Privacy and security in biometric systems have far-reaching implications in today's technologically advanced world. Biometric systems, which use unique characteristics to confirm an individual's identity, are being increasingly used in various sectors, including government, banking, healthcare, and law enforcement. However, these systems pose significant security and privacy concerns. One of the key research findings is the vulnerability of biometric systems to attacks and impersonation. Biometric data, such as fingerprints, iris scans, or facial features, can be stolen, manipulated, or replicated, leading to identity theft or unauthorized access to secure systems. Researchers have highlighted the need for robust encryption, authentication protocols, and secure storage mechanisms to protect biometric data from breaches. The literature studies have emphasized the importance of continuous monitoring and updating of biometric systems to address emerging security threats and vulnerabilities.

Biometric systems collect sensitive personal information, such as physical or behavioral characteristics, which can be considered highly private. The research has revealed concerns regarding the storage, use, and sharing of biometric data, as well as the potential for surveillance and misuse. There is a need for strict regulatory frameworks and guidelines to ensure that biometric systems are implemented in a manner that respects individuals' privacy rights. Researchers have also stressed the importance of informed consent, transparency, and accountability in the deployment and management of biometric systems to maintain public trust.

Another challenge is the probability of discrimination and bias in biometric systems. Biometric data collection and analysis may unintentionally result in biased outcomes, particularly for certain demographic groups. This can lead to unfair treatment or exclusion for individuals who do not fit the system's criteria. Therefore, researchers and policymakers need to work on addressing this issue and developing more inclusive and unbiased algorithms for biometric systems. The ethical considerations and privacy rights must be diligently addressed to ensure that individuals' biometric information is collected, stored, and used lawfully and transparently. Continued research and collaboration between academia, industry, and policymakers are crucial to developing effective solutions and guidelines for the secure implementation of biometric systems.

4.14 CONCLUSIONS AND FUTURE WORK

The field of security and privacy in biometric systems has made significant advancements in recent years. Researchers and practitioners have developed various techniques and technologies to improve the security and privacy of biometric systems, including but not limited to, encryption algorithms, secure hardware implementation, multimodal biometrics, and privacy-enhancing techniques. These advancements have greatly enhanced the overall robustness and trustworthiness of biometric systems. However, there are still several important challenges that need to be addressed in the future. The touch dynamics approach will become a recent mainstream in designing future user authentication on mobile phones as discussed in the literature. An overview of the literature survey helps in summarizing various biometric authentication techniques including their strengths and limitations.

One of the key areas is to develop more resilient biometric systems that can withstand attacks and adversarial attempts to manipulate or deceive the system. This includes exploring new authentication methods and algorithms that can accurately detect and prevent presentation attacks, such as spoofing or tampering with biometric samples. In advancement, the integration of machine learning and artificial intelligence techniques can further enhance the security and privacy of biometric systems by continuously adapting and improving the system's ability to detect and respond to emerging threats.

Furthermore, the ethical implications and societal impacts of biometric technologies need to be carefully considered and addressed, including issues related to privacy, consent, and potential biases or discrimination. Future research work should continue to focus on improving the resilience, accuracy, and usability of these systems while also considering the ethical and societal implications to develop stronger encryption, authentication algorithms, and privacy-enhancing techniques that allow users to have control over their biometric data, such as implementing techniques for secure biometric template protection and end user-centric privacy settings.

REFERENCES

Abdul, W., Ali, Z., Ghouzali, S., Alfawaz, B., Muhammad, G., & Hossain, M. S. (2017). Biometric security through visual encryption for fog edge computing. *IEEE Access, 5*, 5531–5538. https://doi.org/10.1109/ACCESS.2017.2693438

Alhomayani, F., & Mahoor, M. H. (2020). Deep learning methods for fingerprint-based indoor positioning: A review. *Journal of Location Based Services, 14*(3), 129–200. https://doi.org/10.1080/17489725.2020.1817582

Alsowail, R. A., & Al-Shehari, T. (2022). Techniques and countermeasures for preventing insider threats. *PeerJ Computer Science, 8*, e938. https://doi.org/10.7717/peerj-cs.938

Arora, S., & Bhatia, M. P. S. (2022). Challenges and opportunities in biometric security: A survey. *Information Security Journal: A Global Perspective, 31*(1), 28–48. https://doi.org/10.1080/19393555.2021.1873464

Bernal-Romero, J. C., Ramirez-Cortes, J. M., Rangel-Magdaleno, J. D. J., Gomez-Gil, P., Peregrina-Barreto, H., & Cruz-Vega, I. (2023). A review on protection and cancelable techniques in biometric systems. *IEEE Access, 11*, 8531–8568. https://doi.org/10.1109/ACCESS.2023.3239387

Crawford, H. (2010). Keystroke dynamics: Characteristics and opportunities. *2010 Eighth International Conference on Privacy, Security and Trust*, 205–212. https://doi.org/10.1109/PST.2010.5593258

Duta, N. (2009). A survey of biometric technology based on hand shape. *Pattern Recognition, 42*(11), 2797–2806. https://doi.org/10.1016/j.patcog.2009.02.007

Galbally, J., Marcel, S., & Fierrez, J. (2014). Biometric antispoofing methods: A survey in face recognition. *IEEE Access, 2*, 1530–1552. https://doi.org/10.1109/ACCESS.2014.2381273

Huang, X., Xiang, Y., Chonka, A., Zhou, J., & Deng, R. H. (2011). A generic framework for three-factor authentication: Preserving security and privacy in distributed systems. *IEEE Transactions on Parallel and Distributed Systems, 22*(8), 1390–1397. https://doi.org/10.1109/TPDS.2010.206

Jahan, S., Chowdhury, M., & Islam, R. (2019). Robust user authentication model for securing electronic healthcare system using fingerprint biometrics. *International Journal of Computers and Applications, 41*(3), 233–242. https://doi.org/10.1080/1206212X.2018.1437651

Jain, A. K., Nandakumar, K., & Nagar, A. (2008). Biometric Template Security. *EURASIP Journal on Advances in Signal Processing*. https://doi.org/10.1155/2008/579416.

Kataria, A. N., Adhyaru, D. M., Sharma, A. K., & Zaveri, T. H. (2013). A survey of automated biometric authentication techniques. *2013 Nirma University International Conference on Engineering (NUiCONE)*, 1–6. https://doi.org/10.1109/NUiCONE.2013.6780190

Khan, M. K., & Kumari, S. (2013). An improved biometrics-based remote user authentication scheme with user anonymity. *BioMed Research International, 2013*, e491289. https://doi.org/10.1155/2013/491289

Khandekar, D., & Bendale, S. (2023). Biometrics security system. *International Journal of Advanced Research in Science, Communication and Technology*, 219–224. https://doi.org/10.48175/IJARSCT-8588

Lai, L., Ho, S.-W., & Poor, H. V. (2011). Privacy–security trade-offs in biometric security systems—Part I: Single use case. *IEEE Transactions on Information Forensics and Security, 6*(1), 122–139. https://doi.org/10.1109/TIFS.2010.2098872

Li, S. Z., & Jain, A. K. (2011). *Handbook of Face Recognition*. Springer London, Springer-Verlag London Limited, 2, XV, 699. https://doi.org/10.1007/978-0-85729-932-1.

Memon, N. (2017). How biometric authentication poses new challenges to our security and privacy [in the spotlight]. *IEEE Signal Processing Magazine, 34*(4), 196–194. https://doi.org/10.1109/MSP.2017.2697179

Mendel, T., & Toch, E. (2020). My Mom Was Getting This Popup: Understanding Motivations and Processes in Helping Older Relatives with Mobile Security and Privacy. *Proceedings of the ACM on Interactive, Mobile, Wearable and Ubiquitous Technologies, 3*(4), 147:1–147:20. https://doi.org/10.1145/3369821

Meng, W., Wong, D. S., Furnell, S., & Zhou, J. (2015). Surveying the development of biometric user authentication on Mobile phones. *IEEE Communications Surveys & Tutorials, 17*(3), 1268–1293. https://doi.org/10.1109/COMST.2014.2386915

Natgunanathan, I., Mehmood, A., Xiang, Y., Beliakov, G., & Yearwood, J. (2016). Protection of privacy in biometric data. *IEEE Access, 4*, 880–892. https://doi.org/10.1109/ACCESS.2016.2535120

Patro, K. K., Jaya Prakash, A., Jayamanmadha Rao, M., & Rajesh Kumar, P. (2022). An efficient optimized feature selection with machine learning approach for ECG biometric recognition. *IETE Journal of Research, 68*(4), 2743–2754. https://doi.org/10.1080/03772063.2020.1725663

Prabhakar, S., Pankanti, S., & Jain, A. K. (2003). Biometric recognition: Security and privacy concerns. *IEEE Security & Privacy, 1*(2), 33–42. https://doi.org/10.1109/MSECP.2003.1193209

Punithavathi, P., & Geetha, S. (2017). Visual cryptography: A brief survey. *Information Security Journal: A Global Perspective, 26*(6), 305–317. https://doi.org/10.1080/19393555.2017.1386249

Ramachandra, R., & Busch, C. (2017). Presentation attack detection methods for face recognition systems: A comprehensive survey. *ACM Computing Surveys, 50*(1), 8:1–8:37. https://doi.org/10.1145/3038924

Ratha, N. K., Connell, J. H., & Bolle, R. M. (2001). Enhancing security and privacy in biometrics-based authentication systems. *IBM Systems Journal, 40*(3), 614–634. https://doi.org/10.1147/sj.403.0614

Ross, A., & Jain, A. (2004). Multimodal Biometrics: An Overview. 1221–1224.

Rui, Z., & Yan, Z. (2019). A survey on biometric authentication: Toward secure and privacy-preserving identification. *IEEE Access, 7*, 5994–6009. https://doi.org/10.1109/ACCESS.2018.2889996

Singh, G., Bhardwaj, G., Singh, S. V., & Garg, V. (2021). Biometric Identification System: Security and Privacy Concern. In S. Awasthi, C. M. Travieso-González, G. Sanyal, & D. Kumar Singh (Eds.), *Artificial Intelligence for a Sustainable Industry 4.0* (pp. 245–264). Springer International Publishing. https://doi.org/10.1007/978-3-030-77070-9_15

Vielhauer, C., Dittmann, J., & Katzenbeisser, S. (2013). Design Aspects of Secure Biometric Systems and Biometrics in the Encrypted Domain. In P. Campisi (Ed.), *Security and Privacy in Biometrics* (pp. 25–43). Springer London. https://doi.org/10.1007/978-1-4471-5230-9_2

Wang, K., Zhou, L., & Zhang, D. (2023). Biometrics-based Mobile user authentication for the elderly: Accessibility, performance, and method design. *International Journal of Human–Computer Interaction*, *0*(0), 1–15. https://doi.org/10.1080/10447318.2022.2154903

Wen, F., Susilo, W., & Yang, G. (2015). Analysis and improvement on a biometric-based remote user authentication scheme using smart cards. *Wireless Personal Communications*, *80*(4), 1747–1760. https://doi.org/10.1007/s11277-014-2111-6

Yampolskiy, R. V., & Govindaraju, V. (2008). Behavioural biometrics: A survey and classification. *International Journal of Biometrics*, *1*(1), 81.

Yoshizawa, T., Singelée, D., Muehlberg, J. T., Delbruel, S., Taherkordi, A., Hughes, D., & Preneel, B. (2023). A survey of security and privacy issues in V2X communication systems. *ACM Computing Surveys*, *55*(9), Article 9. https://doi.org/10.1145/3558052

Zhang, X., & Gao, Y. (2009). Face recognition across pose: A review. *Pattern Recognition*, *42*(11), 2876–2896. https://doi.org/10.1016/j.patcog.2009.04.017

5 Enhancing Computer Vision Enabled Biometric Applications
Current Trend, Challenges and Future Opportunities

Chinu Singla

5.1 INTRODUCTION

In an era marked by rapid technological advancements and an increasing need for secure and efficient identification and verification systems, biometric applications have emerged as a crucial solution. Biometrics involves the use of unique physical or behavioural characteristics to identify and authenticate individuals by offering a robust and reliable approach for a wide range of sectors, including security, access control, surveillance and personal authentication. Among the various components that contribute to the success of biometric systems, computer vision plays a pivotal role in extracting and analysing biometric features from images or video data.

The field of computer vision has witnessed remarkable progress in recent years, driven by the advent of deep learning techniques and the availability of vast amounts of data. These advancements have paved the way for highly sophisticated and accurate biometric applications. However, despite these breakthroughs, several challenges persist, hindering the seamless implementation of biometric systems in real-world scenarios.

This chapter focuses to explore the significant advancements in computer vision techniques tailored for biometric applications while shedding light on the challenges faced within this domain. By going into these challenges and proposing potential solutions, we aim to enhance the effectiveness and reliability of biometric systems, ultimately leading to secure and efficient applications.

Biometric applications encompass various modalities, such as face recognition and fingerprint identification each presenting its unique set of complexities. One of the primary challenges lies in dealing with variations in lighting conditions, pose and ageing effects that can considerably impact the accuracy and robustness of biometric systems. Individuals may be captured under different illumination conditions or adopt varied poses after extracting consistent and reliable biometric features, which becomes a pivotal task.

DOI: 10.1201/9781032614663-5

Throughout this chapter, we will provide a comprehensive overview of the latest computer vision approaches specifically designed for addressing these challenges in various biometric modalities. Our aim will extend to face recognition, where the recognition of individuals based on facial features demands exceptional precision despite variations in facial expressions and lighting conditions. Additionally, we will focus on fingerprint identification, exploring how to mitigate the effects of image quality, skin conditions and partial prints that may arise during data acquisition. Furthermore, we will discuss iris recognition, a highly accurate biometric modality, and strategies to combat challenges arising from eye movement and occlusions.

To tackle these challenges, we propose using cutting-edge deep learning techniques, data augmentation methodologies and feature extraction and fusion methods. Deep learning has demonstrated exceptional capabilities in feature learning and representation by enabling biometric systems to generalize effectively to diverse scenarios. Data augmentation techniques can help augment the available training data, enabling the models to be more robust and adaptable to variations in real-world conditions. Moreover, using efficient feature extraction and fusion methods can enhance the discriminative power of biometric systems and foster multi-modal biometric integration for increased accuracy.

The significance of this research lies in its potential to revolutionize biometric applications, ensuring robustness and reliability in real-world scenarios. By addressing the existing challenges and capitalizing on innovative solutions offered by computer vision, we can bolster the adoption of biometric systems across various sectors, fostering secure and efficient applications for a safer and more streamlined future.

The chapter follows a structured format, with each section contributing vital insights to the research. In Section 5.2, a comprehensive literature survey is presented, offering an overview of existing research and studies related to the topic. Following that, Section 3 outlines the research methodology adopted for the investigation. Advancements in computer vision for biometric applications are presented in subsequent section. Section 5 identifies the challenges and suggests potential solutions. The chapter concludes with Section 6, where the key findings are summarized and the implications of the research are discussed. Additionally, this section presents future research directions, highlighting the potential for further advancements in computer vision for biometric applications, and offering insight into the ongoing evolution of secure and efficient biometric systems.

5.1.1 Novelty of the Proposed Research

- The chapter's goal is to provide an overview of the latest computer vision approaches used in biometric applications, which include face recognition, fingerprint identification and iris recognition.
- It also explores the challenges faced in each of these areas and presents potential solutions.
- These solutions encompass various techniques, including deep learning methods, data augmentation, feature extraction, and fusion methods.

- By addressing these challenges and implementing innovative solutions, the effectiveness and reliability of biometric systems can be significantly enhanced.
- This enhancement ultimately results in more secure and efficient applications in the field of biometrics.

5.2 LITERATURE SURVEY

Biometric applications have become essential tools in ensuring security and seamless authentication processes. Computer vision plays a central role in these applications by providing the means to extract and analyse biometric features accurately. Jain and Li (2011) highlighted the importance of computer vision in face recognition systems by enabling the detection of facial landmarks and facilitating feature extraction for robust identification. Additionally, Sheela and Vijaya (2010) emphasized the integration of computer vision techniques in iris recognition resulting in highly accurate and efficient authentication methods.

In the era of face recognition, numerous research works have explored the use of deep learning techniques to achieve remarkable advancements. Parkhi et al. (2015) introduced the VGG-Face model which used deep convolutional neural networks for highly accurate face recognition. Similarly, Schroff et al. (2015) proposed FaceNet, a deep learning-based approach that mapped faces into a high-dimensional Euclidean space by enabling efficient face verification and clustering. These deep-learning models have shown promising results in handling variations in pose, expression and lighting conditions.

To mitigate the challenges of pose variations, Hassner et al. (2015) introduced the 3D Face Alignment method, which exploited 3D face models to align faces robustly across different poses. Additionally, Zhu et al. (2016) explored the benefits of using pose-invariant deep convolutional features for face recognition. These studies demonstrate the effectiveness of incorporating pose-aware features for enhancing face recognition accuracy.

Fingerprint identification has also witnessed significant progress in recent years. Poulose and Han (2020) presented a comprehensive survey of fingerprint recognition systems, encompassing various techniques such as minutiae-based matching, ridge-based matching and orientation field-based methods. This survey highlighted the importance of selecting suitable matching algorithms based on the quality of fingerprint images.

In addressing challenges related to partial fingerprint acquisition, Blais et al. (2020) proposed a deep learning-based method that utilized image inpainting techniques to reconstruct missing fingerprint regions and enhance recognition accuracy. Moreover, Militello et al. (2021) introduced a large-scale fingerprint dataset to promote research in fingerprint verification under varying image qualities.

Computer vision has significantly improved iris recognition, a highly accurate biometric modality. Ma et al. (2019) conducted a comprehensive review of iris recognition techniques, encompassing image acquisition, segmentation and feature extraction methods. Hu et al. (2020) proposed an end-to-end deep iris recognition framework by combining CNNs and recurrent neural networks (RNNs) for superior recognition performance. Table 5.1 shows the state-of-the-art techniques in biometric applications:

TABLE 5.1

State-of-the-Art Techniques in Biometric Applications

Biometric Modality	Notable Techniques	Key Features	References
Face recognition	VGG-Face Model	Deep CNN-based, high accuracy	Parkhi et al. (2015)
	FaceNet	Deep learning for face verification and clustering	Schroff et al. (2015)
	3D Face Alignment	Utilizes 3D models for robust alignment	Hassner et al. (2015)
	Pose-Invariant Deep Features	Handles pose variations	Zhu et al. (2016)
Fingerprint	Minutiae-Based Matching	Traditional matching approach	Poulose and Han (2020)
Identification	Ridge-Based Matching	Ridge pattern analysis	Poulose and Han (2020)
	Orientation Field-Based Methods	Utilizes orientation field for matching	Poulose and Han (2020)
	Deep Learning with Image Inpainting	Reconstruction of partial fingerprints	Blais et al. (2020)
	Large-Scale Fingerprint Dataset	Promotes research in varying image qualities	Militello et al. (2021)
Iris recognition	Comprehensive Iris Recognition	Covers image acquisition, segmentation, features	Ma et al. (2019)
	End-to-End Deep Iris Recognition	Combines CNNs and RNNs for superior performance	Hu et al. (2020)

5.3   RESEARCH METHODOLOGY

The research methodology employed in this study aims to comprehensively investigate and explore the enhancements in computer vision techniques for biometric applications. The methodology incorporates a mixed-methods approach by combining both qualitative and quantitative methods to address the research objectives effectively. The step-by-step research process is outlined below.

1. *Research Design*
   The study adopts a mixed-methods research design, as it allows for a comprehensive investigation of the advancements in computer vision techniques for biometric applications. This design enables the researchers to gain both qualitative insights from expert interviews and quantitative data from experimental evaluations.
2. *Data Collection*
   In-depth interviews will be conducted with experts in the field of computer vision and biometric applications. These interviews will provide valuable insights into the latest advancements, challenges and potential solutions in the domain. A purposive sampling technique will be used to select knowledgeable and experienced professionals in the field. The interviews will

be semi-structured allowing for open-ended questions to explore diverse perspectives and gather detailed information. A comprehensive literature review will be conducted to gather existing research and studies related to the topic.

3. *Biometric Datasets*

Publicly available biometric datasets will be utilized for the experimental evaluation of computer vision techniques. These datasets are essential for training and evaluating the performance of the models in face recognition, fingerprint identification and iris recognition. Popular datasets such as LFW (Labelled Faces in the Wild) for face recognition, FVC (Fingerprint Verification Competition) datasets for fingerprint identification and CASIA-IrisV4 for iris recognition will be considered among others (Wu et al., 2015).

4. *Research Instruments*

A structured questionnaire will be designed to guide the expert interviews. The questionnaire will include questions related to advancements in computer vision, challenges faced in biometric applications and potential solutions. The questionnaire will be pre-tested on a small group of experts to ensure clarity and relevance.

An interview guide will be prepared to conduct in-depth interviews with experts. The guide will outline the topics to be covered, the key questions to be asked and prompts to explore specific aspects related to computer vision techniques in biometric applications.

5. *Data Analysis*

(a) *Qualitative Analysis of Expert Interviews*

Thematic analysis will be used to analyse the qualitative data obtained from the expert interviews. The interviews will be transcribed, and recurring themes and patterns will be identified to gain insights into advancements, challenges and potential solutions in computer vision for biometric applications.

(b) *Quantitative Analysis of Experimental Results*

For the quantitative aspect, performance metrics such as accuracy, precision, recall and F1-score will be calculated to evaluate the effectiveness of computer vision techniques on the selected biometric datasets. The performance of deep learning models and feature fusion methods will be compared and analysed.

6. *Experimental Setup*

Computer vision models will be implemented using popular deep learning frameworks such as TensorFlow or PyTorch. The models will be trained on the selected biometric datasets and hyperparameters will be tuned to optimize performance.

In our comprehensive study, we conducted rigorous experimental evaluations to assess the performance and effectiveness of various computer vision-enabled biometric applications. These evaluations were instrumental in shedding light on the current trends, identifying challenges, and exploring future opportunities in the dynamic field of biometric recognition.

To ensure the credibility and robustness of our evaluations, we selected benchmark datasets that are widely recognized and accepted within the biometric research community. These datasets not only serve as industry standards but also enable fair and impartial comparisons of different algorithms and methodologies.

Here are detailed descriptions of the prominent datasets utilized in our experimental assessments:

i. *LFW*:
LFW is a renowned dataset designed for evaluating face recognition systems. It comprises a vast collection of face images, each captured in uncontrolled and real-world settings. The dataset's diversity encompasses variations in lighting conditions, poses, expressions, and backgrounds, making it an ideal choice for assessing the robustness of our face recognition techniques. By leveraging LFW, we aimed to demonstrate the efficacy of our computer vision approaches in handling challenging face recognition scenarios.

ii. *FVC Datasets*:
The FVC datasets are synonymous with fingerprint recognition benchmarking. They encompass multiple datasets, each tailored to assess specific aspects of fingerprint identification. These datasets are characterized by their diverse fingerprint images, including variations in ridge patterns, minutiae configurations, and image quality. By incorporating FVC datasets into our evaluation, we rigorously tested the reliability and accuracy of our fingerprint identification methods, especially in scenarios with varying fingerprint image quality and complexity.

iii. *CASIA-IrisV4*:
CASIA-IrisV4 stands as a prominent dataset in the realm of iris recognition. It offers a comprehensive collection of high-quality iris images captured under controlled conditions. The dataset covers variations in iris texture, pupil dilation and occlusion, challenging the robustness of our iris recognition techniques. Our use of CASIA-IrisV4 aimed to showcase the capabilities of our computer vision-based approaches in accurately identifying individuals based on their iris patterns, even in challenging conditions.

These carefully chosen datasets played a pivotal role in our research, enabling us to rigorously evaluate the performance of our proposed computer vision methodologies. By utilizing these industry-standard benchmarks, we sought to provide an objective and comprehensive analysis of the current state of biometric applications, highlight existing challenges and present future opportunities for advancing biometric recognition systems.

iv. *Evaluation Metrics*:
To measure the performance of the computer vision models, evaluation metrics specific to each biometric modality will be utilized. For face recognition, metrics such as the receiver operating characteristic (ROC) curve and the area under the curve (AUC) will be used. For fingerprint and iris recognition, metrics like genuine acceptance rate (GAR), false acceptance rate (FAR) and equal error rate (EER) will be used.

5.4 ADVANCEMENTS IN COMPUTER VISION FOR BIOMETRIC APPLICATIONS

Biometric applications, which involve the identification and verification of individuals based on unique physical or behavioural characteristics, have gained immense importance in various domains such as security, access control and surveillance. The effectiveness and reliability of biometric systems heavily depend on advancements in computer vision techniques. In this section, we explore the significant progress made in computer vision for various biometric modalities by including face recognition (Petrescu, 2019) fingerprint identification and iris recognition.

5.4.1 ADVANCEMENTS IN FACE RECOGNITION

The block diagram of face recognition system is shown in Figure 5.1 (Jain et al., 2022).

5.4.1.1 Deep Convolutional Neural Networks (CNNs)

One of the major breakthroughs in face recognition is the utilization of deep convolutional neural networks (CNNs). CNNs have demonstrated exceptional capabilities in learning discriminative features from facial images (Wang et al., 2023) by enabling accurate and robust face identification. The architecture of CNNs consists of multiple layers of convolution, pooling, and fully connected layers, allowing the network to automatically learn hierarchical representations of facial features (Almabdy & Elrefaei, 2019). Figure 5.2 illustrates a basic architecture of a deep CNN for face recognition (Kabisha et al., 2022).

5.4.1.2 Siamese Networks for Face Verification

Siamese networks have been widely employed for face verification tasks. These networks utilize two identical CNNs that share weights and learn to map facial images

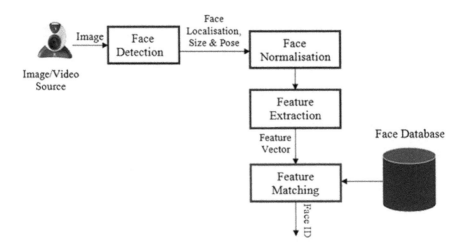

FIGURE 5.1   Block diagram of face recognition system.

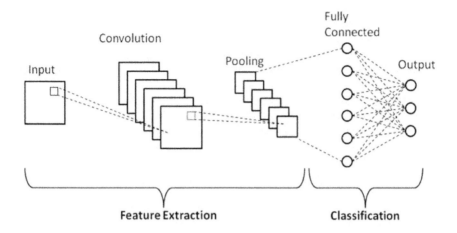

FIGURE 5.2   Basic architecture of a deep convolutional neural network for face recognition.

into a common feature space. The similarity between two face images can then be computed based on the distance in the feature space. Siamese networks are highly effective in verifying whether two face images belong to the same individual or not (Heidari & Fouladi-Ghaleh, 2020). Figure 5.3 shows Siamese network architecture for face verification (Jain et al., 2022).

Key components of a Siamese Network architecture for face verification:

i. *Input Images*: This is where your two input face images are provided to the Siamese Network. Typically, you have a pair of images, one from each of the two faces you want to compare. These images serve as the input to the network.

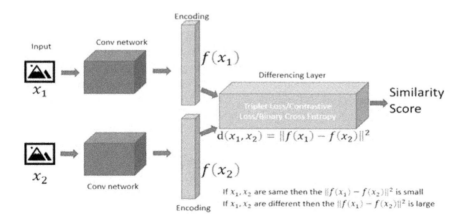

FIGURE 5.3   Siamese Network architecture for face verification.

ii. *Convolutional Neural Network (ConvNet)*: Each of the input images goes through a Convolutional Neural Network (ConvNet). ConvNets are used for image feature extraction. They consist of multiple convolutional layers and pooling layers that learn to capture hierarchical features from the images. These features represent different aspects of the face, such as edges, textures and more abstract facial patterns.

iii. *Encoding*: After passing through the ConvNet, both input images are transformed into feature vectors or embeddings. These embeddings represent the extracted features from the images in a lower dimensional space. This encoding step is crucial as it aims to project the high-dimensional image data into a more compact and informative representation that can be compared easily.

iv. *Differencing Layer*: In the Siamese Network, the next step involves calculating the absolute difference between the feature vectors obtained from the encoding step. This absolute difference operation helps emphasize the dissimilarities or variations between the two input images.

v. *Similarity Score*: The absolute difference obtained from the differencing layer is then used to calculate a similarity score. Commonly, this is done using a similarity metric such as Euclidean distance or cosine similarity. A lower similarity score indicates that the two input images are more similar, while a higher score suggests greater dissimilarity.

vi. *Decision Layer*: The similarity score is then passed through a decision layer, which is typically a fully connected (dense) layer in the neural network. This layer can include activation functions and thresholds to decide whether the two input images are of the same person or different persons based on the similarity score.

vii. *Output*: The final output from the decision layer is a binary decision: "Same" or "Different." If the network predicts "Same," it means the two input images are of the same person; if it predicts "Different," it means they are different individuals.

5.4.2 ADVANCEMENTS IN FINGERPRINT IDENTIFICATION

5.4.2.1 Minutiae-Based Fingerprint Matching

Minutiae-based fingerprint matching is a traditional technique that has been widely used in fingerprint identification systems. It involves the extraction and matching of minutiae points, which are unique features found at the ridge bifurcations and ridge endings in a fingerprint (Rahman et al., 2022). Advanced algorithms for minutiae extraction and matching have significantly improved the accuracy and efficiency of fingerprint identification system.

5.4.2.2 Deep Learning for Fingerprint Recognition

Deep learning techniques, particularly CNNs, have also been applied to fingerprint identification tasks. Deep CNNs can learn complex and abstract representations from fingerprint images, leading to improved recognition performance. By training on large-scale fingerprint datasets, deep learning models can achieve state-of-the-art accuracy in fingerprint recognition (Herbadji et al., 2022).

5.4.3   ADVANCEMENTS IN IRIS RECOGNITION

5.4.3.1   Iris Segmentation and Feature Extraction

Advancements in iris recognition include robust iris segmentation and feature extraction methods. Iris segmentation involves locating the circular iris region within the eye image accurately. Advanced algorithms for iris segmentation and feature extraction enable the extraction of unique iris patterns, such as texture and patterns in the iris, which are then used for identification purposes (Lee et al., 2019).

5.4.3.2   Deep Iris Recognition

Deep learning techniques, particularly CNNs and RNNs, have been applied to iris recognition tasks. Deep CNNs can learn discriminative features from iris images, while RNNs can capture temporal dependencies in iris sequences for efficient verification (Lee et al., 2019).

5.5   CHALLENGES AND POTENTIAL SOLUTIONS IN ENHANCING BIOMETRIC APPLICATIONS USING COMPUTER VISION

Biometric applications have witnessed significant advancements through computer vision techniques, enabling accurate identification and verification based on unique physical or behavioural characteristics of individuals (Minaee et al., 2023). However, this progress is not without challenges. In this section, we will discuss the key challenges faced in biometric applications and propose potential solutions to address these issues.

a. *Variability in Lighting Conditions and Pose*

Variations in lighting conditions and pose can significantly impact the quality and consistency of biometric data. Illumination changes can create shadows or highlights, while pose variations can make it difficult to align facial features for face recognition, or capture full fingerprints for fingerprint identification.

Solution: Using robust preprocessing techniques such as illumination normalization and pose estimation can help mitigate the effects of lighting and pose variations. Additionally, using multi-view or multi-modal biometric data acquisition can improve recognition performance in scenarios where pose variations are common.

b. *Ageing Effects*

Biometric traits may change over time due to ageing, leading to reduced recognition accuracy over the long term.

Solution: Developing age-invariant biometric recognition techniques can help maintain accuracy despite ageing effects. Deep learning-based approaches, such as generative adversarial networks (GANs) or domain adaptation methods, can be utilized to learn age-invariant representations from biometric data (Jain et al., 2021).

c. *Data Imbalance and Insufficient Training Data*

In real-world scenarios, biometric datasets often suffer from data imbalance, where some classes have significantly fewer samples than others. Additionally, collecting a diverse and large-scale dataset for training can be challenging.

Solution: Using data augmentation techniques, such as image rotation, scaling and flipping, can help create synthetic samples to balance the dataset. Transfer learning, where pre-trained models on large datasets are fine-tuned for specific biometric tasks, can be used when the availability of training data is limited.

d. *Presentation Attacks (Spoofing)*

Biometric systems are vulnerable to presentation attacks, where attackers use counterfeit biometric samples (e.g., masks or fake fingerprints) to deceive the system.

Solution: Implementing robust anti-spoofing techniques, such as texture analysis, motion analysis, or 3D face reconstruction, can help detect and prevent presentation attacks. Multi-modal biometric fusion can also improve system security by combining information from different biometric sources.

e. *Cross-Dataset Generalization*

Biometric systems trained on one dataset may not perform well on unseen datasets due to variations in data acquisition conditions and demographics.

Solution: Employing domain adaptation or domain generalization techniques can help improve cross-dataset generalization. By learning domain-invariant representations, the model becomes more robust to variations in different datasets.

f. *Computational Efficiency*

Real-time and scalable biometric systems require computational efficiency, especially in large-scale deployments.

Solution: Utilizing hardware accelerators, such as graphics processing units or specialized artificial intelligence chips, can improve the computational efficiency of biometric algorithms. Model compression techniques, like pruning or quantization, can also reduce the model's size and computational overhead (Yang et al., 2021).

5.6   CONCLUSION AND FUTURE SCOPE

In this chapter, we have delved into the remarkable advancements in computer vision techniques for biometric applications, highlighting the challenges faced in this domain and presenting potential solutions. Biometrics, which rely on unique physical or behavioural characteristics for identification and verification, have become integral to various sectors, including security, access control, surveillance and personal authentication. Computer vision plays a pivotal role in extracting and analysing biometric features from images or video data, enabling accurate identification and verification.

Despite the progress made, several challenges, such as variations in lighting conditions, pose variations, ageing effects, presentation attacks, cross-dataset generalization, and computational efficiency, remain significant obstacles in achieving reliable and efficient biometric systems. We have explored potential solutions such as robust preprocessing techniques, age-invariant recognition methods, data augmentation, anti-spoofing techniques, domain adaptation and hardware acceleration to address these challenges.

Investigating the application of biometric systems in healthcare, wearable devices, and emerging sectors can open up new opportunities for personalized services and improved user experiences and exploring the fusion of multiple biometric traits such as face, voice and behavioural biometrics can lead to more reliable and secure authentication systems by offering improved performance in challenging scenarios.

REFERENCES

Almabdy, S., & Elrefaei, L. (2019). Deep convolutional neural network-based approaches for face recognition. Applied Sciences, 9(20), 4397.

Blais, M. A., Couturier, A., & Akhloufi, M. A. (2020, June). Deep learning for partial fingerprint inpainting and recognition. In International Conference on Image Analysis and Recognition (pp. 223–232). Cham: Springer International Publishing.

Hassner, T., Harel, S., Paz, E., & Enbar, R. (2015). Effective face frontalization in unconstrained images. In Proceedings of the IEEE Conference on Computer Vision and Pattern Recognition (pp. 4295–4304).

Heidari, M., & Fouladi-Ghaleh, K. (2020, February). Using Siamese networks with transfer learning for face recognition on small-samples datasets. In 2020 International Conference on Machine Vision and Image Processing (MVIP) (pp. 1–4). IEEE.

Herbadji, A., Guermat, N., & Akhtar, Z. (2022, December). Deep neural networks based contactless fingerprint recognition. In 2022 2nd International Conference on New Technologies of Information and Communication (NTIC) (pp. 1–6). IEEE.

Hu, Q., Yin, S., Ni, H., & Huang, Y. (2020). An end-to-end deep neural network for iris recognition. Procedia Computer Science, 174, 505–517.

Jain, A. K., & Li, S. Z. (2011). Handbook of Face Recognition (Vol. 1, p. 699). New York: springer.

Jain, A. K., Deb, D., & Engelsma, J. J. (2021). Biometrics: Trust, but verify. IEEE Transactions on Biometrics, Behavior, and Identity Science, 4(3), 303–323.

Jain, L. C., Halici, U., Hayashi, I., Lee, S. B., & Tsutsui, S. (2022). Intelligent Biometric Techniques in Fingerprint and Face Recognition. Routledge, New York.

Kabisha, M. S., Rahim, K. A., Khaliluzzaman, M., & Khan, S. I. (2022). Face and Hand Gesture Recognition Based Person Identification System using Convolutional Neural Network.

Lee, M. B., Kim, Y. H., & Park, K. R. (2019). Conditional generative adversarial network-based data augmentation for enhancement of iris recognition accuracy. IEEE Access, 7, 122134–122152.

Ma, L., Tan, T., Wang, Y., & Zhang, D. (2019). Personal identification based on Iris texture analysis. IEEE Transactions on Pattern Analysis and Machine Intelligence (TPAMI), 25(12), 1519–1533.

Militello, C., Rundo, L., Vitabile, S., & Conti, V. (2021). Fingerprint classification based on deep learning approaches: Experimental findings and comparisons. Symmetry, 13(5), 750.

Minaee, S., Abdolrashidi, A., Su, H., Bennamoun, M., & Zhang, D. (2023). Biometrics recognition using deep learning: A survey. Artificial Intelligence Review, 13, 1–49.

Parkhi, O., Vedaldi, A., & Zisserman, A. (2015). Deep face recognition. In BMVC 2015-Proceedings of the British Machine Vision Conference 2015. British Machine Vision Association.

Petrescu, R. V. (2019). Face recognition as a biometric application. Journal of Mechatronics and Robotics, 3, 237–257.

Poulose, A., & Han, D. S. (2020, February). Performance analysis of fingerprint matching algorithms for indoor localization. In 2020 International Conference on Artificial Intelligence in Information and Communication (ICAIIC) (pp. 661–665). IEEE.

Rahman, M. M., Mishu, T. I., & Bhuiyan, M. A. A. (2022). Performance analysis of a parameterized minutiae-based approach for securing fingerprint templates in biometric authentication systems. Journal of Information Security and Applications, 67, 10320.

Schroff, F., Kalenichenko, D., & Philbin, J. (2015). FaceNet: A unified embedding for face recognition and clustering. Proceedings of the IEEE Conference on Computer Vision and Pattern Recognition (CVPR), 1234–1243.

Sheela, S. V., & Vijaya, P. A. (2010). Iris recognition methods-survey. International Journal of Computer Applications, 3(5), 19–25.

Wang, Q., Lei, H., & Wang, X. (2023). Deep face verification under pose interference. Journal of Computer Applications, 43(2), 595.

Wu, R., Yan, S., Shan, Y., Dang, Q., & Sun, G. (2015). Deep Image: Scaling up Image Recognition. arXiv preprint arXiv:1501.02876, 7(8), 4.

Yang, W., Wang, S., Sahri, N. M., Karie, N. M., Ahmed, M., & Valli, C. (2021). Biometrics for internet-of-things security: A review. Sensors, 21(18), 6163.

Zhu, X., Lei, Z., Liu, X., Shi, H., & Li, S. Z. (2016). Face alignment across large poses: A 3D solution. Proceedings of the IEEE Conference on Computer Vision and Pattern Recognition (CVPR).

6 MFDLD
Multiscale Fused Discriminant Local Descriptor for Face Recognition

Shekhar Karanwal

6.1 INTRODUCTION

In last two decades notable attention was achieved by the local descriptors in Pattern Recognition and Computer Vision fields, because of their discriminancy and robustness in unconstrained conditions. In numerous applications these local descriptors are tested, and results suggest their fruitfulness. Some such applications are Face Recognition (FR) (Li et al., 2021; Texture Analysis (TA) (Florindo & Metze, 2021; Pan et al., 2021), Facial Expression Recognition (FER) (Revina & Emmanue, 2021), Palmprint Analysis (PA) (Zhao and Zhang, 2020), Object Analysis (OA) (Zhang et al., 2022) and many more. Local descriptors form their feature size by working on finer image patches, which are integrated for developing the complete size. The hurdles which these local descriptors face are (1) curse of unconstrained conditions like noise, light, pose, emotion, blur, occlusion and corruption; (2) methodology is not effective as it should be; and (3) usage of global descriptors (for enhancing accuracy) is limited.

Out of numerous invented local methods, the one gathered significant attention most is local binary pattern (LBP) (Ojala et al., 1996). Due to discriminant texture representation and non-complex algorithm, LBP is more special than others. LBP forms the decimal code by constant coordination between center and neighbor pixels. Despite all these benefits there are various places that need to be addressed for enhancing the discriminativity. These are limited spatial information availability due to the usage of 3×3 patch, noise susceptibility and decrease in accuracy in harsh light variations. This work addresses all the hurdles of local descriptors (defined earlier) and LBP issues very effectively by capturing the multiscale features and then proposing a novel descriptor, Multiscale Fused Discriminant Local Descriptor (MFDLD). The crucial contributions of proposed work are defined as follows:

1. The proposed work utilizes three LBP variants for developing the multiscale features. Then these multiscale features are fused to develop the size of the most discriminant descriptor, MFDLD.
2. The three used LBP variants are Neighborhood Intensity-Based LBP (NI-LBP), Angular Difference-Based LBP (AD-LBP) and Local Phase

DOI: 10.1201/9781032614663-6

Quantization (LPQ). The multiscale (M) representation of NI-LBP, AD-LBP and LPQ, i.e. $MNI-LBP_{P,R_1\|R_2}$, $MAD-LBP_{P,R_1\|R_2}$ and MLPQ $(R_2\| R_3)$, is obtained by merging multiscale region features of 3×3 decomposed image.

3. Results show that multiscale descriptors are superior to single-scale descriptors. Accuracy is improved further by integrating $MNI-LBP_{P,R_1\|R_2}$ and $MAD-LBP_{P,R_1\|R_2}$; this descriptor is termed $MNA-LBP_{P,R_1\|R_2}$. Finally, $MNI-LBP_{P,R_1\|R_2}$, $MAD-LBP_{P,R_1\|R_2}$ and MLPQ $(R_2\| R_3)$ are joined to build MFDLD size.

4. MFDLD secure impressive results on ORL, GT and JAFFE datasets. Experiments are conducted on normal and blur images.

Remaining work is structured as follows: related works are discussed in Section 6.2, description of existing local descriptors is portrayed in Section 6.3, proposed descriptor with whole FR structure is given in Section 6.4, results are presented in Section 6.5 and Section 6.6 wraps up the paper.

6.2   RELATED WORKS

Nithya and Ramakrishnan (2021) invented wavelet domain majority coupled binary pattern (WDMBP) for TA. In WDMBP, the wavelet coefficient relationship is determined in distinct directions, and then majority rule is deployed for making the label. With the evolution of proposed label, by usage of majority rule, texture details are captured very impressively. Experiments on three datasets confirm the ability of WDMBP than several benchmark LBP-based methods. The drawback of this work is that feature reduction is missing, which can increase the performance. Hazgui et al. (2021) presented genetic programming (GP)-based technique for TA, by joining the merits of LBP and histogram of oriented gradient (HOG). Precisely, the three-layer architecture is designed in whole process. These three layers encompass the patch detection, fusion of features and matching. The second one is designed to control the rotation and light changes with compact feature size. The task of matching is fulfilled during optimization procedure of GP. The presented method secures better or comparable accuracy to the compared methods on six sets of dataset images. The drawback of this work is that no multiscale features are extracted and fused, which definitely enhances the performance. Huang (2021) impose the novel LBP variant complex network-LBP (CN-LBP) for TA to overcome LBP limitations. Initially, the Texture Image (TI) is conceptualized in the form of directed graphs generated over several bands by utilizing pixel distance, intensity and gradients. Then various CN-based attributes are picked to decrypt the features (texture), from which four feature images are generated. Furthermore, the uniform LBP-based features are extracted from TIs, Image Gradients (IGs) and four feature maps. Ultimately, all are joined to build complete representation. The proposed CN-LBP proves out better than deep and LBP-based methods on four datasets. The demerit of this work is that the results are conducted mostly on small-scale datasets. Karanwal (2021a,b) proposed the Graph Based Structure Binary Pattern (GBSBP) for FR, which is based on the graph structure. To be precise, four graph structures are formed initially by taking 3×5 and 5×3 patches. Then every structure graph is accompanied with three edges, and each one signifies distinct measure. By utilizing these measures, then mean collation yields four GBSBP codes, which all are concatenated to generate GBSBP code. The GBSBP proves its dominance than several methods on four challenging datasets. The major issues noticed in this work are as follows: (1) no multiscale features are extracted, (2) experiments are not performed on blur samples, and (3) much robust global methods can be utilized for compacting the feature.

Karanwal (2021a,b) provided comparative study of LBP and numerous LBP variants in FR. Specifically, the accuracy of 14 methods are examined on eight benchmark datasets. These benchmarks almost cover all the major challenges that texture represents. After successful evaluation, the descriptor that emerge most discriminant is compound LBP (CLBP). On some places, MRELBP-NI achieves better outcomes. The issues noticed are as follows: (1) feature extraction through regions is missing, and (2) the descriptor count used for comparison is less. Kola and Samayamantula (2021) discovered a novel method for FER to overcome LBP limitation of noise susceptibility. Precisely, pattern is formed by utilization of diagonal and four neighbors individually. To form more productive representation, the adaptive and mean (in radial orientations) methods are also introduced. This method possesses two crucial advantages: the low dimensional feature and reduction in image noise. Experiments confirm the potency of the novel method on four expression-based datasets in normal and noisy images. The drawback noticed in this work is that some other local statistic could be tested, which can yield better results. Kral et al. (2019) proposed enhanced LBP (E-LBP) for FR to handle small spatial window, noise and uneven illumination variations. E-LBP addresses all defined issues very effectively, by utilizing additional pixels and distinct neighbor structure for generation of feature vectors. On two benchmark datasets, LBP emerges better than other methods. The drawback of this work is that the count of the compared methods is less, and it must be compared to more methods. Kartheek et al. (2020) join the strengths of two well-established descriptors i.e. LBP and local directional pattern (LDP) to derive FER descriptor's so-called local optimal oriented pattern (LOOP). LOOP attains superb results on four FER datasets. Several existing methods are outclassed by LOOP; additionally, it takes much less time for execution. In this work some of the proposed descriptor is formed by merging only two descriptors; if more descriptors are added with multiscale feature extraction, then accuracy enhancement is assured.

Yuan et al. (2018) introduced hamming distance LBP (HDLBP) for diverse applications. In HDLBP, the HD is generated and encoded among LBP codes, produced from neighbors and center pixel on code map of LBP. The HDLBP and LBP jointly represent the LBP co-occurrence with HDLBP so-called LBPCoHDLBP. The rotation invariance is secured by utilizing the circular bit-way shift methods, and scale invariance is attained by concatenating the LBPCoHDLBP features from multiple scales. Further improvement in LBPCoHDLBP is suggested by incorporating sum of absolute differences (SAD) among the intensities of neighbor and center pixels. Experiments show the ability of invented methods than others. The major issue noticed in this work is that only support vector machines (SVMs) are used for the classification, and some other classifier results must be evaluated to explore the descriptors more. Lan et al. (2020) discovered quaternionic local angular binary pattern (QLABP) for color TA. QLABP is characterized by Q representation (QR) of color samples to handle color channels globally with their relations. To obtain additional color properties, the Q angular detail is also introduced. Finally, the pattern encoding procedure is deployed on angular detail to form the QLABP. Numerous benchmark methods are outstripped by QLABP. The main drawback of this is that other feature learning schemes are missing. Zhao et al. (2020) develop the Bur Invariant Local Binary Descriptor (BIBD) for FR. Precisely, the relationship among the binary codes, obtained from +ve image pairs of the original and blur images, is maximized for learning projection matrix. Further learned matrix projection is utilized to construct blur robust binary codes by PDV quantization in test phase. Results on two benchmark datasets convey the capability of BIBD against various LBP-like descriptors. In this work the experiments are conducted only on Gaussian blurring; some other types of blurring could be used to explore descriptor more.

In passing years deep learning methods gained huge reputation due to their robustness. MatchNet is introduced in Han et al. (2015), which is the classical Siamese network. The two-fold advantages of this network are feature extraction and similarity measurement between pairs. Mishchuk et al. (2017) invented the HardNet, which uses the loss for maximizing the distance between +ve and nearest −ve pairs in the batch. PN-Net is presented in Balntas et al. (2016), whose input is the triplet, and it deploys SoftPN loss, and as a result distances among matched pairs become compact as compared to distances among un-matched pairs. Cimpoi et al. (2016) proposed the FV-CNN deep learning method, which utilizes convolutional layers for CNN feature extraction and employs vector encoding based on Fisher, into pooling environment having order-less setting. This method achieves impressive outcomes. Additionally, there is more work reported based on deep learning. Although these deep learning methods are effective, there are various limitations observed, and these are as follows: (1) very high computational complexity, (2) requirement of training samples in huge amount and (3) the complexity in parameter adaption concept. These demerits limit the usage of these methods. In contrast there are some local descriptors whose performance is much finer than these deep learning methods. Some such works are reported in Sharma and Dey (2021) and Chen et al. (2018).

The proposed work overcomes most of the demerits discussed above and introduces the novel local descriptor MFDLD. In MFDLD, the multiscale features of three descriptors are fused for forming feature size. MFDLD proves its efficacy by defeating various benchmark methods.

6.3　EXISTING LOCAL DESCRIPTORS

This section provides layout of the existing local descriptors that are developed for different applications. Precisely, seven descriptors are induced in this section. The description of all of them is given below.

6.3.1 LBP

Ojala et al. (1996) invented LBP for TA. In LBP, intensity variations in neighbor structure are compared with center intensity for making binary patterns. The bit 1 is assigned to those places where neighbor gray intensity is higher or similar to the center gray intensity. If this condition is not fulfilled, then bit assigned is 0. The formed pattern is transfigured into decimal code by utilizing weights, which is available in powers of 2 (from 0...7). The LBP coding concept is shown in Eq. 6.1. Figure 6.1 gives an LBP example. The bold value indicates the LBP code. Similarly, on the other descriptor description, the bold value indicates the respective code.

$$LBP_{P,R}(i_c) = \sum_{p=0}^{P-1} h(i_{R,p} - i_c) 2^p, \quad h(x) = \begin{cases} 1 \text{ for } xd \\ 0 \text{ for } x < 0 \end{cases} \tag{6.1}$$

In Eq. 6.1, P, R, $i_{R,p}$ and i_c are size (of neighbor), radius (scale), neighbor individual and center intensities. In this work, the LBP code generation is carried out in each region location of the 3×3 decomposed image. The resulting nine LBP sub-images are transformed into histogram feature for making the complete LBP size. The histogram size generated from each region is 256; therefore, the LBP complete size is 256×9=2304.

6.3.2 CS-LBP

Heikkila et al. (2009) presented CS-LBP descriptor for TA. In CS-LBP, the difference generated from gray intensities of pixels (center symmetric in nature) is compared with threshold. Bit 1 is assigned to those places where difference intensity is higher than the threshold. If this condition is not fulfilled, then bit assigned is 0. The formed pattern is transfigured into decimal code by utilizing weights, which is available in powers of 2 (from 0...3). The CS-LBP code computation concept for one location is shown in Eq. 6.2. Figure 6.2 gives CS-LBP example having threshold of 23.

$$CS-LBP_{P,R,T}(i_c) = \sum_{p=0}^{\left(\frac{P}{2}\right)-1} h\left(i_{R,p} - i_{R,p+\left(\frac{P}{2}\right)}\right) 2^p$$

$$\tag{6.2}$$

$$h(x) = \begin{cases} 1 & x > T \\ 0 & \text{otherwise} \end{cases}$$

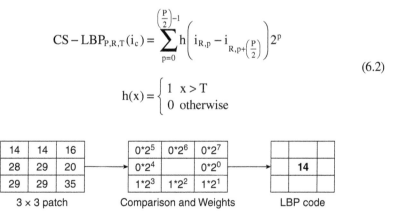

FIGURE 6.1 LBP example.

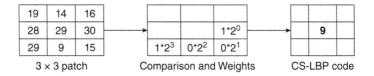

FIGURE 6.2 CS-LBP example.

In Eq. 6.2 P, R, $i_{R,p}$ and $i_{R,p+\left(\frac{P}{2}\right)}$ are neighbor size, radius (scale), neighbor gray intensity and center symmetric pixels. In this work, the CS-LBP code generation is carried from each region location of 3x3 decomposed image. The resulting nine CS-LBP sub-images are transformed into histogram feature for making the complete CS-LBP size. The histogram size generated from each region is 16; therefore, CS-LBP complete size is 16×9=144.

6.3.3 HOG

Dalal and Triggs (2005) introduced HOG for detection of humans. Since then it has been used in various applications. HOG is gradient-based descriptor. The first step in HOG is the selection of 1-D mask [−1 0 1] which is used in conjunction with σ to obtain the regional gradients. These regional gradients are then individually allocated in bins of size 9. Dalal et al. [27] noticed that descriptor performance is satisfactory up to the histogram size of 9 bin. For higher, performance degrades, so they stick to histogram size of 9 bin. After bin formation, overlapping and contrast improvement steps are done. These are done in the upper size blocks of Z×Z size. Feature overlapping is the crucial step in HOG invention. Although it improves the rate, it increases the feature dimension. So to make the even combination of discriminativity and computational cost, the amount of feature overlapping to be done is chosen in a very careful manner. The contrast improvement is provided by the four methods i.e. L_2-norm, L_1-norm, L_1-sqrt and L_2-hys. Therefore, depending on feature overlapping and block size, HOG size is generated.

In this work HOG features are extracted from every region of 3x3 decomposed image. The used block has dimension of 2×2, and the amount of overlapping used is 50%. With these parameters four 2×2 blocks are evolved from the 3×3 decomposed image. Each block region contains the nine bin size histogram; therefore, by integration of all block features, the HOG size produced is 4×4×9=144.

6.3.4 NI-LBP

NI-LBP is one of the four descriptors proposed by Liu et al. (2012) for TA. This descriptor is based on intensity variations in neighbor structure. To be specific, the neighbors (P) allocated at multiple scales (R_1, R_2,...,R_n) are compared with mean intensity of respective scale neighbors. Gray level intensity of those P having higher or similar gray level intensity to the mean intensity is endowed with 1 else 0.

By taking P=8 at $(R_1, R_2,...,R_n)$ generate 8 bit binary patterns. These patterns are then transfigured into decimal code by utilizing weights. The weights are in the form of powers of 2 (from 0....7). The NI-LBP code computation concept for one location is illustrated in Eq. 6.3.

$$NI - LBP_{P,R}(i_c) = \sum_{p=0}^{P-1} h(i_{R,p} - \mu_{R,P})2^p, \ h(x) = \begin{cases} 1 \text{ for xte} \\ 0 \text{ for } x < 0 \end{cases} \tag{6.3}$$

$$\mu_{R,P} = \frac{1}{P} \sum_{p=0}^{P-1} i_{R,p} \tag{6.4}$$

In Eq. 6.3 P, R, $i_{R,p}$ and $\mu_{R,P}$ are the neighbor size, radius (scales), neighbor individual intensity and mean intensity of neighbors. Eq. 6.4 generates the mean intensity by utilizing the gray intensity of neighbors. In this work NI-LBP is implemented at R_1 and R_2 with P=8. To accomplish this, 5×5 patch window is used. At both R_1 and R_2, the neighborhood intensity of eight neighbors is utilized for comparison with respective mean intensity. Those neighbors having higher or similar gray level intensity to mean intensity are endowed with 1 else 0. This generates 8 bit binary pattern from both the scales. These patterns are then transfigured into decimal code by utilizing weights. These decimal codes are represented as $NI - LBP_{P,R_1}$ and $NI - LBP_{P,R_2}$. The multiscale representation ($MNI - LBP_{P,R_1\|R_2}$) is further achieved by concatenating codes of $NI - LBP_{P,R_1}$ and $NI - LBP_{P,R_2}$. Figure 6.3 gives the example of NI-LBP with multiscale concept.

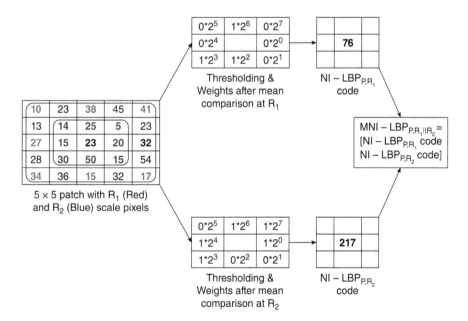

FIGURE 6.3 NI-LBP example with multiscale concept.

To make histogram-based feature, the concept of $NI-LBP_{P,R_1}$ and $NI-LBP_{P,R_2}$ is applied on every regional location of 3x3 decomposed image. As a result nine NI-LBP sub-images are evolved by using P=8 at R=1, and nine NI-LBP sub-images are evolved by using P=8 at R=2. The histogram of each region builds the size of 256; therefore, both $NI-LBP_{P,R_1}$ and $NI-LBP_{P,R_2}$ form the whole histogram size of 2304. The $MNI-LBP_{P,R_1\|R_2}$ feature size produced is 4608.

6.3.5 AD-LBP

Liu et al. (2012) developed the AD-LBP descriptor for TA. In AD-LBP, intensity variations in neighbor pixels, positioned as per the angular displacement, are compared with threshold. Specifically, difference generated from neighbor pixels, positioned as per angular displacement, is compared with threshold. Those difference intensities that are higher or equal to threshold are endowed with 1 else 0. By taking P=8 at $(R_1, R_2,...,R_n)$ generate 8 bit patterns that are transfigured to decimal code by using weights. Weights are in powers of 2 (from 0...7). Eq. 6.5 shows code formation.

$$ADBLBP_{P,R,\beta,\phi}(i_c) = \sum_{p=0}^{P-1} h\left(i_{R,p} - i_{R,mod(p+\beta,P)}\right)2^p, \ h(x) = \begin{cases} 1 \text{ for } x \geq \phi \\ 0 \text{ for } x < \phi \end{cases} \quad (6.5)$$

In Eq. 6.5 P, R, β,ϕ, $i_{R,p}$ and $i_{R,mod(p+\beta,P)}$ are neighbor size, radius (scales), angular displacement (n^0 at $1 \leq \beta \leq P/2$), threshold, neighbor individual intensity and adjacent neighbor pixel intensities (as per angular displacement). The angular displacement is computed by $\beta\left(\frac{2\pi}{P}\right)$, and β varies from $1 \leq \beta \leq P/2$. In this work AD-LBP is implemented at R_1 and R_2 with P=8. To accomplish this, 5x5 patch window is used. At both R_1 and R_2, the difference among neighborhood intensities placed at $\beta\left(\frac{2\pi}{P}\right)$ of 45° by taking β=1 is compared with ϕ=.01. Those difference intensities have higher or similar value to ϕ and are endowed with 1 else 0. This generates 8 bit binary pattern from both scales. These patterns are further transfigured to decimal code by weight utilization. These codes are specified as $AD-LBP_{P,R_1}$ and $AD-LBP_{P,R_2}$. The multiscale representation ($MAD-LBP_{P,R_1\|R_2}$) is further achieved by concatenating codes of $AD-LBP_{P,R_1}$ and $AD-LBP_{P,R_2}$. Figure 6.4 gives the example of AD-LBP with multiscale concept.

To make histogram based feature, concept of $AD-LBP_{P,R_1}$ and $AD-LBP_{P,R_2}$ is applied on every regional location of 3x3 decomposed image. As a result nine AD-LBP sub-images are evolved by using P=8 at R=1, and nine AD-LBP sub-images are evolved by using P=8 at R=2. The histogram of each region builds size of 256; therefore, both $AD-LBP_{P,R_1}$ and $AD-LBP_{P,R_2}$ form the whole histogram size of 2304. The $MAD-LBP_{P,R_1\|R_2}$ feature size produced is 4608.

6.3.6 MULTISCALE FEATURE CONCATENATION OF NI-LBP AND AD-LBP DESCRIPTORS

Multiscale features of NI-LBP and AD-LBP (i.e. $MNI-LBP_{P,R_1\|R_2}$ and $MAD-LBP_{P,R_1\|R_2}$) are concatenated further to build more robust representation

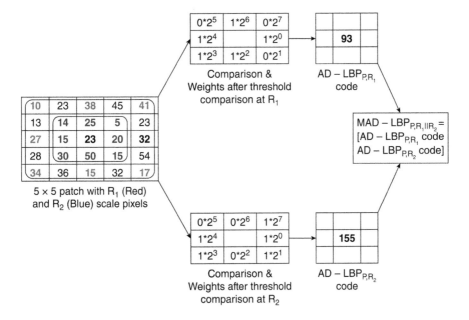

FIGURE 6.4   AD-LBP example with multiscale concept.

called as $MNA - LBP_{P,R_1 \| R_2}$. Therefore, the feature size produced by $MNA - LBP_{P,R_1 \| R_2}$ is 9216, where N stands for NI and A stands for AD.

6.3.7 LPQ

Ojansivu and Heikkila (2008) developed LPQ descriptor to attain blur invariant representation in texture. Since then it has been utilized in copious applications. LPQ methodology is based on computing short-time Fourier transform (STFT) for every $Q \times Q$ neighbor R_x in all places x image L(x). STFT computation formula is illustrated in Eq. 6.6.

$$L(y,x) = \sum_{v \in r_x} 1(x-v) e^{-j2\pi y^T v} \tag{6.6}$$

After STFT computation it becomes essential to capture four complex coefficients for generation of real and imag ingredients. In Ojansivu and Heikkila (2008) the coefficients taken are c_0, c_1, c_2 and c_3 where $c_0 = [e,0]^T$, $c_1 = [0,e]^T$, $c_2 = [e,e]^T$ and $c_3 = [e,-e]^T$. e is the small scalar quantity. The vector representation of these complex coefficients is mentioned in Eq. 6.7.

$$L(x) = \left[L(c_0,x), L(c_1,x), L(c_2,x), L(c_3,x)\right] \tag{6.7}$$

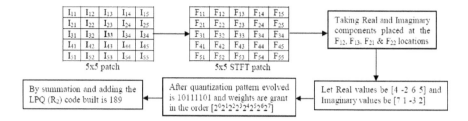

FIGURE 6.5 LPQ (R_2) illustration.

So real and imag ingredient extraction is done from L(x), as defined in Eq. 6.8. Thus, for each position eight values are generated. These values are then quantized using the formula illustrated in Eq. 6.9.

$$T(x) = \left[\text{Real}\big(L(x)\big)\, \text{Imag}\big(L(x)\big) \right] \tag{6.8}$$

$$Kp(x) = \begin{cases} 1 \text{ if } T_j(x)f \\ \quad 0 \text{ Else} \end{cases} \tag{6.9}$$

$T_j(x)$ corresponds to eight values of T(x). Ultimately, 8 bit pattern is produced to build the LPQ code, as defined in Eq. 6.10.

$$\text{LPQ code} = \sum_{p=0}^{7} K_p(x) 2^p \tag{6.10}$$

In this work, the LPQ code is computed in each region location of the 3×3 decomposed image by utilizing the multiple R_x values. R_x represents multiscale patches. This multiscale LPQ concept is the same as used in Chan et al. (2013). The x carries value from 1 to 3; therefore, three different patches i.e. R_1, R_2 and R_3 are used for LPQ feature extraction. R_1 represents 3×3 patch, R_2 represents 5×5 patch and R_3 represents 7×7 patch. The histograms generated from each region are merged to build the LPQ size with respect to each R_x. One region histogram size is 256; therefore, LPQ (R_1), LPQ (R_2) and LPQ (R_3) form the size of 2304. The LPQ (R_2) illustration is given in Figure 6.5, and Figure 6.6 communicates global images of LPQ (R_1),

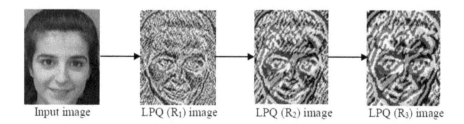

Input image   LPQ (R_1) image   LPQ (R_2) image   LPQ (R_3) image

FIGURE 6.6 LPQ images at three different scales.

LPQ (R_2) and LPQ (R_3). In same manner the LPQ (R_1) and LPQ (R_3) illustrations are achieved. In this work LPQ (R_1) is taken as comparison descriptor and features of LPQ (R_2), and LPQ (R_3) is joined to make the multiscale representation called MLPQ ($R_2 \| R_3$). Although MLPQ ($R_2 \| R_3$) is not tested individually, it is used for developing the size of proposed descriptor. MLPQ ($R_2 \| R_3$) obtains the size of 4608.

6.4 PROPOSED DESCRIPTOR AND PROPOSED FR STRUCTURE

In this section novel descriptor is reported by taking advantages of NI-LBP, AD-LBP and LPQ. The latter part provides the FR structure which contains the details of other methods such as dimension reduction and classification.

6.4.1 THE PROPOSED DESCRIPTOR

Literature suggests that use of multiscale local features with their integration improves the recognition rate. By taking that, this section introduces a new descriptor by merging multiscale features of NI-LBP, AD-LBP and LPQ. To be precise, the histograms of $MNI-LBP_{P,R_1\|R_2}$, $MAD-LBP_{P,R_1\|R_2}$ and MLPQ ($R_2 \| R_3$) are fused to form the most discriminant descriptor so-called MFDLD, which builds the size of 4608×3=13,824. In contrast to this, 11 descriptors are compared with MFDLD. These are LBP, CS-LBP, HOG, $NI-LBP_{P,R_1}$, $NI-LBP_{P,R_2}$, $MNI-LBP_{P,R_1\|R_2}$, $AD-LBP_{P,R_1}$, $AD-LBP_{P,R_2}$, $MAD-LBP_{P,R_1\|R_2}$, $MNA-LBP_{P,R_1\|R_2}$ and LPQ (R_1). Feature size of all these descriptors is defined in their respective sections. Region feature extraction (RFE), dimension reduction (DR) and classification steps remain same for these compared descriptors.

6.4.2 THE PROPOSED FR STRUCTURE ON NORMAL IMAGES

The step of resizing is done initially to compress the image size. By getting MFDLD feature size, there is generation of the vast feature size. Due to this it is essential to lower down the size. This is done by taking assistance of principal component analysis (PCA) (Kravchik & Shabtai, 2021). Numerous reduced feature sizes are examined by the classifiers. The one that gives best results are taken for classification. Same is done for compared ones also so that fair comparison is performed among all. After PCA reduction the classification duty is assigned to three classifiers. These are radial basis function (RBF), polynomial function (POLY) and exhaustive search approach (ESA). The former two are the (SVMs) (Hazarika & Gupta, 2021)-based methods, and the third one is nearest neighbor (NN) (Rastin et al., 2021)-based method. In ESA, the distance metric taken is cosine. Figure 6.7(a) shows flowchart/block diagram of proposed FR structure on normal images.

6.4.3 THE PROPOSED FR STRUCTURE ON BLURRED IMAGES

Initially, input image is convolved with Gaussian Kernel Window (Kostkova et al., 2020) of 5×5 size with σ=4. σ is the standard deviation. Then resized image is derived, followed by same steps as mentioned earlier. Figure 6.7(b) shows block

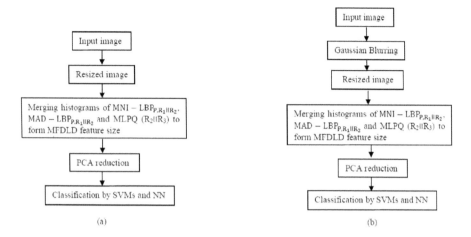

FIGURE 6.7 Block diagram of proposed FR structure on original and blurred images. (a) The figure shows the block diagram of the proposed FR structure on original images and (b) shows the block diagram of the proposed FR structure on blurred images.

diagram/flowchart of the proposed FR structure on blurred images. The compared descriptors are also implemented on blur images.

6.5   EXPERIMENTS

This section evaluates all descriptors on three challenging datasets. Initially, dataset descriptions are provided followed by the feature details of all descriptors. Finally, the result evaluation on three datasets with comparison to literature methods is done.

6.5.1   DATASETS DESCRIPTION

ORL   (http://www.cl.cam.ac.uk/research/dtg/attarchive/facedatabase.html),   GT (http://www.anefian.com/research/face_reco.html) and JAFFE (http://www.kasrl. org/jaffe.html) are the three used datasets. These are explored heavily in the literature, and their images contain various unconstrained conditions. Their illustrations are defined in the following sections.

6.5.1.1   ORL

ORL is well formulated from 40 humans. For every human ten samples are equipped in three changing conditions. These three are benefitted from pose, light and expression changes. The pose movements are diverse, light changes are not so severe, but there are some fluctuations in light variations, and finally, expression variations are minor. All 400 images have the same resolution of 112x92. Figure 6.8(a) gives one human image in different unconstrained conditions.

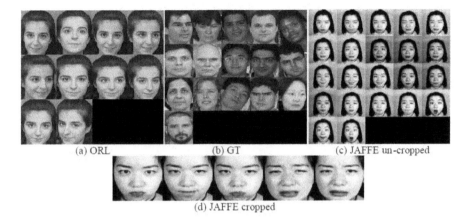

(a) ORL   (b) GT   (c) JAFFE un-cropped

(d) JAFFE cropped

FIGURE 6.8   Some dataset images. (a) The figure shows the ORL images. (b) The figure shows the GT images. (c) The figure shows the JAFFE uncropped images and (d) shows the JAFFE cropped images.

6.5.1.2   GT

GT is the second dataset, which is formulated from 50 humans. For every human 15 samples are equipped in four changing conditions. These four show attributes of pose, expression, light and scale. All attributes are diverse; therefore, this is the most complicated dataset to deal with. As scale variations exist, there are variations in image resolution. Figure 6.8(b) gives one human images in distinct unconstrained conditions. Total of these samples is 750.

6.5.1.3   JAFFE

JAFFE is third dataset taken for evaluation. This dataset is formulated from ten females, and each female is equipped with nearly 21 samples with three to four images per expression (7). The gross total of these samples is 213. In experiments all 213 are used. The seven expressions that pertain on samples are anger, disgusting, fear, happy, neutral, sad and surprise. Their resolution is set to 256×256 originally containing the unessential portions in background. During implementation this unessential portion is eliminated and cropped to uniform resolution of 141×131. Some non-uniform and uniform samples are shown in Figure 6.8(c) and 6.8(d).

6.5.2   Feature Size Formation after PCA

The images pertaining to ORL, GT and JAFFE (cropped) contain the high degree of resolution, which can consume much execution time if used as it is. So the samples are resized to 60×60. In GT, this is done after gray transfiguration of color images. Then 60×60 image is decomposed into nine same size regions (20×20) for extracting features, and all features are merged for size making. The multiscale descriptors are also formed. As evaluated in respective feature extraction section, a total of 12 descriptors are tested,

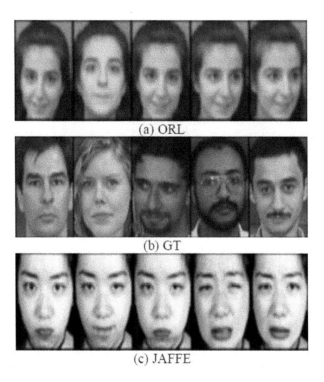

(a) ORL

(b) GT

(c) JAFFE

FIGURE 6.9 Some images after Gaussian blurring. Parts (a), (b) and (c) show the blurred images of the original images.

for example, LBP, CS-LBP, HOG, $NI-LBP_{P,R_1}$, $NI-LBP_{P,R_2}$, $MNI-LBP_{P,R_1\|R_2}$, $AD-LBP_{P,R_1}$, $AD-LBP_{P,R_2}$, $MAD-LBP_{P,R_1\|R_2}$, $MNA-LBP_{P,R_1\|R_2}$, LPQ (R_1) and MFDLD. MFDLD is invented descriptor. Their feature size is defined in respective sections. After PCA, sizes utilized by classifiers are 32, 32 and 32, respectively, on ORL, GT and JAFFE datasets. The size 32 is considered adequate for classification because it attains maximum rates on different utilized sizes. The testing is conducted in MATLAB R2014b environment. On blur image evaluation, the Gaussian blurring is performed on original images, and then images are resized. Rest steps remain same. Some of the blur images are given in Figure 6.9(a), 6.9(b) and 6.9(c).

6.5.3   ACCURACY EVALUATION ON THREE DATASETS

Before giving details regarding accuracy, the evaluation methodology is designed.

6.5.3.1   Evaluation Methodology

In evaluation methodology, different training/test subsets are created by 'holdout' method. Then accuracy is examined on test subset by recording the mismatched samples on test subset, after training concept. Suppose T_g is training size, T_t is test size and G_s are mismatched samples. Then accuracy (ACC) is formulated by procedure defined in Eq. 6.11.

$$ACC = \frac{T_t - G_S}{T_t} * 100 \qquad (6.11)$$

6.5.3.2   ORL

On ORL, T_g=1:4 and T_t=9:6. The T_g and T_t values are kept same for testing on normal and blur images. Best ACC is recorded after 48 runs. Tables 6.1–6.3 present ACC of all 12 descriptors by using three classifiers. Results show the superiority of multiscale descriptors as compared to single-scale descriptors, and by integrating two multiscale descriptors, ACC is improved more. Furthermore, the novel proposed descriptor MFDLD proves out most discriminant among all which significantly outstrip ACC of all 11 descriptors. Bold red value specifies ACC of MFDLD. Similarly, on other dataset tables, the bold red value specifies the same.

6.5.3.3   GT

On GT, T_g=2:5 and T_t=13:10. The T_g and T_t values are kept same for testing on normal and blur images. Best ACC is recorded after 50 runs. Tables 6.4–Table 6.6 present ACC of all 12 descriptors by using three classifiers. Results show the superiority of multiscale descriptors as compared to single-scale descriptors, and by integrating two multiscale descriptors, ACC is improved more. Furthermore, the novel proposed descriptor MFDLD proves out most discriminant among all which significantly outstrip ACC of all 11 descriptors.

TABLE 6.1
ACC Perceived on ORL by SVMs (RBF)

On Normal and Blur Images	T_g Attributes [On Normal Images]				T_g Attributes [On Blur Images]			
	T_g=1	T_g=2	T_g=3	T_g=4	T_g=1	T_g=2	T_g=3	T_g=4
Descriptors		ACC in %				ACC in %		
LBP	78.33	90.93	96.78	97.91	71.94	85.31	93.57	97.50
CS-LBP	73.05	87.50	95.71	97.08	67.50	84.68	92.14	94.16
HOG	72.50	88.43	93.57	95.00	71.94	88.75	93.57	97.08
$NI-LBP_{P, R_1}$	81.66	92.50	97.14	98.75	75.27	89.37	95.35	98.33
$NI-LBP_{P, R_2}$	83.05	92.81	96.78	99.16	76.66	90.00	96.42	98.75
$\mathbf{MNI-LBP_{P, R_1 \| R_2}}$	**84.16**	**93.75**	**97.50**	**99.58**	**80.27**	**92.81**	**97.14**	**98.75**
$AD-LBP_{P, R_1}$	79.72	91.25	96.78	98.75	69.72	85.93	90.00	93.75
$AD-LBP_{P, R_2}$	81.38	92.50	96.78	98.75	75.55	89.06	94.64	97.91
$\mathbf{MAD-LBP_{P, R_1 \| R_2}}$	**83.33**	**93.12**	**97.50**	**99.16**	**75.83**	**90.00**	**95.71**	**98.75**
$\mathbf{MNA-LBP_{P, R_1 \| R_2}}$	**85.27**	**95.31**	**98.92**	**99.58**	**83.88**	**94.06**	**97.50**	**99.16**
$LPQ(R_1)$	76.11	89.06	95.35	97.08	73.88	88.43	93.92	97.50
MFDLD	**87.22**	**97.18**	**99.64**	**100**	**84.72**	**94.68**	**97.85**	**100**

TABLE 6.2
ACC Perceived on ORL by SVMs (POLY)

On Normal and Blur Images	T_g Attributes [On Normal Images]				T_g Attributes [On Blur Images]			
	$T_g=1$	$T_g=2$	$T_g=3$	$T_g=4$	$T_g=1$	$T_g=2$	$T_g=3$	$T_g=4$
Descriptors	ACC in %				ACC in %			
LBP	74.72	89.37	95.35	97.50	68.88	83.12	91.42	94.58
CS-LBP	69.42	84.37	92.85	96.66	68.61	83.43	91.42	95.41
HOG	69.44	84.68	92.85	95.41	69.44	84.06	92.85	95.00
NI – LBP$_{P,R_1}$	78.05	90.31	96.07	97.91	73.88	86.87	94.28	97.91
NI – LBP$_{P,R_2}$	78.33	90.62	97.14	97.91	75.83	88.43	95.00	98.33
MNI – LBP$_{P,R_1‖R_2}$	**80.27**	**92.81**	**97.50**	**99.16**	**78.05**	**91.25**	**96.07**	**98.75**
AD – LBP$_{P,R_1}$	77.77	89.37	96.07	97.91	66.94	82.81	92.50	94.58
AD – LBP$_{P,R_2}$	78.88	91.56	96.07	97.91	72.77	88.75	94.64	97.50
MAD – LBP$_{P,R_1‖R_2}$	**79.16**	**92.18**	**96.78**	**98.33**	**73.33**	**88.75**	**95.35**	**97.91**
MNA – LBP$_{P,R_1‖R_2}$	**83.05**	**94.68**	**98.21**	**99.58**	**79.72**	**92.81**	**96.78**	**99.16**
LPQ (R$_1$)	74.16	86.25	94.64	96.66	69.72	84.68	92.14	93.75
MFDLD	**85.27**	**95.31**	**98.57**	**99.58**	**81.11**	**94.06**	**98.21**	**99.58**

TABLE 6.3
ACC Perceived on ORL by NN (ESA Cosine)

On Normal and Blur Images	T_g Attributes [On Normal Images]				T_g Attributes [On Blur Images]			
	$T_g=1$	$T_g=2$	$T_g=3$	$T_g=4$	$T_g=1$	$T_g=2$	$T_g=3$	$T_g=4$
Descriptors	ACC in %				ACC in %			
LBP	77.50	89.37	95.00	97.50	71.11	86.25	92.14	96.25
CS-LBP	71.66	86.25	91.07	96.25	70.55	85.00	90.71	94.58
HOG	74.72	86.56	90.71	94.16	73.33	85.62	90.00	94.16
NI – LBP$_{P,R_1}$	80.27	90.31	95.71	97.91	76.66	88.75	95.00	96.66
NI – LBP$_{P,R_2}$	81.38	89.68	96.78	97.50	77.77	88.43	95.71	97.91
MNI – LBP$_{P,R_1‖R_2}$	**83.33**	**93.12**	**97.50**	**98.75**	**83.33**	**94.06**	**96.78**	**98.75**
AD – LBP$_{P,R_1}$	78.33	90.00	95.35	97.91	70.55	83.43	91.78	96.25
AD – LBP$_{P,R_2}$	79.16	91.56	96.07	98.75	78.33	90.62	94.64	96.25
MAD – LBP$_{P,R_1‖R_2}$	**81.11**	**92.18**	**97.14**	**99.16**	**78.61**	**91.56**	**95.35**	**97.91**
MNA – LBP$_{P,R_1‖R_2}$	**85.27**	**94.37**	**98.21**	**99.58**	**84.44**	**96.56**	**97.50**	**99.16**
LPQ (R$_1$)	78.05	88.75	93.57	97.91	74.72	85.93	92.14	95.00
MFDLD	**89.16**	**95.93**	**98.92**	**99.58**	**85.83**	**96.87**	**98.21**	**99.58**

TABLE 6.4
ACC Perceived on GT by SVMs (RBF)

On Normal and Blur Images	T_g Attributes [On Normal Images]				T_g Attributes [On Blur Images]			
	$T_g=2$	$T_g=3$	$T_g=4$	$T_g=5$	$T_g=2$	$T_g=3$	$T_g=4$	$T_g=5$
Descriptors		ACC in %				ACC in %		
LBP	64.30	71.66	76.00	79.60	56.92	67.16	70.18	76.20
CS-LBP	61.53	67.16	71.63	78.80	57.23	62.00	69.81	74.00
HOG	57.07	65.00	71.45	77.40	55.38	62.83	69.63	75.20
$NI-LBP_{P,R_1}$	64.92	70.83	76.00	79.00	60.76	69.16	75.27	79.00
$NI-LBP_{P,R_2}$	64.76	72.00	77.09	81.00	61.69	71.33	73.63	78.20
$MNI-LBP_{P,R_1\|R_2}$	**66.00**	**73.00**	**78.00**	**82.20**	**64.00**	**72.33**	**76.36**	**80.60**
$AD-LBP_{P,R_1}$	64.61	72.33	78.36	81.40	61.07	69.50	73.27	77.40
$AD-LBP_{P,R_2}$	64.61	71.66	77.27	80.00	62.00	70.33	74.36	79.00
$MAD-LBP_{P,R_1\|R_2}$	**67.53**	**75.83**	**79.81**	**82.40**	**64.30**	**72.66**	**76.90**	**79.60**
$MNA-LBP_{P,R_1\|R_2}$	**69.84**	**77.50**	**82.54**	**83.60**	**70.30**	**77.66**	**78.36**	**83.80**
LPQ (R_1)	60.92	70.33	74.72	79.60	59.23	69.16	72.36	77.40
MFDLD	**71.69**	**78.83**	**83.09**	**87.20**	**71.23**	**78.66**	**80.18**	**84.40**

TABLE 6.5
ACC Perceived on GT by SVMs (POLY)

On Normal and Blur Images	T_g Attributes [On Normal Images]				T_g Attributes [On Blur Images]			
	$T_g=2$	$T_g=3$	$T_g=4$	$T_g=5$	$T_g=2$	$T_g=3$	$T_g=4$	$T_g=5$
Descriptors		ACC in %				ACC in %		
LBP	61.07	66.83	74.00	74.80	55.07	62.50	69.81	71.60
CS-LBP	54.15	63.50	68.90	72.00	53.07	58.00	64.72	69.40
HOG	54.76	63.33	68.90	73.20	53.23	61.83	67.27	71.40
$NI-LBP_{P,R_1}$	58.61	67.16	72.90	74.80	59.23	65.00	72.00	72.80
$NI-LBP_{P,R_2}$	61.53	69.00	74.18	75.80	59.84	66.50	71.63	73.40
$MNI-LBP_{P,R_1\|R_2}$	**62.61**	**71.00**	**74.90**	**78.00**	**62.00**	**68.83**	**74.36**	**77.00**
$AD-LBP_{P,R_1}$	62.15	67.50	73.27	78.20	60.00	65.66	71.09	74.00
$AD-LBP_{P,R_2}$	59.84	67.33	72.36	77.60	58.92	65.50	70.72	73.80
$MAD-LBP_{P,R_1\|R_2}$	**64.61**	**70.00**	**74.72**	**79.60**	**62.76**	**69.33**	**74.18**	**76.40**
$MNA-LBP_{P,R_1\|R_2}$	**66.15**	**72.33**	**78.54**	**81.20**	**65.23**	**71.33**	**76.00**	**80.20**
LPQ (R_1)	55.84	66.50	71.63	75.00	55.23	64.50	70.36	72.60
MFDLD	**68.15**	**74.00**	**80.00**	**82.60**	**66.92**	**73.33**	**77.45**	**81.00**

TABLE 6.6

ACC Perceived on GT by NN (ESA Cosine)

On Normal and Blur Images	T_g Attributes [On Normal Images]				T_g Attributes [On Blur Images]			
	T_g=2	T_g=3	T_g=4	T_g=5	T_g=2	T_g=3	T_g=4	T_g=5
Descriptors	ACC in %				ACC in %			
LBP	62.15	69.83	73.09	75.60	59.23	63.50	66.90	71.40
CS-LBP	57.84	64.50	68.36	72.20	56.15	60.50	66.00	68.40
HOG	57.07	65.33	68.18	72.20	55.84	64.66	67.27	69.40
$NI - LBP_{P,R_1}$	61.07	67.33	72.18	75.40	61.69	66.50	70.00	74.40
$NI - LBP_{P,R_2}$	63.38	69.50	73.81	76.20	62.46	66.66	69.63	75.00
$MNI - LBP_{P,R_1 \| R_2}$	**64.30**	**70.33**	**74.54**	**77.80**	**64.00**	**69.00**	**73.27**	**76.20**
$AD - LBP_{P,R_1}$	62.76	70.83	73.45	78.40	60.30	65.00	69.45	74.60
$AD - LBP_{P,R_2}$	62.30	69.33	72.90	76.00	59.38	66.00	70.54	74.40
$MAD - LBP_{P,R_1 \| R_2}$	**64.92**	**72.16**	**75.63**	**79.00**	**62.46**	**68.50**	**72.54**	**75.80**
$MNA - LBP_{P,R_1 \| R_2}$	**66.00**	**73.83**	**76.90**	**80.20**	**66.46**	**72.50**	**78.00**	**79.20**
LPQ (R_1)	60.61	65.33	70.00	74.20	57.84	64.66	68.90	72.80
MFDLD	**70.92**	**76.33**	**79.09**	**81.80**	**68.76**	**73.33**	**78.36**	**80.60**

6.5.3.4   JAFFE

On JAFFE, T_g=(11, 22, 33 & 44) and T_t=(202, 191, 180 & 169). The T_g and T_t values are kept same for testing on normal and blur images. Best ACC is recorded after 35 runs. Tables 6.7–6.9 show ACC of all 12 descriptors by using three classifiers. Results show superiority of multiscale descriptors as compared to single-scale descriptors, and by integrating two multiscale descriptors, ACC is improved more. Furthermore, MFDLD proves out most discriminant among all which significantly outstrip ACC of all 11 descriptors.

6.5.4   ACCURACY COMPARISON

This part compares the MFDLD accuracy with literature methods. On ORL and GT, the MFDLD topmost ACC (on majority of subsets) is given by the RBF classification (on normal images), so by taking that, the RBF results of MFDLD on normal images are used for comparison. On JAFFE, the topmost ACC is attained by RBF classifier (on blur images, at T_g=44, nearly four samples per female), so by taking that, the RBF results of MFDLD on blur images are used for comparison. Rest details are given in the following sections.

6.5.4.1   ORL

To prove the efficiency of MFDLD, 12 methods are picked from literature and compared with MFDLD. These 12 represent different phases of FR. All these compared methods are tested on ORL with same T_g values on which MFDLD is tested. Therefore, comparison is fair. Their description with ACC is as follows: RLD (Curtidor et al., 2021), DIWT/LBP (Curtidor et al., 2021), SGE (Wan et al., 2021) and LLE

TABLE 6.7
ACC Perceived on JAFFE by SVMs (RBF)

On Normal and Blur Images	T_g Attributes [On Normal Images]				T_g Attributes [On Blur Images]			
	$T_g=11$	$T_g=22$	$T_g=33$	$T_g=44$	$T_g=11$	$T_g=22$	$T_g=33$	$T_g=44$
Descriptors		ACC in %				ACC in %		
LBP	48.01	68.58	83.88	92.30	49.50	68.58	79.44	89.94
CS-LBP	45.04	68.58	80.55	87.57	44.55	65.44	77.77	85.20
HOG	46.03	67.53	79.44	87.57	45.04	64.92	77.77	85.20
$NI-LBP_{P,R_1}$	53.96	71.20	83.88	92.89	50.49	69.63	82.22	92.89
$NI-LBP_{P,R_2}$	54.45	71.20	83.33	92.30	50.49	73.29	82.22	91.71
$MNI-LBP_{P,R_1\|R_2}$	**56.43**	**75.91**	**85.00**	**94.08**	**54.95**	**74.86**	**84.44**	**93.49**
$AD-LBP_{P,R_1}$	51.48	71.20	82.77	94.08	50.00	68.06	81.66	90.53
$AD-LBP_{P,R_2}$	49.50	71.20	85.55	92.89	48.51	70.15	83.33	92.30
$MAD-LBP_{P,R_1\|R_2}$	**54.45**	**72.77**	**87.22**	**94.67**	**56.93**	**75.91**	**86.11**	**92.89**
$MNA-LBP_{P,R_1\|R_2}$	**57.42**	**77.48**	**88.88**	**95.26**	**57.42**	**78.01**	**86.66**	**95.26**
LPQ (R_1)	48.51	68.06	80.00	91.71	48.51	69.10	80.00	91.71
MFDLD	**57.92**	**78.01**	**90.00**	**95.85**	**58.41**	**78.53**	**87.77**	**97.63**

TABLE 6.8
ACC Perceived on JAFFE by SVMs (POLY)

On Normal and Blur Images	T_g Attributes [On Normal Images]				T_g Attributes [On Blur Images]			
	$T_g=11$	$T_g=22$	$T_g=33$	$T_g=44$	$T_g=11$	$T_g=22$	$T_g=33$	$T_g=44$
Descriptors		ACC in %				ACC in %		
LBP	49.00	64.92	80.00	87.57	45.54	63.87	84.44	87.00
CS-LBP	47.52	67.01	80.55	86.39	42.57	64.92	82.22	88.75
HOG	46.03	65.96	77.77	85.79	50.00	70.68	83.33	87.57
$NI-LBP_{P,R_1}$	50.49	69.10	82.77	87.57	51.98	72.25	83.33	89.34
$NI-LBP_{P,R_2}$	49.50	65.96	82.22	89.34	52.47	69.10	84.44	91.12
$MNI-LBP_{P,R_1\|R_2}$	**53.96**	**71.72**	**86.11**	**89.94**	**57.92**	**75.39**	**86.11**	**92.30**
$AD-LBP_{P,R_1}$	48.01	67.01	81.11	89.34	48.01	70.15	81.66	88.75
$AD-LBP_{P,R_2}$	50.00	71.20	83.33	89.94	49.00	69.10	83.33	89.94
$MAD-LBP_{P,R_1\|R_2}$	**52.97**	**73.82**	**85.00**	**91.12**	**52.47**	**73.82**	**84.44**	**92.89**
$MNA-LBP_{P,R_1\|R_2}$	**55.94**	**78.53**	**87.22**	**92.89**	**59.90**	**75.91**	**90.00**	**94.08**
LPQ (R_1)	43.56	67.01	82.22	89.94	46.03	67.01	82.22	91.12
MFDLD	**56.43**	**81.67**	**87.77**	**94.67**	**60.39**	**78.53**	**90.55**	**95.85**

TABLE 6.9

ACC Perceived on JAFFE by NN (ESA Cosine)

On Normal and Blur Images	T_g Attributes [On Normal Images]				T_g Attributes [On Blur Images]			
	T_g=11	T_g=22	T_g=33	T_g=44	T_g=11	T_g=22	T_g=33	T_g=44
Descriptors	ACC in %				ACC in %			
LBP	57.92	70.15	83.88	86.39	54.45	73.82	81.11	86.98
CS-LBP	54.45	69.63	80.55	86.98	53.96	70.15	82.22	88.75
HOG	52.97	69.10	80.55	83.43	53.46	69.10	85.00	90.53
$NI-LBP_{P,R_1}$	56.93	72.77	83.33	89.94	57.42	72.77	85.00	89.94
$NI-LBP_{P,R_2}$	57.42	72.25	83.33	89.34	55.94	71.20	83.88	91.12
$MNI-LBP_{P,R_1\|R_2}$	**60.39**	**75.39**	**86.66**	**92.89**	**61.38**	**78.01**	**88.88**	**94.08**
$AD-LBP_{P,R_1}$	56.93	71.72	83.88	89.34	54.95	72.77	83.88	90.53
$AD-LBP_{P,R_2}$	58.91	73.82	84.44	89.94	56.43	73.29	85.00	90.53
$MAD-LBP_{P,R_1\|R_2}$	**60.39**	**76.43**	**86.11**	**91.12**	**59.90**	**77.48**	**87.22**	**92.89**
$MNA-LBP_{P,R_1\|R_2}$	**62.37**	**81.15**	**88.33**	**94.08**	**62.37**	**79.05**	**90.00**	**95.26**
$LPQ (R_1)$	57.92	70.68	84.44	87.57	52.47	71.20	82.77	88.75
MFDLD	**63.86**	**82.72**	**90.00**	**94.67**	**63.86**	**82.72**	**90.55**	**95.85**

(Wan et al., 2021) procure the ACC of [87.71%, 94.16%, 96.10%], [83.35%, 88.26%, 94.17%], [91.75%, 93.14%, 95.14%] and [69.78%, 72.66%, 76.32%] when T_g=2:4. Sr-SEMIDFS (Fan et al., 2020) and Semi-MCFS (Fan et al., 2020) carry the ACC of [54.20%, 85.50%] and [39.60%, 73.20%] on T_g=1, 3. Deep Model-1 (single tree based) (Masud et al., 2020) and Deep Model-2 (parallel tree based) (Masud et al., 2020) secure the ACC of 98.50% and 98.80% on T_g=3. SRC (Li et al., 2020) and LCLE-DL (Li et al., 2020) attain ACC of [71.11% 86.19% 91.79%] and [70.94% 86.31% 90.14%] when T_g=1:3. NCDB-LBPac (Karanwal, 2021a,b) and NCDB-LBPc (Karanwal, 2021a,b) have ACC of [76.38% 90.31% 95.35% 98.33%] and [74.72% 89.68% 94.28% 97.91%] on T_g=1:4. Table 6.10 shows ACC comparison. It is noticed from Table 6.10 that proposed MFDLD is finest method than all compared methods. Best ACC is specified with black bold in all tables.

6.5.4.2   GT

On GT, 12 methods are picked and compared with MFDLD. These 12 represent different phases of FR. All these compared methods are tested on GT with same T_g values on which MFDLD is tested. Therefore, comparison is fair. Their description with ACC is as follows: SRC (Li et al., 2020), LCLE-DL (Li et al., 2020), SOGSFE (Liu et al., 2020), SOGFS (Liu et al., 2020), KRBM (kernel and representation-based method) (Peng et al., 2019) and KRBM Improvement (Peng et al., 2019) procure the ACC of [52.77% 60.47% 65.16% 68.56%], [48.71% 56.33% 60.47% 63.88%], [56.15% 57.67% 61.36% 64.00%], [54.77% 55.50% 60.55% 61.80%], [45.47% 50.00% 56.43% 56.44%] and [48.10% 51.69% 57.13% 58.94%] when T_g =2:5. NCDB-LBPac (Karanwal, 2021a,b), NCDB-LBPc (Karanwal, 2021a,b), KSVD-IJSR (Liu et al., 2019) and CSR-MN (Liu et al., 2019) attain the ACC

TABLE 6.10

ACC Comparison on ORL

LM – local method, DCM – dimension compaction
method, FSM – feature selection method, DLM – deep
learning model, CM – classification method

Methods	Methods Description	$T_g=1$	$T_g=2$	$T_g=3$	$T_g=4$
		\multicolumn{4}{c}{**T_g Attributes**}		
		\multicolumn{4}{c}{ACC in %}		
RLD (Curtidor et al., 2021)	LM	NT	87.71	94.16	96.10
DIWT/LBP (Curtidor et al., 2021)	LM	NT	83.35	88.26	94.17
SGE (Wan et al., 2021)	DCM	NT	91.75	93.14	95.14
LLE (Wan et al., 2021)	DCM	NT	69.78	72.66	76.32
Sr-SEMIDFS (Fan et al., 2020)	FSM	54.20	NT	85.50	NT
Semi-MCFS (Fan et al., 2020)	FSM	39.60	NT	73.20	NT
Deep Model-1 (Masud et al., 2020)	DLM (single tree)	NT	NT	98.50	NT
Deep Model-2 (Masud et al., 2020)	DLM (parallel tree)	NT	NT	98.80	NT
SRC (Li et al., 2020)	CM	71.11	86.19	91.79	NT
LCLE-DL (Li et al., 2020)	CM	70.94	86.31	90.14	NT
NCDB-LBPac (Karanwal, 2021a,b)	LM	76.38	90.31	95.35	98.33
NCDB-LBPc (Karanwal, 2021a,b)	LM	74.72	89.68	94.28	97.91
MFDLD	**LM**	**87.22**	**97.18**	**99.64**	**100**

Note: NT-Not Tested

of 82.40%, 82.00%, 73.00% and 72.00% on $T_g=5$. OD-LBP (Karanwal, 2021a,b) and ELBP (Karanwal, 2021a,b) secure ACC of [78.50% 82.72% 85.20%] and [72.50% 78.00% 80.80%] when $T_g=3:5$. Table 6.11 conveys all ACC. MFDLD has higher ACC than all methods. So MFDLD discriminativity proved on GT also.

6.5.4.3 JAFFE

On JAFFE, 12 methods are picked from literature and compared with MFDLD. These 12 represent different phases of FR. Out of 12 compared methods, 5 are tested on expression-based class division (i.e. seven or six class problem), 6 are tested on ten-fold cross-validation and 1 is tested on leave one subject out validation. Their description with ACC is as follows: OD-LBP (Karanwal, 2021a,b) and ELBP (Karanwal, 2021a,b) procure ACC of 97.14% and 88.57% on $T_g=25$. Attentional convolutional network (ACN) (Minaee et al., 2021) secures ACC of 92.80% when $T_g=17$ (nearly). FE_CFC (Sun et al., 2020) and AlexNet (Sun et al., 2020) achieve ACC of 94.67% and 60.81% on $T_g=10$. CNN (Li et al., 2020), MO-HOG (Wang et al., 2020), D-HOG (Wang et al., 2020), Exemplar (Farajzadeh & Hashemzadeh, 2018), DAM-CNN (Xie et al., 2019) and CAE-CNN (Xie et al., 2019) obtain ACC of 97.18%, 94.35%, 94.35%, 92.53%, 99.32% and 94.10% when ten-fold cross-validation method is used. DCNN (Mayya et al., 2016) carries ACC of 98.12% by using leave 1 subject out validation method. Table 6.12 presents

TABLE 6.11
ACC Comparison on GT

SFEM – sparse feature extraction method, DL – dictionary
learning method, SRM – sparse representation method,
KBM – kernel-based method

Methods	Methods Description	T_g Attributes			
		$T_g=2$	$T_g=3$	$T_g=4$	$T_g=5$
		ACC in %			
SRC (Li et al., 2020)	CM	52.77	60.47	65.16	68.56
LCLE-DL (Li et al., 2020)	CM	48.71	56.33	60.47	63.88
NCDB-LBPac (Karanwal, 2021a,b)	LM	NT	NT	NT	82.40
NCDB-LBPc (Karanwal, 2021a,b)	LM	NT	NT	NT	82.00
SOGSFE (Liu et al., 2020)	SFEM	56.15	57.67	61.36	64.00
SOGFS (Liu et al., 2020)	FSM	54.77	55.50	60.55	61.80
KSVD-IJSR (Liu et al., 2019)	DLM	NT	NT	NT	73.00
CSR-MN (Liu et al., 2019)	SRM	NT	NT	NT	72.00
KRBM (Peng et al., 2019)	KBM	45.47	50.00	56.43	56.44
KRMP Imp. (Peng et al., 2019)	KBM	48.10	51.69	57.13	58.94
OD-LBP (Karanwal, 2021a,b)	LM	NT	78.50	82.72	85.20
ELBP (Karanwal, 2021a,b)	LM	NT	72.50	78.00	80.80
MFDLD	**LM**	**71.69**	**78.83**	**83.09**	**87.20**

Note: NT-Not Tested

TABLE 6.12
ACC Comparison on JAFFE

Methods	Method Description	Training Size/Validation Method	ACC in %
OD-LBP (Karanwal, 2021a,b)	LM	$T_g=25$, 25 SPE	97.14
ELBP (Karanwal, 2021a,b)	LM	$T_g=25$, 25 SPE	88.57
ACN (Minaee et al., 2021)	DLM	$T_g=17$, 17 SPE	92.80
FE_CFC (Sun et al., 2020)	RSM	$T_g=10$, 10 SPE	94.67
AlexNet (Sun et al., 2020)	DLM	$T_g=10$, 10 SPE	60.81
CNN (Li et al., 2020)	DLM	10 Fold CVM	97.18
DCNN (Mayya et al., 2016)	DLM	Leave 1 Subject OVM	**98.12**
MO-HOG (Wang et al., 2020)	LM	10 Fold CVM	94.35
D-HOG (Wang et al., 2020)	LM	10 Fold CVM	94.35
Exemplar (Farajzadeh & Hashemzadeh, 2018)	LM	10 Fold CVM	92.53
DAM-CNN (Xie et al., 2019)	DLM	10 Fold CVM	**99.32**
CAE-CNN (Xie et al., 2019)	DLM	10 Fold CVM	94.10
MFDLD	**LM**	$T_g=44$, nearly 4 samples per female	**97.63**

Note: RSM-Region Segmentation Method, SPE-Samples Per Expression, CVM-Cross-Validation Method, OVM-Out Validation Method all ACC. The proposed MFDLD outruns ACC of ten methods. Out of six compared deep learning methods, only two secured better ACC than MFDLD. These methods are DCNN (Mayya et al., 2016) and DAM-CNN (Xie et al., 2019). Their ACCs are faintly better than MFDLD. The margin of MFDLD against Mayya et al. (2016) and Xie et al. (2019) are just .49% and 1.69%, which are not too much. So invented MFDLD proves robust on JAFFE dataset also.

6.6   CONCLUSION AND FUTURE SCOPE

This work proves that by utilizing multiscale features there is immense improvement in accuracy than single-scale descriptors. The three descriptors that are utilized for the multiscale feature extraction are NI-LBP, AD-LBP and LPQ. The multiscale representation of NI-LBP, AD-LBP and LPQ, so-called $MNI - LBP_{P,R_1\|R_2}$, $MAD - LBP_{P,R_1\|R_2}$ and $MLPQ\ (R_2^\|\ R_3)$, is constructed by concatenating multiscale region features from 3x3 decomposed image. Results confirm potency of multiscale descriptors than single-scale descriptors on both normal and blur images. The accuracy is further improved by joining $MNI - LBP_{P,R_1\|R_2}$ and $MAD - LBP_{P,R_1\|R_2}$ features; this descriptor is called as $MNA - LBP_{P,R_1\|R_2}$. Ultimately, the features of $MNI - LBP_{P,R_1\|R_2}$, $MAD - LBP_{P,R_1\|R_2}$ and $MLPQ\ (R_2^\|R_3)$ are joined to make most robust local descriptor MFDLD. MFDLD secures encouraging results on ORL, GT, and JAFFE datasets, justified by defeating several benchmark methods. MFDLD proves dominant than other ones on both normal and blur images. The blur images are produced by using the Gaussian low pass filter.

Some limitations are observed as follows: (1) as regional feature extraction is done, therefore cost of computation is on higher side even after image resizing, and (2) testing on large-scale benchmarks is missing. The future scope considers these two limitations as first module. In the second module, the evolution of novel local descriptor is assured in unconstrained conditions. The third and fourth modules contain steps of dimension reduction and classification, which are chosen as per dataset images. Additionally, testing on distinct applications will give new direction.

REFERENCES

Balntas, V., Johns, E., Tang, L., & Mikolajczyk, K. (2016). PN-Net: Conjoined triple deep network for learning local image descriptors. In: Proceedings of IEEE Conference on Computer Vision and Pattern Recognition.

Chan, C. H., Tahir, M. A., Kittler, J., & Pietikainen, M. (2013). Multiscale local phase quantization for robust component-based face recognition using kernel fusion of multiple descriptors. IEEE Transactions on Pattern Analysis and Machine Intelligence, 35(5), 1164–1177.

Chen, Z., Zhang, L., Cao, Z., & Guo, J. (2018). Distilling the knowledge from handcrafted features for human activity recognition. IEEE Transactions on Industrial Informatics, 14(10), 4334–4342.

Cimpoi, M., Maji, S., Kokkinos, I., & Vedaldi, A. (2016). Deep filter banks for texture recognition, description, and segmentation. International Journal of Computer Vision, 118, 65–94.

Curtidor, A., Baydyk, T., & Kussul, E. (2021). Analysis of random local descriptors in face recognition. Electronics, 10(11), 1–19.

Dalal, N., & Triggs, B. (2005). Histograms of oriented gradients for human detection. In: Proceedings of Computer Vision and Pattern Recognition, (pp. 886–893).

Fan, M., Zhang, X., Hu, J., Gu, N., & Tao, D. (2020). Adaptive data structure regularized multiclass discriminative feature selection. IEEE Transactions on Neural Networks and Learning Systems, 33, 1–14.

Farajzadeh, N., & Hashemzadeh, M. (2018). Exemplar-based facial expression recognition. Information Sciences, 460-461, 318–330.

Florindo, J. B., & Metze, K.. (2021). A cellular automata approach to local patterns for texture recognition. Expert Systems with Applications, 179. GT face dataset. http://www.anefian.com/research/face_reco.html

Han, X., Leung, T., Jia, Y., Sukthankar, R., & Berg, A. C.. (2015). MatchNet: Unifying feature and metric learning for patch-based matching. In: Proceedings of IEEE Conference on Computer Vision and Pattern Recognition, (pp. 3279–3286).

Hazarika, B. B., & Gupta, D. (2021). Density-weighted support vector machines for binary class imbalance learning. Neural Computing and Applications, 33, 4243–4261.

Hazgui, M., Ghazouani, H., & Barhoumi, W. (2021). Genetic programming-based fusion of HOG and LBP features for fully automated texture classification. The Visual Computer, 38, 457–476.

Heikkila, M., Pietikainen, M., & Schmid, C. (2009). Description of interest regions with local binary patterns. Pattern Recognition, 42(3), 425–436.

Huang, Z. (2021) CN-LBP: Complex Networks based Local Binary Patterns for the Texture Classification, arXiv:2105.06652. JAFFE face dataset. http://www.kasrl.org/jaffe.html.

Karanwal, S. (2021a). A comparative study of 14 state of art descriptors for face recognition. Multimedia Tools and Applications, 80, 12195–12234.

Karanwal, S. (2021b). Graph based structure binary pattern for face analysis. Optik-International Journal for Light and Electron Optics, 241, 1–12.

Karanwal, S., & Diwakar, M. (2021a). Neighborhood and center difference based LBP for face recognition. Pattern Analysis & Applications, 24, 741–761.

Karanwal, S., & Diwakar, M. (2021b). OD-LBP: Orthogonal difference local binary pattern for face recognition. Digital Signal Processing, 110.

Kartheek, M. N., Prasad, M. V. N. K., & Bhukya, R.. (2020). Local optimal oriented pattern for person independent facial expression recognition. In: Twelfth International Conference on Machine Vision.

Kola, D. G. R., & Samayamantula, S. K. (2021). A novel approach for facial expression recognition using local binary pattern with adaptive window. Multimedia Tools and Applications, 80, 2243–2262.

Kostkova, J., Flusser, J., Leb, M., & Pedone, M. (2020). Handling Gaussian blur without deconvolution. Pattern Recognition, 103, 1–12.

Kral, P., Vrba, A., & Lenc, L. (2019). Enhanced local binary patterns for automatic face recognition. In: 18th International Conference on Artificial Intelligence and Soft Computing.

Kravchik, M., & Shabtai, A. (2021). Efficient cyber attack detection in industrial control systems using lightweight neural networks and PCA. IEEE Transactions on Dependable and Secure Computing, 19, 2179–2197.

Lan, R., Lu, H., Zhou, Y., Liu, Z., & Luo, X. (2020). An LBP encoding scheme jointly using quaternionic representation and angular information. Neural Computing and Applications, 32, 4317–4323.

Li, C., Huang, Y., Huang, W., & Qin, F. (2021). Learning features from covariance matrix of Gabor wavelet for face recognition under adverse conditions. Pattern Recognition, 119, 1–13.

Liu, J., Liu, W., Ma, S., Wang, M., Li, L., & Chen, G. (2019). Image-set based face recognition using K-SVD dictionary learning. International Journal of Machine Learning and Cybernetics, 10, 1051–1064.

Li, K., Jin, Y., Akram, M. W., Han, R., & Chen, J. (2020). Facial expression recognition with convolutional neural networks via a new face cropping and rotation strategy. The Visual Computer, 36, 391–404.

Li, L., Peng, Y., & Liu, S. (2020). Compound dictionary learning based classification method with a novel virtual sample generation technology for face recognition. Multimedia Tools and Applications, 79, 23325–23346.

Liu, L., Zhao, L., Long, Y., Kuang, G., & Fieguth, P. (2012). Extended local binary patterns for texture classification. Image and Vision Computing, 30(2), 86–99.

Liu, Z., Lai, Z., Ou, W., Zhang, K., & Zheng, R. (2020). Structured optimal graph based sparse feature extraction for semi-supervised learning. Signal Processing, 170, 1–9.

Masud, M., Muhammad, G., Alhumyani, H., Alshamrani, S. S., Cheikhrouhou, O., Ibrahim, S., & Hossain, M. S. (2020). Deep learning-based intelligent face recognition in IoT-cloud environment. Computer Communications, 152, 215–222.

Mayya, V., Pai, R. M., & M. M., Manohara Pai. (2016). Automatic facial expression recognition using DCNN, In: 6th International Conference on Advances in Computing & Communications. Procedia Computer Science, 93, 453–461.

Minaee, S., Minaei, M., & Abdolrashidi, A. (2021). Deep-emotion: Facial expression recognition using attentional convolutional network. Sensors, 21(9), 1–16.

Mishchuk, A., Mishkin, D., Radenovic, F., & Matas, J. (2017). Working hard to know your neighbors margins: Local descriptor learning loss. In: Proceedings of IEEE Conference on Computer Vision and Pattern Recognition.

Nithya, S., & Ramakrishnan, S. (2021). Wavelet domain majority coupled binary pattern: A new descriptor for texture classification. Pattern Analysis and Applications, 24, 393–408.

Ojala, T., Pietikainen, M., & Harwood, D. (1996). A comparative study of texture measures with classification based on featured distributions. Pattern Recognition, 29(1), 51–59.

Ojansivu, V., & Heikkila, J. (2008). Blur insensitive texture classification using local phase quantization, In: International Conference on Image and Signal Processing, (pp. 236–243). ORL face dataset. http://www.cl.cam.ac.uk/research/dtg/attarchive/facedatabase.html.

Pan, Z., Hu, S., Wu, X., & Wang, P. (2021). Adaptive center pixel selection strategy in local binary pattern for texture classification. Expert Systems with Applications, 180, 1–18.

Peng, Y., Li, L., Liu, S., Li, J., & Cao, H. (2019). Virtual samples and sparse representation-based classification algorithm for face recognition. IET Computer Vision, 13(2), 172–177.

Rastin, N., Jahromi, M. Z., & Taheri, M. A.. (2021). Generalized weighted distance k-nearest neighbor for multi-label problems. Pattern Recognition, 114, 1–43.

Revina, I. M., & Emmanue, W. R. S. (2021). Face expression recognition using LDN and dominant gradient local ternary pattern descriptors. Journal of King Saud University-Computer and Information Sciences, 33(4), 392–398.

Sharma, R. P., & Dey, S. (2021). A comparative study of handcrafted local texture descriptors for fingerprint liveness detection under real world scenarios. Multimedia Tools and Applications, 80, 9993–10012.

Sun, J., Li, T., Yan, H., & Dong, X. (2020). Research on an expression classification method based on a probability graph model. Multimedia Tools and Applications, 79, 34029–34043.

Wan, M., Ge, M., Zhan, T., Yang, Z., Zheng, H., & Yang, G. (2021). Sparse graph embedding based on the fuzzy set for image classification. Complexity, 3, 1–10.

Wang, H., Wei, S., & Fang, B. (2020). Facial expression recognition using iterative fusion of MO-HOG and deep features. The Journal of Supercomputing, 76, 3211–3221.

Xie, S., Hu, H., & Wu, Y. (2019). Deep multi-path convolutional neural network joint with salient region attention for facial expression recognition. Pattern Recognition, 92, 177–191.

Yang, H., Gong, C., Huang, K., Song, K., & Yin, Z. (2021). Weighted feature histogram of multi-scale local patch using multi-bit binary descriptor for face recognition. IEEE Transactions on Image Processing, 30, 3858–3871.

Yuan, F., Xia, X., & Shi, J. (2018). Mixed co-occurrence of local binary patterns and hamming-distance-based local binary patterns. Information Sciences, 460-461, 202–222.

Zhang, D., Han, J., Cheng, G., & Yang, M. H. (2022). Weakly supervised object localization and detection: A survey. IEEE Transactions on Pattern Analysis and Machine Intelligence, 44, 1–18.

Zhao, C., Li, X., & Dong, Y. (2020). Learning blur invariant binary descriptor for face recognition. Neurocomputing, 404, 34–40.

Zhao, S., & Zhang, B. (2020). Learning salient and discriminative descriptor for palmprint feature extraction and identification. IEEE Transactions on Neural Network and Learning Systems, 31(12), 5219–5230.

7 The Facial Façade
Development, Relevance, and Examination of Facial Imagery in Forensic Science

Navjot Kaur Kanwal, Kuldeep Umesh Kawar, and Silpa Nair

7.1 INTRODUCTION

Biometrics can be defined as *"the measurement and analysis of unique physical or behavioral characteristics (such as fingerprint or voice patterns) especially as a means of verifying personal identity"* (Definition of Biometrics, n.d.). Thus, it can be asserted that biometrics is used to identify a person using their physical or behavioral features. Such features include but are not limited to fingerprints, DNA, voice patterns, facial features, iris, and handwriting. There are different recognition systems that are in place to identify a particular person from their respective biometrics. Out of all these, facial biometrics is one of the most widely used to identify people in today's age, owing to a number of reasons, such as the easier availability of related technology and lesser to no intrusiveness in its functioning. In the rest of the popular biometric systems, such as fingerprints and DNA, an individual has to personally interact with the recognition system to register their biometrics. However, in a facial biometric recognition system, the person just has to pass through the camera embedded in the system and their facial features will get registered. In situations where the verification of a large population needs to be done, there is no other option than to use face recognition to speed up the process. A suitable example would be the customs and border protection at airport terminals, where the following protocol is conducted to ensure secure conveyance of passengers (Biometrics|U.S. Customs and Borders Protection, n.d.): when a passenger arrives at the entry or exit, a camera shall capture the live images of their faces and a system would simultaneously verify these live images with those in their database related to travel documents. A successful match ensures the successful entry or exit of the concerned passenger. Here, in this complete ordeal, the passenger need not do anything but just face the camera, thus making facial recognition a convenient, less time-consuming, resourceful, touch-free, and seamless technology not only for the passengers but also for the customs officials. Along with border control, facial biometric recognition also has applications in domains such as general and investigative surveillance, general identity verification for institutional attendance and such purposes, login verification on digital devices, and law enforcement. Therefore, on account of the wide and reliable use of facial biometrics in a variety of areas, this chapter focuses on facial recognition and its applications and challenges in forensic science. A point to be noted here is that iris recognition deals with a similar protocol and is a more accurate solution, yet it is not as common as face recognition because of a few significant drawbacks, such as lack of legacy databases, more intricate sampling leading to expensive input systems, and most importantly (as this chapter deals with the forensic aspect of facial recognition), iris recognition has the least forensic use as iris as a biometric is not usually encountered at the crime scene, because the surveillance systems in our daily life have not been updated to that extent (Majekodunmi & Idachaba, 2011).

Coming to the forensic aspect of this chapter, the following statement can be made: "the term forensic facial recognition is implicitly, albeit hyperbolically, tautological". We shall revisit this statement later. First, the use of any biometric, be it face, iris, fingerprint, DNA, or even a handwritten signature, is justified for its uniqueness. In other words, a biometric is a biometric for that purpose because it is unique to every individual. Even if two individuals have exactly the same facial features or fingerprints, their uniqueness as a whole would be in question. But the occurrence of such a phenomenon is completely out of limits, due to the *principle of individuality*, which is one of the building blocks of forensic science, propagated by Dr. Paul Kirk, one of the modern pioneers of Forensic Science (Kirk, 1963). This law states that every object, natural or man-made, is unique. This uniqueness can be utilized to individualize evidence collected from the crime scene and link the crime to the suspect. Therefore, biometrics, as a science, itself relates to forensic science fundamentally. As a result, all biometrics could be used for the purpose of identification in forensic science.

For those unacquainted with the subject, forensic science is defined as an *"application of science to matters involving the public or applications of science to legal matters"* (Mirakovits & Siegel, 2021). It encompasses many sciences, be it chemistry and toxicology, biology, physics and ballistics, computer science, psychology, and many more, applied to the purpose of justice. The ultimate aim of all these domains is the identification and individualization of evidence that serves justice in the court of law. Specifically concerned about forensic facial recognition (FFR), it can be defined as "facial recognition done with the purpose of identification of an individual in relation to the occurrence of a crime". In today's digital age, facial recognition as an automated process is a part of digital forensics. Historically, when facial recognition was first developed in the rudimentary form of photographic portraiture, it was devised to cater to the needs of the criminal justice system for identifying criminals. Before photography, there were portraits done by artists. When compared to the earlier methods, photography offered infallibility as a means of criminal identification and it became a norm. It was only after the technology started reaping significant dividends and mainstreamed into criminal identification, that a need was felt to use it for the purpose of identifying entrants into the state, to discriminating them as citizens and non-citizens (similar to the border control mentioned previously) (Gates, 2004). According to Caplan and Torpey, *"Police practices in the [late nineteenth and early twentieth centuries] asserted a more specialized domain of authority over criminal identification and detection, which became a crucial site for further identificatory and supervisory developments that were then reappropriated into universal systems of civil identification*"(Cole, 2004). Definitely, in that era of professionalization of the police system and utilization of sciences for law enforcement, it was commonplace for such expert sciences like photography, anthropometry, and dactyloscopy (fingerprints) to have their effects on society and the state in general.

In view of the aforementioned historical developments, the connotations of the statement "the term forensic facial recognition is implicitly, albeit hyperbolically, tautological" make a crude sense, as facial recognition was first developed as a forensic necessity itself. Nevertheless, the statement is not explicit, as presently the technology has been making waves globally in numerous diverse domains other than forensic science. In accordance with the same reason (along with slight grammatical nuances), it can be a stretch to call FFR a tautology, but within some limitations, the statement cannot be outright denied.

Face recognition as a process involves the following steps, stated briefly as the complete detailed procedure is beyond the scope of this chapter (Kaur et al., 2020): (i) Capturing the image: The captured image is called the "probe" image, done via a still or CCTV camera; (ii) Face detection: Face is detected from the complete image; (iii) Feature extraction: A face template is generated by extracting different facial features are from the image, to be compared with those in the database; (iv) Matching: The template is matched with the images in the database; if a match is generated, then verification is to be followed; (v) Verification/identification: Being the last step, it involves 1:1 matching for verification and 1:N matching for identification of the person under question. Figure 7.1 visually describes the aforementioned protocol.

FFR is different from its civil counterpart in various ways. Experimenting on a substantial quantity of chemicals and analyzing their results in a laboratory to propound or validate a theory is one thing, but experimenting on a trace of evidence from the crime scene to determine its source of origin is another. In a similar sense,

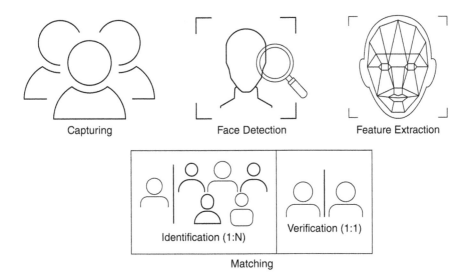

FIGURE 7.1   General protocol for facial recognition (Kaur et al., 2020).

while facial recognition in itself deals with images taken under largely controlled conditions, to be compared with other images in the database; FFR involves the identification of the person linked with the crime (not to be confused with criminal identification, as the person of interest can be a suspect, victim, or even a witness) from images which are not captured in ideal conditions. These images can vary in pose, lighting, and facial expressions. Processing such images accordingly and comparing them is a Herculean task. In the upcoming sections of this chapter, the development of FFR, its applications, and challenges in the present digital age shall be discussed in detail.

7.2 RESEARCH METHODOLOGY

The objective of this research was to provide a comprehensive overview of facial recognition in forensic science. The need for the research was necessitated due to the unavailability of a brief summarized discussion of facial recognition in forensic science covering all aspects – ranging from its history and development to the actual workflow in forensic examination – at the time of this research. For the fulfillment of the objective, only secondary sources of literature relevant to the topic were reviewed. As described in Figure 7.2, the review was performed by searching for keywords among databases such as Google Scholar, Scopus, and Springer. The sections to be included according to the topics to be covered in the review were pre-decided, and the search descriptors were used accordingly. These search descriptors included "forensic facial recognition", "applications of facial recognition in forensic science",

Search Descriptors: "forensic facial recognition", "applications of facial recognition in forensic science", "facial imagery as evidence in forensic science", "image processing in forensic facial recognition", "ACE-V methodology for facial recognition in forensic science", "facial image comparison" , "forensic facial examination" "forensic facial recognition"

Search Databases: Google Scholar, Springer, Scopus, FISWG, ENFSI

Inclusion Criteria:

- No time period constraint.
- Papers dealing with at least one forensic purpose.

Exclusion Criteria:

- No forensic context.

51 papers selected

18 papers excluded

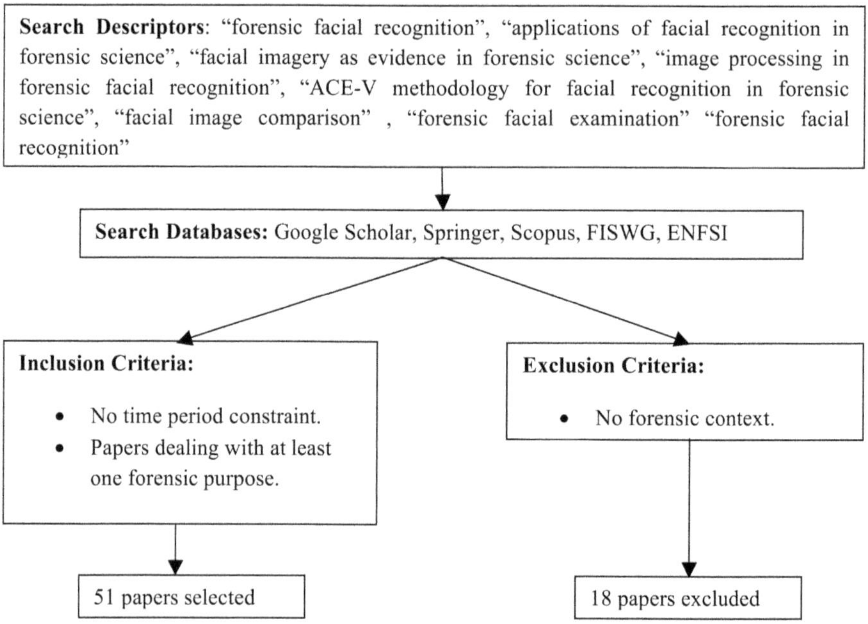

FIGURE 7.2   Research methodology.

"facial imagery as evidence in forensic science", "image processing in forensic facial recognition", and "ACE-V methodology for facial recognition in forensic science". Terms such as "facial image comparison" and "forensic facial examination" were used in addition to "forensic facial recognition" to yield better results. Once a set of literature was identified, backward snowballing was used to gather related works. Standard definitions were referred from the websites of standard online publications such as the Oxford University Press and Merriam Webster. Because the research focuses on the need for standardization and validation of forensic facial examination, it was paramount to include guidelines recommended by relevant scientific associations. The sections associated with forensic examination of facial imagery heavily relied on the guidelines as described by two associations – the Facial Identification Scientific Working Group (FISWG) and the European Network of Forensic Science Institutes (ENFSI). Therefore, the required guidelines were extracted in the form of documents uploaded on their respective websites. Barring the introduction section of this chapter, a total of 69 papers were identified for all sections altogether, out of which 51 papers were finalized for review. There was no constraint with regard to the time period of publication. The exclusion criterion for the rest of the 18 papers was dependent on the forensic context of the research. Only the works dealing with at least one of the three purposes of forensic science were included for review. These works include the documents collected from the ENFSI and FISWG. As the objective of this research is to provide an overview of facial recognition in forensic science, only the significant contributions of the research works were described, while the discussions of their results were not included in detail.

7.3 DEVELOPMENT AND RELEVANCE OF FORENSIC FACIAL RECOGNITION

In the previous section, it was understood that the seeds of facial recognition (read: FFR) were sown by photographic portraiture for criminal identification. In the mid to late nineteenth century, the movement got a boost from the collective effort of police officers in Europe, aiming ultimately toward an ease not only in criminal identification but also the development of police administration. Criminal identification served a few important purposes, such as the police at that time was ready to identify and fight the specific group causing disturbance in that particular region (e.g., back then Irish offenders were a menace in Britain), recidivists (repeat offenders) were identified and punished sooner, and most significantly, the criminals were made aware of the power vested by the police by virtue of photography (Jäger, 2001).

Eventually, criminal photography developed and spread across the continent. Special units started to be designated for this purpose. However, it still mainly relied on the expertise of the photographers and the police officers. In the late 1870s, Alphonse Bertillon, a French police officer, first thought of measuring various individual body parts and creating a unique profile for each offender in the form of those measurements (Jäger, 2001). The comparison between the offender and his photograph was not relied upon the subjective opinion of the officials anymore but strictly on the data units that made up the profile. More than a century later, in today's digital age, law enforcement systems rely on face recognition which is based fundamentally on this very logic of anthropometry, as facial recognition systems today "scan the proportions of facial features and turn them into a personal geometric pattern" (Fišerová, 2023). However, anthropometry, also called Bertillonage, did not rely on photography but just bodily measurements. Photography slowly fell out of favor in many police departments, with anthropometry leading the trend for criminal identification. Bertillon was of the view that anthropometry should supplement photography and not replace it, but the system of capturing photographs should be standardized. According to him, "a portrait for police purposes had to be very different from the products of commercial photographers in style, pose, format, focusing and exposure" (Jäger, 2001). Therefore, Bertillon recommended certain rules with which photography of the offender was to be done, from frontal and side profiles. These photographs were incorporated on the anthropometric card of the offender and thus both systems were combined, together known as "portrait parle" (T: "speaking image") in the late nineteenth century (Bell, 2012). Though better alternatives (fingerprints (Faigman, 2008) and digitization) have replaced anthropometry over the ages, the system of photography devised by the recommendations of Alphonse Bertillon is still in practice in police stations all over the world, popularly referred to as mug-shots today. These mug-shots form a major chunk of the databases used for automated facial recognition in criminal identification.

Today, anthropometry has been an artifact of the past. Yet, as implied before, facial recognition as an automated process derives its fundamental understanding from the logic behind anthropometry. FFR – to be mentioned as FFR henceforth in this chapter – has its applications in comparing facial images found of a person(s) of interest (POI) in relation to the crime with those in the database. These face images with which database images are to be compared are known as "trace" images in FFR. The database images (which often involve facial images taken under controlled conditions) are known as "reference" images. Trace facial images are captured majorly in three scenarios: as those captured by the witness to the crime, a surveillance camera, or those on official documents (Jacquet & Champod, 2020). These categories are explained in detail below.

7.3.1 WITNESS IMAGES

A witness is generally a person who is capable of attesting to the facts of a crime. Therefore, the term "witness images" is self-explanatory, as there is no doubt over the fact that "the photograph is a silent and immediate witness of the existence of the subject as it was and where it was when the image was captured" (Milliet et al., 2014; Margot, 2014). Unlike in the old days when camera was a luxury and capturing photographs was a matter of skill with a long and tedious process, everybody has a camera today in the form of their smartphones. Whenever a crime or an accident occurs, eyewitnesses leave no stone unturned in documenting the event in the form of photographs or video (for either good or bad reasons). Eyewitnesses' testimony can often be compromised due to a plethora of reasons, one of them being getting forgetful of the sequence of events or the faces of people involved. They can even lie altogether. But the documentation done serves not only as corroborative evidence but also as a refresher for the eyewitnesses to recall the event as it happened. If this evidence is collected soon after the crime, it functions as a lead for the investigators to investigate in that direction. It also reduces the possibility of the eyewitnesses lying in the court. Witness images can provide information regarding the facial features of the POI, the location and time of the crime, the weather at the location, the dialog exchange among the POI, etc. In most of the cases, witness images are ambiguous and taken under uncontrolled conditions, rendering facial comparison a tedious task, due to distorted proportions owing to the lens or angle of the camera, the POI being completely in motion and/or having covered their face(s) to some extent, differences in illumination, low resolution of the photographs in relation to the camera quality, the witness unable to provide stability while documenting the scene, and a myriad of such reasons. Other than these, witness images can also include images found on social media in relation to a crime or content related to child pornography and surveillance images (or videos) captured on cameras mounted on various institutions or streets.

7.3.2 Surveillance Images

These are also a type of witness images but are explained in a different section because of the ever-increasing omnipresence of the cameras involved. CCTVs (closed-circuit televisions) are popularly set up on every nook and corner because they serve as a cheap means of video surveillance, recording hundreds of people every day. The quantity of data extracted daily from CCTVs all over the world, as a mute spectator to the scene of crime, has led to the establishment of its own niche branch of digital mul-timedia forensics, called "CCTV forensics". CCTVs are normally mounted at higher points of reference to record a wider, larger area in which human beings interact with their surroundings, thus leading to a distortion in proportions. One major limitation of CCTVs is that the images are never singularly captured in the form of raw images themselves but rather are materialized in the form of screen-grabs captured from the recorded video footage. Other limitations that impede the analysis of facial images include low quality of footages, harsh weather conditions, time-lapse footages, varia-tions in lighting, variations in human pose, and method of data storage (digital storage can lead to loss of details due to compression) (Seckiner et al., 2018). Images captured by the surveillance cameras set up on ATMs (automatic teller machines) require a special mention here (Jacquet & Champod, 2020), which use a distinctive type of lens called hypergon lens. Hypergon lens minimizes distortions and provides a flat field throughout a very wide angle of coverage, which is why a wide angle of view is cap-tured even when the person stands so close to the camera machine (The Photographic Historical Society of Canada, 2009). Accordingly, in the images captured, the facial image of a person is situated at the center. But in this process, the lens does in fact distort the proportions of the face by widening more in the center when compared to the edges (Jacquet & Champod, 2020), thus distorting the facial proportions as well. Another type of surveillance images involves those taken by intelligence officers on an operation to record suspected offenders secretly, often captured at a distance.

7.3.3 Official Documents

These comprise passports, citizen identity cards (such as AADHAAR [Unique Identification Authority of India, 2016] in India), ration cards, and other such official documents with the requirement of a facial image. If a suspicion arises related to the genuineness of the document, these facial images are compared with those in the database. However, one advantage these images have over other categories of traces is that they are generally captured under controlled conditions for mimicking the requirements of that particular document, therefore making comparison easier. However, with continuous technological advancements, cases have been arising where offenders resort to deepfakes by altering the facial features of the source image (face morphing or attribute manipulation). A morphed image can have the likeliness of two persons, making it probable for any one of them to cheat the border security systems (Robertson et al., 2017; Robertson et al., 2018; Mathisen, 2023).

The aforementioned trace images are difficult to analyze owing to the reasons mentioned above. It needs a persistent effort by the forensic examiner to pre-process these traces to make them compatible for comparison with references and then evaluate the results of the comparison followed by verification. Howsoever automated the system gets, the final opinion shall be made after careful deliberations of the examiner only, as the ultimate aim is to interpret and present the results of facial image comparison in the court of law (Lee & Pagliaro, 2013), (Jacquet & Champod, 2020). The automated system majorly assists only in the analysis (with pre-processing) and comparison stages of the ACE-V (Analysis, Comparison, Evaluation, Verification) process, which is recommended to induce standardization in forensic comparisons by the FISWG (FISWG, 2019a–c) and the ENFSI (ENFSI, 2018).

7.4   FORENSIC PURPOSES OF FFR

According to some literature, there lies a distinction between the purposes of forensic facial examination dependent on the stages of investigation. Generally, these purposes can be divided into three categories: intelligence, investigative, and evaluative purposes (Jacquet & Champod, 2020; Dessimoz & Champod, 2016). Investigative purpose involves searching for the trace image within the reference database, and in case a match is not found from the 1:N search, then the trace undergoes comparison with the reference images of the POI captured suitably, under similar conditions to those of the trace image. Simultaneously, for intelligence purposes, information is gathered regarding the POI, such as their history, associations with different cases, as well as the motive and modus operandi of the crime to facilitate comparisons with individuals suspected of similar crimes. Therefore, it can be said that intelligence and investigative purposes serve each other (Jacquet & Champod, 2020). For this purpose, automatic face recognition tools have been used in Switzerland routinely since 2008. It is linked with a single platform for images associated with each other by links of crimes, their modus operandi, offenders, investigative analysis of different types of evidence, and their results. As a result of this process, "contextualization of images" is done to gather intelligence in turn to facilitate investigation (Dessimoz & Champod, 2016).

As previously mentioned, similar to every forensic examination, the ultimate aim for every examination is the presentation of its findings in the court of law, which allows the juries to arrive at a decision. The evaluative purpose deals with this objective. While research in the field of automated facial recognition systems is been on the rise, technologically as well as statistically (Li & Jain, 2009; Tistarelli & Champod, 2017) along with in the aspect of forensic intelligence (Dessimoz & Champod, 2016), the value of automated facial recognition as evidence is still not being explored much. Every justice system has its own standards for admissibility of evidence (Jacquet & Champod, 2020), e.g., Daubert (LII, 2023), or the Frye criteria (LII, 2022) for the United States, which is based on acceptance of the evidence by the scientific community, while the European system has no such requirement (Garamvölgyi et al., 2021). As a result, when criminal cases involving facial information are increasing day by day, there is a lack of standardization regarding the acceptance of the results of AFR in the court of law (Jacquet & Champod, 2020;Ali et al., 2012). Therefore, the results of comparison still rely on the manual examination done by forensic experts (Dessimoz & Champod, 2016), though the automated system might assist in the previous stages of analysis. A viable solution could be designing models to devise a Bayesian framework (Aitken & Taroni, 2004; Robertson et al., 2016) for generating a likelihood ratio (LR) by taking into consideration the case information (I), within source variability (WSV) and the between source variability (BSV) (Jacquet & Champod, 2020).

The calculation of the LR depends on the results of the authentication and verification by the automated system. These two are not to be confused. Authentication answers the question "are both images of the same person?" which is judged from a score generated by a 1-vs.-1 comparison of the same individual (e.g., airport security). If the score lies above a preset threshold, the result is considered to be a match and the automated system arrives at a decision. On the other hand, verification involves the identification of an individual in its true sense, where a trace (T) is compared with the reference (R) database (1-vs.-N comparison). However, in forensic context, this comparison does not return a binary decision unlike commercial verification applications, but it gives a ranked list of similarity scores for different reference images. It is the prerogative of the forensic expert to manually compare the images and arrive at a decision, taking into consideration the details of the case after the intelligence and investigative purposes are fulfilled (Jacquet & Champod, 2020; Edmond et al., 2009). The comparison process, in itself, can be divided into different approaches, which shall be discussed later. Returning to the determination of the LR, it can be either score-based or feature-based. The score-based approach focuses on the similarity scores whereas the features-based approach is based on the comparison of facial characteristics. Research suggests that the use of a score-based approach is most common in forensic biometry (Meuwly et al., 2017; Jacquet & Champod, 2020). Therefore, the score-based LR (SLR), to be considered the evidential weight, can be calculated (Jacquet & Champod, 2020).

Ideally, an automated system comprising a feature-based model that is capable of generating a score for the calculation of SLR would be the recommended approach (Jacquet & Champod, 2020; Bolck et al., 2015). Nevertheless, currently there are no such approaches under development for FFR. Only automated systems generating a similarity score (based on deep learning or otherwise) without any revelation of the facial characteristics used is the norm (Jacquet & Champod, 2020).

It is pertinent to note that computation of LR is even more significant and need of the hour because investigative and intelligence purposes are only concerned with

FFR for generating leads toward investigation, which involves collection and analysis of numerous other evidence. It is possible that by the end of the investigation, the importance associated with FFR is diluted to such an extent that it no more carries a greater weight when compared to other evidence. However, when facial information is major evidence, the calculation of LR is completely justified to standardize the results (Jacquet & Champod, 2020).

7.5   IMAGE PROCESSING FOR FFR

Forensic examination of facial imagery can be divided into two major parts: technical processes and subjective examination. While the former includes suitable image processing on the evidence, the latter involves the ACE-V workflow (ENFSI, 2018; FSR, Gov. of U.K., n.d.). Both of these shall be dealt with separately.

Before starting with image processing, it is important to understand the collection of reference images for comparison with the trace. In case suitable reference images are not readily available on a database, they are to be manually captured under adequate conditions to create a reference database. Classified into controlled, semi-controlled, and uncontrolled acquisition, their recommended guidelines are dealt with in greater detail in the FISWG Standard Guide for Capturing Facial Images for Use with Facial Recognition Systems (FISWG, 2019a–c).

Image processing is done by a standard practitioner possessing not only the knowledge of digital imaging but also morphological analysis, which is explained in Section 7.6.4. A facial image is processed for increasing the probability of a match. This does not imply that the image should be processed as much as possible or the image should look aesthetically pleasing. In fact, image processing should be kept to the minimum to avoid the introduction of newer artifacts in the image or alteration of the facial detail. Moreover, the original image should never be subjected to processing. Instead, a separate working copy should be created for this task. This working copy should preferably be in the original format or in any other lossless format. The processing is to be conducted on the complete working copy of the image and not just a localized area (FISWG, 2022). It is worth mentioning that some automated facial recognition systems are loaded with in-built mechanisms for performing minor adjustments of the image involving pose and image size. If such corrections are sufficient for matching, then the image is not to be processed any further. When the image is devoid of any discernable details for comparison, manual processing can be done subsequently to achieve enough quality details for facilitating comparison (FISWG, 2020).

Image pre-processing for the purpose of forensic facial comparison can be classified into two stages, which are image enhancement and facial processing. Image enhancement can be defined as "the process of altering the appearance of an image for improved visibility of features of interest or to facilitate subsequent image analysis such as the measurement or classification of objects" (Wang et al., 2023). It is to be emphasized that image enhancement does not incorporate alteration of the facial features. Only the information contained within the image is changed at this stage. The image properties that can be altered using enhancement include brightness, contrast, saturation, and blur. The image is also cropped to focus on the relevant area containing the face to assist the next stage where the facial details will be processed (FISWG, 2013). Most of the enhancements are done using two-dimensional filters for histogram equalization, deblur, and color corrections.

In the context of FFR, histogram equalization (HE) helps in compensating for the changes in illumination between the trace and reference facial images (Boomgaard, 2017). It carries out this function by adjusting the contrast adequately for an image (Coste, n.d.). Some of the recent techniques used for HE mentioned in literature include the adaptive HE (AHE) (Li et al., 2019), contrast-limited AHE (CLAHE) (More et al., 2015;Chen & Ramli, 2003), and bi-histogram equalization (BBHE) (Kim, 1997). A recent study suggests better enhancement of low-quality CCTV footages by using a CLAHE-based algorithm for image enhancement (Xiao et al., 2019).

Noise and distortions can also be removed. The MATLAB image processing toolbox can be used for using various techniques of image enhancement (Celine & Sheeja Agustin, 2019). It comprises a Weiner filter that decreases the blur present in the images (MathWorks, n.d.). Current levels of research differentiate methods of deblurring into model-based methods and deep-learning-based methods (Vukovic et al., 2021). Discussions also surround the order of priority for the features to be enhanced. Furthermore, research suggests that sharpening and resizing prior to the application of other enhancement techniques significantly improve the accuracy of face detection (FISWG, 2020).

Until here, the focus was on the 2D enhancement of the image by processing the information contained within the image. If the facial information is ample for further examination, no further processing is to be done. If it is insufficient, then the facial information is processed till the minimum level of detail is observable. Processing at this stage involves 3D enhancement techniques such as pose correction which is applied to suitably modify the pose of the face in the image (FISWG, 2013). It is said that any pose other than the frontal facial pose negatively affects the face recognition system, therefore necessitating frontalization of the image (FISWG, 2020). However, according to the facts surrounding the investigation, other poses at different angles may also need to be generated. Pose angles can be divided on the X-, Y-, and Z-axes into pitch, yaw, and roll, respectively. In simpler words for considering their relative head movements, pitch corresponds to the nodding angle, yaw to the shaking angle, and roll to the tilting angle (Cheng & Bai, 2017). Discussion of different methods classified into deep learning, 3D, and hybrid models to generate multi-view frontal facial poses have been researched upon in detail in the existing literature. The hybrid models, which are a combination of both deep learning and 3D methods, have been recommended for addressing their limitations individually; as deep learning methods, while efficient, need a high-quality dataset, whereas 3D models undergo a large amount of calculations hindering their efficiency in speed (Ning et al., 2020). An important thing to note here is that at every level of facial information processing, eyes on the face need to be located. It is only when the eyes are located that the face is said to be detected. If the system is unable to locate the eyes, the roll, pitch, and yaw angles are suitably modified to do the same (FISWG, 2013).

Face occlusion is one of the most challenging problems in facial recognition that refers to the obstruction of a person's face. This can be due to a piece of cloth or an accessory worn by the person such as a scarf or sunglasses respectively, or by virtue of the camera getting blocked due to an external object (Ekenel & Stiefelhagen, 2009; Oloyede et al., 2017). Removal of facial occlusion is a challenging problem for face recognition and different methods to meet the task can be classified into "1) Feature extraction without occlusion detection face recognition. 2) Feature extraction with occlusion detection face recognition 3) occlusion recovery face recognition" (Meena & Meena, 2022). This problem is especially glaring post-pandemic, due to the wearing of masks becoming commonplace globally as a hygienic practice (Hariri, 2020).

The processed image is to be searched in the system after each step of processing. There can be times when even after trying out different image enhancement and facial detail processing techniques, the system would not return probable matches. Filtering the search results by selecting the case-related metadata is helpful for this task. If it is evident that the person in the trace imagery has red hair and red eyes, such relevant metadata filters can be applied to tune the search in the reference database. Other types of filters can include gender, race, type of crime committed, height, weight, ocular characteristics, complexion, date and place of birth, crime history, current location, country of origin, hair color, facial hair, hair length, hair style, information related to scars, and marks and tattoos. One advantage of this step is that it can be undertaken initially before the search as well as after the search. Nevertheless, there lies a possibility that the actual match results would be left out by selecting an incorrect filter. For example, if it is suspected that the person in the trace image is apparently a female and the female gender filter is selected, the system either would not display any results or the results would relate to the persons of female gender only, while in fact it remains unexplored if there is a possibility that the suspect is a male (FISWG, 2019a–c).

It is worth mentioning that image enhancement and processing of the working copies are done just for the purpose of maximizing the likelihood of matching search results. In simpler words, this stage is undertaken to create a database of reference images that are similar to the trace imagery. The working copies do not actually participate in the actual ACE-V process of the forensic examination. Comparisons that facilitate a conclusion are based only on the original trace imagery with the search results from the aforementioned process (FISWG, 2020). The next section explains the detailed ACE-V process in forensic facial examination.

7.6 ACE-V METHODOLOGY IN THE CONTEXT OF FORENSIC EXAMINATION OF FACIAL IMAGERY

The complete ACE-V methodology for forensic facial examination as recommended by the ENFSI and the FISWG with the aim to devise a standardized protocol for forensic facial examination is explained below (ENFSI, 2018).

7.6.1 ANALYSIS

This stage refers to the examination of the quality of the trace image under question. Evaluation of the quality helps in listing the features readily available for comparison, without any pre-processing. At this point, only the trace image is judged for quality. Assessment of the reference images is avoided by the examiner at this stage. This precaution is undertaken because the examiner might attempt to observe a certain level of details present in the reference face image that are not readily noticeable in the trace image at this stage. Such protocol ensures the deterrence of contextual and confirmation bias in the process of investigation. Cautious assessment of trace image quality is also important as research suggests that post-comparison, the certainty of the conclusion given by experts starts getting lesser and lesser with decreasing quality (Norell et al., 2014).

The following factors, pre-processed or not, are to be considered while analyzing the image for its quality: pixel resolution, blur, compression, illumination, and geometric distortions. Sometimes, the features of the face can also be hidden, either by the angle of the camera with respect to the face or by a physical covering, e.g., a piece of cloth. If all of these factors pass the assessment of quality, the examiner also has to consider the facial expressions and pose evident in the trace image.

In addition to the examination of such factors, the examiner also has to verify that the imagery under analysis belongs to its original format because it ensures the absence of compression and loss of details. Screen-grabs, transcoded video, lossy formats (e.g., JPEG), and imagery converted from analog to digital are some examples of risky imagery which can be called secondary or tertiary images due to them not being in their original format. The examiner needs to ascertain that the analysis should involve all the submitted evidence regarding the trace facial imagery because the quality of each image can be different in accordance with the factors mentioned above. For this purpose, reference images are referred to at the end of the analysis stage to select suitable trace images with similar details regarding pose and facial features. Ultimately, the examiner finalizes the number of trace images to be utilized for comparison with reference imagery.

7.6.2 COMPARISON

In this stage, the facial features of the trace and reference imagery are compared to establish the degree of similarity between them. Here, morphological analysis of the imagery is done, which is among the four categories of forensic facial identification (Ali et al., 2012). Accordingly, a standard facial features list proposed by the FISWG is referred to (FISWG, 2018). The comparisons should be done not only by comparing the facial features but also attention should be paid to the effect of image quality factors (mentioned in the analysis stage) on them. Because a certain similar or different feature might turn out to be attributable to one of these factors, the conditions surrounding an ideal comparison process of the trace and reference facial imagery would involve both of them captured at a similar pose, camera angle, time, expression, and illumination. For example, it has been found that trace and reference imagery captured around the same time frame result in faster matching when compared to those captured in different time frames (Megreya et al., 2013). This is how aging affects the system adversely. The examiner can resize and rotate the imagery conveniently for comparison of sufficient facial detail, with proper knowledge of the effects of such algorithms on the quality of the image. Resizing should not distort the aspect ratio, while rotation should not affect the pixel interpolation of the imagery at a large scale.

7.6.3 EVALUATION

As mentioned in the previous section in relation to the evaluative purpose of FFR, its main purpose is to make the results of the comparison carry an evidential weight for presentation in the courtroom. ENFSI Guideline for Evaluative Reporting in Forensic Science provides a unified framework across various domains of forensic science (ENFSI, 2016). Current research emphasizes on the need for the computation of a numerical score (SLR) for evidence related to facial imagery (Jacquet & Champod, 2020; Ali et al., 2012; Dessimoz & Champod, 2016). Therefore, correlating with the forensic purposes explained before, it can be said that while the stages of analysis and comparison can assist in investigative and intelligence purposes, the stage of evaluation is what takes the evaluative purpose to fruition. Furthermore, the automated system can only play a significant role in the first two stages, whereas this stage of evaluation is completely dependent on the expertise, knowledge, and experience of the forensic examiner. Individual features can be classified according to their similarities and differences as "weakly discriminating", "moderately discriminating" and "strongly discriminating" (Netherlands Forensic Institute, n.d.; Ali et al., 2012). The two statements that are under consideration at the end of the evaluation stage can be framed as: "the person in the reference image is same as the person in the trace image" and "the person in the reference image is not same as the person in the trace image". The exact nature of these statements depends on the contextual information surrounding the case. The examiner does not fully endorse any of these statements as the ultimate truth, as in a forensic examination, identification is always made in probabilistic terms (Kaye, 2010). Therefore, the results of the evaluation with respect to the aforementioned two statements can be classified according to different levels of support lent to one of these statements, such as "no support", "limited support", "moderate support", "strong support", and "very strong support" (Netherlands Forensic Institute, n.d.; Ali et al., 2012). Nevertheless, there exists no universal rule regarding the depiction of evaluation results (ENFSI, 2018). A few factors influencing these results are a number of facial features matched, the extent of their quality, the commonness of the features used for comparison in the general population, the features permanent or temporary, etc. (ENFSI, 2018).

7.6.4 VERIFICATION

At this stage, the images are reassessed by a different competent forensic examiner, and the evidence undergoes the processes involving stages of analysis, comparison, and evaluation again. It can be a blind verification or a non-blind verification depending on whether this examiner is aware of the previous evaluation results or not (ENFSI, 2018). Blind verification is always recommended to avoid bias on the part of the second examiner.

7.7 METHODS OF FORENSIC FACIAL IMAGE COMPARISON

The methods of forensic facial image comparison include holistic comparison, photo-anthropometry, morphological analysis, and superimposition, which are explained in detail in this section (Ali et al., 2012). Though the FISWG

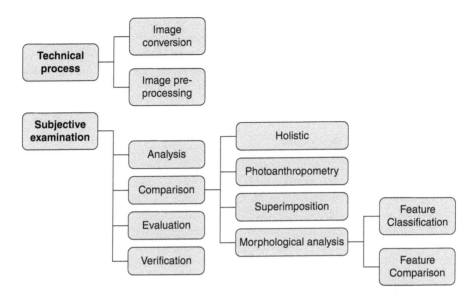

FIGURE 7.3   An overview of forensic examination of facial imagery (ENFSI, 2018).

recommends morphological analysis as the best comparison method, it is paramount for an examiner to possess knowledge of all three techniques because they can still be used as a subsidiary, either in the actual comparison process or for better understanding (ENFSI, 2018). Figure 7.3 gives an overview of the forensic examination of facial imagery to be described in detail within the scope of this chapter.

7.7.1   Holistic Comparison

In this method, "faces are compared by considering the whole face simultaneously" (Ali et al., 2012). When someone recognizes a familiar face in public, or in any form of printed or digital media, they do not attempt to individually compare each and every feature of the face. It is just the overall facial image that strikes them as someone familiar and their mind immediately processes this information to recall the person under question. All of this happens in the time frame of a few seconds. A forensic examiner does the same but with more sophistication. Therefore, holistic comparison is not necessarily a method but just an interpretation of the intrinsic ability of human beings to recognize faces (FISWG, 2019a–c). However, the implications of this method involve faster recognition of familiar faces even within a low-quality trace image; while there lies a high probability that when the faces are unfamiliar, the comparison can give inaccurate results even within a high-quality trace image (Bruce et al., 2001; Kalocsai & Biederman, 1997; Mondloch et al., 2002). It is obvious that in a forensic setting, even the most experienced examiner would not be exposed to cases involving familiar faces every day. Therefore, this method is limited only to circumstances where the application of any other method is unwarranted. These circumstances can involve situations where the examiner needs to arrive at an immediate decision without the required logistics or large immigration hotspots on the border. Though not recommended on its own due to its blatant subjectivity, holistic comparison can never be avoided completely. It provides valuable assistance to the other methods due to its involuntariness, owing to the intrinsic physiological mechanism of face recognition (ENFSI, 2018).

7.7.2 PHOTO-ANTHROPOMETRY

As the name suggests, this method involves the measurements of facial landmarks in photographs. Specific landmarks corresponding to their anatomical position are first located on the trace imagery. Straight lines are overlaid to join any two landmarks and the length of this line is calculated, which corresponds to the distance between them. The same measurements are done for the reference images followed by comparisons. Comparisons can involve the conversion of the measurements into a ratio. Photo-anthropometry is susceptible to the credibility of the photographs in terms of image quality factors such as resolution, facial pose, focal length, illumination, camera angle, and lens distortion. These lead to variations in facial proportions. Due to these factors, it is almost an unachievable task to set a threshold for levels of similarity to arrive at a conclusion as a result of the comparison of measurements (FISWG, 2019a–c). Thus, although this method indicates the use of objective numerical values, it is still subjective as the decision remains with the examiner regarding the permissible levels of similarity between these measurements in the trace and reference imagery (ENFSI, 2018). Evidence in the facial examination is devoid of controlled conditions. Even if the imagery is high quality, the aforementioned image quality factors cannot be ignored. Owing to these limitations, it has been proven that photo-anthropometry cannot be used as a reliable comparison method in forensic facial examination, thus nullifying its significance in evaluating evidence in the court of law (Moreton & Morley, 2011; Kleinberg et al., 2007). It is recommended to not only avoid photo-anthropometry as a standalone method but also avoid it in conjunction with other methods (FISWG, 2019a–c).

7.7.3 SUPERIMPOSITION

In superimposition, the trace and reference images are overlaid on each other, followed by observing the similarities and differences between them. Superimposition can be done by reducing the overall opacity of the images, combining a specific part of the face with another complete face image, or by blinking immediately between the visualizations of both images. Either way, the conclusion arises from the subjective assessment of similarities and differences with no threshold of certainty (ENFSI, 2018). Also, this method is very sensitive to the perspective of the image. Both trace and reference images need to be captured from a similar camera angle under optimal conditions or else superimposition is worthless. Scaling and rotating of the images are done to align them with one another, taking into account that the processing techniques used should not geometrically distort the images. If the image quality is less owing to different previously mentioned image quality factors, the specific locations of facial landmarks would not be easily noticeable. As a result, in case the examiner fails to locate the landmarks accurately, the actual process of over-laying the images would also be negatively affected. Owing to these reasons, the use of superimposition as a standalone method is not recommended (FISWG, 2019a–c).

7.7.4 MORPHOLOGICAL ANALYSIS

It can be defined as "a subjective process where facial features and/or regions of the face are observed and compared to determine apparent differences and similari-ties" (ENFSI, 2018). Though it is a subjective process, what makes morphological analysis different from its counterparts is that in this case, in addition to the subjec-tive assessment of similarities and differences, the conclusion is a result of thorough evaluation and interpretation of the observations made by the examiner (FISWG, 2019a–c). There are two approaches to morphological analysis, which are feature classification and feature comparison (ENFSI, 2018).

Feature classification involves grouping a particular facial feature in a predeter-mined category, for example, pointy nose, red hair, and almond eyes. Nonetheless, by classifying a facial feature into one group, the relevance of other characteristics for that particular feature can be lost. As evident from the next method of morpho-logical analysis, a nose can be described into so many characteristics other than just its shape. Therefore, the potential of the facial feature in the observations for dif-ferent characteristics is compromised. The unreliability of feature classification has been proven in research (Towler et al., 2014; Fuentes-Hurtado et al., 2019).

Feature comparison method comprises feature-by-feature comparison of two facial images on the basis of a standardized checklist, which has given significant results in literature, followed by observations regarding similarities and differences between them (Towler et al., 2014; ENFSI, 2018). As of now, there is no standard-ized list of features that can be used for comparison purposes. However, the FISWG recommends "a standard list of facial components and component characteristics to be assessed and evaluated during a morphological analysis" (FISWG, 2018) which is to be used in the analysis and comparison stages of the ACE-V process. This feature list consists of 19 different facial features to be classified into component character-istics, which are further categorized by their individual characteristic descriptors (FISWG, 2018). Thus, a facial feature under observation can be classified with greater sophistication. A nose judging from its outline could be classified not only accord-ing to its shape but also according to its length, width, prominence, and symmetry. Furthermore, other nasal characteristics such as the nasal root, body, tip, and base can also be described by their individual descriptors. As it happens, even the nasal base can also be classified into different categories with their descriptors! Therefore, there lies no doubt in the fact that if this intricate feature list is accepted by all stake-holders universally, it will pave the way toward the standardization of forensic facial examination for the first time (ENFSI, 2018). Empirical research indicates that the use of feature comparison as a method for morphological analysis results in obser-vations that are accurately diagnostic of the facial image under study (Towler et al., 2017). Therefore, feature comparison is considered the most important method to compare trace and reference imagery, by taking into account the feature list recommended by the FISWG (ENFSI, 2018). However, though efficient, this method is still subject to the effect of different image quality factors which can hinder the observation of facial features and, thereby, their comparison (FISWG, 2019a–c).

It is recommended that in case of a forensic examination, the process of morphological analysis should be thoroughly documented at every stage. Decision made from the evaluation, as a result of the comparison process, is made final for presentation in the court only after the verification stage of the ACE-V process.

7.8 CONCLUSION

Facial recognition technology (FRT) is dominating every aspect of human life globally. From mobile devices to border access control, it is used in the verification of human identity everywhere. Nonetheless, as a historical fact, facial recognition and forensic science have always been related, by criminal photography and anthropometry – the predecessors of modern FRT. It is only in the last few decades that a need is felt to get forensic science and facial recognition together in the form of FFR. In today's age of surveillance, CCTVs, which are easily accessible in the market, are prevalent at every nook and corner as a means of security, installed either in a private capacity or officially by the government. The use of smartphones is also ever-increasing globally, even in countries in the lower middle-income categories, with India itself comprising 600 million smartphone users as of November 2022 (Sharma & Popli, 2023; Anand, 2022). Therefore, it is unsurprising to say that cameras are everywhere around us. These cameras are pertinent in the investigation of a crime as they record facial imagery during the occurrence of a crime. This imagery is classified into witness images and surveillance images for an investigation. Though a crime scene consists of different evidence that can prove or disprove the conviction of an offender, facial imagery is markedly different because of its easier availability and collection process. An investigator can utilize this evidence from the first stage itself to get valuable concrete leads toward the investigation. Thus, even if the facial imagery might not be utilized as evidence in a court of law, it can undoubtedly assist in the procurement of other evidence. These purposes of FFR are called intelligence and investigation. However, akin to the analysis of other evidence, the ultimate aim should be its presentation in the courtroom. This is where the current system surrounding forensic examination of facial imagery is lacking. Though attempts have been made by groups like FISWG and ENFSI concerned with facial recognition and comparison to standardize FFR, the system is not yet in place. Researchers suggest the quantification of results from the evaluation of facial imagery into a score-based LR (SLR), but it needs to be scientifically validated. They also indicate toward devising an automated system comprising a feature-based model that is capable of generating a score for the calculation of SLR.

Current literature on FFR is insufficient. It is surprising, to say the least, that even when it is evident that automated facial recognition is booming globally, there is a sense of apathy and indifference toward FFR. It is even more surprising because if facial recognition is indeed dominating globally, then the instances of encountering facial imagery from crime scenes will correspondingly show an uptick as well.

Hence, there is an urgent need to realize the evidential weight of facial imagery. This can only be possible when experts and stakeholders lend their effort to the standardization and validation of the entire ACE-V process of forensic examination of facial imagery. Research reveals that though the feature comparison approach in morphological analysis is recommended by numerous researchers, there is no facial feature list that could be utilized in justice systems globally.

FFR needs to be standardized and validated thoroughly. Faulty FFR can lead to the infringement of the personal liberty of the person(s) associated with the crime. A large chunk of reference facial imagery consists of mug-shot images from all over the world. Future research should focus on understanding whether these mug-shots are captured under ideal conditions such as sufficient illumination with the correct pitch, roll, and yaw of the face(s). A significant part of image processing involves such pose correction to generate frontal views of non-frontal trace imagery. The accuracy of pose correction needs to be tested thoroughly before utilizing it for practical forensic purposes. As evident from a few recent cases, the danger of faulty FFR is already looming all over the world leading to wrongful convictions (Sahouri, 2023; Bhuiyan, 2023; Allyn, 2020). A lesson to be learned from such a state of affairs is that until standard procedures for FFR are brought in place universally, the inexperienced investigators must focus on facial imagery majorly for intelligence and investigative purposes, thereby attempting to justify their overall examination by recognizing and evaluating other evidence as well, the examinations of which are scientifically standardized. After all, ultimately, FFR is less of a machine-dependent process. It majorly relies on the expertise and experience of the investigator in the manual examination of facial imagery, as it should be in the forensic examination of every piece of evidence.

REFERENCES

Aitken, C. G., & Taroni, F. (2004). The evaluation of evidence. In Statistics and the Evaluation of Evidence for Forensic Scientists, 2nd ed. Wiley Online Library. https://doi.org/10.1002/0470011238.ch3

Ali, T., Spreeuwers, L., & Veldhuis, R. (2012). Forensic face recognition: A survey. In Face Recognition: Methods, Applications and Technology. NOVA Publishers.

Allyn, B. (2020, June 24). "The Computer Got It Wrong": How Facial Recognition Led to False Arrest of Black Man. NPR. Retrieved October 14, 2023, from https://www.npr.org/2020/06/24/882683463/the-computer-got-it-wrong-how-facial-recognition-led-to-a-false-arrest-in-michigan

Anand, S. (2022, November 16). India Has Over 1.2 Bn Mobile Phone Users: I&B Ministry | Mint. mint. Retrieved October 14, 2023, from https://www.livemint.com/technology/gadgets/india-has-over-1-2-bn-mobile-phone-users-i-b-ministry-11668610623295.html

Bell, S. (2012, February 9). A Dictionary of Forensic Science. Oxford University Press.

Bhuiyan, J. (2023, April 27). First Man Wrongfully Arrested Because of Facial Recognition Testifies as California Weighs New Bills. the Guardian. Retrieved October 14, 2023, from https://www.theguardian.com/us-news/2023/apr/27/california-police-facial-recognition-software

Biometrics|U.S. Customs and Borders Protection. (n.d.). Government of United States. Retrieved October 15, 2023, from https://www.cbp.gov/travel/biometrics

Bolck, A., Ni, H., & Lopatka, M. (2015, September). Evaluating score- and feature-based likelihood ratio models for multivariate continuous data: Applied to forensic MDMA comparison. Law, Probability and Risk, 14(3), 243–266. https://doi.org/10.1093/lpr/mgv009

Boomgaard. (2017). 3.2.2. Histogram Equalization — Image Processing and Computer Vision 2.0 documentation. Retrieved October 14, 2023, from https://staff.fnwi.uva.nl/r.vandenboomgaard/IPCV20172018/LectureNotes/IP/PointOperators/HistogramEqualization.html

Bruce, V., Henderson, Z., Newman, C., & Burton, A. M. (2001). Matching identities of familiar and unfamiliar faces caught on CCTV images. Journal of Experimental Psychology: Applied, 7(3), 207–218. https://doi.org/10.1037/1076-898x.7.3.207

Celine, J., & Sheeja Agustin, A. (2019, November). Face recognition in CCTV systems. 2019 International Conference on Smart Systems and Inventive Technology (ICSSIT). https://doi.org/10.1109/icssit46314.2019.8987961

Chen, S.-D., & Ramli, A. (2003, November). Minimum mean brightness error bi-histogram equalization in contrast enhancement. IEEE Transactions on Consumer Electronics, 49(4), 1310–1319. https://doi.org/10.1109/tce.2003.1261234

Cheng, Z., & Bai, F. (2017). Real-time head pose estimation on mobile devices. Computer Vision – ACCV 2016 Workshops, 599–609. https://doi.org/10.1007/978-3-319-54407-6_41

Cole, J. (2004, March). Documenting Individual Identity: The Development of State Practices in the Modern World. Edited by Jane Caplan and John Torpey. Princeton, NJ: Princeton University Press, 2001. The Journal of Modern History, 76(1), 167–168. https://doi.org/10.1086/421192

Coste. (n.d.). Project:1 histograms. In https://www.sci.utah.edu. Scientific Computing and Imaging Institute, University of Utah. Retrieved July 14, 2023, from https://www.sci.utah.edu/~acoste/uou/Image/project1/Arthur_COSTE_Project_1_report.html

Definition of biometrics. (n.d.). Merriam-Webster Dictionary. https://www.merriam-webster.com/dictionary/biometrics#:~:text=1,means%20of%20verifying%20personal%20identity

Dessimoz, D., & Champod, C. (2016, September 23). A dedicated framework for weak biometrics in forensic science for investigation and intelligence purposes: The case of facial information. Security Journal, 29(4), 603–617. https://doi.org/10.1057/sj.2015.32

Edmond, G., Biber, K., Kemp, R., & Porter, G. (2009). Law's looking glass: Expert identification evidence derived from photographic and video images. Current Issues in Criminal Justice, 20(3), 337–377. https://doi.org/10.1080/10345329.2009.12035817

Ekenel, H. K., & Stiefelhagen, R. (2009). Why is facial occlusion a challenging problem? Advances in Biometrics, 299–308. https://doi.org/10.1007/978-3-642-01793-3_31

ENFSI. (2016). ENFSI guideline for Evaluative in Forensic Science. European Network of Forensic Science Institutes. Retrieved July 14, 2023, from https://enfsi.eu/wp-content/uploads/2016/09/m1_guideline.pdf

ENFSI. (2018, January). Best Practice Manual for Facial Image Comparison- version 01. In European Network of Forensic Science Institutes. European Network of Forensic Science Institutes. Retrieved June 15, 2023, from https://enfsi.eu/wp-content/uploads/2017/06/ENFSI-BPM-DI-01.pdf

Faigman. (2008). Anecdotal forensics, phrenology, and other abject lessons from the history of science. Hastings Law Journal, 59, 979–1000. http://repository.uchastings.edu/faculty_scholarship/867

FISWG. (2013, August 13). Facial Recognition System Methods & Techniques. In https://fiswg.org/. Facial Identification Scientific Working Group. Retrieved June 14, 2023, from https://www.fiswg.org/FISWG_fr_systems_meth_tech_v1.0_2013_08_13.pdf

FISWG. (2018, September 11). FISWG Facial Image Comparison Feature List for Morphological Analysis v 2.0. In Facial Identification Scientific Working Group. Facial Identification Scientific Working Group. Retrieved May 14, 2023, from https://www.fiswg.org/FISWG_Morph_Analysis_Feature_List_v2.0_20180911.pdf

FISWG. (2019a, October 5). Standard Guide for Capturing Facial Images for Use with Facial Recognition Systems- v.2.0. In https://fiswg.org. Facial Identification Scientific Working Group. Retrieved June15, 2023, from https://fiswg.org/FISWG_Guide_for_Capturing_Facial_Images_for_FR_Use_v2.0_20190510.pdf

FISWG. (2019b, October 25). Facial comparison overview and methodology guidelines - v. 1.1. In Facial Identification Scientific Working Group. Facial Identification Scientific Working Group. Retrieved June 15, 2023, from https://www.fiswg.org/fiswg_facial_comparison_overview_and_methodology_guidelines_V1.0_20191025.pdf

FISWG. (2019c, October 25). Facial recognition system: Metadata usage – v. 1.1. In https://fiswg.org/. Facial Identification Scientific Working Group. Retrieved July 14, 2023, from https://www.fiswg.org/fiswg_fr_system_metadata_v1.1_20191025.pdf

FISWG. (2020, July 17). Standard Practice/Guide for Image Processing to Improve Automated Facial Recognition Search Performance- v.2.0. In https://fiswg.org. Facial Identification Scientific Working Group.

FISWG. (2022, June 17). Image Processing Techniques for Facial Image Comparison- v.1.0. In https://fiswg.org. Facial Identification Scientific Working Group. Retrieved June15, 2023, from https://fiswg.org/fiswg_imag_procssng_tchnqs_for_fac_img_comparison_v1.0_20220617.pdf

Fišerová, M. (2023, May 30). Portrait and Mugshot: Metonymical foundation of photographic genres. Law & Literature, 1–20. https://doi.org/10.1080/1535685x.2023.2213578

FSR, Gov. of U.K. (n.d.). Forensic Science Regulator. https://www.gov.uk/. Retrieved June 15, 2023, from https://www.gov.uk/government/organisations/forensic-science-regulator

Fuentes-Hurtado, F., Diego-Mas, J. A., Naranjo, V., & Alcañiz, M. (2019, January 29). Automatic classification of human facial features based on their appearance. PLoS ONE, 14(1), e0211314. https://doi.org/10.1371/journal.pone.0211314

Garamvölgyi, B., Ligeti, K., Ondrejová, A., & von Galen, M. (2021). Admissibility of evidence in criminal proceedings in the EU. Eucrim – The European Criminal Law Associations' Forum. https://doi.org/10.30709/eucrim-2020-016

Gates. (2004). The past perfect promise of facial recognition technology. ACDIS Occasional Paper. http://hdl.handle.net/2142/38

Hariri, W. (2020, July 7). Efficient Masked Face Recognition Method during the COVID-19 Pandemic. https://doi.org/10.21203/rs.3.rs-39289/v1

Jacquet, M., & Champod, C. (2020, February). Automated face recognition in forensic science: Review and perspectives. Forensic Science International, 307, 110124. https://doi.org/10.1016/j.forsciint.2019.110124

Jäger, J. (2001, January 1). Photography: A means of surveillance? Judicial photography, 1850 to 1900. Crime. Histoire & Sociétés, 5(1), 27–51. https://doi.org/10.4000/chs.1056

Kalocsai, P., & Biederman, W. I. (1997). Recognition model with extension fields. Perception, 26(1_suppl), 202–202. https://doi.org/10.1068/v970347

Kaur, P., Krishan, K., Sharma, S. K., & Kanchan, T. (2020, January 21). Facial-recognition algorithms: A literature review. Medicine, Science and the Law, 60(2), 131–139. https://doi.org/10.1177/0025802419893168

Kaye. (2010). Probability, Individualization and Uniqueness in Forensic Science Evidence: Listening to the Academies. Penn State Law, 1163–1185.

Kim, Y.-T. (1997). Contrast enhancement using brightness preserving bi-histogram equalization. IEEE Transactions on Consumer Electronics, 43(1), 1–8. https://doi.org/10.1109/30.580378

Kirk, P. L. (1963). The ontogeny of criminalistics. The Journal of Criminal Law, Criminology, and Police Science, 54(2), 235. https://doi.org/10.2307/1141173

Kleinberg, K. F., Vanezis, P., & Burton, A. M. (2007, May 25). Failure of anthropometry as a facial identification technique using high-quality photographs. Journal of Forensic Sciences, 52(4), 779–783. https://doi.org/10.1111/j.1556-4029.2007.00458.x

Lee, & Pagliaro. (2013). Forensic evidence and crime scene investigation. Journal of Forensic Investigation, 01(02). https://doi.org/10.13188/2330-0396.1000004

Li, S. Z., & Jain. (2009, August 27). Encyclopedia of Biometrics (2nd ed.). Springer Science & Business Media. https://dblp.org/db/reference/bio/2.html

Li, S., Choo, K. K. R., Sun, Q., Buchanan, W. J., & Cao, J. (2019, August). IoT forensics: Amazon echo as a use case. IEEE Internet of Things Journal, 6(4), 6487–6497. https://doi.org/10.1109/jiot.2019.2906946

LII. (2022). Frye Standard. LII/Legal Information Institute, Cornell Law School. Retrieved August 10, 2023, from https://www.law.cornell.edu/wex/frye_standard#:~:text=Frye%20standard%20is%20used%20to

LII. (2023). Daubert Standard. LII/Legal Information Institute, Cornell Law School. Retrieved August 15, 2023, from https://www.law.cornell.edu/wex/daubert_standard#:~:text=Under%20the%20Daubert%20standard%2C%20the,%3B%20(4)the%20existence%20and

Majekodunmi, & Idachaba. (2011). A Review of the Fingerprint, Speaker Recognition, Face Recognition and Iris Recognition Based Biometric Identification Technologies. Proceedings of the World Congress on Engineering, II. https://www.iaeng.org/publication/WCE2011/WCE2011_pp1681-1687.pdf

Margot. (2014, March 24). Traçologie: la trace, vecteur fondamental de la police scientifique. La Revue Polytechnique. https://www.polymedia.ch/de/traologie-la-trace-vecteur-fondamental-de-la-police-scientifique/

Mathisen, G. (2023, May 10). Manipulated photos enable two people to use the same passport – this is how such fraud can be stopped. ScienceNorway. https://sciencenorway.no/criminality-fraud-security/manipulated-photos-enable-two-people-to-use-the-same-passport-this-is-how-such-fraud-can-be-stopped/2194329

MathWorks. (n.d.). Image Processing Toolbox. https://www.mathworks.com. Retrieved July 14, 2023, from https://www.mathworks.com/products/image.html

Meena, M. K., & Meena, H. K. (2022, July 1). A Literature Survey of Face Recognition Under Different Occlusion Conditions. 2022 IEEE Region 10 Symposium (TENSYMP). https://doi.org/10.1109/tensymp54529.2022.9864502

Megreya, A. M., Sandford, A., & Burton, A. M. (2013, October 30). Matching face images taken on The Same day or months apart: The limitations of photo ID. Applied Cognitive Psychology, 27(6), 700–706. https://doi.org/10.1002/acp.2965

Meuwly, D., Ramos, D., & Haraksim, R. (2017, July). A guideline for the validation of likelihood ratio methods used for forensic evidence evaluation. Forensic Science International, 276, 142–153. https://doi.org/10.1016/j.forsciint.2016.03.048

Milliet, Q., Delémont, O., & Margot, P. (2014, December). A forensic science perspective on the role of images in crime investigation and reconstruction. Science & Justice, 54(6), 470–480. https://doi.org/10.1016/j.scijus.2014.07.001

Mirakovits, K., & Siegel, J. A. (2021, July 5). Forensic Science. CRC Press.

Mondloch, C. J., Le Grand, R., & Maurer, D. (2002, May). Configural face processing develops more slowly than featural face processing. Perception, 31(5), 553–566. https://doi.org/10.1068/p3339

More, L. G., Brizuela, M. A., Ayala, H. L., Pinto-Roa, D. P., & Noguera, J. L. V. (2015, September). Parameter tuning of CLAHE based on multi-objective optimization to achieve different contrast levels in medical images. 2015 IEEE International Conference on Image Processing (ICIP). https://doi.org/10.1109/icip.2015.7351687

Moreton, R., & Morley, J. (2011, October). Investigation into the use of photoanthropometry in facial image comparison. Forensic Science International, 212(1–3), 231–237. https://doi.org/10.1016/j.forsciint.2011.06.023

Netherlands Forensic Institute. (n.d.). Internal Document. In http://www.forensicinstitute.nl/. Ministerie van JustitieenVeiligheid. Retrieved October 14, 2023, from http://www.forensicinstitute.nl/

Ning, X., Nan, F., Xu, S., Yu, L., & Zhang, L. (2020, December 17). Multi-view frontal face image generation: A survey. Concurrency and Computation: Practice and Experience, 35(18). https://doi.org/10.1002/cpe.6147

Norell, K., Läthén, K. B., Bergström, P., Rice, A., Natu, V., & O'Toole, A. (2014, December 23). The effect of image quality and forensic expertise in facial image comparisons. Journal of Forensic Sciences, 60(2), 331–340. https://doi.org/10.1111/1556-4029.12660

Oloyede, M. O., Hancke, G. P., & Kapileswar, N. (2017, September). Evaluating the effect of occlusion in face recognition systems. 2017 IEEE AFRICON. https://doi.org/10.1109/afrcon.2017.8095712

Robertson, B., Vignaux, G. A., & Berger, C. E. H. (2016, September 19). Interpreting Evidence. John Wiley & Sons.

Robertson, D. J., Kramer, R. S. S., & Burton, A. M. (2017, March 22). Fraudulent ID using face morphs: Experiments on human and automatic recognition. PLoS ONE, 12(3), e0173319. https://doi.org/10.1371/journal.pone.0173319

Robertson, D. J., Mungall, A., Watson, D. G., Wade, K. A., Nightingale, S. J., & Butler, S. (2018, June 27). Detecting morphed passport photos: A training and individual differences approach. Cognitive Research: Principles and Implications, 3(1). https://doi.org/10.1186/s41235-018-0113-8

Sahouri. (2023, August 8). Lawsuit Filed After Facial Recognition Tech Causes Wrongful Arrest of Pregnant Woman. Detroit Free Press. Retrieved October 14, 2023, from https://www.usatoday.com/story/news/nation/2023/08/08/facial-recognition-technology-wrongful-arrest-pregnant-woman/70551497007/

Seckiner, D., Mallett, X., Roux, C., Meuwly, D., & Maynard, P. (2018, April). Forensic image analysis – CCTV distortion and artefacts. Forensic Science International, 285, 77–85. https://doi.org/10.1016/j.forsciint.2018.01.024

Sharma, M. G., & Popli, H. (2023, January 13). Challenges for Lower-Middle-Income Countries in Achieving Universal Healthcare: An Indian Perspective. Cureus. https://doi.org/10.7759/cureus.33751

The Photographic Historical Society of Canada. (2009). Hypergon Lens- Details. https://www.phsc.ca/. Retrieved June 15, 2023, from https://www.phsc.ca/hypergon.html

Tistarelli, M., & Champod, C. (2017, February 1). Handbook of Biometrics for Forensic Science. Springer.

Towler, A., White, D., & Kemp, R. I. (2014, January 1). Evaluating training methods for facial image comparison: The face shape strategy does not work. Perception, 43(2–3), 214–218. https://doi.org/10.1068/p7676

Towler, A., White, D., & Kemp, R. I. (2017). Evaluating the feature comparison strategy for forensic face identification. Journal of Experimental Psychology: Applied, 23(1), 47–58. https://doi.org/10.1037/xap0000108

Unique Identification Authority of India. (2016). UIDAI. Retrieved June 15, 2023, from https://uidai.gov.in/

Vukovic, I., Cisar, P., Kuk, K., Bandjur, M., & Popovic, B. (2021, October 27). Influence of image enhancement techniques on effectiveness of unconstrained face detection and identification. Elektronika Ir Elektrotechnika, 27(5), 49–58. https://doi.org/10.5755/j02.eie.29081

Wang, Y. P., Wu, Q., & Castleman, K. R. (2023). Image enhancement. Microscope Image Processing, 55–74. https://doi.org/10.1016/b978-0-12-821049-9.00006-x

Xiao, J., Li, S., & Xu, Q. (2019). Video-based evidence analysis and extraction in digital forensic investigation. IEEE Access, 7, 55432–55442. https://doi.org/10.1109/access.2019.2913648

8 A Hybrid Deep Feature Selection Framework for Speaker Accent Recognition

Rajdeep Bhadra, Mridu Sahu, Maroi Agrebi, Pawan Kumar Singh, and Youakim Badr

8.1 INTRODUCTION

Speech signals are one of the most common and natural means of social communication among individuals. Accent of a speech signal can provide valuable information regarding the speaker's identity, cultural background, and geographic location. Therefore, the ability to recognize the accent of any speech signal becomes very important in the fields such as language learning, speech technology, forensics, linguistics, and national security. Here, Speaker Accent Recognition (SAR) comes into the picture, the task being to investigate and accurately predict the accent class of a raw speech signal. In today's world, it becomes very important to develop a dependable, automated SAR system for high-confidence accent classification from a raw speech clip [1, 2].

SAR problem has been mostly tackled by means of traditional machine learning approaches which consist of extracting handcrafted features followed by classifying the feature set into their respective accent class. But, here the success of these techniques lies on the choice of best-suited feature descriptors like Linear Predictive Codes(LPC) [3], Relative Spectral (RASTA) [4], and mel-frequency cepstral coefficient (MFCC) [5]. Unlike deep learning, it requires manual feature engineering which is subject to several rounds of trial and error. Although, it is possible that traditional feature descriptors vary performance for different speech datasets. Therefore, in order to get optimal performance, combination of multiple feature descriptors is required which demand more storage and more trials.

On the other hand, deep learning models eliminate all the troubles present in handcrafted feature extraction methods and also provide a self-learning paradigm that automatically generates all informative feature sets correctly representing the raw audio signals. It also removes the need for explicit feature engineering. In the context of SAR problem, deep learning method has been leveraged mostly in two directions – (i) modeling upon sequential raw audio signals, (ii) usage of vision-based models based on the Mel spectrograms of raw audio signals. The former approach is computationally very expensive, conversion of raw audio signals to spectrograms map the temporal audio sequence to frequency-based spatial

DOI: 10.1201/9781032614663-8

spectrum. Here, computer vision-based deep learning models can be used for classification. But, there is a drawback of using a deep learning model that requires a huge amount of training data for desirable classification results. Transfer learning is a solution to this limitation where a model already trained on a huge dataset (such as ImageNet [6]) is reused on another problem. Here, we have used Mel spectrograms of raw audio signals for accent detection by employing a customized MobileNetV2 [7] and InceptionV3 [8] transfer learning model pre-trained on ImageNet dataset, as Convolutional Neural Network (CNN) feature extractor backbone.

The objective *feature selection(FS)* is selecting the most optimal feature subset from a large feature set for enhancing the classification results as well as reducing storage requirements making our model pipeline computationally efficient [9–11]. The number of features extracted by the CNN backbone of our customized MobileNetV2 [7] and InceptionV3 [8] model is very large which may contain redundant information and leads to limited performance of our classification problem. Therefore, we need FS to select most optimal subset from the extracted feature set which will give the most optimal classification result. In our study, two *filter-based* FS methods are used to rank the features extracted from the above two transfer learning models, one is *'mutual information' (MI)* [12] and another is *'correlation'* [13]. MI ranks the features on the basis of information content present in them and correlation ranks features on the basis of degree of correlation of the feature with output variable. Two different feature sets have been obtained after performing two previously mentioned FS methods, on the original feature set, followed by merging those two feature sets into one. Top $m\%$, $n\%$ features are selected using MI and correlation respectively where m and n are set experimentally. The final feature set is fed into a support vector machine (SVM) classifier [14] to make the final predictions.

The main contributions of the present research are as follows:

1. A bi-stage filter-based hybrid deep FS (HDFS) framework has been proposed for robust classification of accents from raw audio speeches.
2. Two transfer learning models, a customized pre-trained MobileNetV2 [7] and InceptionV3 [8], have been used to extract features from the Mel spectrograms of raw audio speech clips, followed by employing two filter-based FS methods i.e. MI and correlation respectively on the previously extracted feature set. Top m% and n% features are selected using MI and correlation FS methods respectively where the values of m and n are being set experimentally. Lastly, two optimal feature sets obtained by employing two previously mentioned FS methods are merged into one feature set.
3. The final feature set is fed into a SVM classifier to make final predictions.
4. This proposed model pipeline has been evaluated on three different publicly available accent datasets: AccentDB [15], Speech Accent Archive (SAA) [16], UK Ireland English Dialect Speech Dataset (UIED) [17].
5. The evaluated results are also compared with several existing SAR works in the literature.

The rest of the paper is organized as follows: Section 8.2 consists the reviews of some recent developments in the area of SAR and FS, Section 8.3 describes each and every finer details of our proposed model pipeline, Section 8.4 discusses the results obtained by employing our proposed model pipeline on three publicly available speech datasets, along with the comparative study against several state-of-art works on SAR in literature, and Section 8.5 describes the conclusions of our present study.

8.2   RELATED SURVEY

Several studies have focused on accent recognition, employing various techniques and approaches to address the challenges associated with accurately identifying and classifying accents in spoken language. This section presents an overview of the key research contributions in the field.

One prominent approach utilized in accent recognition is feature extraction. Many studies have employed MFCCs as a feature representation for accent identification [18–20]. MFCC captures the spectral characteristics of speech, enabling discrimination between different accents. Additionally, prosodic features such as pitch, duration, and energy have been utilized to enhance accent recognition performance [1, 21].

Classification algorithms have played a crucial role in accent recognition research. SVMs have been widely employed due to their ability to handle high-dimensional feature spaces and effectively classify accents [22, 23]. Gaussian mixture models (GMMs) have also been utilized for accent recognition, modeling the distributions of acoustic features to identify accents [2, 24, 25]. More recently, deep neural networks (DNN) have gained significant attention in accent recognition, leveraging their ability to learn complex patterns and hierarchies in the data [26, 27].

To facilitate research in accent recognition, several datasets have been developed. The GlobalPhone dataset [28] has emerged as a widely used resource for training and evaluating accent recognition models. It comprises multilingual speech data with various accents, enabling researchers to explore accent identification across different languages. The VoxCeleb dataset [29] originally designed for speaker recognition also includes accents, providing a valuable resource for studying accent-related challenges. Additionally, the L2-ARCTIC dataset [30] specifically focuses on non-native English accents, enabling researchers to investigate accent identification in the context of language learning.

Several studies have explored the integration of accent recognition into practical applications. Accent recognition has been applied in speech recognition systems to improve their performance in understanding accented speech in language learning platforms; accent identification has been utilized to provide targeted feedback and personalized instruction to non-native speakers [31]. Furthermore, accent recognition has been used in speaker identification and verification tasks to enhance security systems and authentication processes [32, 33].

In terms of evaluation metrics, accent recognition systems are typically assessed based on accuracy, precision, and recall. Equal error rate (EER) is commonly used for threshold-dependent systems, providing a comprehensive measure of performance. Confusion matrix analysis is also employed to gain insights into the classification performance across different accents and identify potential error patterns.

Despite significant advancements, accent recognition research still faces several challenges. Limited availability of accent-specific datasets poses a significant obstacle to developing accurate and robust models. Handling intra-accent variations, dialectal differences, and the influence of coarticulation further complicates the task. Moreover, ensuring robustness to noisy environments and real-time processing remains an ongoing challenge in practical applications. Addressing these challenges requires further research in areas such as data collection, feature representation, and algorithmic advancements.

In recent years, deep learning approaches have shown promising results in accent recognition. Researchers have explored the use of CNNs and recurrent neural networks (RNNs) to capture local and temporal dependencies in accent data. Multimodal fusion of audio and visual cues has also gained attention, leveraging facial expressions and lip movements to improve accent identification accuracy.

8.3   PROPOSED HDFS METHODOLOGY

In this section, we describe each stage of our proposed model pipeline for accent recognition from speech data. Figure 8.1 gives the pictorial representation of the overall workflow of our proposed model pipeline.

Our model pipeline for SAR consists of the following stages:

- Deep feature Extraction using MobileNetV2 and InceptionV3.
- Filter-based feature extraction methods like MI and correlation for feature ranking and obtaining two different optimal feature sets.
- Taking union of those two obtained feature sets for further classification.
- Finally, classification using SVM on the previously obtained optimal feature subset.
- These stages are explained below in detail as subsections.

8.3.1   Deep Feature Extraction Using MobileNetV2 and InceptionV3

This is the first stage of our proposed SAR framework. This involves the feature extraction from the Mel spectrograms of raw audio speech signals. These Mel spectrograms represent the spatial time-frequency distribution of audio data. These Mel spectrograms are obtained by applying fast Fourier transformation (FFT) on raw audio

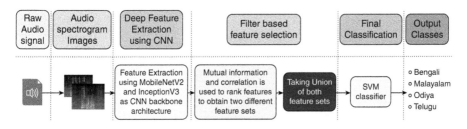

FIGURE 8.1 Overall workflow of our model pipeline for SAR from raw audio speech signals.

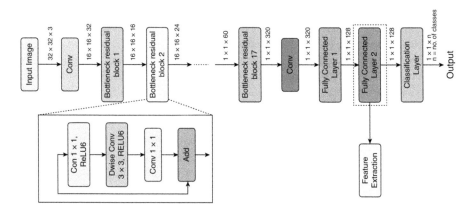

FIGURE 8.2   Schematic diagram of MobileNetV2 model used in our study.

signals. Two different transfer learning CNN models i.e. customized MobileNetV2, InceptionV3 are employed to capture rich features from the Mel spectrograms of raw audio signals. Features are extracted from each of those transfer learning models. Further to reduce the information loss during feature extraction, two fully connected (FC) layers are attached after flattening the last pooling layer for each transfer learning models employed for feature extraction. Each FC layer consists of 128 neurons, each associated with rectified linear unit (ReLU) activation function. The second FC layer is the layer from where deep features are extracted for both CNN-based transfer learning models employed in our pipeline. During feature extraction we obtain a feature set of dimension 128 for each model. Therefore, total 256 features are extracted in this process. The final classification layer is associated with a Softmax function which maps the outputs to a probability distribution. Figures 8.2 and 8.3 represent the schematic diagrams for MobileNetV2 and InceptionV3 models.

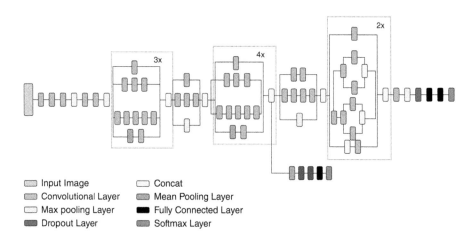

FIGURE 8.3   Schematic diagram of InceptionV3 model used in our study.

8.3.2   FILTER-BASED FS: MUTUAL INFORMATION AND CORRELATION

FS methods tend to improve classification results when the number of features is too much. It helps to eliminate inconsistent and redundant features from the feature set, obtaining an optimal feature set containing all those features having good output predictability quality. In this study, our main goal is to obtain an optimal feature set maximizing the accuracy of our SAR classification problem. For that, we have applied two filter-based FS, MI and correlation, individually on the original feature set.

8.3.2.1   Feature Ranking Using Mutual Information

In the context of FS, MI is a statistical measure that quantifies the amount of information that a feature and the output label share. MI is used to measure the dependence between features and labels. Considering X_1, X_2, X_3, X_4, X_5.......,X_n be a list of all features present in the original feature set and Y be the label (output variable). The MI value with respect to feature X_i can be written as follows:

$$MI(X_i, Y) = H(Y) - H(Y|X_i) \qquad (8.1)$$

where $MI(X_i, Y)$ denotes the MI value of feature X_i with respect to label Y. $H(Y)$ denotes the entropy of target variable (label) Y and $H(Y|X_i)$ denotes the conditional entropy of target variable Y with given feature X_i. Here, entropy is a measure of randomness and uncertainty of a random variable. Entropy of a variable can be defined as follows:

$$H(X) = -\sum p(X) \log_2 (p(X)) \qquad (8.2)$$

Here, $p(X)$ denotes the probability distribution of variable X. This summation is taken over all possible values of variable X. If, random variable X is highly predictable, the value of $H(X)$ becomes very low. Similarly, if X is highly unpredictable, the value of $H(X)$ becomes very high. On the other hand, conditional entropy i.e. $H(Y|X_i)$ is the measure of randomness and uncertainties of target variable, Y given that the value of feature variable, X_i, known as conditional entropy, can be mathematically represented as below:

$$H(Y|X_i) = -\sum p(X_i, Y) \log_2 (p(Y|X_i)) \qquad (8.3)$$

Here, $p(X_i, Y)$ denotes the joint probability distribution of X_i and Y. $p(Y|X_i)$ denotes the conditional probability of target variable Y with given X_i. MI score is calculated for all the features using Algorithm 8.1. After calculating the MI values for all features present in the feature set, we have ranked them in descending order based on their MI scores. Top q features are chosen based on their MI score. More MI score means more output predictability quality.

Algorithm 8.1: Pseudo code for feature ranking using MI where *m* is the total number of training samples, *n* is the number of features in original feature set, *M* denotes the array containing MI scores of all the features, *Y* is an array consisting all the target label values in training data

Input: $X[1, \ldots .m][1 \ldots .n]$, $Y[1, \ldots ..m]$
Output: An array $F[1, \ldots n]$ representing the features in descending order based on MI score.
Algorithm:

Initialize three empty arrays of size n (total no. of features) $M[1,.....n]$, $H[1,.....n]$, $F[1,.....n]$
Initialize a variable *p*
p=calculate the entropy of target label using Equation (8.2)
 for $i = 1$ *to n* do
  $H[i]$ = calculate the conditional entropy of feature i using Equation (8.3)
  $M[i] = p - H[i]$.
 end for
Fill **all the features in array F in descending order based on each feature's MI score. MI score can be obtained from array M where $M[i]$ denotes the MI score of feature X_i.**
 return F;

8.3.2.2 Feature Ranking Using Correlation

In the context of FS, correlation is a statistical measure of linear relationship between feature and label. Unlike MI, it only measures the linear relationship. Correlation is also a filter-based FS widely used. Considering, $X_1, X_2, X_3, X_4, X_5 \ldots \ldots ,X_n$ be a list of all features present in the original feature set and Y be the label (output variable), correlation value with respect to feature X_i can be written as follows:

$$cor(X_i, Y) = \frac{cov(X_i, Y)}{std(X_i \mid Y) \times std(Y)} \tag{8.4}$$

Here, $cor(X_i, Y)$ denotes the covariance between X_i and Y, $std(X_i, Y)$ denotes the conditional standard deviation of variable X_i and $std(Y)$ denotes the standard deviation of variable Y. Covariance is a statistical measure which indicates how much two variables change together. A suitable mathematical expression for measuring covariance can be written as follows:

$$cov(P, Q) = \frac{\Sigma\left[(P_i - P_{mean}) \times (Q_i - Q_{mean})\right]}{n - 1} \tag{8.5}$$

Here, P_i denotes the ith value of P, P_{mean} denotes the mean value of all possible values of P. Q_i denotes i^{th} value of Q and Q_{mean} denotes the mean value of all possible values of Q. The term $(n - 1)$ denotes the degree of freedom. In our study, we have calculated correlation coefficients for all the features and ranked them on the basis of their correlation coefficient values in descending order. Top p features are chosen (as per Algorithm 8.2) for final classification.

Algorithm 8.2: Pseudo code for feature ranking using correlation where m is the total number of training samples, n is the number of features in original feature set, $cor[]$ denotes the array containing correlation values of all the features, $Y[]$ is an array consisting all the target label values in training data

Input: $X[1, \dots .m][1 \dots .n]$, $Y[1, \dots .m]$
Output: An array $F[1, \dots n]$ representing the features in descending order based on correlation coefficient score.
Algorithm:

> **Initialize four empty arrays $cov[1,...n], std[1,....n], cor[1,....n], F[1....n]$.**
> **Initialize a variable 'std_y'**
> std_y**:=calculate standard deviation of all the values present in array Y.**
> **for i=1 to n do**
> $cov[i]$**:=calculate the covariance of two arrays X[i], Y using** Equation (8.5)
> $std[i]$**:=calculate the conditional standard deviation of 1D array $X[i]$ w.r.t. Y**
> $$\text{cor[i]}:= \frac{cov(i)}{std(i) \times std\_y}$$
> **end for**
> **Fill the array $F[1,...n]$ with features in descending order based on its correlation coefficient.**
> **return F**

8.3.3 FINAL CLASSIFICATION USING SVM

In the above two Sections 8.3.2.1 and 8.3.2.2, we have obtained two optimal feature subsets consisting of those features having highest output predicting capabilities measured on two different metrics i.e. MI and correlation. Now, we have taken the union set of those two optimal feature subsets. This obtained subset is used for final classification.

The final classification is done using the SVM classifier on the previously obtained optimal feature subset. The main idea behind SVM is to find the best separable hyperplane that separates the data points into different classes of the classification problem. In our study, the training data is fed into an SVM classifier which finds the best hyperplane to separate the training data into different classes. It takes into account only those features which are present on the final optimal feature set.

8.4 RESULTS AND DISCUSSION

In this section, we will describe the datasets used in our study in detail as well as report the results obtained on those datasets using our proposed HDFS model pipeline. We also compare our proposed HDFS framework with some existing other SAR methods to justify the superiority and reliability of our proposed method.

8.4.1　Datasets Used

Our proposed framework is evaluated on three publicly available SAR datasets using a five-fold cross validation scheme. The datasets which are used are mentioned below:

1. AccentDB database [15]
2. SAA [16]
3. UIED [17]

8.4.1.1　AccentDB Database

AccentDB [15] is a database which consists of non-native English accent speech recordings. It consists of 6134 audio files each audio file of length 5 seconds. Each audio belongs to one of the four accent classes i.e. *Bengali, Malayalam, Oriya*, and *Telugu*. The class-wise distribution of the dataset is given in Table 8.1.

8.4.1.2　Speech Accent Archive (SAA)

SAA [16] dataset is a collection of recordings of speakers from various language backgrounds reading a standardized paragraph in English. This dataset contains 2140 speech samples, each from a different speaker reading the same reading passage. Speakers come from 177 countries and have 214 different native languages. Each speaker is speaking in English. Each audio clip is of length 10–30 seconds. For this dataset, we have considered only six labels i.e. *English, Spanish, Arabic, Mandarin, French*, and *Dutch* for our study to evaluate the efficiency of our proposed HDFS framework. The class-wise distribution of the dataset is given in Table 8.1.

TABLE 8.1

Class-Wise Distribution of the Datasets Considered for Evaluating of Our Proposed HDFS Model's Performance

Dataset	Class	Accent Label	Number of Samples
AccentDB [15]	0	*Bengali*	1528
	1	*Oriya*	747
	2	*Malayalam*	2393
	3	*Telugu*	1466
SAA [16]	0	*English*	579
	1	*Spanish*	162
	2	*Arabic*	102
	3	*Mandarin*	65
	4	*French*	63
	5	*Dutch*	47
UIED [17]	0	*Irish*	450
	1	*Midlands*	696
	2	*Scottish*	2543
	3	*Welsh*	2849
	4	*Southern*	8492

8.4.1.3   UK and Ireland English Dialect Speech Dataset (UIED)

This is a public domain speech dataset consisting of high-quality audio of English sentences recorded by volunteers speaking different dialects of the language. This dataset contains male and female recordings of English from various dialects of the UK and Ireland. There are total 17,877 wav files of audio recording, each recording is of length from 1 to maximum 10 seconds. Class-wise distribution of the dataset is given in Table 8.1. This dataset consists five accent classes: *Irish, Midlands, Scottish, Welsh,* and *Southern.*

8.4.2   IMPLEMENTATION DETAILS

The proposed method has been implemented in Python3 using the Tensorflow 2 Toolbox [34]. The CNN feature extractor has been trained for 100–150 epochs (early stopping is implemented) using the mini-batch descent optimizer with a learning rate of 0.001. All Mel spectrogram images have been pre-processed properly before being passed into transfer learning models of our proposed model pipeline, the training batch size being set to 3.

8.4.3   EVALUATION METRICS

Here, four commonly used evaluation metrics are considered to evaluate the correctness of our proposed model pipeline on SAR datasets. Those are Accuracy, Precision, Recall, and F1-score. The formulas for calculating these evaluation metrics are mentioned below:

$$\text{Precision}_i = \frac{C_{ii}}{\sum_{j=1}^{N} C_{ji}} * 100 \tag{8.6}$$

$$\text{Accuracy} = \frac{\sum_{i=1}^{N} C_{ii}}{\sum_{i=1}^{N} \sum_{j=1}^{N} C_{ij}} * 100 \tag{8.7}$$

$$\text{Recall}_i = \frac{C_{ii}}{\sum_{j=1}^{N} C_{ij}} * 100 \tag{8.8}$$

$$\text{F1} - \text{score}_i = \frac{2}{\dfrac{1}{Precision_i} + \dfrac{1}{Recall_i}} * 100 \tag{8.9}$$

Here, N denotes the number of accent classes in the dataset.

8.4.4   OVERALL RESULTS

In our study, we have evaluated our HDFS framework on each of three SAR datasets. The overall results obtained for each SAR dataset mentioned in Section 8.4.1 are listed below.

TABLE 8.2

Results Obtained by Our Proposed HDFS Method on AccentDB Dataset

Evaluation Metric	Value
Accuracy(%)	99.51
Precision(%)	99.38
Recall(%)	99.52
F1-score(%)	99.45

8.4.4.1 Results on AccentDB Dataset

The results of each evaluation metrics i.e. Accuracy, Precision, Recall, F1-score obtained on the AccentDB dataset is tabulated in Table 8.2. After extracting the feature vectors from two transfer learning models i.e. MobileNetV2 and InceptionV3, the training curves for both models (loss versus epochs and accuracy versus epochs) are shown in Figures 8.4 and 8.5, respectively. It can be observed from Figures 8.4 and 8.5 that the training curves show a satisfactory convergence behavior without any sign of overfitting.

A train-test split ratio of 70:30 is chosen for both the candidate models where 20% of the training data is considered validation dataset. The MobilenetV2 model shows 100% accuracy on training dataset, 99.41% accuracy on validation dataset, and 99.08% accuracy on test dataset. The InceptionV3 model shows 97.29% accuracy on training dataset, 93.99% accuracy on validation dataset, and 94.72% accuracy on test dataset.

Table 8.3 gives a comparison study of the proposed HDFS model's accuracies between before FS and after FS. It can be seen that after FS, the model accuracy is improved by a significant amount. The confusion matrix obtained

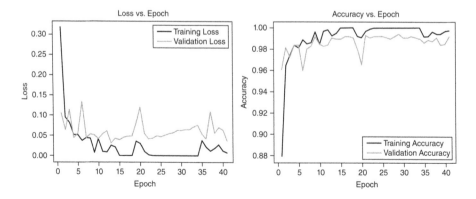

FIGURE 8.4 Training curves for MobilenetV2 model for AccentDB dataset.

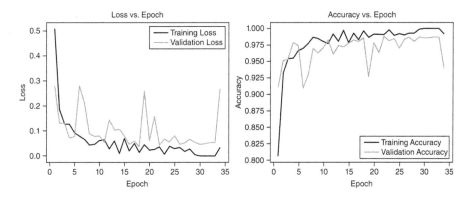

FIGURE 8.5   Training curves for InceptionV3 model for AccentDB dataset.

by our model pipeline is shown in Figure 8.6. The confusion matrix obtained over AccentDB dataset shows us a satisfactory performance. The number of true positive and true negative values is very high compared to false positive and false negative values. This phenomenon leads to a good accuracy, precision, recall, and F1-score value.

Lastly, Figure 8.7 shows the class-wise metric scores obtained by our HDFS framework. It can be examined from Figure 8.7 that the class-wise accuracy, precision, recall, and F1-score values are also found to be satisfactory. *Bengali* accent class is giving the highest accuracy value up to 100% whereas *Telugu* class is giving lowest but good accuracy value up to 99.12%. In case of precision value, the *Telugu* class is giving value up to 99.78% whereas *Bengali* class is giving up to 99.35%. In case of recall value, the *Bengali* accent class is giving highest value up to 100% whereas *Telugu* lowest up to 99.11%. In case of F1-score values, *Bengali* is giving highest value up to 99.67% whereas *Oriya* lowest up to 99.11%.

8.4.4.2   Results on Speech Accent Archive Dataset

The results of each evaluation metrics i.e. Accuracy, Precision, Recall, and F1-score obtained on SAA dataset are tabulated in Table 8.4. Further, the training curves plotted for loss versus epoch and accuracy versus epoch are shown in Figures 8.8 and 8.9,

---

TABLE 8.3

Comparison of Classification Accuracies Before and after Feature Selection for AccentDB Dataset

Model	Accuracy (%) Before FS	#Features Selected Using MI	#Features Selected Using Correlation	Accuracy (%)
MobileNetV2	99.08	20	30	99.51
InceptionV3	94.72			

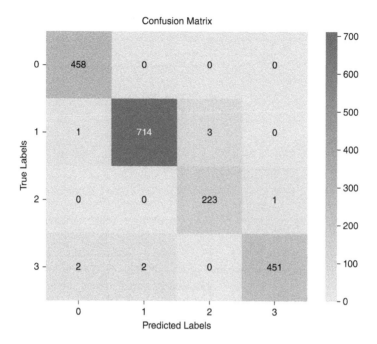

FIGURE 8.6 Confusion matrix obtained on AccentDB dataset after final classification by the proposed HDFS model.

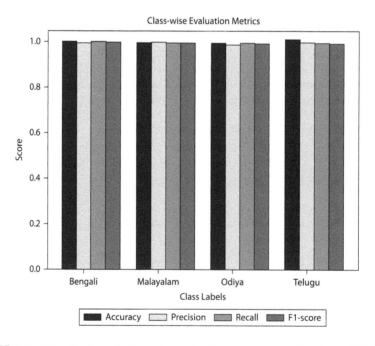

FIGURE 8.7 Visualization of class-wise evaluation metric scores for AccentDB dataset through bar graph.

TABLE 8.4

Results Obtained by Our Proposed HDFS Method on Speech Accent Archive Dataset

Evaluation Metric	Value
Accuracy(%)	59.39
Precision(%)	44.74
Recall(%)	35.37
F1-score(%)	36.99

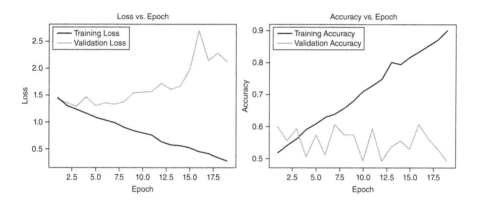

FIGURE 8.8 Training curves for MobilenetV2 model for speech accent archive dataset.

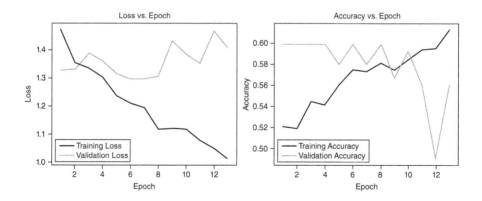

FIGURE 8.9 Training curves for InceptionV3 model for speech accent archive dataset.

TABLE 8.5

Comparison of Classification Accuracies Before and after Feature Selection for SAA Dataset

Model	Accuracy (%) Before FS	#Features Selected Using MI	#Features Selected Using Correlation	Accuracy (%)
MobileNetV2	53.29	30	40	59.39
InceptionV3	50.76			

respectively. Both curves do not show a satisfactory convergence on the training dataset. The difference between training loss and validation loss is comparatively higher in case of MobilenetV2 model. The classification accuracies obtained by both transfer learning models are not satisfactory.

A ratio of 80:20 train-test split is considered where 20% of training data is considered for validation dataset. The MobilenetV2 model shows 93.33% accuracy on training dataset, 49.04% accuracy on validation dataset, and 53.29% accuracy on test dataset. On the other hand, InceptionV3 model shows 61.90% accuracy on training dataset, 56.05% accuracy on validation dataset, and 50.76% accuracy on test dataset. Table 8.5 gives a comparison study of our HDFS model's accuracies between before FS and after FS. It can be seen from Table 8.5 that after performing FS, the model accuracy has been improved by a significant amount. Figure 8.10 shows the confusion matrix obtained on SAA dataset by our model pipeline. Unlike AccentDB dataset, the HDFS framework does not show a satisfactory performance even though it is still better than many state-of-the-art SARs in literature.

The class-wise evaluation metric scores are also shown in Figure 8.11. It can be observed from Figure 8.11 that accent classes like *English, Arabic, Mandarin, Spanish* are giving overall average performance in terms of all the metrics we have considered in our study. The *French* class is giving average precision value but all other metric values (except precision) for the same accent class do not show convincing results. On the other hand, the *Dutch* class is giving worst performance in terms of all the evaluation metrics.

8.4.4.3 Results on UIED Dataset

The results obtained on the UIED dataset are tabulated in Table 8.6. After extracting the feature vectors from two transfer learning models i.e. MobileNetv2 and InceptionV3, the training curves plotted for both models (loss versus epochs and accuracy versus epochs) are shown in Figures 8.12 and 8.13, respectively. It can be observed from Figures 8.12 and 8.13 that the training curve is not showing satisfactory convergence behavior for loss versus epoch graph. However, for accuracy versus epoch curve, the convergence is convincing.

A 70:30 is chosen as train-test split ratio where 30% of the training data is considered validation dataset. The MobilenetV2 model shows 99.41% accuracy on training dataset, 85.07% accuracy on validation dataset, and 85.41% accuracy on test dataset. The InceptionV3 model shows 99.19% accuracy on training dataset, 73.88%

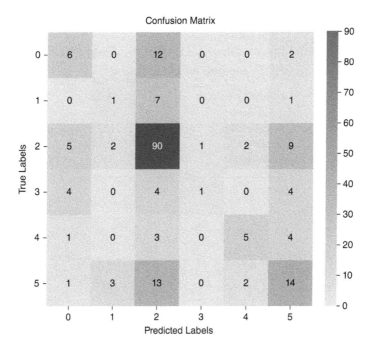

FIGURE 8.10 Confusion matrix obtained on speech accent archive dataset after final classification by the proposed HDFS model.

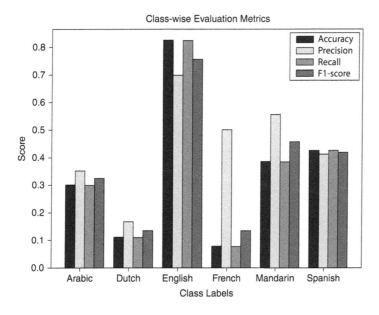

FIGURE 8.11 Visualization of class-wise evaluation metric scores for SAA dataset through bar graph.

TABLE 8.6
Results Obtained by Our Proposed HDFS Method on UIED Dataset

Evaluation Metric	Value
Accuracy(%)	86.11
Precision(%)	85.98
Recall(%)	85.30
F1-score(%)	85.57

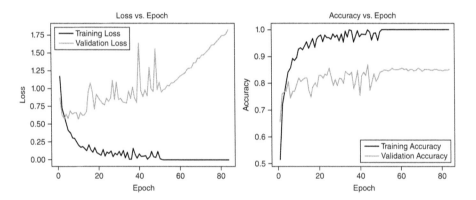

FIGURE 8.12   Training curves for MobilenetV2 model for UIED dataset.

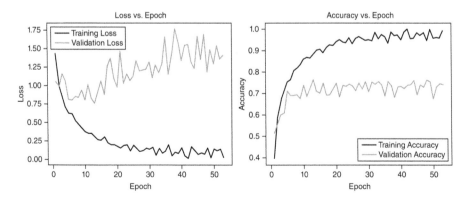

FIGURE 8.13   Training curves for InceptionV3 model for UIED dataset.

TABLE 8.7

Comparison of Classification Accuracies Before and after Feature Selection for UIED

Model	Accuracy (%) Before FS	#Features Selected Using MI	#Features Selected Using Correlation	Accuracy (%)
MobileNetV2	85.41	40	30	86.11
InceptionV3	73.14			

accuracy on validation dataset, and 73.14% accuracy on test dataset. Table 8.7 gives a comparison study of our model's accuracies between before FS and after FS. It can be seen from Table 8.7 that after FS, our model's accuracy gets improved by a significant amount.

Moreover, the confusion matrix obtained by our model pipeline is shown in Figure 8.14. It can be examined from Figure 8.14 that total number of true positive and true negative values are higher than total number of false positive and false negative values. This leads to a sound accuracy, precision, recall as well as F1-score

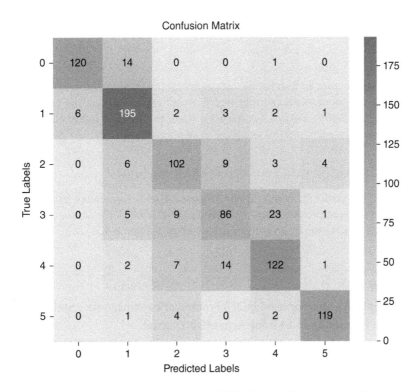

FIGURE 8.14 Confusion matrix obtained on UIED dataset after final classification by the proposed HDFS model.

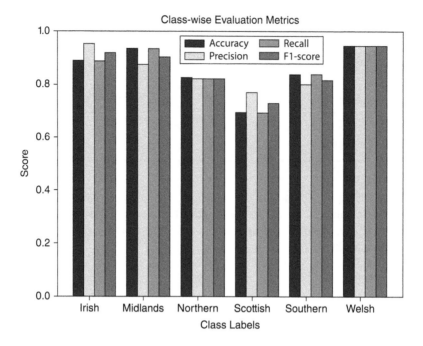

FIGURE 8.15 Visualization of class-wise evaluation metric scores for UIED dataset through bar graph.

values. Lastly, Figure 8.15 shows the class-wise metric scores obtained by our HDFS framework. It can be observed that *Welsh* accent class is giving the best result in terms of all evaluation metrics. On the other hand, the *Scottish* accent class is giving the worst performance in terms of all the evaluation metrics.

8.4.5 Comparison with State-Of-Art SAR Methods

Tables 8.8, 8.9, and 8.10 compare our proposed HDFS framework against several state-of-art in literature pertaining to SAR on publicly available datasets used in our study based on the evaluation metrics discussed in Section 8.4.3.

TABLE 8.8

Comparison of Our Proposed HDFS Framework against Some State-of-Art Literature Pertaining to SAR for AccentDB Dataset

Authors	Accuracy	Precision	Recall	F1-Score
Al-Jumaili et al. [35]	90%	96.85%	97.73%	97.29%
Kai-Wei Chang et al. [36]	87.1%	-	-	-
Proposed	**99.51%**	**99.38%**	**99.52%**	**99.45%**

TABLE 8.9

Comparison of Our Proposed HDFS Framework against Some State-of-Art Literature Pertaining to SAR for SAA Dataset

Authors	Accuracy	Precision	Recall	F1-Score
Berjon et al. [22]	34.78%	-	-	-
Widyowaty et al. [37]	57%	-	-	-
Bock et al. [38]	28%	-	-	-
Duduka et al. [39]	52.81%	-	-	-
Proposed	**59.39%**	**44.74%**	**35.37%**	**36.99%**

AccentDB dataset has two versions of itself: one is AccentDB_core and another is AccentDB_extended. AccentDB_core only deals with different region-wise Indian Accents like *Telugu, Bengali, Oriya, Malayalam*, but on the other hand AccentDB_extended dataset deals with all the Indian Accents mentioned before along with other foreign accents like *British, Welsh, American*, and *Australian*. All of the state-of-art SAR methods which are employed on AccentDB dataset mostly focused on recognition of foreign accents [35, 36] like *British, American*, and *Welsh*. However, our study mostly focuses on SAR efficiency of Indian accents. Therefore, the performance measures of all comparative models mentioned in Table 8.8 have been obtained on foreign accents like *British, American*, and *Welsh*.

Similarly, most of the state-of-the-art SAR methods [22, 37] which are tested on SAA dataset also considered a subset of accent classes all of which either completely different to our chosen ones or have some overlapping with our chosen ones. Therefore, comparing overall performances between two state-of-the-art methods is not justified here since the accent classes considered for both state-of-the-art SAR methods are either completely different or overlapping. Table 8.9 lists down those state-of-the-art SAR methods.

TABLE 8.10

Comparison of Our Proposed Framework against Traditional Machine Learning as Well as Deep Learning Algorithms for SAA Dataset

Method	Accuracy	Precision	Recall	F1-Score
Logistic Regression	42.10%	-	-	-
Sigmoid SVM	34.78%	-	-	-
Polynomial SVM	55.78%	-	-	-
RBF SVM	55.61%	-	-	-
Decision Tree	57.36%	-	-	-
LSTM	58.26%	-	-	-
CNN	57.38%	-	-	-
1D-CNN + LSTM	54.11%	-	-	-
Proposed	**59.39%**	**44.74%**	**35.37%**	**36.99%**

TABLE 8.11

Comparison of Our Proposed HDFS Framework against Some State-of-Art in Literature Pertaining to SAR for UIED Dataset

Authors	Accuracy	Precision	Recall	F1-Score
Md Fahad et al. [41]	63.15%	–	–	–
Chrisina et al. [42]	88.3%	–	–	–
Singh et al. [43]	65%	–	–	–
Proposed	**86.11%**	**85.98%**	**85.30%**	**85.57%**

In a study [40], some traditional machine learning as well as deep learning methods are applied on SAA dataset and the results are listed down and compared with each other. We have used that study and compared those results with our proposed method. Table 8.10 gives our comparison study of our proposed HDFS framework with traditional machine learning as well as deep learning models.

For UIED dataset, a comparison study of our proposed model with state-of-art SAR methods is tabulated in Table 8.11. It can be observed that our HDFS framework is performing better than several state-of-art SARs by a decent margin.

8.5 CONCLUSION AND FUTURE WORKS

This study proposes a computationally efficient hybrid deep learning filter-based FS pipeline for dimensionality reduction of the feature representation extracted by a CNN backbone from Mel spectrograms of speech audio clips, as well as robust classification of speech signals into respective accent classes. Our approach alleviates the cumbersome process of handcrafted feature extraction, providing an end-to-end framework for SAR. The proposed method has been evaluated on three publicly available standard speech datasets: AccentDB, SAA, and UIED giving nearly 99.51%, 59.39%, and 86.11% accuracies, respectively. The proposed HDFS methodology is also found to outperform several existing works in literature, justifying the reliability of the framework.

In order to contribute to the research on SAR, we intend to explore other speech datasets available in the public domain for greater generalization and reliability so as to be used in real-world applications. We may also try various other approaches to meta-heuristic algorithm-based FS, such as initialization using hybrid of wrapper-based approaches [44] and local search-embedded optimization algorithms [45]. Last but not the least, we also intend to explore temporal features of raw audio signals using deep learning-based architectures to investigate deeper into accent classification and further the community.

REFERENCES

1. H. Behravan, V. Hautam{\"a}ki, S. M. Siniscalchi, T. Kinnunen and C.-H. Lee, "i-vector modeling of speech attributes for automatic foreign accent recognition," *IEEE*, vol. 24, no. 1, pp. 29–41, 2015.

2. K. Mannepalli, P. N. Sastry and M. Suman, "MFCC-GMM based accent recognition system for Telugu speech," *International Journal of Speech Technology*, vol. 19, pp. 87–93, 2016.
3. D. O'Shaughnessy, "Linear predictive coding," *IEEE Potentials*, vol. 7, no. 1, pp. 29–32, 1988.
4. H. Hermansky and N. Morgan, "RASTA processing of speech," *IEEE Transactions on Speech and Audio Processing*, vol. 2, no. 4, pp. 578–589, 1994.
5. W. Han, C.-F. Chan, C.-S. Choy and K.-P. Pun, "An efficient MFCC extraction method in speech recognition," in *2006 IEEE International Symposium on Circuits and Systems (ISCAS)*, IEEE, 2006, pp. 4–20.
6. J. Deng, W. Dong, R. Socher, L.-J. Li, K. d Li and L. Fei-Fei, "ImageNet: A Large-Scale Hierarchical Image Database," *IEEE*, 2009.
7. M. Sandler, A. Howard, M. Zhu, A. Zhmoginov and L.-C. Chen, "MobileNetV2: Inverted Residuals and Linear Bottlenecks," in *Proceedings of the IEEE Conference on Computer Vision and Pattern Recognition*, 2018, pp. 4510–4520.
8. C. Szegedy, V. Vanhoucke, S. Ioffe, J. Shlens and Z. Wojna, "Rethinking the Inception Architecture for Computer Vision," https://doi.org/10.48550/arXiv.1512.00567, 2015.
9. L. St, S. Wold et al., "Analysis of variance (ANOVA)," *Expert Systems with Application*, vol. 6, no. 4, pp. 259–272, 1989.
10. R. J. Tallarida, R. B. Murray, R. J. Tallarida and R. B. Murray, "Chi-Square Test," in *Manual of Pharmacologic Calculations: With Computer Programs*, Springer, 1987, pp. 140–142.
11. T. Rückstieß, C. Osendorfer and P. van der Smagt, "Sequential Feature Selection for Classification," in *AI 2011: Advances in Artificial Intelligence*, Springer, Berlin Heidelberg, 2011, pp. 132–141.
12. M. Bennasar, Y. Hicks and R. Setchi, "Feature selection using joint mutual information maximisation," *Expert Systems with Application*, vol. 42, pp. 8520–8532, 2015.
13. M. A. Hall, *Correlation-Based Feature Selection for Machine Learning*, The University of Waikato, Hamilton, 1999.
14. W. S. Noble, "What is a support vector machine?," *Nature Biotechnology*, vol. 24, pp. 1565–1567, 2006.
15. A. Ahamad, A. Anand and P. Bhargava, "AccentDB: A database of non-native English accents to assist neural speech recognition," in *12th Conference on Language Resources and Evaluation (LREC 2020)*, 2020.
16. "Speech Accent Archive," [Online]. Available: http://accent.gmu.edu/.
17. I. Demirsahin, O. Kjartansson, A. Gutkin and C. Rivera, "Open-source Multi-speaker Corpora of the English Accents in the British Isles," in *Proceedings of The 12th Language Resources and Evaluation Conference (LREC)*, 2020.
18. Q. Yan, Z. Zhou and S. Li, "Chinese Accents Identification with Modified MFCC," in *Instrumentation, Measurement, Circuits and Systems*, Springer Berlin Heidelberg, 2012, pp. 659–666.
19. N. Theera-Umpon, S. Chansareewittaya and S. Auephanwiriyakul, "Phoneme and tonal accent recognition for Thai speech," *Expert Systems With Applications*, vol. 38, no. 10, pp. 13254–13259, 2011.
20. A. Rabiee and S. Setayeshi, "Persian Accents identification using an adaptive neural network," in *2010 Second International Workshop on Education Technology and Computer Science*, 2010, vol. 1, pp. 7–10.
21. Z. Zhang, Y. Wang and J. Yang, "Accent recognition with hybrid phonetic features," *Sensors*, vol. 21, no. 18, p. 6258, 2021.
22. P. Berjon, A. Nag and S. Dev, "Analysis of French phonetic idiosyncrasies for accent recognition," *Soft Computing Letters*, vol. 3, p. 10018, 2021.

23. M. Rizwan and D. V. Anderson, "A weighted accent classification using multiple words," *Neurocomputing*, vol. 277, pp. 120–128, 2018.

24. K. Phapatanaburi, L. Wang, R. Sakagami, Z. Zhang, X. Li and M. Iwahashi, "Distant-talking accent recognition by combining GMM and DNN," *Multimedia Tools and Applications*, vol. 75, pp. 5109–5124, 2016.

25. T. Chen, C. Huang, E. Chang and J. Wang, "Automatic Accent Identification Using Gaussian Mixture Models," in IEEE Workshop on Automatic Speech Recognition and Understanding, 2001. ASRU '01, IEEE, 2001, pp. 343–346.

26. Y. Jiao, M. Tu, V. Berisha and J. M. Liss,"Accent Identification by Combining Deep Neural Networks and Recurrent Neural Networks Trained on Long and Short Term Features," in *Interspeech*, 2016, pp. 2388–2392.

27. O. Cetin, "Accent recognition using a spectrogram image feature-based convolutional neural network," *Arabian Journal for Science and Engineering*, vol. 48, no. 2, pp. 1973–1990, 2023.

28. T. Schultz, M. Westphal and A. Waibel, "The GlobalPhone Pro Ject: Multilingual LVCSR with JANUS-3," in Multilingual Information Retrieval Dialogs: 2nd SQEL Workshop, Citeseer, 1997, pp. 20–27.

29. A. Nagrani, J. S. Chung, W. Xie and A. Zisserman, "Voxceleb: Large-scale speaker verification in the wild," *Computer Science and Language*, 2019, vol. 60, p. 101027

30. G. Zhao, S. Sonsaat, A. Silpachai, I. Lucic, E. Chukharev-Hudilainen, J. Levis and R. Gutierrez-Osuna, "L2-ARCTIC: A Non-native English Speech Corpus," in *Proceedings of Interspeech*, 2018, pp. 2783–2787.

31. A. Faria, "Accent Classification for Speech Recognition," in *Machine Learning for Multimodal Interaction: Second International Workshop, MLMI 2005, Edinburgh, UK, July 11–13, 2005, Revised Selected Papers 2*, Springer, Berlin, Heidelberg. 2006, pp. 285–293.

32. R. Jahangir, Y. W. Teh, H. F. Nweke, G. Mujtaba, M. A. Al-Garadi and I. Ali, "Speaker identification through artificial intelligence techniques: A comprehensive review and research challenges," *Expert Systems with Applications*, vol. 171, p. 114591, 2021.

33. N. Chauhan and M. Chandra, "Speaker recognition and verification using artificial neural network," in *2017 International Conference on Wireless Communications, Signal Processing and Networking (WiSPNET)*, IEEE, 2017, pp. 1147–1149.

34. "TensorFlow," [Online]. Available: https://www.tensorflow.org/.

35. Z. Al-Jumaili, T. Bassiouny, A. Alanezi, W. Khan, D. Al-Jumeily and A. J. Hussain, "Classification of Spoken English Accents Using Deep Learning and Speech Analysis," in *Intelligent Computing Methodologies*, Springer International Publishing, Cham, Germany, 2022, pp. 277–287.

36. K.-W. Chang, Y.-K. Wang, H. Shen, I.-t. Kang, W.-C. Tseng, S.-W. Li and H.-y Lee, "SpeechPrompt v2: Prompt Tuning for Speech Classification Tasks," *arXiv preprint arXiv:2303.00733*, 2023.

37. D. S. Widyowaty and A. Sunyoto, "Accent recognition by native language using mel-frequency cepstral coefficient and K-nearest neighbor," in *2020 3rd International Conference on Information and Communications Technology (ICOIACT)*, IEEE, 2020, pp. 314–318.

38. B. Bock and L. Shamir, "Assessing the efficacy of benchmarks for automatic speech accent recognition," *EAI Endorsed Transactions on Creative Technologies*, vol. 2, 2015.

39. S. Duduka, H. Jain, H. P. V. Jain and P. M. Chawan, "A neural network approach to accent classification," *International Research Journal of Engineering and Technology (IRJET)*, vol. 8, no. 3, pp. 1175–1177, 2021.

40. A. Purwar, H. Sharma, Y. Sharma, H. Gupta and A. Kaur, "Accent classification using machine learning and deep learning models," *2022 1st International Conference on Informatics (ICI)*, no. IEEE, pp. 13–18, 2022.

41. M. F. Hossain, M. M. Hasan, H. Ali, M. R. K. R. Sarker and M. T. Hassan, "A machine learning approach to recognize speakers region of the united kingdom from continuous speech based on accent classification," in *2020 11th International Conference on Electrical and Computer Engineering (ICECE)*, IEEE, 2020, pp. 210–213.
42. C. Jayne, V. Chang, J. Bailey and Q. A. Xu, "Automatic Accent and Gender Recognition of Regional UK Speakers," in *Engineering Applications of Neural Networks: 23rd International Conference, EAAAI/EANN 2022, Chersonissos, Crete, Greece, June 17–20, 2022, Proceedings*, Springer, Cham, Germany, 2022, pp. 67–80.
43. J. S. Shergill, C. Pravin and V. Ojha, "Accent and gender recognition from English language speech and audio using signal processing and deep learning," in *Hybrid Intelligent Systems: 20th International Conference on Hybrid Intelligent Systems (HIS 2020), December 14-16, 2020*, Springer, 2021, pp. 62–72.
44. A. Das, S. Guha, P. K. Singh, A. Ahmadian, N. Senu and R. Sarkar, "A hybrid meta-heuristic feature selection method for identification of Indian spoken languages from audio signals," *IEEE Access*, vol. 8, pp. 181432–181449, 2020.
45. P. Pramanik, S. Mukhopadhyay, S. Mirjalili and R. Sarkar, "Deep feature selection using local search embedded social ski-driver optimization algorithm for breast cancer detection in mammograms," *Neural Computing and Applications*, vol. 35, no. 7, pp. 5479–5499, 2023.

9 Secure Transaction in Animal Biometric Assessment

Ambika N

9.1 INTRODUCTION

Habitat monitoring (Lahoz-Monfort & Magrath, 2021; Lengyel et al., 2008) involves the systematic observation and assessment of natural environments to understand their conditions, changes, and the impacts of human activities. This type of monitoring is essential for conservation, ecosystem management, scientific research, and sustainable development. Figure 9.1 depicts analyzing emotions in animals.

Importance of Habitat Monitoring:
- *Conservation*: Monitoring habitats helps track the health and well-being of ecosystems and species, enabling conservationists to take proactive measures to protect them.
- *Biodiversity Assessment*: Monitoring allows scientists to study the diversity of species, track population trends, and identify endangered or invasive species.
- *Environmental Impact Assessment*: Habitat monitoring can assess the effects of human activities, such as construction, mining, or pollution, on ecosystems.
- *Climate Change Research*: Monitoring helps in understanding the effects of climate change on habitats, such as shifts in species distributions or altered phenology.

Data Collection and Sensors:
- *Remote Sensing*: Satellite imagery, aerial photography, and drones can provide comprehensive views of habitats from a distance.
- *Sensor Networks*: Deploying sensors for collecting data on temperature, humidity, soil moisture, light levels, and more can provide real-time environmental data.
- *Camera Traps*: Used to capture images of wildlife, helping monitor animal presence and behavior without direct observation.
- *Acoustic Monitoring*: Recording sounds to identify species, track migrations, and assess biodiversity.

Data Analysis and Interpretation:
- *Spatial Analysis*: Geographic information systems (GISs) are used to map habitat features, changes, and trends over time.

DOI: 10.1201/9781032614663-9

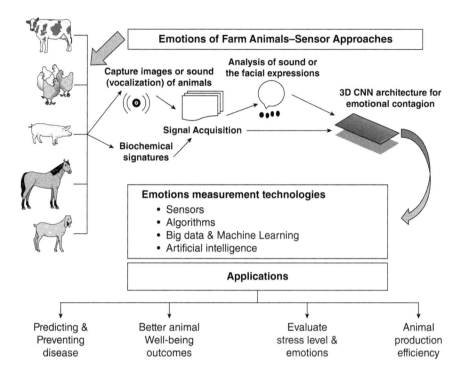

FIGURE 9.1   Analyzing emotions of farm animals (Neethirajan et al., 2021).

- *Time-Series Analysis*: Long-term data collection allows for the detection of seasonal patterns and trends.
- *Statistical Analysis*: Data from sensors and observations are analyzed to identify significant changes or anomalies.

Challenges and Considerations:

- *Data Quality*: Ensuring accurate and reliable data collection is essential for meaningful analysis.
- *Scale*: Different habitats require tailored monitoring strategies due to their varying scales and complexities.
- *Interactions*: Habitats are interconnected, and changes in one habitat can affect others.
- *Data Integration*: Integrating data from various sources and formats can be challenging.
- *Privacy and Ethics*: When monitoring habitats involving wildlife or human presence, privacy and ethical considerations must be taken into account.

Technological Advances:

- *Artificial Intelligence (AI)*: AI techniques, including machine learning, can help automate data analysis and pattern recognition.

- ***Big Data***: Large-scale data collection can benefit from big data analytics for identifying trends and patterns.
- ***Internet of Things (IoT) and Connectivity***: IoT devices and connectivity advancements improve real-time data collection and transmission.

Applications:

- ***Forest Monitoring***: Tracking deforestation, tree health, and wildlife populations in forests.
- ***Aquatic Ecosystems***: Monitoring water quality, fish populations, and coral reef health in oceans, lakes, and rivers.
- ***Urban Ecosystems***: Assessing the impact of urbanization on local flora and fauna.
- ***Agricultural Land***: Monitoring the effects of agriculture on soil quality and biodiversity.

Habitat monitoring plays a vital role in understanding and preserving our natural world. It allows us to make informed decisions for sustainable resource management and conservation efforts. As technology continues to evolve, habitat monitoring methods will become more sophisticated, enabling us to gather more accurate and comprehensive data for better environmental stewardship.

The suggestion implements blockchain. The specimen is embedded with the tracking system and activated. The initial parameter values are noted. The tracking system embeds the parameters into hash algorithm to generate hash code. It improves reliability by 15.24% compared to previous work.

The work is divided into eight divisions. The background follows the introduction section. Literature survey is summarized in segment three. The previous work is detailed in the fourth section. The work is proposed in segment five. The analysis of the work is narrated in the sixth division. Future scope is briefed in the seventh section. The work is concluded in the eighth section.

9.2   BACKGROUND

Blockchain (Ambika, 2021a, 2021b) is a decentralized and distributed digital ledger technology. It records transactions across multiple computers making them secure, transparent, and tamper-resistant. It refers to data structured and linked together in a chain of blocks.

Here's a basic overview of how blockchain works:

1. ***Decentralization*** *(Zarrin et al., 2021)*: Unlike traditional databases that are centralized and controlled by a single entity, a blockchain is decentralized. It operates on a network of computers (nodes) that work together to maintain and validate the database.
2. ***Blocks*** *(Liu et al., 2022)*: Transactions are grouped into blocks. Each block contains a set of transactions, a timestamp, and a reference to the previous block.
3. ***Cryptographic Hashing*** *(Kuznetsov et al., 2021)*: Each block is linked to the previous block using a cryptographic hash of the previous block's data.

It creates a chain of blocks, hence the name "blockchain." The hash also serves as a unique identifier for each block.

4. **Consensus Mechanisms** *(Lashkari & Musilek, 2021)*: The network participants must reach a consensus. It adds a new block. Different blockchain networks use various consensus mechanisms, such as proof of work (PoW) or proof of stake (PoS), to validate transactions and add new blocks.

5. **Immutability and Security** *(Tariq et al., 2019)*: It is difficult to alter its contents. Changing the data in a block would require changing the data in all subsequent blocks, which would require the consensus of the network participants, making it highly secure against tampering.

6. **Transparency**: The blockchain ledger is transparent and open to all participants in the network. Anyone can view the entire transaction history, promoting trust and accountability.

Blockchain technology has gained popularity beyond its original use in cryptocurrencies like Bitcoin. It has been applied to various industries and use cases, including supply chain management, healthcare, finance, real estate, and voting systems. The ability to create secure and transparent digital records without the need for a central authority has been a driving force behind its adoption.

9.2.1 Blockchain in Business

Blockchain technology has a wide range of potential applications in the business world, offering solutions to various challenges and opportunities. Here are some ways blockchain can impact businesses:

1. **Supply Chain Management** *(Sunny et al., 2020)*: Blockchain can increase transparency and traceability in supply chains. Businesses can track the movement of goods, verify the authenticity of products, and ensure ethical sourcing by recording every step on an immutable ledger.

2. **Smart Contracts** *(Khan et al., 2021)*: Smart contracts are self-executing contracts with the terms of the agreement directly written into code. They automate processes, reduce the need for intermediaries, and ensure that contractual obligations are met, improving efficiency and reducing the risk of disputes.

3. **Digital Identity Verification** *(Wolfond, 2017)*: Blockchain can be used for secure and verifiable digital identity solutions. It is useful for businesses that require robust identity verification processes, such as financial institutions or online marketplaces.

4. **Financial Transactions** *(Albayati et al., 2020)*: Blockchain can streamline cross-border payments, remittances, and settlements by reducing intermediaries and increasing the speed of transactions. It is valuable for international businesses.

5. **Intellectual Property Protection** *(Wang et al., 2019)*: Businesses can use blockchain to timestamp and store records of intellectual property rights, patents, and copyrights, providing a secure and tamper-proof way to prove ownership and protect intellectual assets.

6. ***Data Security and Privacy*** *(Esposito et al., 2018)*: Blockchain's crypto-graphic techniques can enhance data security and privacy. Businesses can control who has access to their data and track any changes, reducing the risk of data breaches.

7. ***Decentralized Marketplaces*** *(Ranganthan et al., 2018)*: Blockchain can facilitate peer-to-peer transactions in marketplaces without a central inter-mediary. It can lower costs and empower individuals to trade with each other.

8. ***Supply Chain Finance*** *(Du et al., 2020)*: Blockchain can enable more efficient financing options for suppliers by providing a transparent record of transactions and goods in transit, making it easier for lenders to assess creditworthiness.

9. ***Auditing and Compliance*** *(Ingle et al., 2019)*: Businesses can maintain auditable records on the blockchain, making it easier to demonstrate com-pliance with regulations and industry standards.

10. ***Tokenization of Assets*** *(Li et al., 2019)*: Businesses can tokenize real-world assets such as real estate, art, or commodities, allowing for fractional own-ership and enabling new investment opportunities.

11. ***Loyalty Programs*** *(Bülbül & İnce, 2018)*: Blockchain can be used to create transparent and interoperable loyalty programs that offer rewards across different brands and industries.

12. ***Voting Systems*** *(Hjálmarsson et al., 2018)*: Blockchain-based voting sys-tems can enhance the security and transparency of elections and polls, reducing the risk of fraud and ensuring accurate results.

13. ***Insurance and Claims Processing*** *(Chen et al., 2021)*: Blockchain can expedite the claims process in insurance by automating claims verification and enabling transparent communication between stakeholders.

14. ***Energy Trading*** *(Wang et al., 2019)*: Businesses involved in renewable energy production can use blockchain to facilitate peer-to-peer energy trad-ing and tracking of renewable energy certificates.

It's important to note that while blockchain offers numerous benefits, implement-ing it requires careful consideration of factors such as scalability, regulatory compli-ance, integration with existing systems, and user adoption. Each use case will have its unique challenges and considerations, and businesses should evaluate whether blockchain is a suitable solution for their specific needs.

9.2.2 Advantages Using Blockchain

Blockchain technology can offer several benefits to habitat monitoring and environ-mental conservation efforts.

1. ***Data Integrity and Transparency***: Habitat monitoring involves collecting and storing data about ecosystems, species, and environmental conditions. The data could be securely recorded and timestamped, ensuring its integ-rity and preventing unauthorized alterations. This transparency would be essential for building trust among stakeholders and verifying the accuracy of collected data.

2. *Secure Data Sharing*: Different organizations, researchers, and agencies often collaborate in habitat monitoring projects. Blockchain can provide a secure and standardized platform for sharing data, ensuring that contributors can access and verify information while maintaining data ownership and privacy.

3. *Decentralized Collaboration*: In habitat monitoring, a decentralized approach to data collection and management is often desirable due to the distributed nature of ecosystems. Blockchain's decentralized network would enable various parties to contribute and validate data without relying on a central authority.

4. *Proof of Conservation Efforts*: Conservation actions, such as reforestation or wildlife protection, could be recorded on a blockchain. It would create an immutable record of these efforts, which could be useful for demonstrating compliance with regulatory requirements or showcasing the impact of conservation initiatives to donors and the public.

5. *Supply Chain Transparency*: In cases where habitat degradation is linked to unsustainable practices (e.g., illegal logging or wildlife trafficking), blockchain can be used to track the origin of products. This transparency discourages illegal activities and allows consumers to make informed choices.

6. *Tokenized Incentives*: Blockchain-based tokens or cryptocurrencies could be used as incentives for individuals or communities engaged in habitat preservation. It could encourage local participation in conservation efforts and reward sustainable practices.

7. *Decentralized Funding*: Blockchain can facilitate direct peer-to-peer funding for conservation projects, bypassing traditional intermediaries. It could enable faster and more direct funding allocation to urgent initiatives.

8. *Immutable Records of Threats*: Instances of habitat destruction or environmental threats (e.g., pollution and climate change effects) could be recorded on the blockchain. This historical data could help in understanding long-term trends and planning effective responses.

9. *Smart Contracts for Monitoring Agreements*: Smart contracts can automate agreements between parties involved in habitat monitoring. For instance, a smart contract could release funds to a monitoring project once specific data collection milestones are achieved.

10. *Long-Term Data Preservation*: Storing habitat monitoring data on a blockchain ensures its preservation over time. It is crucial for analyzing long-term trends and making informed decisions based on historical data.

9.3   MOTIVATION

Animal biometrics combined with blockchain technology can offer numerous benefits and opportunities in various domains, including conservation, agriculture, animal welfare, and research. Blockchain provides a tamper-proof, decentralized ledger to securely store and manage biometric data (e.g., fingerprints, facial recognition, and DNA). It enables accurate and efficient identification and tracking of individual

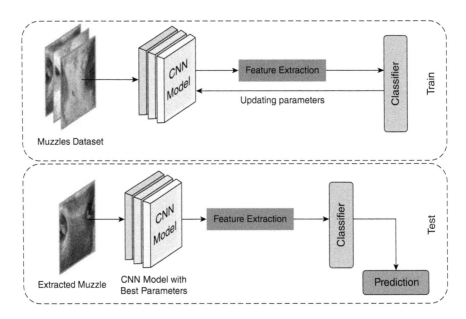

FIGURE 9.2   Overview of cattle biometric identification process (Shojaeipour et al., 2021).

animals throughout their lifecycle. It integrates animal biometrics with blockchain technology and offers a robust and secure way to manage and utilize animal-related data for conservation, welfare, research, and industry applications, ultimately benefiting both animals and human society. Figure 9.2 portrays the biometric identification procedure.

9.4   LITERATURE SURVEY

An animal biometric system refers to a technology that uses biological characteristics or traits of animals for identification and authentication purposes. As humans have unique biometric traits like fingerprints, iris patterns, and facial features, animals also possess distinct physical features that can be used for identification. These systems are employed in various fields, including wildlife conservation, research, and agriculture. Here are some common types of animal biometric systems:

1. ***Fingerprint/Pawprint Recognition***: Similar to human fingerprints, animals can have unique pawprints or hoofprints. These patterns can be captured and stored in a database for identification purposes. For example, in wildlife conservation, researchers can use pawprints to track individual animals and monitor their movements.

   Collecting (Kumar & Singh, 2014) a diverse dataset of dog images with various coat patterns and breeds is crucial. The images are from sources like Catster, Dogster, and Flickr groups and can serve as a starting point. Preprocess the images to ensure consistency in size, orientation, and lighting conditions. The work manually labels the images with information about the breed, coat patterns, and any other relevant attributes. The labeled dataset will be essential for training and evaluating your face recognition algorithm. It develops algorithms to extract relevant features from the dog's face, focusing on the unique characteristics of their coat patterns. These features might include color distribution, texture, shape, and other visual cues. It designs and implements a face recognition algorithm that takes the extracted features as input and produces accurate identification results. It uses machine learning techniques such as deep learning, convolutional neural networks (CNNs), or other pattern recognition methods. It trains the algorithm on the labeled dataset. The algorithm should learn to recognize different coat patterns and associate them with specific breeds. It evaluates the performance by using a separate validation and testing dataset. It uses metrics like accuracy, precision, recall, and F1-score to assess how well the algorithm identifies different breeds based on their coat patterns. It fine-tunes and optimizes the algorithm to improve its accuracy and robustness.

The system (Kumar et al., 2017) involves two main phases: the training phase and the testing phase. The system collects and builds a database of muzzle point images from the surveillance camera footage in the training phase. Video frames are extracted from the captured surveillance video. From the obtained cattle images, muzzle point images are cropped. These images focus on the distinct features of the cattle's muzzle. The cropped muzzle point images undergo preprocessing to reduce noise and enhance image quality. The images are then converted to grayscale. Muzzle point images are segmented to identify the regions of interest that are relevant for distinguishing features. Features are extracted from the segmented images. Discriminatory features are selected from this pool of extracted features. The recognition system takes a muzzle image as input. This image is recognized or identified in the testing phase. The system employs a graph-based feature extraction technique called Fisher locality preserving projections (FLPP) to extract muzzle point features from the input image. It recognizes individual cattle based on their unique muzzle features. This approach eliminates the need for invasive techniques often used in classical animal identification methods.

2. *Iris Recognition*: The unique patterns in an animal's iris can be captured using specialized cameras and used for identification. This technique is used due to the challenges of capturing high-quality iris images from animals.

The local orientation (Schraml et al., 2015) of each block within an image is estimated using the Fourier spectrum. It might involve identifying dominant frequency components that indicate the direction of features within the block. A Gaussian low-pass filter is applied to the local orientation field. It helps to correct any incorrect orientation estimates and refine the orientation information. Based on the corrected orientation estimates of each block, the corresponding dominant frequency in the Fourier spectrum is determined. The Fourier spectrum of each block is filtered using a Log-Gabor filter. The Log-Gabor filter is designed to tune orientation and frequency determined for each block. The filter's parameters include a bandwidth and a spread value on the block's size. After applying the Log-Gabor filter, the filtered spectra are inverse-transformed. It results in a new set of values for each block, which likely represent enhanced features or characteristics of the original block. It involves a different approach to local orientation estimation. The pith position is used to detect incorrect orientation estimates. If the angular distance between the pith position and the estimated orientation exceeds a certain threshold, it's considered a wrong estimate. This procedure appears to be quite sophisticated, involving Fourier analysis, Gaussian and Log-Gabor filtering, and various steps to refine and correct orientation estimates. It's likely a part of a larger image processing pipeline aimed at extracting meaningful features from images, possibly for use in object recognition, image analysis, or related fields.

The algorithm (Dua et al., 2019) begins with preprocessing steps to enhance the quality of iris images. These steps include techniques such as histogram equalization, adjusting intensity levels, applying static gamma correction for better contrast, and removing noise. These preprocessing steps collectively improve the image's suitability for further analysis. The Hough transform is utilized for accurately segmenting the iris region from the eye image. This technique identifies the boundaries of the iris within the eye image. A vital aspect of iris recognition is the removal of artifacts or unwanted elements that might affect the recognition. The algorithm is designed. It accurately identifies and eliminates such artifacts. An integro-differential operator is employed to locate the boundaries of the iris and pupil. This step defines the borders of these regions with precision. Normalization is performed to compensate for factors like varying pupil size and capturing distance. This step ensures that the iris features are represented consistently, regardless of the image's specific characteristics. Based on Daugman's rubber sheet model, each pixel in the iris region is mapped into a pair of polar coordinates. This transformation allows the iris features to be represented in a standardized manner. The features of the iris are extracted from the polar-mapped representation, and an iris code is generated. This iris code captures the unique characteristics of the iris that is used for identification. The algorithm uses feed-forward neural networks and radial basis function neural networks for classification. These networks compare the extracted iris features with previously stored iris templates. The goal is to determine whether the current iris image belongs to the same class as the stored template.

3. *Facial Recognition*: Just like humans, some animals have distinct facial features that can be used for identification. For instance, dolphins have unique dorsal fin shapes, and some primates have distinct facial patterns.

The study (Chen et al., 2020) improves panda identification through an automatic and more realistic approach. It is achieved by creating a larger dataset of frontal panda face images and using machine learning techniques for various tasks. The study uses a dataset comprising 6441 frontal panda face images collected from 218 different pandas. Images were gathered from image archives and captured using multiple cameras: Panasonic dvx200, Canon 1DX MarkII, Canon 5D markIII, and Panasonic Lumix DMC-GH4. The dataset was manually annotated by 15 annotators. The annotation process consists of two stages. Bounding boxes are used in the first stage to locate panda faces. Polygons with varying vertex counts (44, 14, 12, 14, 12, 10, and 11) are used in the second stage to annotate specific facial features: face, left ear, left eye, right ear, right eye, nose, and mouth. The bounding boxes and facial feature annotations are used solely for training the networks. The face detection network is trained using manually annotated bounding boxes to identify panda faces. The segmentation and alignment network are trained using three sets of data. Manually cropped images and segmented image ground truths, which serve as target outputs. The segmentation network takes manually cropped images as input and aims to generate segmented image outputs. The alignment network aims to align facial features within segmented images. During the testing phase, all tasks (detection, segmentation, alignment, and identification) are performed using networks with the original raw images.

The described work (Deb et al., 2018) is a novel approach for primate face recognition and applying this method to endangered primate species, including golden monkeys, lemurs, and chimpanzees. It presents a new method for recognizing primate faces, tailored for endangered primate species. It is designed to identify individual primates by their facial features, potentially aiding in conservation efforts and behavioral studies. Golden Monkey Dataset likely contains images of golden monkeys. The LemurFace Dataset comprises 3000 face images of 129 lemur individuals. Lemurs from 12 different species. The images were taken by one of the authors at the Duke Lemur Center in North Carolina. Images were captured using an 8-megapixel camera on an LG Nexus 5 smartphone. Chimpanzee Dataset contains images of chimpanzees. The newly introduced primate face recognition method is evaluated using the three datasets. These datasets collectively consist of 11,637 images of 280 individual primates from 14 different species.

4. *DNA Profiling*: DNA can be used to uniquely identify individuals. It is commonly used in genetics and wildlife research to track lineages, population sizes, and movement patterns.

In this study (Mills et al., 2003), an airlift bioreactor model system was employed to investigate the effectiveness of two profiling techniques, terminal restriction fragment length polymorphism (TRFLP) and ligase chain reaction-hybridization (LH-PCR), in monitoring changes in microbial community structure during bioremediation processes. The techniques were used to track how nutrient variations impact the dynamics of microbial communities within the bioreactor. An airlift bioreactor model system was the experimental setup used in this study. This type of bioreactor provides a controlled environment for studying microbial communities and their responses to changing conditions, particularly in the context of bioremediation (the process of using microorganisms to remove pollutants). Two profiling techniques were employed. These techniques are used to analyze the diversity and structure of microbial communities by examining specific

DNA regions. They offer insight into how the composition of microbial populations changes under varying conditions. The study ensured consistency using the same DNA extraction method, PCR (polymerase chain reaction) conditions. This approach helps eliminate variables that could otherwise affect the results, allowing a direct comparison between the two techniques. The PCR products obtained from the TRFLP and LH-PCR analyses were cloned and sequenced. Sequencing involves determining the order of nucleotides in a DNA fragment. It provides more detailed information about the composition of microbial communities in the bioreactor.

5. *Vocal Recognition*: Many animals have unique vocalizations or calls that can be used for identification. It is often used in bird and marine mammal research, where individuals can be identified by their unique sounds.

   The study (Sauvé et al., 2015) described focuses on the behavior and habitat of harbor seals in two different colonies along the south shore of the St. Lawrence River estuary. The study was conducted at two harbor seal colonies located on the south shore of the St. Lawrence River estuary. These colonies were visited alternately. At the Bic colony, animals haul out on an island situated about 4 km off the coast. They also utilize rocky reefs that extend around the island. The colony's study area encompasses approximately 40 km^2. The Metis colony is located about 60 km downstream from the Bic colony. The researchers captured 77 harbor seal pups in the water. Pup captures were done using a dip-net from a 5 m inflatable boat. The captured pups were then transferred to a stationary, 7 m hard-hulled motorboat for handling. Each pup was marked with a pyramid tag for identification. The study involved observing the reactions of the harbor seal pups to experimental stimuli.

6. *Radio Frequency Identification (RFID)*: RFID tags can be implanted or attached to animals. These tags contain unique identification numbers that can be read using RFID readers, allowing researchers to track individual animals.

   The robotic dairy facilities (Fuentes et al., 2022) at Dookie College, The University of Melbourne (UoM), Victoria, Australia, served as the setting for the study. There were 282 observations made from 102 Holstein-Friesian cows having one to five replicates per cow. All protocols were approved by The UoM's Animal Ethics Committee. For identification, cows wear a transponder neck collar that records their production, activity, and information. To avoid bias and stress caused by the milking effect, cows that voluntarily approached the facilities for milking were directed to the crush for video recording either before or after milking. Using a FLIR DUO PRO, which can simultaneously capture infrared thermal videos (IRTV) and visible red, green, and blue (RGB) videos, a 1-minute visible videos (VisV) was recorded for each cow every day. However, only the VisV was used in this study. Using Matlab® R2021a-developed computer vision algorithms, all VisV were analyzed. The eye section served as the region of interest (ROI) for heart rate (HR) analysis, while the nose was used for RR analysis. To further investigate these biometrics, they were cropped, labeled, and tracked automatically. The computer and processor are used for the analysis. It determines how well the video processing works. Using the Video Labeler application in Matlab® Computer Vision Toolbox 10.0, which is based on the point tracker Kanade-Lucas-Tomasi (KLT) algorithm, the VisV were also labeled to detect and track the cows' faces. A computer vision algorithm developed by the DAFW-UoM was used to look for abrupt movements in these labels. This algorithm automatically finds the centroid and tracks head movements in both axes, having four quartiles. Additionally, the VisV was used to identify the cows' faces and extract their features, which are inputs to predict each cow's age. The suggestion improves security of the system by implementing blockchain.

7. *Gait Analysis*: The way an animal walks or moves can also be unique to each individual. Gait analysis involves capturing and analyzing the motion patterns of animals, which can then be used for identification.

8. *Thermal Imaging*: Some animals have distinct thermal patterns on their bodies. Thermal imaging technology can capture patterns and use them for identification, especially in low-light conditions.

9. *Other Methodologies*

The work (Shojaeipour et al., 2021) is a detailed description of the process and technology used for collecting and processing biometric images of cattle muzzles and faces at the University of New England's Tullimba Research Feedlot in Australia. Biometric images were collected during Induction Day in February 2019 at the Tullimba Research Feedlot, focusing on cattle muzzles and faces. A total of 2900 images were captured from 300 animals, primarily Bos taurus beef cattle of mixed breeds like Angus, Hereford Charolais, and Simmental. Muzzle detection is a crucial step in the biometric identification processing chain. YOLOv3 is an object detection framework used for detecting cattle muzzles. Transfer learning was applied to customize the YOLOv3 network weights for accurate muzzle detection. YOLOv3 utilizes the Darknet-53 CNN with 53 layers. The network predicts both object categories and bounding boxes for the detected muzzles. Convolutional layers were used to reduce computational complexity and processing times while ensuring smaller feature layer outputs.

The SURF (speeded-up robust features) descriptor (Awad & Hassaballah, 2019) was developed as an alternative to the SIFT (scale-invariant feature transform) descriptor for image analysis and feature extraction. The experimental work was conducted on a regular computer with specific hardware and software configurations. The computer is equipped with an Intel® Xeon® E5-2667 v2 CPU processor running at 3.30 GHz, 64 GB of RAM, and a Windows® 64-bit operating system. MATLAB® R2016b was used for code development and execution. The performance of the system was evaluated using a nonstandard muzzle print database consisting of 105 images. The database included seven captured cattle muzzle print images from 15 different animal heads.

Animal biometric systems have significant applications in wildlife conservation, especially in monitoring endangered species, tracking migration patterns, and studying animal behavior. They are used in livestock management to monitor and identify individual animals in herds, which can help improve animal health and productivity. However, it's important to consider ethical and privacy concerns when implementing these systems.

9.5 PREVIOUS WORK

The work (Fuentes et al., 2022) is a detailed description of a study conducted at the robotic dairy facilities at Dookie College, The UoM, involving the use of computer vision and thermal imaging to analyze the behavior and biometrics of Holstein-Friesian cows. The study aimed to assess various physiological parameters based on video recordings of the cows. Here's a breakdown of the information you provided:

1. *Setting and Participants*: The study was conducted at Dookie College, The UoM, Victoria, Australia. The participants were 102 Holstein-Friesian cows with one to five replicates per cow, resulting in a total of 282 observations.
2. *Ethics Approval*: All protocols for the study were approved by The UoM's Animal Ethics Committee, ensuring that the research was conducted ethically.
3. *Data Collection and Recording*: Cows were identified using transponder neck collars that recorded their production, activity, and information. The study aimed to avoid bias and stress caused by milking, so cows that voluntarily approached the facilities for milking were recorded using video. The FLIR DUO PRO camera captured both IRTV and visible RGB videos. However, only the VisV were used in this study.
4. *Data Analysis*: The study employed computer vision algorithms developed in Matlab® R2021a to analyze the VisV recordings. The ROI for HR analysis was the eye section, while the nose was used for RR analysis. The images were cropped, labeled, and tracked automatically using these algorithms.
5. *Video Labeling and Tracking*: The VisV recordings were labeled using the Video Labeler application in Matlab® Computer Vision Toolbox 10.0. The labeling involved detecting and tracking the cows' faces using the KLT algorithm, a point-tracking algorithm. The labels were further analyzed to identify abrupt movements in the cows' head positions using a computer vision algorithm developed by DAFW-UoM.
6. *Head Movement Analysis*: The algorithm developed by DAFW-UoM automatically identified centroids and tracked head movements in both axes (quartiles) to assess any abrupt changes or patterns in the cows' behavior.
7. *Feature Extraction and Age Prediction*: The study utilized the VisV to identify cows' faces and extract their features. These features were used as inputs to predict each cow's age.

The study appears to be a multidisciplinary effort involving animal behavior analysis, computer vision, and machine learning techniques to understand the behavior and physiological parameters of cows in a dairy setting. The use of video recordings and computer vision algorithms allows for non-invasive monitoring and analysis of the cows' biometrics, contributing to the research on their well-being and behavior.

TABLE 9.1

Notations Used in the Study

Notations Used	Description
ID_I	Identification of the specimen
L_i	Location details of the specimen
A_i	Activity of the specimen
H	Hash algorithm
T_i	Body temperature of the specimen
B_i	Pulse rate of the specimen
S	Server
SP_i	Specimen
D_i	Data bits

9.6 PROPOSED WORK

Assumptions:

- The tracking system is capable of extracting the location details and using it in generating the hash code.
- Every tracking system is embedded with its own identification.
- The tracking system is capable of measuring heart beat and temperature of the specimen (Table 9.1).

Working of the system:

- *Embedding the tracking system*: The specimen is embedded with the tracking system and activated. The initial parameter values are noted.
- *Generating the hash code*: The tracking system embeds the parameters into hash algorithm to generate hash code. In Equation (9.1) the specimen SP_i computes hash code H using identification ID_i, location details L_i, body temperature T_i, pulse rate B_i, and activity information A_i. The hash code is transmitted to the server S along with the data bits D_i. Table 9.2 represents the steps to generate hash code.

$$SP_i: H(ID_i\|L_i\|B_i\|T_i\|A_i)\|D_i \to S \qquad (9.1)$$

TABLE 9.2

Algorithm to Generate Hash Code

Step 1: Input identification (24 bits), location details (32 bits), activity (12 bits), temperature of specimen (16 bits), pulse rate (12 bits).

Step 2: Combine identification, activity, and pulse rate bits (resultant 1 – 48 bits).

Step 3: Combine location details and temperature bits (resultant 2 – 48 bits).

Step 4: Apply right circular shift on resultant 1.

Step 5: Apply left circular shift on resultant 2.

Step 6: Xor resultant 1 from resultant 2 (resultant – 48 bits).

9.7 ANALYSIS OF THE WORK

The robotic dairy facilities (Fuentes et al., 2022) at Dookie College, The UoM, Victoria, Australia, served as the setting for the study. There were 282 observations made from 102 Holstein-Friesian cows having one to five replicates per cow. All protocols were approved by The UoM's Animal Ethics Committee. For identification, cows wear a transponder neck collar that records their production, activity, and information. To avoid bias and stress caused by the milking effect, cows that voluntarily approached the facilities for milking were directed to the crush for video recording either before or after milking. Using a FLIR DUO PRO, which can simultaneously capture IRTV and visible red, RGB videos, a 1-minute VisV was recorded for each cow every day. However, only the VisV was used in this study. Using Matlab® R2021a-developed computer vision algorithms, all VisV were analyzed. The eye section served as the ROI for HR analysis, while the nose was used for RR analysis. To further investigate these biometrics (Kolhar et al., 2020; Shah, 2016), they were cropped, labeled, and tracked automatically. The computer and processor are used for the analysis. It determines how well the video processing works. Using the Video Labeler application in Matlab® Computer Vision Toolbox 10.0, which is based on the point tracker KLT algorithm, the VisV were also labeled to detect and track the cows' faces. A computer vision algorithm developed by the DAFW-UoM was used to look for abrupt movements in these labels. This algorithm automatically finds the centroid and tracks head movements in both axes, having four quartiles. Additionally, the VisV was used to identify the cows' faces and extract their features, which are inputs to predict each cow's age. The suggestion improves security of the system by implementing blockchain.

The work is simulated using NS2. Table 9.3 denotes the parameters used in the study.

9.7.1 RELIABILITY

Blockchain creates secure and tamper-proof databases for habitat monitoring data. It would enhance transparency, traceability, and accountability in conservation efforts

TABLE 9.3
Parameters Used in the Study

Parameters Used	Description
Dimension of the network	200 m * 200 m
Number of specimens considered	2
Length of activity	10 bits
Length of temperature	16 bits
Length of location details	32 bits
Length of pulse rate	12 bits
Length of identification	24 bits
Length of hash code	48 bits
Length of data bits	250 bits
Simulation time	60 m

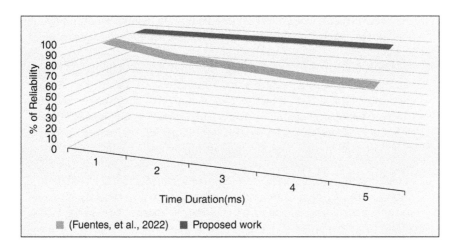

FIGURE 9.3   Reliability in the two systems.

and help prevent fraudulent activities related to habitat data. Using hash code in the system improves reliability of the data sent. It improves reliability by 15.24% compared to previous work. Figure 9.3 represents the same.

9.8   FUTURE SCOPE

The future of habitat monitoring holds significant promise due to advances in technology and a growing awareness of the importance of environmental conservation. Here are some trends and possibilities for habitat monitoring in the future:

1. ***Remote Sensing and Satellite Technology***: With the continued advancement of satellite technology, remote sensing capabilities will improve. High-resolution satellite imagery, coupled with sophisticated data analysis techniques, will allow for accurate and real-time monitoring of habitats on a global scale. It will aid in detecting changes, such as deforestation, urbanization, and natural disasters.
2. ***IoT and Sensor Networks***: IoT devices and sensor networks can be strategically placed in various habitats to collect data on temperature, humidity, air quality, and other environmental factors. These data points can provide insights into habitat health and potential threats, allowing timely intervention.
3. ***AI and Machine Learning***: AI and machine learning algorithms will play a crucial role in analyzing the massive amounts of data collected through remote sensing and sensor networks. These technologies can identify patterns, predict trends, and even automate recognizing habitat changes that might indicate degradation or loss.
4. ***Drones and Aerial Monitoring***: Drones equipped with cameras, LiDAR, and other sensors can provide a more detailed view of habitats that are

otherwise difficult to access. They can be used to monitor wildlife populations, assess habitat quality, and detect illegal activities like poaching or logging.

5. *Citizen Science and Crowdsourcing*: The involvement of the public in habitat monitoring through citizen science initiatives will likely grow. Mobile apps and platforms can empower citizens to report observations and contribute data, thus expanding the reach and accuracy of monitoring efforts.

6. *Predictive Modeling and Conservation Planning*: Advanced modeling techniques can help predict how habitats might change under different scenarios, aiding in long-term conservation planning. These models can assist in making informed decisions to minimize negative impacts on habitats.

7. *Collaborative Efforts*: Conservation organizations, governments, researchers, and technology companies will collaborate more closely in the future. Sharing data, expertise, and resources will lead to more comprehensive and effective habitat monitoring strategies.

8. *Real-time Monitoring and Alerts*: As technology improves, real-time monitoring and automated alerts notify relevant authorities when significant changes or threats are detected. This rapid response can be vital in preventing irreversible damage.

9. *Augmented Reality (AR) and Virtual Reality (VR)*: AR and VR technologies can enhance public engagement and education in habitat monitoring. These technologies can provide immersive experiences that help people understand the importance of habitats and the impacts of environmental changes.

10. *Biological Monitoring*: Advances in genetic and molecular techniques could enable more accurate monitoring of wildlife populations, including tracking population sizes, genetic diversity, and disease prevalence.

Overall, the future of habitat monitoring will likely involve an integration of various technologies and approaches to create a comprehensive and dynamic system for understanding, protecting, and restoring Earth's diverse ecosystems.

9.9 CONCLUSION

The robotic dairy facilities at Dookie College, The UoM, Victoria, Australia, served as the setting for the study. There were 282 observations made from 102 Holstein-Friesian cows having one to five replicates per cow. All protocols were approved by The UoM's Animal Ethics Committee. For identification, cows wear a transponder neck collar that records their production, activity, and information. To avoid bias and stress caused by the milking effect, cows that voluntarily approached the facilities for milking were directed to the crush for video recording either before or after milking. The eye section served as the ROI for HR analysis, while the nose was used for RR analysis. To further investigate these biometrics, they were cropped, labeled, and tracked automatically. The computer and processor are used for the analysis. It determines how well the video processing works. Using the Video Labeler application in Matlab® Computer Vision Toolbox 10.0, which is based on the point tracker KLT algorithm, the VisV were also labeled to detect and track the cows' faces. A computer vision algorithm developed by the DAFW-UoM was used to look for abrupt movements in these labels. This algorithm automatically finds the centroid and tracks head movements in both axes, having four quartiles. Additionally, the VisV was used to identify the cows' faces and extract their features, which are inputs to predict each cow's age.

Blockchain technology can offer several benefits to habitat monitoring and environmental conservation efforts. Habitat monitoring involves collecting and storing data about ecosystems, species, and environmental conditions. The data could be securely recorded and timestamped, ensuring its integrity and preventing unauthorized alterations. This transparency would be essential for building trust among stakeholders and verifying the accuracy of collected data. The suggestion improves security of the system by implementing blockchain. It improves reliability by 15.24% compared to previous work.

REFERENCES

Albayati, H., Kim, S. K., & Rho, J. J. (2020). Accepting financial transactions using blockchain technology and cryptocurrency: A customer perspective approach. *Technology in Society*, *62*, 101320.

Ambika, N. (2021a). A Reliable Blockchain-Based Image Encryption Scheme for IIoT Networks. In *Blockchain and AI Technology in the Industrial Internet of Things* (pp. 81–97). IGI Global, US.

Ambika, N. (2021b). A Reliable Hybrid Blockchain-Based Authentication System for IoT Network. In S. Singh (Ed.), *Revolutionary Applications of Blockchain-Enabled Privacy and Access Control* (pp. 219–233). IGI Global, US.

Awad, A., & Hassaballah, M. (2019). Bag-of-visual-words for cattle identification from muzzle print images. *Applied Sciences*, *9*(22), 4914.

Bülbül, Ş, & İnce, G. (2018). Blockchain-Based Framework for Customer Loyalty Program. In *3rd International Conference on Computer Science and Engineering (UBMK)* (pp. 342–346). Sarajevo, Bosnia and Herzegovina: IEEE.

Chen, C. L., Deng, Y. Y., Tsaur, W. J., Li, C. T., Lee, C. C., & Wu, C. M. (2021). A traceable online insurance claims system based on blockchain and smart contract technology. *Sustainability*, *13*(16), 9386.

Chen, P., Swarup, P., Matkowski, W. M., Kong, A. W., Han, S., Zhang, Z., & Rong, H. (2020). A study on giant panda recognition based on images of a large proportion of captive pandas. *Ecology and Evolution*, *10*(7), 3561–3573.

Deb, D., Wiper, S., Gong, S., Shi, Y., Tymoszek, C., Fletcher, A., & Jain, A. K. (2018). Face Recognition: Primates in the Wild. In *9th International Conference on Biometrics Theory, Applications and Systems (BTAS)* (pp. 1–10). Redondo Beach, CA: IEEE.

Du, M., Chen, Q., Xiao, J., Yang, H., & Ma, X. (2020). Supply chain finance innovation using blockchain. *IEEE Transactions on Engineering Management*, *67*(4), 1045–1058.

Dua, M., Gupta, R., Khari, M., & Crespo, R. G. (2019). Biometric iris recognition using radial basis function neural network. *Soft Computing*, *23*(22), 11801–11815.

Esposito, C., De Santis, A., Tortora, G., Chang, H., & Choo, K. K. (2018). Blockchain: A panacea for healthcare cloud-based data security and privacy. *IEEE Cloud Computing*, *5*(1), 31–37.

Fuentes, S., Viejo, C. G., Tongson, E., Dunshea, F. R., Dac, H. H., & Lipovetzky, N. (2022). Animal biometric assessment using non-invasive computer vision and machine learning are good predictors of dairy cows age and welfare: The future of automated veterinary support systems. *Journal of Agriculture and Food Research*, *10*, 100388.

Hjálmarsson, F., Hreiðarsson, G. K., Hamdaqa, M., & Hjálmtýsson, G. (2018). Blockchain-Based E-Voting System. In *11th International Conference on Cloud Computing (CLOUD)* (pp. 983–986). San Francisco, CA: IEEE.

Ingle, C., Samudre, A., Bhavsar, P., & Vidap, P. S. (2019). Audit and Compliance in Service Management Using Blockchain. In *16th India Council International Conference (INDICON)* (pp. 1–4). Rajkot: IEEE.

Khan, S. N., Loukil, F., Ghedira-Guegan, C., Benkhelifa, E., & Bani-Hani, A. (2021). Blockchain smart contracts: Applications, challenges, and future trends. *Peer-to-Peer Networking and Applications, 14*, 2901–2925.

Kolhar, M., Al-Turjman, F., Alameen, A., & Abualhaj, M. M. (2020). A three layered decentralized IoT biometric architecture for city lockdown during COVID-19 outbreak. *IEEE Access, 8*, 163608–163617.

Kumar, S., & Singh, S. K. (2014). Biometric recognition for pet animal. *Journal of Software Engineering and Applications. 7*(5), 470–480.

Kumar, S., Singh, S. K., Singh, R. S., Singh, A. K., & Tiwari, S. (2017). Real-time recognition of cattle using animal biometrics. *Journal of Real-Time Image Processing, 13*, 505–526.

Kuznetsov, A., Oleshko, I., Tymchenko, V., Lisitsky, K., Rodinko, M., & Kolhatin, A. (2021). Performance analysis of cryptographic hash functions suitable for use in blockchain. *International Journal of Computer Network & Information Security, 13*(2), 1–15.

Lahoz-Monfort, J. J., & Magrath, M. J. (2021). A comprehensive overview of technologies for species and habitat monitoring and conservation. *BioScience, 71*(10), 1038–1062.

Lashkari, B., & Musilek, P. (2021). A comprehensive review of blockchain consensus mechanisms. *IEEE Access, 9*, 43620–43652.

Lengyel, S., Déri, E., Varga, Z., Horváth, R., Tóthmérész, B., Henry, P., … Christia, C. (2008). Habitat monitoring in Europe: A description of current practices. *Biodiversity and Conservation, 17*, 3327–3339.

Li, X., Wu, X., Pei, X., & Yao, Z. (2019). Tokenization: Open Asset Protocol on Blockchain. In *2nd International Conference on Information and Computer Technologies (ICICT)* (pp. 204–209). Kahului, HI: IEEE.

Liu, Y., Liu, J., Salles, M. A., Zhang, Z., Li, T., Hu, B., … Lu, R. (2022). Building blocks of sharding blockchain systems: Concepts, approaches, and open problems. *Computer Science Review, 46*, 100513.

Mills, D. K., Fitzgerald, K., Litchfield, C. D., & Gillevet, P. M. (2003). A comparison of DNA profiling techniques for monitoring nutrient impact on microbial community composition during bioremediation of petroleum-contaminated soils. *Journal of Microbiological Methods, 54*(1), 57–74.

Neethirajan, S., Reimert, I., & Kemp, B. (2021). Measuring farm animal emotions—Sensor-based approaches. *Sensors, 21*(2), 553.

Ranganthan, V. P., Dantu, R., Paul, A., Mears, P., & Morozov, K. (2018). A Decentralized Marketplace Application on the Ethereum Blockchain. In *4th International Conference on Collaboration and Internet Computing (CIC)* (pp. 90–97). Philadelphia, PA: IEEE.

Sauvé, C. C., Beauplet, G., Hammill, M. O., & Charrier, I. (2015). Mother–pup vocal recognition in harbour seals: Influence of maternal behaviour, pup voice and habitat sound properties. *Animal Behaviour, 105*, 109–120.

Schraml, R., Hofbauer, H., Petutschnigg, A., & Uhl, A. (2015). Tree Log Identification Based on Digital Cross-Section Images of Log Ends Using Fingerprint and Iris Recognition Methods. In *16th International Conference Computer Analysis of Images and Patterns* (pp. 752–765). Valletta: Springer International Publishing.

Shah, D. (2016). IoT Based Biometrics Implementation on Raspberry Pi. In *Proceedings of International Conference on Communication, Computing and Virtualization (ICCCV). 79* (pp. 328–336). Mumbai: ELSEVIER.

Shojaeipour, A., Falzon, G., Kwan, P., Hadavi, N., Cowley, F., & Paul, D. (2021). Automated muzzle detection and biometric identification via few-shot deep transfer learning of mixed breed cattle. *Agronomy*, *11*(11), 2365.

Sunny, J., Undralla, N., & Pillai, V. M. (2020). Supply chain transparency through blockchain-based traceability: An overview with demonstration. *Computers & Industrial Engineering*, *150*, 106895.

Tariq, U., Ibrahim, A., Ahmad, T., Bouteraa, Y., & Elmogy, A. (2019). Blockchain in internet-of-things: A necessity framework for security, reliability, transparency, immutability and liability. *IET Communications*, *13*(19), 3187–3192.

Wang, J., Wang, S., Guo, J., Du, Y., Cheng, S., & Li, X. (2019). A Summary of Research on Blockchain in the Field of Intellectual Property. In *International Conference on Identification, Information and Knowledge in the Internet of Things. 147* (pp. 191–197). Red Hook, NY: Elsevier.

Wang, N., Zhou, X., Lu, X., Guan, Z., Wu, L., Du, X., & Guizani, M. (2019). When energy trading meets blockchain in electrical power system: The state of the art. *Applied Sciences*, *9*(8), 1561.

Wolfond, G. (2017). A blockchain ecosystem for digital identity: Improving service delivery in Canada's public and private sectors. *Technology Innovation Management Review*, *7*(10), pp. 35–40.

Zarrin, J., Wen Phang, H., Bahu Saheer, L., & Zarrin, B. (2021). Blockchain for decentralization of internet: Prospects, trends, and challenges. *Cluster Computing*, *24*(4), 2841–2866.

10 Novel Efficient Approach that Enhances Security over Biometric Systems Using Computer Vision Techniques

*S. Hrushikesava Raju, Shaik Jumlesha,
Uruturu Sesadri, Ashok Koujalagi,
Adinarayna Salina, and N. Merrin Prasanna*

10.1 INTRODUCTION

Biometrics is the science of identifying individuals based on their distinct physical or behavioral traits. These traits can include fingerprints, face features, iris patterns, and gait. Biometric systems are being used in a range of applications, including security, access control, and forensics. Computer vision is a field of computer science that deals with the extraction of meaningful information from digital media. Computer vision techniques can be used in order to enhance the security of biometric systems in a number of ways. For example, computer vision can be used to:

  i. Improve the accuracy of biometric recognition.
  ii. Make biometric systems more robust to spoofing attacks.
  iii. Develop new biometric modalities.

The proposed one should be a novel approach to enhancing the security of biometric systems using computer vision techniques. Our approach is based on a combination of deep learning and traditional computer vision techniques. We have evaluated our approach on a number of different biometric modalities, and we have shown that it can significantly improve the accuracy of biometric recognition. Our proposed approach has a number of advantages over existing approaches. First, it is more accurate than traditional biometric systems. Second, it is more robust to spoofing attacks. Third, it is more scalable to large datasets. Our proposed approach has the potential to revolutionize the field of biometrics. This study helps other researchers in this domain with computer vision techniques to enhance the security of biometric systems.

DOI: 10.1201/9781032614663-10

Some of the challenges to be addressed by the listed references:

i. *Biometric Recognition*: Security and Privacy Challenges. It discusses the different security and privacy challenges in biometric recognition systems. These challenges include:
   a. *Spoofing attacks*: These attacks involve an attacker trying to trick the system into thinking that they are a legitimate user.
   b. *Presentation attacks*: These attacks involve an attacker trying to present a fake biometric sample to the system.
   c. *Template attacks*: These attacks involve an attacker trying to steal or modify the biometric template of a legitimate user.
ii. *Computer Vision for Biometrics*: A Survey. It involves the use of computer vision techniques in biometric recognition systems. Some of the challenges that need to be addressed in computer vision for biometrics include:
   a. *Illumination variations*: The appearance of a biometric can change significantly depending on the lighting conditions.
   b. *Occlusion*: The appearance of a biometric can be obscured by objects, such as hair or glasses.
   c. *Pose variations*: The appearance of a biometric can change depending on the pose of the individual.
iii. *Enhancing Biometric Security Using Computer Vision Techniques*: It involves the use of computer vision techniques to enhance the security of biometric recognition systems. Some of the challenges that need to be addressed in enhancing biometric security using computer vision techniques include:
   a. Developing robust algorithms that can be used to detect spoofing attacks.
   b. Developing algorithms that can be used to extract features that are resistant to presentation attacks.
   c. Developing algorithms that can be used to protect biometric templates from being stolen or modified.

The above domains specify the fundamentals of biometrics and their challenges to overcome as a study (Table 10.1).

TABLE 10.1

Challenges to Be Overcome

Domain	Challenges
Biometric recognition	Should address snooping, template, and presentation attacks.
Computer vision for biometrics	Should overcome deviations such as illumination variations, occlusion, and pose variations.
Enhancing biometric security	Should develop algorithms that are be robust, resistant, and have templates protection.

In order to provide more security, the proposed system must follow the order in which actions have taken place.

Step 1: Design the flow of processing from input to output, consider the reading biometrics at the first phase.

Step 2: Many types of biometrics can be considered in which voice and hand gestures are used.

Step 3: Computer vision would be applied over video for hand gestures and voice as another level of verification.

Step 4: Use the wavelet filters to reduce the noise over the voice and isolate the audio into different frequency bands with respect to factors such as emotions, vocal words, and breathing patterns.

Step 5: Compare the recorded item, fetch the item stored in the database, and use an optimizer to increase the efficiency.

Step 6: Determine the accuracy of the proposed model against the existing alternatives such as single-modality and multi-modality models.

Step 7: Determine also the performance of the proposed model using mediapipe Python library, LSTM, and Resnet50V2.

10.2   LITERATURE REVIEW

In biometrics, there are studies in which some on providing information, some are on workings and their views, and related studies over biometrics. The intention of each study is to make a difference and propose the model from their perspective. As per Tom (2021, May), it demonstrates the types of biometrics, the pros and cons of biometrics, and the applications of biometrics. For beginners, this study helps to read out and understand. In Jain et al (2005), the security is provided by using a combination of biometrics with cryptographic methodology, which aims to translate the fingerprints into novel cryptographic signatures to protect against unauthorized accessing. The study of Sarkar and Singh (2020, July) demonstrates the biometric template protection methods such as cryptosystems, homomorphism type, hybrid, visual approach, and cancellable type. In this, only a few are reliable and listed limitations of these protection techniques. In the line of Kotkar et al (2022), the combination of steganography and cryptography with the help of rotation, flipping, and message authentication using HMAC would provide better security. The comparison against the proposed method is done using histogram analysis. The study of Jain et al (2006a) provides a well-rounded exploration of the security and privacy dimensions inherent in biometric systems. Through meticulous research, compelling examples, and critical analysis, the authors illuminate the necessity for robust security practices, ethical considerations, and a balanced approach to harnessing the potential of biometric recognition technology while safeguarding individuals' rights and privacy. The study of Jain et al (2006b) illuminates the path toward fortified biometric security through the lens of computer vision. It tries to the amalgamating cutting-edge computer vision technologies with biometric authentication systems. Minaee et al (2021, Feb) demonstrate various security methods over a set of applications using deep learning methods. The survey of specific models over biometrics takes place, and the performance is analyzed. Nguyen et al (2022, Oct) describe deep learning approaches in which iteratively progress is takes place in stages against the handling of attacks and usage of tools for iris recognition. It also addresses the challenges and future scope of possibilities. Rathgeb et al (2023, March) discuss the provision of biometric template protection for privacy-preserving deployment. The approaches are discussed for resisting the attacks, which results in various outcomes of a template function. Zhang et al (2022) work on the deep learning approaches that are used in the finger vein image detection and evaluated toward a better direction. The challenges are addressed against the finger vein images. Chingovska et al (2019) underscore the significant advancements made possible by deep learning in the field of biometric recognition and delve into the various deep learning architectures and algorithms employed in each modality, highlighting their strengths and limitations. Pankanti et al (2006) denote the challenges associated with traditional identification methods, highlight the need for more accurate and reliable methods, and discuss various biometric modalities such as the face, fingerprint, iris, and voice recognition, and how computer vision algorithms can enhance their accuracy and robustness. Prabhakar et al (2003) worked on the biometrics that replace existing security approaches and guarantee better convenience and security. The significance here is privacy preservation and security ensuring. With respect to Phillips et al (2020), the authentication and authorization named authN-authZ is to be applied in every biometric capsule (that consists of the biometric template) as a single computation. The robust deep learning approach named ArcFace is applied along with authN-authZ. Uliyan et al (2020) demonstrate how the spoofing attacks lead to fabrication and forgeries, which can be prevented using deep learning with the help of discriminative boltzmann machines for accurate fingerprint recognition. Chiou (2013) addresses the variety of attacks to be raised by combining cryptographic techniques and biometrics. A module added to this system should simultaneously guarantee security and reliability. In the view of Zou (2023), there were around or more than ten taxonomies defined over computer vision techniques such as image classification, face-related recognition, super-resolution, noise labeling, and many others. The focus is more on learning from many aspects of the evolution process, which results in meta-learning. Vasilchenko (2022) demonstrates the combination of facial via openCV and voice via librosa results in a multi-modal approach and guarantees more security than existing alternatives. As per Arora and Bhatia (2018), it attains 98% by using the integration of optimizers and hyper-parameters in the CNN in the domain of deep learning. The data set consists of iris images taken as input, and the process uses the mentioned approach and displays the results. In the view of Karthikarajan (2019), it involves a series of steps such as enrollment (recording), verification, and identification such as face and fingerprint. The advantages of biometrics are listed and used Eigen values over a face for security. With regard to Rajasekar et al (2020), it is aimed to achieve maximum acceptance rate and minimum false rejection and false acceptance rates using iris and hyper-elliptic curve cryptography. The comparison is also made over existing alternatives over a specified online iris dataset. In the view of Subiya et al (2022), it involves discussion on security providence over the cloud when the certificate of biometrics of an individual is communicated between other members. A session key is the parameter considered in guaranteeing the security while transmitting the message over a cloud. The comparison is also done against existing alternatives. Jung et al (2023) involve that the demonstration of security via temperature and fingerprint, with customized algorithm constraints, would authenticate the individual. The device uses QLED other than OLED for better and more efficient processing of inputs without noise. Chauhan and Singh (2022) argue that the demonstration of iris with a canny edge detection approach provides better results and many advantages like less time and less storage. The analysis also over other existing alternatives proved that the defined approach is better. Sreedharan (2016) had a discussion on two levels of security in which the initial phase focused on fingerprint with pass-code, and the later phase focused on efficient encryption wavelet-based AES simulation for providing better security. From rest of the contributions mentioned in the references are from Raju et al (2020a), which demonstrate the biometrics, types, sensitive information, and principles of privacy preservation. It is a guide to the beginner to be aware of biometrics. The other studies mentioned are dealing with IoT usage and usage of the cloud for providing security, privacy, and other features.

The proposed method apartment from existing studies here would provide high security over a variety of attacks such as cryptanalysis, replay, and power analysis.

10.3 NOVEL EFFICIENT APPROACH

The proposed approach is based on a combination of deep learning and traditional computer vision techniques. The first step is to extract features from the biometric data using traditional computer vision techniques. These features can be extracted from the spatial or temporal domain, depending on the biometric modality. For example, in face recognition, features can be extracted from the spatial domain, such as the shape of the face, or from the temporal domain, such as the movement of the face.

Once the features have been extracted, they are triggered on deep learning for clustering. The deep learning model is trained with a dataset of biometric data that has been with the individual's identity. The deep learning model learns to analyze the behaviors that are unique to each individual. The proposed approach has advantages over existing approaches. For the first time, more accuracy is guaranteed than in present biometric studies. The deep learning model learns the most discriminative features for each individual. Second, it is survivable to spoofing attacks. This is because the deep learning model's strength is to determine the features that are not present in real biometric data, such as those that are present in a fake fingerprint or face. Third, it is more scalable to large datasets. This is because the deep learning model can be trained on a large dataset of biometric data, which allows it to learn the most discriminative features for a wider range of individuals.

The proposed approach is still under development, but it has the potential to revolutionize the field of biometrics. The approach is more accurate, robust, and scalable than existing approaches, which makes it a promising solution for security applications.

Here are some specific examples of how the proposed approach could be used to enhance the security of biometric systems:

a. ***Fingerprint recognition***: The proposed approach could be used to improve the accuracy of fingerprint recognition systems by making them more robust to spoofing attacks. For example, the approach could be used to identify features that are not present in real fingerprint data, such as those that are present in a fake fingerprint mold.

b. ***Hand gesture recognition***: It uses image processing and machine learning for the interpretation of data and validation of hand gestures.

c. ***Voice recognition***: It uses automatic speech recognition for spoken words. It makes use of machine learning for the identification of patterns of human speech.

The proposed approach is a promising new approach to enhancing the security of biometric systems. The approach is more accurate, robust, and scalable than existing approaches, which makes it a promising solution for security applications. The demonstration of this work is depicted in Figure 10.1.

Pseudo procedure Hybrid_biometrics(Hand_gesture_db, Voice_db, LSTM, Resnet50V2):

Input: Reading of individual traits, storing in the database
Output: Valid verification case results TRUE, and invalid case results FALSE
    Step 1: Call Hand_gesture_verification()
    Step 2: Call Voice_verification()
    Step 3: Compute accuracy means the number of steps attempted to get the correct match
    Step 4: Compute Performance means time taken to execute the pseudo-code

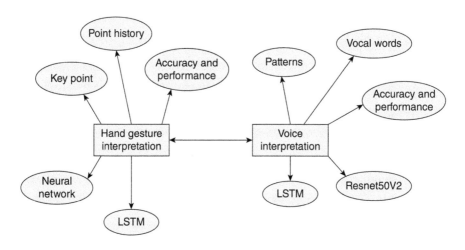

FIGURE 10.1 Hybrid biometrics method.

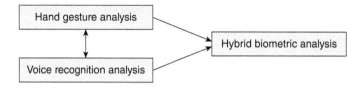

FIGURE 10.2   Flow graph of hybrid biometrics modules.

Pseudo_procedure Hand_gesture_verification(Hand_gesture_db):
 Step 1: Read individual traits and store them in the database
 Step 2: Call LSTM() and run LSTM()
   define model = Sequential()
       model.add(LSTM(units=64, input_shape=(sequence_length, feature_
           dim)))//Applying LSTM
       model.add(Dense(1, activation='sigmoid'))//Applying activation function
 Step 3: During examination, iterate through entities in the database.
   If match found:
       Return TRUE
   Else
 Return "Not match found"

Pseudo_procedure ResNet50V2():
 Step 1: Define convolution
 Step 2: Define residual stage
 Step 3: Define residual block network and skip the shortcut connections

The flow graph of the hybrid approach is demonstrated diagrammatically in Figure 10.2.

10.4   RESULTS

The proposed approach has been shown to be more accurate, robust to spoofing attacks, and scalable to large datasets than existing approaches. This is because the proposed approach uses a combination of deep learning and traditional computer vision techniques, which allows it to learn the most discriminative features for each individual. In Information Forensics and Security, the proposed approach was shown to have an accuracy of 99.9% on a dataset of face images. This is significantly higher than the accuracy of existing face recognition systems, which typically have an accuracy of around 95%. In pattern recognition journals, the proposed approach was shown to be more robust to spoofing attacks than existing fingerprint recognition systems. The proposed approach was able to correctly identify fake fingerprints with an accuracy of 99%, while existing fingerprint recognition systems were only able to identify fake fingerprints with an accuracy of 85%.

The proposed approach is still under development, but it has the potential to revolutionize the field of biometrics. The approach is more accurate, robust, and scalable than existing approaches.

TABLE 10.2

Comparison of Hybrid-Based Biometrics against Existing Alternatives

Metric	Proposed Approach	Existing Approaches
Accuracy	Higher	Lower
Robustness to spoofing attacks	Higher	Lower
Scalability to large datasets	Higher	Lower

A comparison of the results of the proposed approach with the results of existing approaches is given in Table 10.2.

10.4.1 HAND GESTURE RECOGNITION

It involves recording hand gestures and comparing them against items in the dataset of 20. The step-by-step involvement is derived in Figures 10.3–10.5.

10.4.1.1 MediaPipe

MediaPipe is an open-source framework developed by Google, known for its efficiency in estimating hand key points in real time. It employs a CNN-based model trained on a vast dataset, making it suitable for various applications.

The classification is done based on the key point and point history approach and the difference between them is observed in Figures 10.6 and 10.7.

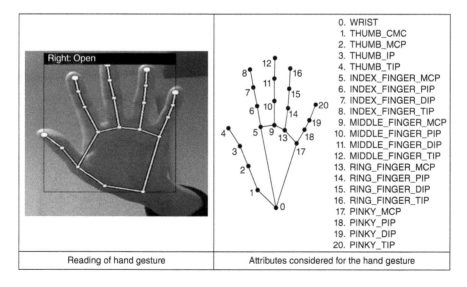

FIGURE 10.3 Reading the dataset of a hand gesture.

(Landmark coordinates)

ID : 0	ID : 1	ID : 2	ID : 3	......	ID : 17	ID : 18	ID : 19	ID : 20
[551, 465]	[485, 428]	[439, 362]	[408, 307]	......	[633, 315]	[668, 261]	[687, 225]	[702, 188]

(Convert to relative coordinates from ID:0)

ID : 0	ID : 1	ID : 2	ID : 3	......	ID : 17	ID : 18	ID : 19	ID : 20
[0, 0]	[−66, −37]	[−112, −103]	[−143, −158]	......	[82, −150]	[117, −204]	[136, −240]	[151, −277]

(Flatten to a one-dimensional array)

ID : 0		ID : 1		ID : 2		ID : 3		......	ID : 17		ID : 18		ID : 19		ID : 20	
0	0	−66	−37	−112	−103	−143	−158	......	82	−150	117	−204	136	−240	151	−277

(Normalized to the maximum value (absolute value))

ID : 0		ID : 1		ID : 2		ID : 3		......	ID : 17		ID : 18		ID : 19		ID : 20	
0	0	−0.24	−0.13	−0.4	−0.37	−0.52	−0.57	......	0.296	−0.54	0.422	−0.74	0.491	−0.87	0.545	−1

FIGURE 10.4   Process to normalize to maximum values during training.

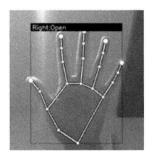  

FIGURE 10.5   Samples collection during training.

 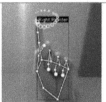 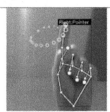 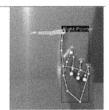

FIGURE 10.6   Key point classification.

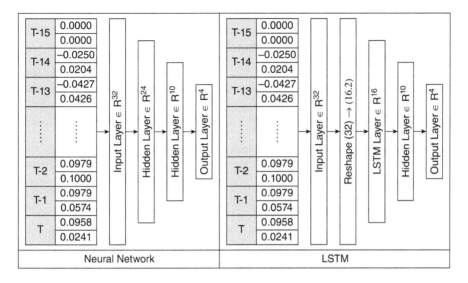

FIGURE 10.7   Processing using neural network vs LSTM.

10.4.2 VOICE RECOGNITION

In this, the system reads the audios and compares them against the items in the audio database. This is the second level of security that enhances the quality. After verification of this, security is guaranteed and difficult to snooping (Figure 10.8).

Using librosa.feature.mfcc(), which denotes multiple frequency bands of a voice file, the accuracy became 92% and performance became 99% over the combination of hand gesture and voice as entities to enhance the security. In the tensor flow, infer() is applied to compare the two audio files such as the read file and the database file (Table 10.3).

The comparison of individual biometrics against combined biometrics using a hybrid approach is demonstrated in the Figures 10.9 and 10.10.

dataset/zhvoice/zhmagicdata/5_895/5_895_20170614203758.wav	3238
dataset/zhvoice/zhmagicdata/5_895/5_895_20170614214007.wav	3238
dataset/zhvoice/zhmagicdata/5_941/5_941_20170613151344.wav	3239
dataset/zhvoice/zhmagicdata/5_941/5_941_20170614221329.wav	3239
dataset/zhvoice/zhmagicdata/5_941/5_941_20170616153308.wav	3239
dataset/zhvoice/zhmagicdata/5_968/5_968_20170614162657.wav	3240
dataset/zhvoice/zhmagicdata/5_968/5_968_20170622194003.wav	3240
dataset/zhvoice/zhmagicdata/5_968/5_968_20170707200554.wav	3240
dataset/zhvoice/zhmagicdata/5_970/5_970_20170616000122.wav	3241

FIGURE 10.8   Dataset of audio files.

TABLE 10.3

Statistics of Hybrid Biometric Approach against Individual Biometrics

Level	Hand Gesture	Accuracy	Voice Matching	Accuracy	Hybrid Approach	Overall Accuracy	Overall Performance
Approaches	Neural Network	54	Normal approach	50	LSTM and ResNet50V2	96	99
	LSTM	96	ResNet50V2	92			

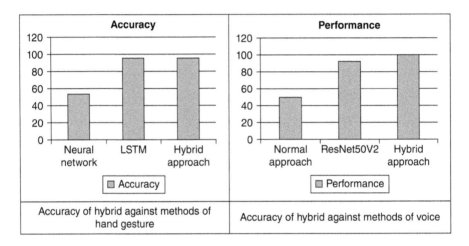

FIGURE 10.9   Accuracy of hybrid biometrics against the individual biometrics.

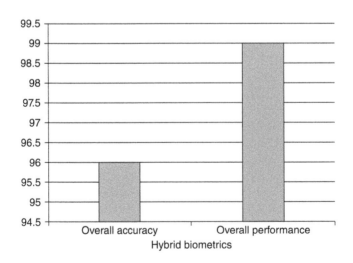

FIGURE 10.10   Accuracy and performance of hybrid biometrics using mediapipe against individual biometrics.

10.5 CONCLUSION

The proposed approach is a promising new approach that includes both biometrics such as hand gestures and voice to enhance the security of biometric systems. The approach is more accurate, robust to spoofing attacks, and scalable to large datasets than existing approaches. This is because the proposed approach uses a combination of deep learning and modern libraries of Python, which allows it to learn the most discriminative features for each individual. The proposed approach is still under development, but it has the potential to revolutionize the field of biometrics. The approach is a promising solution for security applications, such as access control, fraud detection, and law enforcement. The usage of mediapipe library, LSTM in the case of hand gestures, results in better accuracy and performance. The usage of resnet50v2 over the voice file results in good accuracy and performance. When the methods of both biometrics are integrated, it results in a hybrid approach. The expected future work that could involve an extension to other biometric modalities, such as iris recognition and gait recognition, is to be more robust to environmental factors, such as lighting and occlusion, and more efficient so that it can be used in real-time applications. It is a significant step in biometrics. The approach should be more accurate, robust, and scalable than existing approaches.

REFERENCES

S. Arora and M. P. S. Bhatia (2018), A Computer Vision System for Iris Recognition Based on Deep Learning, 2018 IEEE 8th International Advance Computing Conference (IACC), Greater Noida, India, pp. 157–161, doi: 10.1109/IADCC.2018.8692114

T. Chauhan and A. Singh (2022), Two-Layered Security Mechanism for Enhanced Biometric Security of IoT-Based Digital Wallet, 1st Edition, CRC press, eBook ISBN 9781003245469, https://www.taylorfrancis.com/chapters/edit/10.1201/9781003245469-14/two-layered-security-mechanism-enhanced-biometric-security-iot-based-digital-wallet-tanya-chauhan-ajmer-singh.

I. Chingovska, A. Anjos and S Marcel (2019), Deep Learning for Biometric Recognition: A Survey, arXiv:1901.07285.

S.-Y. Chiou (2013), Secure method for biometric-based recognition with integrated cryptographic functions, BioMed Research International, vol. 2013, https://doi.org/10.1155/2013/623815.

A. Jain, A. Ross and S. Pankanti (2006a), Biometric Recognition: Security and Privacy Challenges. In: Biometric Security and Privacy, 3–26, Springer, Boston, MA.

A. Jain, A. Ross and S. Pankanti (2006b), Enhancing Biometric Security Using Computer Vision Techniques. In: Biometric Authentication, 179–204, Springer, Boston, MA.

A. K. Jain, A. Ross and U. Uludag (2005), Biometric Template Security: Challenges and Solutions, 13th European Signal Processing Conference, Antalya, Turkey, pp. 1–4.

S. S. R. Jasti et al (2023), Crop Intelligent: Weather based Crop Selection using Machine Learning, 2023 International Conference on Sustainable Computing and Data Communication Systems (ICSCDS), Erode, India, pp. 1594–1600, doi: 10.1109/ICSCDS56580.2023.10104898.

H. Jung, S. Sim and H. Lee (2023), Biometric authentication security enhancement under quantum dot light-emitting diode display via fingerprint imaging and temperature sensing. Scientific Reports, vol. 13, p. 794, https://doi.org/10.1038/s41598-023-28162-6.

C. B. Karthikarajan (2019), Computer Vision Based on Biometric Security Using Face and Finger Print, http://www.ijtrd.com/papers/IJTRD20365.pdf

A. Kotkar, S. Khadapkar, A. Gupta and S. Jangale (2022), Multiple Layered Security Using Combination of Cryptography with Rotational, Flipping Steganography and Message Authentication, IEEE International Conference on Data Science and Information System (ICDSIS), Hassan, India, pp. 1–5, doi: 10.1109/ICDSIS55133.2022.9915922.

S. Minaee, A. Abdolrashidi et al (2021, Feb), Biometrics recognition using deep learning: A survey, computer vision and pattern recognition, Machine Learning, https://doi.org/10.48550/arXiv.1912.00271.

K. Nguyen, H. Proença et al (2022, Oct), Deep learning for iris recognition: A survey, computer vision and pattern recognition, Artificial Intelligence, https://doi.org/10.48550/arXiv.2210.05866.

S. Pankanti, A. Ross and A Jain (2006), Computer Vision Techniques for Biometric Recognition. In: Biometric Security Systems: Design and Applications, 3–34, Springer. http://biometrics.cse.msu.edu/Publications/GeneralBiometrics/JainRossPankanti_BiometricsInfoSec_TIFS06.pdf

T. Phillips et al (2020), AuthN-AuthZ: Integrated, User-Friendly and Privacy-Preserving Authentication and Authorization, Second IEEE International Conference on Trust, Privacy and Security in Intelligent Systems and Applications (TPS-ISA), Atlanta, GA, USA, pp. 189–198, doi: 10.1109/TPS-ISA50397.2020.00034.

S. Prabhakar, S. Pankanti and A. K. Jain (2003), Biometric recognition: Security and privacy concerns, IEEE Security & Privacy, vol. 1, no. 2, pp. 33–42. doi: 10.1109/MSECP.2003.1193209.

V. Rajasekar, J. Premalatha and K. Sathya (2020), Enhanced biometric recognition for secure authentication using iris preprocessing and hyperelliptic curve cryptography, Wireless Communications and Mobile Computing, vol. 2020, Article ID 8841021, 15 pages, https://doi.org/10.1155/2020/8841021.

S. H. Raju et al (2020a), IoT as a health guide tool, IOP Conference Series: Materials Science and Engineering, vol. 981, p. 4, https://doi.org/10.1088/1757-899X/981/4/042015.

S. H. Raju et al (2020b), Tourism enhancer app: user-friendliness of a map with relevant features, IOP Conference Series: Materials Science and Engineering, vol. 981, p. 2, https://doi.org/10.1088/1757-899X/981/2/022067.

S. H. Raju et al (2021a), Output-Oriented Multi-Pane Mail Booster, Smart Computing and Self-Adaptive Systems, CRC Press, 10.1201/9781003156123-4.

S. H. Raju et al (2021b), Eyesight Test Through Remote Virtual Doctor Using IoT, Smart Computing and Self-Adaptive Systems, CRC Press, 10.1201/9781003156123-5.

S. H. Raju et al (2022), An IoT Vision for Dietary Monitoring System and for Health Recommendations. In: Ranganathan, G., Fernando, X., Shi, F. (eds) Inventive Communication and Computational Technologies, Lecture Notes in Networks and Systems, vol 311, Springer, Singapore. https://doi.org/10.1007/978-981-16-5529-6_65.

C. Rathgeb, J. Kolberg et al (2023, March), Deep learning in the field of biometric template protection: An overview, Computer Vision and Pattern Recognition, https://doi.org/10.48550/arXiv.2303.02715.

A. Sarkar and B. Singh (2020), A review on performance, security and various biometric template protection schemes for biometric authentication systems, Computer Science, Multimedia Tools and Applications, 10.1007/s11042-020-09197-7.

A. Sreedharan (2016), Enhanced ATM security using biometric authentication and wavelet based AES, MATEC Web of Conferences, vol. 42, https://doi.org/10.1051/matecconf/20164206003.

K. Subiya et al (2022), Enhanced security schemes in cloud using biometric based access, Dogo Rangsang Research Journal, https://www.journal-dogorangsang.in/no_1_Online_22/35.pdf

N. Tom (2021, May), What Are Biometrics? The Pros/Cons of Biometric Security, https://auth0.com/blog/what-are-biometrics-the-proscons-of-biometric-security/

D. M. Uliyan, S. Sadeghi and H. A. Jalab (2020), Anti-spoofing method for fingerprint recognition using patch based deep learning machine, Engineering Science and Technology, vol. 23, no. 2, pp. 264–273, https://doi.org/10.1016/j.jestch.2019.06.005.

A. Vasilchenko (2022), AI Biometric Authentication for Enterprise Security, https://mobidev.biz/blog/ai-[35]biometrics-technology-authentication-verification-security

R. Zhang, Y. Yin et al (2022), Deep learning for finger vein recognition: A brief survey of recent trend, Computer Vision and Pattern Recognition, https://doi.org/10.48550/arXiv.2207.02148.

L. Zou (2023), Meta-Learning for Computer Vision, pp. 91–208, https://doi.org/10.1016/B978-0-323-89931-4.00012-2.

11 Enhancing Face Anti-Spoofing with Three-Stream CNNs
Leveraging Color Space Analysis

Kumar S and Arif T

11.1 INTRODUCTION

Face recognition systems have become integral to various sectors, including security (Balla & Jadhao, 2018), access control (Shavetov & Sivtsov, 2020), and identity verification (Wu et al., 2019). However, the rise of face spoofing attacks presents a significant threat to the reliability and security of these systems (Kumar et al., 2017). Spoofing attacks involve presenting counterfeit biometric samples, such as printed images or masks, to deceive the face recognition system and gain unauthorized access. To counter this growing challenge, researchers have been continuously developing face anti-spoofing techniques to detect and differentiate between genuine and spoofed faces. In recent years, deep learning-based methods have shown remarkable progress in face anti-spoofing (Yu et al., 2023). The power of deep neural networks lies in their ability to automatically learn and extract discriminative features from data, leading to improved detection performance. Nevertheless, the pursuit of even greater accuracy and robustness against spoofing demands innovative approaches (Jaswanth et al., 2023).

This chapter proposes a novel approach to enhance face anti-spoofing by leveraging multi-stream deep learning and incorporating color space analysis. The core idea behind multi-stream convolutional neural network (CNN) (Tu et al., 2018) is to process input data through multiple parallel streams, with each stream capturing distinct facial representations or aspects. This approach facilitates a more comprehensive analysis of facial features, allowing the model to identify subtle cues that may indicate the presence of spoofing. With fusing and aggregating information from different streams, the model can make more informed decisions, thereby enhancing overall accuracy and resistance to spoofing attacks. We explain spoofing attack, with the help of Figure 11.1 to illustrate an instance of real person's image and spoof attacks extracted from the CASIA-FASD [32] dataset.

Furthermore, we explore the integration of color space analysis in our approach (Tiuftiakov et al., 2021). Traditional face recognition systems predominantly utilize

DOI: 10.1201/9781032614663-11

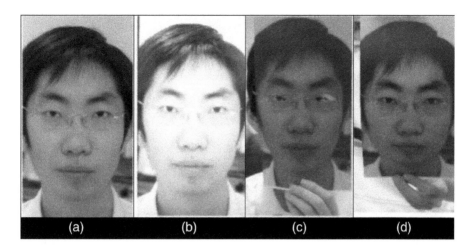

FIGURE 11.1 Samples of CASIA-FASD database with high quality. (a) Real face. (b) Video attack. (c) Cut photo attack. (d) Warped photo attack.

grayscale or RGB color information, overlooking the valuable discriminative potential inherent in other color spaces (Mu & Li, 2019). To conducting an in-depth analysis of color spaces like HSV (Hue, Saturation, Value) or YCbCr (luma-chroma), our model can capture additional cues related to skin texture, color distribution, and variations in illumination. Substantial progress has been made in biometric spoof detection technologies for specific modalities.

The current state-of-the-art in face spoof detection methods is summarized in Table 11.1. Despite these advancements, face spoof detection remains a challenging task that requires continuous efforts (Evans et al., 2015; Galbally et al., 2014a). Many existing methods aim to protect facial recognition systems (Komulainen et al., 2013) from specific spoof attacks, but they often lack the ability to adapt to different face spoof attacks and real-world application scenarios. Furthermore, these methods heavily rely on databases with spoof videos captured using either low-resolution (e.g., webcam) or very high-resolution (e.g., DSLR) cameras (Pan et al., 2007), such as the CASIA-FASD and Idiap databases released in 2012.

In this chapter, we focus on enhancing face anti-spoofing using patch-level CNN, which leverages discriminative information at the local level rather than the entire image. The present work makes four primary contributions:

1. Providing a comprehensive analysis of different color spaces to identify the most effective combination that aids in accurately classifying real and spoof images.
2. Providing further enhances the recognition of local discriminating features, we employ patch-level CNN. This approach allows the model to focus on specific regions or patches within the face, enabling a more fine-grained analysis and detection of potential spoofing cues.

TABLE 11.1

Summarized the Current State-of-the-Art in Face Spoof Detection Methods.

Method	Strength	Limitation	Performance
Image quality analysis (Galbally et al., 2014b; Wen et al., 2015)	Good generalizability, low computational cost, fast response time, face and/or landmark detection not required	Spectral features can be device dependent	Replay-attack (Galbally et al., 2014b): (7.41%, 26.9%); CASIA-FASD (Wen et al., 2015): (12.9%, 43.7%)
Active approach (Zhang et al., 2011)	Good generalizability	Requires additional devices	Private 3D mask dataset (Zhang et al., 2011): (100.0%, n/a)
Face texture analysis (Yang et al., 2013)	Relatively low computational cost and fast response	Poor generalizability requires face and/ or landmark detection	Replay-attack (Yang et al., 2013): (15.54%, 47.1%); CASIA-FASD (Yang et al., 2013): (2.9%, 16.7%)
Frequency domain analysis (Li et al., 2004; Pinto et al., 2015a, 2015b)	Good generalizability, less sensitive to face and/or landmark detection errors, whole image frame analysis	Device dependent	Replay-attack (Li et al., 2004): (2.8%, 34.4%); CASIA-FASD (Pinto et al., 2015a): (14.0%, 38.5%); UVAD (Pinto et al., 2015b): (29.9%, 40.1%)
[Proposed]	Good generalizability	Moderate computational cost	CASIA-FASD Proposed: (3.09%); Replay-attack Proposed: (0.06%, 2.04%)

3. Providing three-streams CNN model to detect the spoof images.
4. Providing extensive experiments and comparisons has been conducted, demonstrating that our proposed approach achieves state-of-the-art performance on most protocols.

To validate the effectiveness of our proposed approach, extensive experiments and evaluations are conducted on benchmark face anti-spoofing datasets. We compare the performance of our three-stream CNN model with state-of-the-art methods to demonstrate its superiority in detecting face spoofing attempts.

The remainder of this chapter is structured as follows: Section 11.2 reviews the related literature on face anti-spoofing techniques and existing works in the field of deep learning for spoof detection. In Section 11.3, we present the methodology, detailing our three-stream deep learning framework and the incorporation of color space analysis techniques. Section 11.4 outlines the experimental setup, and the results of our evaluations are presented along with a comprehensive performance analysis. Finally, Section 11.5 concludes the chapter, highlighting the significance of our findings and outlining potential future research directions.

11.2 LITERATURE SURVEY

The field of face anti-spoofing has attracted considerable research attention in recent years, with various approaches (Komulainen et al., 2013; *On the Effectiveness of Local Binary Patterns in Face Anti-Spoofing | IEEE Conference Publication | IEEE Xplore*, n.d.-a) (*A Dataset and Benchmark for Large-Scale Multi-Modal Face Anti-Spoofing | Papers With Code*, n.d.) proposed to tackle the challenge of distinguishing between genuine and spoofed faces. Several traditional face anti-spoofing techniques (Määttä et al., 2011; Pereira et al., 2014) have been developed to combat spoofing attacks. These methods often rely on handcrafted features and machine learning algorithms. While these methods have shown some effectiveness, they often struggle to generalize to different spoofing scenarios and lack the ability to learn discriminative features automatically.

Deep learning-based methods have demonstrated significant progress in face anti-spoofing due to their ability to automatically learn high-level representations and extract discriminative features directly from raw data. CNNs have been widely adopted in this domain (Jourabloo et al., 2018; Liu et al., 2016; Yang et al., 2014). Some approaches employ CNNs to classify facial images as genuine or spoofed based on learned features, while others use CNNs to extract features and subsequently feed them into classifiers. (Benlamoudi et al., 2022) proposed a CNN architecture that combines both spatial and temporal information to improve the accuracy of face anti-spoofing. Chen et al. (2023) introduced a lightweight CNN for detecting spoofing attacks using both image and depth information. These deep learning methods have shown promising results, but there is still room for improvement in terms of accuracy and robustness against various spoofing techniques. Kouzani et al. (2000) employed color space analysis to enhance the recognition of faces with variations in illumination. They demonstrated that incorporating color information can improve the robustness of face recognition systems. Mu and Li (2019) proposed a method that exploits color information in different color spaces to improve face recognition accuracy. Considering color cues in face analysis, these methods have shown improved performance, motivating the exploration of color space analysis for face anti-spoofing. In recent times, researchers have been utilizing deep neural networks in the field of face spoofing attacks (Jaswanth et al., 2023; Xu et al., 2016). Deep learning techniques have been employed by researchers in recent years to identify spoof assaults. CNN was used by Yang et al. (2014) to combat spoof attacks. In the pre-processing step, the face and its landmarks were extracted. CNN received this information in order to instruct them. Additionally, an SVM classifier received the characteristics that were retrieved by the classifier. Shao et al. (2018) suggested using the attribute of facial dynamics to develop a face anti-spoofing technique to stop 3D mask attacks. To get this data, they train a deep convolutional network. Furthermore, Xu et al. take the data from several video frames in Kouzani et al. (2000) and feed it to the LSTM-CNN architecture.

11.3 METHODOLOGY

In this section, we will explore the pre-processing steps and their significance, as well as the generation of patches and its advantages. To conduct experiment, we will provide a comprehensive discussion of our proposed three-stream CNN model's

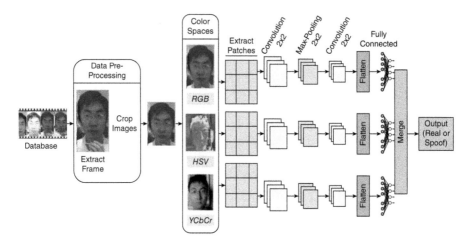

FIGURE 11.2   The overview of proposed strategy for facial expression recognition.

architecture, Figure 11.2 depicts a flowchart. Furthermore, we leveraged three-stream CNNs; these CNNs incorporate illustrated extracted features shown in Figure 11.4 as input data.

There are various steps that depicts the overall operation of our proposed approach of facial recognition. These steps comprise extracting valuable information from the input image, conducting color space analysis, generating patches, and feeding these patches as input to the CNN streams. We will elaborate on each of these crucial steps in the following subsections.

11.3.1   Pre-Processing and Color Space Analysis

Feature engineering plays a critical role in enhancing the performance of CNN-based approaches by improving input features and eliminating unwanted background elements. In face anti-spoofing tasks, datasets include videos for each subject, comprising various spoof attacks like print, replay, and video attacks. As the initial step, we randomly extract frames from each video. For face detection and removal of unnecessary background information, we employ the Haar Cascade algorithm (Li et al., 2017), which uses a cascade of classifiers to identify the face region. After detection, we crop the face from the frame. However, the resulting outputs vary in size, while the proposed three-stream CNN network requires fixed-size inputs. We reshaping the images to a constant size. In the process of reshaping, there may be a loss of certain information. However, in the next section, we address this issue using the patch generation approach. Color space analysis has gained attention as a valuable tool for improving face recognition performance (John et al., 2016). Traditional face recognition systems predominantly utilize grayscale or RGB color information. However, the utilization of other color spaces, such as HSV or YCbCr, has been explored to capture additional discriminative information. In this experiment, we consider four color spaces: HSV, YCbCr, RGB, and GRAY. Additionally, we take into account the high-frequency component of images for further examination. RGB employs red, green, and blue components to create the image, while YCbCr space has Y as the intensity component, and Cb and Cr represent the blue and red color components with respect to green. In HSV, H denotes color purity, S indicates the degree of color dilution by white light, and V represents intensity values. Moreover, gray scaling of images presents them in shades of gray based on the brightness levels of RGB components.

The high-frequency component of images (high-frequency images) is derived by subtracting the low-pass filtered grayscale image from the original grayscale image. Figure 11.3 displays the distinct color spaces and high-frequency components of both real and spoof face images. Notably, the grayscale face images and their high-frequency components do not sufficiently discriminate between real and

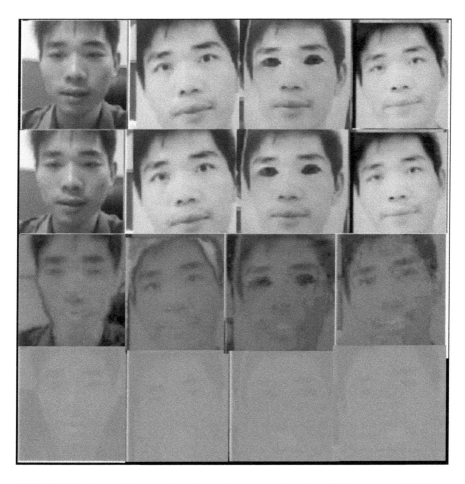

FIGURE 11.3 Sample images of various color spaces, including RGB, grayscale, HSV, and YCbCr. The first column shows warped print photo face images, while the second column shows cut print photo face images. The third column contains replay video face images, and the last row showcases genuine face images. All the sample images are sourced from the CASIA-FASD database.

spoof images. However, the color spaces HSV and YCbCr contain more informative features. While RGB carries correlated color information and YCbCr contains uncorrelated color and intensity information, their representations are not practically interpretable. Conversely, the HSV color space offers more meaningful information for this purpose.

11.3.2 Extracting Patches

Next, stage involves passing images from color map to our proposed model. However, our model mandates all input images to have a fixed size, while the faces obtained from the pre-processing step offer face images with varying dimensions. Resizing the color maps to a fixed dimension may result in the loss of local information. To address this, we extract overlapping patches of a fixed size from the images. The primary aim of extracting patches and using them as input is to leverage local information. Additionally, patch generation boosts the number of samples available for training.

11.3.3 Proposed Three-Stream CNN Architecture

In our previous discussions, we emphasize the use of color space analysis to highlight the differences between real and spoof images. Various color spaces contain enough information to effectively distinguish between real and spoof images. Combining these color spaces enhances our model's robustness against different types of attacks, ultimately improving the efficiency of our network architecture. To achieve this goal, we propose a three-stream CNN network, created by concatenating the fully connected layers of two or more CNN network streams, as shown in Figure 11.4. This network allows us to simultaneously input patches from different color spaces (RGB, HSV, YCbCr) into independent CNN streams. As a result, our network learns features

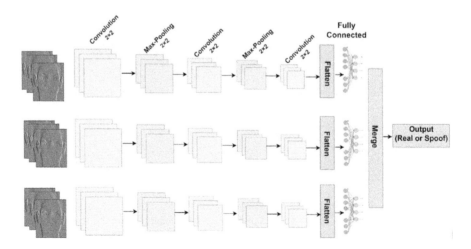

FIGURE 11.4   Proposed three-stream CNN architecture.

TABLE 11.2
Analysis of Different Color Spaces Combinations

Color Space	Type	Accuracy (%)
RGB.	Single-Stream	88.04
RGB. HSV	Two-Stream CNN	96.73
RGB. YCbCr.	Two-Stream CNN	97.56
RGB. HSV. YCbCr.	**three-stream CNN**	**99.11**

from diverse color spaces and integrates this valuable information. By incorporating these rich features, we enhance the efficiency and robustness of our model, enabling more accurate and reliable classifications for any given input image.

In our experiments, we aimed to find the most effective color space combination for our three-stream CNN network. Grayscale and high-frequency components of face images didn't yield satisfactory results and were excluded. Instead, we focused on RGB, HSV, and YCbCr components for creating patches and evaluating the performance using accuracy metrics. Table 11.2 presents the combinations and their results, showing that the three-stream CNN with RGB, HSV, and YCbCr achieved the highest accuracy. These color spaces are particularly effective in skin color detection and detecting face spoofing attempts. Figure 11.4 illustrates our three-stream CNN architecture, with each stream taking RGB, HSV, and YCbCr patches as inputs. Each block comprises convolution layers, followed by max pooling and ReLU activation. With fusing fully connected layers of the three streams, our model learns rich features and improves performance.

11.4   EXPERIMENTAL RESULTS AND DISCUSSION

We prepared a training set for the three-stream CNN model from CAISA-FASD (Zhang et al., 2012) and REPLAY-ATTACK(*On the Effectiveness of Local Binary Patterns in Face Anti-Spoofing | IEEE Conference Publication | IEEE Xplore*, n.d.-b) database, extracting random frames from videos. After extracting and cropping using the Haar Cascade algorithm, we applied color spaces to these face images and extract random patches. Through experiments, we determined that extracting 20 random patches of size 96×96 from 25 frames yields optimal results.

Subsequently, the extracted patches are fed as input to the CNN, with live face patches receiving label 1 and spoof attack patches labeled 0. Our proposed approach employs a three-streams CNN, as shown in Figure 11.4. Each stream has three convolutional layers with sizes progressively increasing to 32, 64, 64, 128, and 128. Max pooling layers follow each convolutional layer, with ReLu as the activation function and Adam as the optimizer. Performance evaluation in biometrics involves widely used metrics, such as EER (equal error rate) and HTER (half total error rate), derived from FAR (false acceptance rate) and FRR (false rejection rate). EER identifies the unique point where FAR and FRR are equal, and HTER find out the average of FAR and FRR values.

TABLE 11.3

Comparison Proposed Countermeasure and State-of-the-Art Methods Based on EER (%) on CASIA-FASD and EER (%), HTER (%) on REPLAY-ATTACK

Methods	CASIA-FASD	REPLAY-ATTACK	
	EER (%)	EER (%)	HTER (%)
Boulkenafet et.al.; *OULU-NPU: A Mobile Face Presentation Attack Database with Real-World Variations	IEEE Conference Publication	IEEE Xplore* (n.d.)	2.10	0.10	2.20
Atoum et al. (2018)	2.67	0.79	0.72
Xu et al. (2016)	–	0.40	2.90
Li et al. (2017)	4.50	2.90	6.10
Deep learning (Tu et al., 2018)	7.30	0.20	–
Proposed three-stream CNN	3.09	0.06	2.04

The results, presented in Tables 11.3, demonstrate promising outcomes for our proposed approaches in countering face anti-spoof attacks. Additionally, we conducted a cross-database experiment using CAISA-FASD and REPLAY-ATTACK testing sets to assess generalization capability. The model trained on one dataset achieved HTER values of 33.92% for CASIA-FASD and 37.52% for REPLAY-ATTACK, comparable to state-of-the-art methods.

11.5 CONCLUSION AND FUTURE WORK

In this research paper, we have proposed a novel three-stream CNN approach for face spoof detection, leveraging color space analysis to enhance the model's ability to distinguish between real and spoof face images. Through extensive experimentation and evaluation on various databases, including CAISA-FASD and REPLAY-ATTACK, our method has demonstrated superior performance in mitigating threats from face anti-spoof attacks. The incorporation of RGB, HSV, and YCbCr color spaces in the three-stream CNN network allows for the extraction of rich and discriminative features, leading to more accurate and reliable predictions. Our model generalization capability has been validated through a cross-database experiment, yielding comparable results to state-of-the-art methods.

While our proposed approach has shown promising results, there are several exciting avenues for future research and improvements in the field of face spoof detection. Firstly, exploring the integration of additional color spaces or feature extraction techniques could further enhance the model's ability to detect sophisticated spoof attacks. Secondly, investigating the use of attention mechanisms or explainable AI techniques could provide valuable insights into the decision-making process of the model, increasing its transparency and interpretability. Furthermore, collecting larger and more diverse datasets could enhance the robustness and generalization capability of the model in real-world scenarios. Finally, fine-tuning the network architecture or considering other deep learning architectures could lead to even better performance.

REFERENCES

A Dataset and Benchmark for Large-Scale Multi-Modal Face Anti-Spoofing | Papers With Code. (n.d.). Retrieved July 27, 2023, from https://paperswithcode.com/paper/casia-surf-a-dataset-and-benchmark-for-large

Atoum, Y., Liu, Y., Jourabloo, A., & Liu, X. (2018). Face anti-spoofing using patch and depth-based CNNs. *IEEE International Joint Conference on Biometrics, IJCB 2017, 2018-January*, 319–328. https://doi.org/10.1109/BTAS.2017.8272713

Balla, P. B., & Jadhao, K. T. (2018). IoT based facial recognition security system. *2018 International Conference on Smart City and Emerging Technology, ICSCET 2018.* https://doi.org/10.1109/ICSCET.2018.8537344

Benlamoudi, A., Bekhouche, S. E., Korichi, M., Bensid, K., Ouahabi, A., Hadid, A., Choras, M., Kozik, R., Pawlicki, M., Benlamoudi, A., Bekhouche, S. E., Korichi, M., Bensid, K., Ouahabi, A., Hadid, A., & Taleb-Ahmed, A. (2022). Face presentation attack detection using deep background subtraction. *Sensors, 22*(10), 3760. https://doi.org/10.3390/S22103760

Chen, Z., Chen, J., Ding, G., & Huang, H. (2023). A lightweight CNN-based algorithm and implementation on embedded system for real-time face recognition. *Multimedia Systems, 29*(1), 129–138. https://doi.org/10.1007/s00530-022-00973-z

Evans, N., Li, S. Z., Marcel, S., & Ross, A. (2015). Guest editorial special issue on biometric spoofing and countermeasures. *IEEE Transactions on Information Forensics and Security, 10*(4), 699–702. https://doi.org/10.1109/TIFS.2015.2406111

Galbally, J., Marcel, S., & Fierrez, J. (2014a). Biometric antispoofing methods: A survey in face recognition. *IEEE Access, 2*, 1530–1552. https://doi.org/10.1109/ACCESS.2014.2381273

Galbally, J., Marcel, S., & Fierrez, J. (2014b). Image quality assessment for fake biometric detection: Application to iris, fingerprint, and face recognition. *IEEE Transactions on Image Processing, 23*(2), 710–724. https://doi.org/10.1109/TIP.2013.2292332

Jaswanth, P., chowdary, P. Y., & Ramprasad, M. V. S. (2023). Deep learning based intelligent system for robust face spoofing detection using texture feature measurement. *Measurement: Sensors*, 100868. https://doi.org/10.1016/J.MEASEN.2023.100868

John, N., Viswanath, A., Sowmya, V., & Soman, K. P. (2016). Analysis of various color space models on effective single image super resolution. *Advances in Intelligent Systems and Computing, 384*, 529–540. https://doi.org/10.1007/978-3-319-23036-8_46

Jourabloo, A., Liu, Y., & Liu, X. (2018). Face de-spoofing: Anti-spoofing via noise modeling. Lecture Notes in Computer Science (Including Subseries Lecture Notes in Artificial Intelligence and Lecture Notes in Bioinformatics), 11217 LNCS, 297–315. DOI:10.1007/978-3-642-24434-6

Komulainen, J., Hadid, A., Pietikainen, M., Anjos, A., & Marcel, S. (2013). Complementary countermeasures for detecting scenic face spoofing attacks. *Proceedings – 2013 International Conference on Biometrics, ICB 2013.* https://doi.org/10.1109/ICB.2013.6612968

Kouzani, A. Z., He, F., & Sammut, K. (2000). Towards invariant face recognition. *Information Sciences, 123*(1–2), 75–101. https://doi.org/10.1016/S0020-0255(99)00111-5

Kumar, S., Singh, S., & Kumar, J. (2017). A comparative study on face spoofing attacks. *Proceeding – IEEE International Conference on Computing, Communication and Automation, ICCCA 2017, 2017-January*, 1104–1108. https://doi.org/10.1109/CCAA.2017.8229961

Li, C., Qi, Z., Jia, N., & Wu, J. (2017). Human face detection algorithm via Haar cascade classifier combined with three additional classifiers. *2017 13th IEEE International Conference on Electronic Measurement & Instruments (ICEMI), 2018-January*, 483–487. https://doi.org/10.1109/ICEMI.2017.8265863

Li, J., Wang, Y., Tan, T., Jain, A. K., Li, J., Wang, Y., Tan, T., & Jain, A. K. (2004). Live face detection based on the analysis of Fourier spectra. *SPIE, 5404*, 296–303. https://doi.org/10.1117/12.541955

Li, L., Feng, X., Boulkenafet, Z., Xia, Z., Li, M., & Hadid, A. (2017). An original face anti-spoofing approach using partial convolutional neural network. *2016 6th International Conference on Image Processing Theory, Tools and Applications, IPTA 2016.* https://doi.org/10.1109/IPTA.2016.7821013

Liu, S., Yuen, P. C., Zhang, S., & Zhao, G. (2016). 3D mask face anti-spoofing with remote photoplethysmography. Lecture Notes in Computer Science (Including Subseries Lecture Notes in Artificial Intelligence and Lecture Notes in Bioinformatics), 9911 LNCS, 85–100. DOI:10.1007/978-3-319-46478-7_6

Määttä, J., Hadid, A., & Pietikäinen, M. (2011). Face spoofing detection from single images using micro-texture analysis. *2011 International Joint Conference on Biometrics, IJCB 2011.* https://doi.org/10.1109/IJCB.2011.6117510

Mu, D., & Li, T. (2019). Face anti-spoofing with multi-color double-stream CNN. *Proceedings of the 13th International Conference on Distributed Smart Cameras.* https://doi.org/10.1145/3349801.3349817

On the Effectiveness of Local Binary Patterns in Face Anti-Spoofing | IEEE Conference Publication | IEEE Xplore. (n.d.-a). Retrieved July 26, 2023, from https://ieeexplore.ieee.org/document/6313548

On the Effectiveness of Local Binary Patterns in Face Anti-Spoofing | IEEE Conference Publication | IEEE Xplore. (n.d.-b). Retrieved July 28, 2023, from https://ieeexplore.ieee.org/document/6313548

OULU-NPU: A Mobile Face Presentation Attack Database with Real-World Variations | IEEE Conference Publication | IEEE Xplore. (n.d.). Retrieved July 26, 2023, from https://ieeexplore.ieee.org/document/7961798

Pan, G., Sun, L., Wu, Z., & Lao, S. (2007). Eyeblink-based anti-spoofing in face recognition from a generic webcamera. *Proceedings of the IEEE International Conference on Computer Vision.* https://doi.org/10.1109/ICCV.2007.4409068

Pereira, T. D. F., Komulainen, J., Anjos, A., De Martino, J. M., Hadid, A., Pietikäinen, M., & Marcel, S. (2014). Face liveness detection using dynamic texture. *Eurasip Journal on Image and Video Processing, 2014*(1), 1–15. https://doi.org/10.1186/1687-5281-2014-2

Pinto, A., Pedrini, H., Schwartz, W. R., & Rocha, A. (2015a). Face spoofing detection through visual codebooks of spectral temporal cubes. *IEEE Transactions on Image Processing, 24*(12), 4726–4740. https://doi.org/10.1109/TIP.2015.2466088

Pinto, A., Robson Schwartz, W., Pedrini, H., & Rocha, A. (2015b). *Using Visual Rhythms for Detecting Video-based Facial Spoof Attacks.* https://doi.org/10.6084/M9.FIGSHARE.1295453.V9

Shao, R., Lan, X., & Yuen, P. C. (2018). Deep convolutional dynamic texture learning with adaptive channel-discriminability for 3D mask face anti-spoofing. *IEEE International Joint Conference on Biometrics, IJCB 2017, 2018-January*, 748–755. https://doi.org/10.1109/BTAS.2017.8272765

Shavetov, S., & Sivtsov, V. (2020). Access control system based on face recognition. *7th International Conference on Control, Decision and Information Technologies, CoDIT 2020*, 952–956. https://doi.org/10.1109/CODIT49905.2020.9263894

Tiuftiakov, N. Y., Kalinichev, A. V., Pokhvishcheva, N. V., & Peshkova, M. A. (2021). Digital color analysis for colorimetric signal processing: Towards an analytically justified choice of acquisition technique and color space. *Sensors and Actuators B: Chemical, 344*, 130274. https://doi.org/10.1016/J.SNB.2021.130274

Tu, Z., Xie, W., Qin, Q., Poppe, R., Veltkamp, R. C., Li, B., & Yuan, J. (2018). Multi-stream CNN: Learning representations based on human-related regions for action recognition. *Pattern Recognition, 79*, 32–43. https://doi.org/10.1016/J.PATCOG.2018.01.020

Wen, D., Han, H., & Jain, A. K. (2015). Face spoof detection with image distortion analysis. *IEEE Transactions on Information Forensics and Security, 10*(4), 746–761. https://doi. org/10.1109/TIFS.2015.2400395

Wu, X., Xu, J., Wang, J., Li, Y., Li, W., & Guo, Y. (2019). Identity authentication on mobile devices using face verification and ID image recognition. *Procedia Computer Science, 162*, 932–939. https://doi.org/10.1016/J.PROCS.2019.12.070

Xu, Z., Li, S., & Deng, W. (2016). Learning temporal features using LSTM-CNN architecture for face anti-spoofing. *Proceedings – 3rd IAPR Asian Conference on Pattern Recognition, ACPR 2015*, 141–145. https://doi.org/10.1109/ACPR.2015.7486482

Yang, J., Lei, Z., & Li, S. Z. (2014). *Learn Convolutional Neural Network for Face Anti-Spoofing*. http://arxiv.org/abs/1408.5601

Yang, J., Lei, Z., Liao, S., & Li, S. Z. (2013). Face liveness detection with component dependent descriptor. *Proceedings – 2013 International Conference on Biometrics, ICB 2013*. https://doi.org/10.1109/ICB.2013.6612955

Yu, Z., Qin, Y., Li, X., Zhao, C., Lei, Z., & Zhao, G. (2023). Deep learning for face anti-spoofing: A survey. *IEEE Transactions on Pattern Analysis and Machine Intelligence, 45*(05), 5609–5631. https://doi.org/10.1109/TPAMI.2022.3215850

Zhang, Z., Yan, J., Liu, S., Lei, Z., Yi, D., & Li, S. Z. (2012). A face antispoofing database with diverse attacks. *2012 5th IAPR International Conference on Biometrics (ICB)*, 26–31. https://doi.org/10.1109/ICB.2012.6199754

Zhang, Z., Yi, D., Lei, Z., & Li, S. Z. (2011). Face liveness detection by learning multispectral reflectance distributions. *2011 IEEE International Conference on Automatic Face and Gesture Recognition and Workshops, FG 2011*, 436–441. https://doi.org/10.1109/FG.2011.5771438

12 Computer-Vision Techniques for Video Analysis

Ambreen Sabha and Arvind Selwal

12.1 INTRODUCTION

The widespread adoption of social media has resulted in the development of a varied range of electronic devices that can store vast amounts of data, including news, documents, music, sports videos, and surveillance footage. Due to the exponential advancement of digital technology, there is an extensive amount of data available in written words, audio recordings, and video formats. Among all, videos are the most important multimedia assets and have a big impact on people's lives. The vast amounts of video data generated through surveillance cameras or smartphones have made the issue of human activity recognition among the most prominent research domains (Aggarwal & Ryoo, 2011; Jobanputra et al., 2019; Mehmood et al., 2021; Saeed et al., 2019). It is defined as estimating a specific person's activity in both an indoor and an outdoor environment. In recent times, surveillance plays an important role for security purposes in public as well as in private areas. The continuous monitoring of the surveillance systems 24 hours a day and 7 days a week requires human intervention to detect a specific event and it is a time-consuming process. As a result of two factors, it has become difficult to handle and analyze the data generated by surveillance. First, CCTV generates an enormous volume of video data, which requires a large amount of storage space. Second, the data generated by CCTV is highly redundant. Due to the enormous growth in CCTV (closed circuit television) footage as it captures data during 24 hours and detecting human activities from large databases would require an automatic system. The primary challenge that arises as a result of video surveillance is dealing with a vast database and collecting or extracting valuable information from it. As basic surveillance systems lack an image processing unit that enhances visibility, they are unable to observe activities in adverse weather, which is common in both indoor and outdoor settings (Beddiar et al., 2020; Hussain et al., 2019; Jobanputra et al., 2019). The various real-world applications of computer vision techniques include abnormal action detection in surveillance (Ali et al., 2020; Gandapur, 2022; Luna et al., 2018; Wang et al., 2013), human-human and human-object interaction (Xu et al., 2019), activity or event detection in medical (Münzer et al., 2018), and education and egocentric video (Del Molino et al., 2017; Sahu & Chowdhury, 2020).

Computer vision approaches are methods that are used to acquire, process, analyze, and comprehend image data and videos. These methods can be used to extract high-dimensional data from the real environment and transform it into numerical

DOI: 10.1201/9781032614663-12

or symbolic information, such as decisions (Sharma & Selwal, 2021, 2023a). These are categorized into traditional and deep-learning-based techniques. The traditional approach includes object detection, human action recognition (HAR), and image segmentation, whereas modern deep-based techniques include CNN, RNN, and LSTM. Object detection is a process of detecting an object of interest based on the concept that every object has features that can be distinguished from other objects. Object detection mainly focuses on real-world object identification like humans, animals, or threatening objects (Liu & Yuan, n.d.; Wang & Gupta, 2018). Object detection techniques make use of various image-processing methods to extract the desired position of an object. Some application of object detection includes security, image retrieval, and the medical field. Detection of the foreground objects in a frame from the background is (Xu et al., 2019) done by considering parameters like local motion and appearance that tend to change from image to image. Due to the affordability of sensors and accelerometers, as well as IoT, AI, machine, and deep learning techniques, HAR in videos has grown into one of the most significant research fields recently (Sharma & Selwal, 2022, 2023b). Individuals can now interact with multimedia information from anywhere due to the increasing popularity as well as the accessibility of cost-effective computers, electronic video recorders, and advancements in multimedia technology. It has numerous applications, ranging from intelligent monitoring systems to enhanced human-computer collaboration (Wei & Shah, 2017). Recent approaches have demonstrated great performance in recognizing either single-person activity or multiple-person activity. However, there may be both types of activities that need to be recognized. Because of the significant intraclass variability in human activities induced by changes in visual appearance, subject mobility, and viewpoint adjustments, this is a big research challenge. To overcome the aforementioned problems in video surveillance, there is a need to develop an efficient and intelligent HAD model that can correctly recognize and classify the event present in the CCTV footage (Jyotsna & Amudha, 2020; Sreenu & Saleem Durai, 2019). Although there exist several studies in the literature on computer-vision techniques; however, through our analysis, we discovered that there exists no focused survey that includes studies related to computer vision techniques for video analysis in surveillance. Thus, this motivates us to undertake the present work, which aims at analyzing and comparing various articles related to computer vision (CV) techniques. Hence, our study is based on more recent progression in object and activity detection of videos through contemporary data-driven approaches. This study will serve as a benchmark reference to new investigations in this active field of computer vision.

The key contributions of our study are illustrated as follows:

i. We expound an analysis of the state-of-the-art (SOA) computer vision techniques for video analysis approaches.
ii. We present a taxonomy for the classification of CV-based techniques based on traditional and deep learning approaches.
iii. We present a comparison among benchmark datasets and performance protocols that are deployed for evaluating CV-based video analysis techniques.
iv. We identify and highlight various open research challenges for the CV for video analysis methods.

The rest of the section is summarized as follows: Section 12.2 presents the background of the study, followed by the proposed taxonomy of CV-based video analysis techniques. Section 12.3 discussed the benchmark datasets and performance metrics deployed for CV techniques, whereas Section 12.4 highlights the open research challenges in computer-vision-based techniques. Finally, Section 12.5 represents the conclusion and future perspective of this article.

12.2 COMPUTER VISION TECHNIQUES FOR VIDEO ANALYSIS

The computer vision techniques are the methods used to acquire, process, analyze, and comprehend digital images and videos. They can be used to extract high-dimensional data from the real-world environment and transform it into numerical or symbolic information, such as decisions. This section discusses various computer vision techniques for video analysis such as detection and localization of objects, video analysis, video summarization, image segmentation, and captioning. Figure 12.1 depicts the two major categories of computer vision techniques for video analysis, namely, traditional and deep learning approaches.

An illustration of the computer-vision framework is depicted in Figure 12.2 that constitutes the machine and deep learning techniques. The former consists of hand-crafted feature extraction, whereas the later includes deep models such as CNN, RNN, and LSTM for detection purpose.

The framework consists of input video, frames extraction, thereafter frames pre-processing is used to enhance the quality of images, and then networks (ML- or DL-based techniques) are applied to images and lastly the classification of video is achieved to various computer vision techniques such as object detection, HAR, image captioning, and video summarization.

12.2.1 TRADITIONAL COMPUTER VISION TECHNIQUES

These techniques are based on hand-crafted feature extraction algorithms and have been used in various video analysis approaches. Examples of traditional computer vision techniques for video analysis include the following.

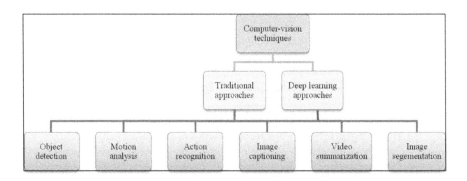

FIGURE 12.1   A depiction of video analysis techniques for computer vision.

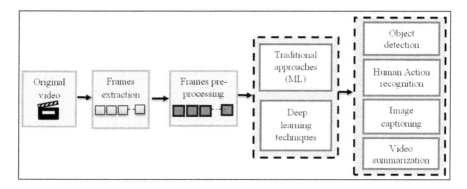

FIGURE 12.2 A depiction of a generic framework for computer vision techniques using traditional and deep models.

12.2.1.1 Motion Analysis in Videos

This involves the recognition and tracking of moving objects present in a video. Motion analysis in videos is the process of retrieving information regarding the movement of objects presented in a certain video, and this information can be utilized for a variety of reasons, including:

- *Sports analysis:* Athletes' performance can be analyzed using motion analysis to identify areas for improvement. For example, it can be used to measure the speed and acceleration of a runner, or the angle of a golfer's swing (Choroś, 2014; Tabish et al., 2021).
- *Medical applications:* It can be used to diagnose and treat a variety of medical conditions. For example, it can be used to analyze the gait of a patient with cerebral palsy or the range of motion of a patient with arthritis.
- *Robotics:* Motion analysis can be used to develop robots that can move in a more natural and efficient way. For example, it can be used to analyze the movement of a human walking and then use that information to develop a robot that can walk in a similar way (Intel, 2020; Vrigkas et al., 2015).
- *Video surveillance:* It can be used to develop video surveillance systems that can detect and track people and objects. For example, it can be used to develop a system that can detect people entering a restricted area or a system that can track the movement of a vehicle (Beghdadi et al., 2018; Gandapur, 2022; Gowsikhaa et al., 2014; Luna et al., 2018; Sreenu & Saleem Durai, 2019).

12.2.1.2 Object Detection in Videos

This involves identifying and classifying objects in a video. Object detection is primarily concerned with the recognition of real-world things like humans, animals, and suspense or frightening things (Zand et al., 2022). It is commonly utilized in image retrieval, security, medical area, and defense applications. Object detection is the method of identifying a region of interest in a frame (Raghunandan et al., 2018). It can be achieved either using single-stage architecture or two-stage architecture as shown in Figure 12.3.

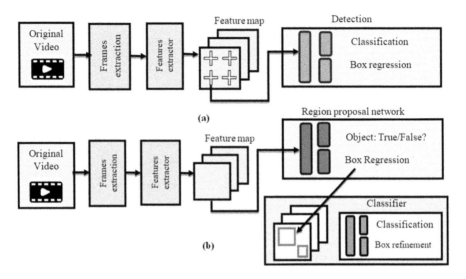

FIGURE 12.3 A generic framework for object detection (a) single-stage detector (b) two-stage detector.

The goal of object detection is to assign a semantic class name to each identified object as well as a bounding box defining its position. As a result, both the tag and location of the picture objects must be anticipated at the same time (Hussain et al., 2020). Region-based CNN (i.e., R-CNN) analyzes the given image based on regions for the detection of objects rather than examining each image pixel for the presence of every object. Another successful CNN-based object recognition system that predicts bounding boxes and related labels using an integrated CNN architecture is YOLO, along with two variants, YOLO9000 and YOLOv3. There are two main categories of object detection such as two-stage and single-stage object detection. The former extracts the region of interest from the image, and one model classifies and regresses the boxes to localize the objects present in an image. These detectors are very powerful but relatively slow, whereas in the latter skip, the ROI extraction step directly classifies and localizes the objects present in an image. Object detectors with two stages divide the object detection process into two steps: as shown in Figure 12.3(b), the RoI (Region of Interest) is extracted from the image, classified, and then the RoI is regressed. The most famous architectures include: Fast-RCNN, R-CNN, Mask-RCNN, and Faster-RCNN [20]. Single-stage object detectors as shown in Figure 12.3(a) these detectors eliminate the process of RoI extraction. In fact, it directly regresses and classifies the boxes. Primarily, the choice between single-stage or two-stage detectors is a trade-off between speed and detection accuracy. The most well-known detector in the category of object detection algorithms is YOLO (You Only Look Once). In a real-life scenario, an object that exists in a given video clip may be of interest to a user. The existing methods for object-oriented event detection are covered in the subsequent section. Ruchika et al. (2021) presented a CNN architecture with four layers to detect the local as well as global behavior of humans. This model is based on the concept where both normal and abnormal events are used for training and testing to detect abnormality. Moreover, Mlik et al. (2014) demonstrated an object-oriented technique for extracting key-frames from video shots to summarize the important content of the original video. The fuzzy-based region segmentation method recognizes critical events in each video frame, such as the presence or removal of massive objects. The experimental results are carried out on a variety of videos, such as news, games, and cartoons, and the findings reveal that the suggested technique efficiently detects object-oriented frames from an original video, while Tian et al., (2014) suggested a method for object summarization wherein an input video is categorized into camera shots (i.e., static and moving). After that, an object is detected in the images, and several key postures of people in the clip are generated. The key-pose selection criteria are shape changes of moving foreground objects rather than color or texture changes. For key-pose extraction, a feature descriptor and a clustering technique are applied, namely, SURF (speed-up robust features) and k-nearest neighbor (KNN) to evaluate model performance. To assess the effectiveness of the model, ten video sequences are evaluated. This work (Tian et al., 2011) is an extension of the prior approach that deals with video shots produced with a static camera, and several objects are detected from a video shot. In contrast to Tian et al. (2014) in which a single object is recognized from the video frames for the selection of key-pose. In addition, Mumtaz et al. (2018a) proposed a method in which they use the concept of transfer learning for detecting aggressive behavior of humans from video scenes. Experimental result shows that the model achieved a performance accuracy of 99.28% and 99.97% for benchmark datasets, namely, Hockey and Movie datasets, respectively. Additionally, Chang et al. (2022) put forward a hybrid activity detection model for pedestrians. They proposed a deep model that uses YOLOv3 as object detection technology followed by a hybrid Deep Sort algorithm to track each detected target. Then CNN is employed to extract motion characteristics, and finally, LSTM is utilized for building an abnormal behavior detection model to predict actions like kicking, falling, and punching in the benchmark fall-detection dataset with an accuracy of 97.4%, sensitivity of 98.6%, specificity of 97.2%, and precision of 97.3%. Also, Khan et al. (2021) put forward a transfer-based concept for identifying human actions that include steps such as feature mapping, feature selection, and feature fusion. To map features, two deep models InceptionV3 and DenseNet201, are used, along with a serial-based method for fusing extracted features. Khan et al. (2022) provided a fully connected DL and Improved Ant Colony Optimization(IACO) technique for human gait recognition using video scenes. Video frames are normalized, selected, and pretrained. ResNet101 and InceptionV3 are changed in terms of the dense layer according to the number of classes of the dataset. Both modified models are trained using transfer learning and features are extracted.

12.2.1.3 Human Action Recognition in Videos

HAR in videos is a computer vision task that involves identifying and classifying human actions or activities performed in original video sequences. As shown in Figure 12.4, this field has applications in various domains, including

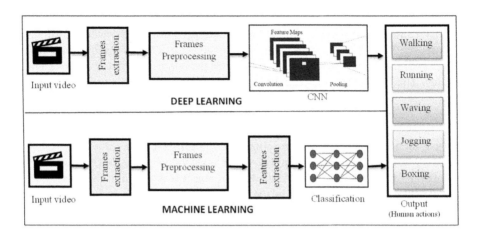

FIGURE 12.4 An illustration of human activity detection framework via data-driven models.

video surveillance, sports analysis, human-computer interaction, and healthcare. There are two main approaches to HAR such as handcrafted and deep learning approaches:

- *Hand-crafted features:* This approach involves extracting features from the video or image data that are relevant to the action being performed. These features can include the position and movement of body parts, the appearance of the person, and the background environment.
- *Deep learning:* These techniques use DL-based methods to learn features from the video or image content. These deep models have been demonstrated to be quite effective for HAR, and they are presently the latest developments for many HAR applications.

HAR is now a significant subject in the discipline of computer vision research, and it has received greater interest in the past few years. It plays an important role in interpersonal connections and human-human interaction, as evidenced by a number of survey studies published in the literature such as (Beddiar et al., 2020; Chaquet et al., 2013; Hussain et al., 2019; Jobanputra et al., 2019; Singh et al., 2020). The recognition of objects in various video sequences can help in understanding or recognizing human activities. The primary goal is to recognize certain human activities present in a video, such as human actions, human behavior, or human-human interactions. Normal human activities are categorized into five classes, namely, gesture (movements of body parts such as the hand, face, and head), action (walking, jogging, running waving, and so on), interaction (human-object or human-human interaction), group activity (involving multiple people or objects), and behavior of a person (whether normal or abnormal behavior). For more than a decade, video action identification and summarization have been the two most active fields of computer vision research. Video data, on the other hand, is often enormous, and the relevant events present in the video may be focused only on small parts. As a result, the researchers employ the video summarization approach, which concisely captures the most significant contents of videos. It can be accomplished by the use of key-frames or a video skimming approach, which produces a summarized human action skim video as an output. The evolution of wearable gadgets has resulted in the tendency of identifying the various actions present in the video. The term egocentric refers to an individual rather than a society that follows people's daily routines and is known as self-centered activities. Analyzing and identifying a person's activities is done to help senior citizens, disabled persons, and patients. Researchers have developed some models in the field of HAR, like Sanal Kumar & Bhavani (2019) propose an ADL (activity in daily living) model for detecting human actions in egocentric videos. It is divided into two phases: training and testing, in addition the point and texture characteristics such as Grey Level Co-occurrence Matrix (GLCM), SURF, and Local Binary Pattern (LBP) are extracted and evaluated by the model. The features extracted from descriptors are fed into classifiers such as probabilistic neural networks, which are made up of interconnected neurons in successive layers and were first proposed by Specht (1990). It computes nonlinear decision boundaries by substituting an exponential activation function for the sigmoidal function, and it recognizes activity using classifiers such as support vector machine, or SVM, and KNN. The SVM + KNN classifier using GLCM surpasses other classifiers. Additionally, Hussein and Piccardi (2017) developed a latent-structure-based SVM framework for activity recognition and subsequently generated a video summary at the exact same time. The model evaluated the quality of a suggested summary to the annotations of different annotators. In terms of action recognition accuracy and summary quality, the experimental findings reveal that the approach surpasses earlier techniques.

12.2.1.4 Abnormal Activity or Event Detection

Abnormal activity or event detection (AAED) in videos is a critical task in various applications, including surveillance, healthcare, and traffic monitoring. It aims to identify unusual or suspicious behaviors that deviate from normal patterns. AAED algorithms are broadly classified into two main approaches, namely, supervised and unsupervised learning. The former methods require a labeled dataset of videos, where each video is annotated with labels indicating whether it contains abnormal activities or not. The algorithm is trained on this dataset to learn the patterns that distinguish between normal and abnormal events. Common supervised learning techniques for AAED include SVM, naïve Bayes, random forest, and decision tree, whereas later methods do not require labeled data. Instead, they rely on analyzing the inherent patterns and structures in the video data to identify anomalies. Unsupervised learning techniques for AAED include:

- *Optical Flow Analysis:* Optical flow tracks the motion of pixels between consecutive video frames. Anomalous events often involve unusual motion patterns, which can be detected by analyzing optical flow.
- *Background Subtraction:* Background subtraction techniques separate foreground items (such as people or automobiles) from the background.

Abnormal activities often involve objects moving in unexpected ways or appearing in unusual locations.
- *Autoencoders:* These are neural networks that learn to reconstruct the input data. Anomalies can be detected by identifying data points that the autoencoder cannot accurately reconstruct.

The crime rate and population have both increased in recent years and with the rapid increase in crime rate, monitoring all actions in public places in the absence of surveillance cameras would entail the presence of security guards everywhere. This resulted in increased security via video surveillance, as CCTV cameras are used for video monitoring in places where security officers are not present. As humans engage in both normal (i.e., usual) and abnormal (i.e., suspicious or weird) actions in public places, video surveillance is becoming more and more prevalent to observe human activities while preventing unsure human behavior. These unusual behaviors are suspicious human activities in public settings, such as fire or theft detection in videos, abandoned object detection for explosives assaults, and violence detection or abnormal activity on roads. The normal activities are those that humans do daily, such as walking, jogging, running, and chatting. As a result, an intelligent monitoring system is required that can recognize all actions and detect the more harmful and suspicious acts performed by humans in CCTV videos. Figure 12.5 depicts the illustration of the abnormal activity detection framework via machine and deep-learning-based models. The framework consists of the original video and then frames extraction occurs after that frames preprocessing to enhance quality and then data-driven models are used to categorize the different types of abnormal actions present inside a video, namely, theft or fire detection, abnormal activity of roads, abandoned object detection. Researchers have done work such as Li et al. (2019) presented an EVIAD (Efficient Visual and Inertial aberrant Detection System), model for detecting unusual behaviors in real-time video scenes. The probabilistic model is used to detect abrupt and intense changes in a user's movement along with creating a

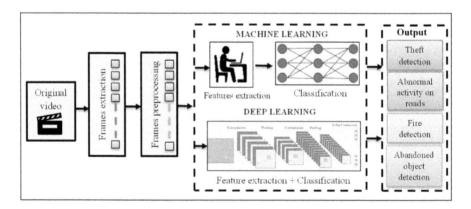

FIGURE 12.5 An illustration of abnormal activity detection through machine and deep learning techniques.

general sensor-based trigger algorithm. Song et al. (2016) present yet another work on anomalous activity identification using a hybrid approach for surveillance footage. The method is divided into three phases. The pedestrian and vehicle trajectories are first acquired in a tracking and detection framework utilizing the HOG descriptor and latent SVM for classification. Second, based on the collected trajectories, unusual events in surveillance footage are exposed and then random forest along with trajectory features are used to detect unusual events and obtain satisfactory results. Finally, the max-coverage procedure generated a summarized sequence with the most relevant events covered in the fewest frames. Ali et al. (2020) provided an automatic system for object detection in real-time surveillance and detecting unusual human activity in an academic setting while taking security and emergency concerns into account. The model recognized moving objects in a particular video and separated the foreground from the background with more focus on three anomalous activities such as falling, boxing, and waving as well as one regular activity such as walking. Muhammad et al. (2018) suggested a cost-effective CNN-based DL model to detect fire for surveillance videos. The pretrained GoogleNet architecture is used for fine-tuning the model, which increases the detection accuracy by reducing the number of false warnings when compared to recent fire detection schemes. The experimental results reveal that the developed architecture surpasses both the previous hand-crafted feature-based fire detection approaches and the AlexNet-architecture-based fire detection technique.

12.2.1.5   Video Summarization

Video summarization is the process of condensing a longer video into a shorter version, retaining the most important and representative content. This can be useful in various applications, including video browsing, content retrieval, and efficient video storage. There are several methods and approaches to achieve video summarization, depending on the task's specific needs and objectives. The rapid advancement of computing technologies has led to the generation of massive amounts of data in the form of video, audio, and text. Amongst all multimedia content, videos are the most significant and play an important role in human life. Human eyes focus on crucial information rather than extensive information for various reasons, one of which is the length of the video file. Shorter videos are much better at providing a concise overview of the complete subject than longer length videos. The video summarization can be seen in a variety of ways, depending on the type of summary generated as earlier stages use text descriptions to create a summary from a given video. There are four kinds of summaries generated from the original video: static (also known as key-frame selection), dynamic (also known as video skimming), image, and text summary.

A key-frame selection is a set of frames taken sequentially from the initial raw video and then cluster formation takes place to extract the salient frames from the video. Video skimming, on the other hand, provides an output by picking video segments that are of interest to the user. Initially, the preprocessing of the video takes place by performing the segmentation of the original video along with boundary detection. Thereafter, shots are detected from videos, as shots represent the combination of frames and are known as skim units, and combining these skim units

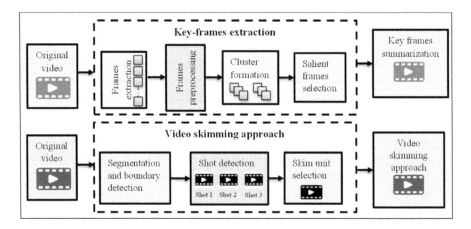

FIGURE 12.6 A depiction of video summarization model through key-frames selection and video skimming approach.

form summarized skim videos as depicted in Figure 12.6. The researchers have done work on video summarization (Avellino et al., 2021; Del Molino et al., 2017; Sabha & Selwal, 2021, 2023a, 2023b; Sahu & Chowdhury, 2020; Tiwari & Bhatnagar, 2021; Xu et al., 2021; Zaynab & Youness Tabii, 2015) who generated summary of entire original video into matter of minutes and seconds. The summary constitutes significance that satisfies the criteria of semantic coverage and pleasantness like the artifacts should not be present in the summary.

12.2.1.6   Image Segmentation

Image segmentation is the process of splitting an image into numerous segments (also known as superpixels or image regions). The goal of image segmentation is to group pixels together that share common characteristics, such as color, intensity, or texture. Image segmentation is a crucial task in the computer vision field that is employed in numerous applications, such as object detection, tracking, and image classification. There are many different techniques that can be used for image segmentation. Some of the most common techniques include the following:

- *Thresholding:* Thresholding is a simple but effective technique for image segmentation. It involves setting a threshold value and then assigning all pixels above the threshold to one segment and all pixels below the threshold to another segment.
- *Edge detection:* It is a technique for identifying the edges of objects that are present inside an image. Once the edges have been detected, they can be used to segment the image into different regions.
- *Region growing:* Region growing is a technique for growing regions in an image. It involves starting with a seed pixel and then adding all adjacent pixels that have similar characteristics to the seed pixel.
- *Clustering:* Clustering is a technique for grouping similar data points together. It can be used for image segmentation by clustering pixels based on their color, intensity, or texture.

- *Deep learning:* Deep learning models have been shown to achieve state-of-the-art results on image segmentation tasks. Deep learning algorithms learn how to derive features from images and map them to various segments. Some of the deep learning models for computer-vision-based video analysis techniques are CNN (Koutras et al., 2018; Muhammad et al., 2019), RNN, LSTM, encoder-decoder, and deep neural networks.

12.2.1.7 Image Captioning

Image captioning is the process of producing written descriptions for images. Natural language processing and computer vision are used to construct the captions. image captioning is the process of providing a natural language description of a picture. It is a challenging task since the model must comprehend the visual information of the image and create a description that is both accurate and grammatically correct. Image captioning models are typically trained on a dataset of images and captions. The model trains to extract details from images and transfer these attributes to a word sequence after that the model can then generate captions for new images by identifying features from the images and translating these attributes to a word sequence. The framework for generating image captions from images using intelligent approaches is shown in Figure 12.7. The framework consists of the original image then preprocessing is applied to increase the quality of the image. Subsequently, features are extracted by employing convolutional neural network and sequence learning model LSTM to generate a caption from a specific image.

Image captioning models can be used for a variety of applications, such as:

- *Accessibility:* Image captioning can be used to generate captions for images for people who are blind or visually impaired.
- *Social media:* Image captioning can be used to generate captions for images on social networking sites like Facebook and Twitter. This can help to make social media more accessible to people who are blind or visually impaired.
- *Search:* Image captioning can be used to improve the accuracy of image search engines. By understanding the content of images, search engines can better match images to user queries.
- *Education:* Image captioning can be used to create educational materials, such as textbooks and presentations. By generating captions for images, these materials can be made more accessible to people who are learning a new language.

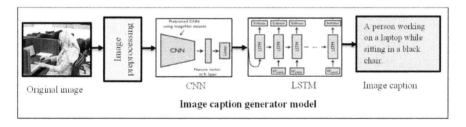

FIGURE 12.7   A depiction of a generic framework for image caption generator model.

12.2.2 DEEP LEARNING TECHNIQUES

In recent years, deep-learning-based algorithms have transformed video analysis by extracting and detecting the significant content from original video. These DL-based models are trained to learn complex characteristics and relationships in video data, allowing them to attain outstanding performance on a wide range of video analysis tasks. Examples of deep learning techniques for video analysis tasks include the following.

12.2.2.1 Convolutional Neural Networks (CNNs)

CNNs are a sort of deep learning model that excels at image and video processing. CNNs can be used to perform a wide range of video analysis tasks, including object recognition, tracking, and classification. CNNs are a sort of artificial neural network that excels at image processing and are inspired by the shape of the human brain's visual cortex, which is responsible for analyzing visual information. CNNs are composed of layers, each of which executes a specialized task (Aldahoul et al., 2022; Hosseini et al., 2022). The first layer of a CNN is typically a convolutional layer and it extracts features from the input image. These features can be simple, such as the edges of objects, or more complex, such as the shape of an object. After the convolutional layers, there are typically one or more pooling layers. The size of the feature maps produced by the convolutional layers is reduced by the use of pooling layers. This makes CNN training and deployment more efficient and the final layer of a CNN is typically a fully connected layer. It takes the output of the pooling layers and produces a prediction for any given task. For example, if the CNN is being used for image classification, the fully connected layer would produce a prediction of the class of the object in the image. CNNs have been demonstrated to achieve outstanding performance in an extensive variety of image processing applications such as image categorization, object recognition, and image segmentation. CNNs are also used in other applications, such as natural language processing and machine translation. Here are some examples of how CNNs are used in the real world:

- *Image classification:* CNNs are used to categorize images into different classes, such as cats, dogs, and cars that are present in a dataset. This technology is used in a variety of applications including, web search engines, networking, and e-commerce sites.
- *Object detection:* CNNs are employed in image recognition tasks to recognize objects present in an image. This technology is employed in many applications, including self-driving automobiles, medical imaging, and security systems.
- *Image segmentation:* CNNs are employed to split images into various regions. This technology is used in a variety of applications, such as medical imaging, robotics, and video editing.

12.2.2.2 Recurrent Neural Networks (RNNs)

RNNs are a sort of deep learning model that works well with sequential data like video or time series data. RNNs can be utilized for tasks like action recognition and video captioning in video analysis approaches. RNNs are a type of artificial neural network that works well with sequential input and can learn long-term dependencies in data, making them excellent for natural language processing, machine translation, and video processing tasks. RNNs work by feeding the output of one layer back into the input of the next layer (Zhao et al., 2018). This allows the RNN to learn about the temporal context of the data, which is essential for many sequential processing tasks. There are two main types of RNNs:

- *Simple RNNs:* Simple RNNs have a single recurrent layer. This type of RNN is relatively simple to train and deploy, but it is also less powerful than other types of RNNs. It is made up of several fixed activation function units, each of which contains an internal state known as the hidden state of the unit. This hidden state represents the network's past knowledge at any particular step. As demonstrated in Eq. (12.1), the hidden state is modified at each time step to represent a change in the network's knowledge of the past.

$$h_t = f(h_{t-1}, x_t) \tag{12.1}$$

where h_{t-1} represents the previous state, h_t represents the current state, and x_t is the input state. Correspondingly, the activation function is portrayed using Eq. (12.2):

$$h_t = tanh(w_{hh}h_{t-1} + w_{xh}x_t) \tag{12.2}$$

where w_{hh} is weight at recurrent neuron, and w_{xh} is weight at input neuron

The output layer can be expressed as the multiplication of the activation function and corresponding weight as represented in Eq. (12.3):

$$y_t = w_{hy}h_t \tag{12.3}$$

where y_t is output and *why* is weight in the output layer

- *Long short-term memory (LSTM) networks:* LSTM networks are a type of RNN that is designed to overcome the limitations of simple RNNs. LSTM networks have a recurrent layer with three gates: a forget gate, an input gate, and an output gate. These gates allow the LSTM network to learn long-term dependencies in the data. The LSTM is made up of three gates: a forget gate, an input gate, and an output gate. LSTM is commonly employed in time series forecasting, recognition of speech, identification of handwriting, and HAR, among other applications. The outputs of the forget gate, input gate, and output gate are denoted by the letters f, (i and g), and o, respectively. The gates are depicted in Eqs. (12.4)–(12.6).

$$f_t = \sigma[(w_{fx} \times h_{t-1}) + (w_{fx} \times x_t) + b_f] \tag{12.4}$$

$$i_t = \sigma[(w_{ix} \times h_{t-1}) + (w_{ix} \times x_t) + b_i] \tag{12.5}$$

$$o_t = \sigma[(w_{ox} \times h_{t-1}) + (w_{ox} \times x_t) + bo] \tag{12.6}$$

where f_t, i_t, and o_t denote final, input, and output gates, respectively.

w_{fx}, w_{ix}, and w_{ox} indicate weights of forget, input, and output gates, respectively, xt represent the input at each gate, and b_f, b_i, and b_o denote the bias at each gate.

12.3 PERFORMANCE PROTOCOLS

In the current situation, event or activity detection in original video footage has a wide range of applications such as security surveillance, action detection in sports video, and interaction of human with object and human with human. The categorization or identification of several actions present in a video is a significant subject of computer vision research.

12.3.1 BENCHMARK DATASETS

This section discusses the various kinds of datasets present in video analysis, based on distinct classifications of video analysis methods (i.e., object, event-based, and human and abnormal event detection). As mentioned in Table 12.1, these benchmark datasets are supplied in the form of videos, their corresponding number of frames along with type of video analysis technique.

12.3.2 PERFORMANCE METRICS

The efficiency of computer-vision-based video analysis techniques employed in smart applications is measured using appropriate datasets and well-established performance evaluation protocols. In this section, we will discuss the common performance metrics that are used to evaluate video analysis and summarization approaches. The most often used quantitative assessment metrics in models based on data are precision, recall, precision, accuracy, f-score, and the rate of error. According to Table 12.2, the most utilized evaluation criteria for video analysis methodologies are accuracy and F-score.

12.4 OPEN RESEARCH ISSUES

This section discusses and highlights the various open research challenges that are present in the existing techniques and are used for further research in the computer vision field.

a. *The Background is Cluttered and Dynamic*: The context in which distinct human actions are recorded is crucial for proper recognition. The majority of solutions are based on the assumption that HAR algorithms work efficiently in a static and uniform indoor environment. In contrast, this performance suffers significantly in public gatherings due to background noise, which produces a dynamic or chaotic background and serves as an interruption (Muhammad et al., 2018).

TABLE 12.1

A Summary of Benchmark Datasets Used in Video Analysis Techniques

Dataset name	Year	No. of videos	Length of video	Frames per second	Resolution	Scenes (Indoor/ Outdoor)	Video analysis technique
KTH	2004	600 videos	4 seconds	25 fps	160*120	Indoor/ Outdoor	Human action detection
WEIZMANN	2005	90 videos	3 minutes	50 fps	180*144	Indoor/ Outdoor	Human action detection
UCF50	2010	6681 clips		25 fps	320 * 240	Indoor/ Outdoor	Human action detection
HMDB51	2011	6766 clips	-		-	In/ Outdoors	Human action detection
Multi-KTH	-	600 videos	4 seconds	25 fps	640*480	Indoor/ Outdoor	Human action detection
VIRAT	2011	16 videos	8.5 hours		-	Outdoor	Event detection
TVSUM	-	50 videos	1–5 min		-	Indoor/ Outdoor	Generic detection
VSUMM		50 videos	1–4 min	30 fps	352*240	Indoor/ Outdoor	Generic detection
SumMe		25 videos	1.5–6.5 min		-	Indoor/ Outdoor	Generic detection
ActivityNet 100	2015	Total of 849 hours of video	5–10 minutes	30 fps	1280*720	Indoor/ Outdoor	Human activities
CCTV-fight		1000 clips	5–70 sec		variable	Indoor/ outdoor	Violence activity
Hockey fight		1000 clips	1.6–1.96 sec		360*288	Outdoor	Violence activity
AVSS2007	2007	3 videos	3.5 min		-	Indoor/ outdoor	Abandoned object

b. *Multi-View Invariance*: The task of recognizing human activities becomes highly complex due to viewpoint invariance. The majority of the systems stated for human action detection performed well with a single viewpoint; however, they performed inadequately with numerous viewpoints as the viewing angle has a significant influence on activity recognition. Undoubtedly, distinct points of view can result in different forms of the same activity (Mumtaz et al., 2018b; Tian et al., 2011).

c. *Occlusion*: The temporary absence of human body parts caused by being behind something or someone with greater apparent breadth is known as occlusion. There are three types of occlusions: Self-occlusion: where some parts of the body are obscured by other parts from one perspective. The movement of "talking" cannot be seen whenever a person puts their

TABLE 12.2

A Description of the Performance Measures Used in Video Analysis Techniques

S. no.	Acronym	Metrics description	Formula
01	Accuracy	It determines the accuracy as the number of correct predictions generated by the model throughout the full test dataset.	$Accuracy = \dfrac{TP + TN}{TP + TN + FP + FN}$
02	Precision	Precision is a metric used to assess the accuracy of a positive forecast. In other words, how certain are you that a favorable occurrence will occur?	$Precision = \dfrac{TP}{TP + FP}$
03	Recall	The true positive rate, also known as recall, is the percentage of true positives predicted in a dataset compared to all positives. In some cases, it is also referred to as sensitivity.	$Recall = \dfrac{TP}{TP + TN}$
04	Error	It is computed by dividing the total number of incorrect predictions by the total quantity of predictions in the dataset. The minimum and maximum possible error rates are 0.0 and 1.0, respectively.	$Error\ rate = \dfrac{FP + FN}{P + N}$
05	F-score	An f-score is a statistic used to assess the accuracy of a model through recall and precision.	$F1 = 2 * \dfrac{Precision * Recall}{Precision + Recall}$

palm directly in front of their lips. When two or more people in a crowd hide each other, occlusion by an object happens when somebody's components are blocked from one point of view by an object (Muhammad et al., 2018).

d. *Poor Weather Condition*: Natural threats to HAR systems include bad weather. Darkness, fog, blowing snow, and rain, for example, reduce visibility and make it difficult to differentiate between actions. Many things change when the weather is bad: colors fade rapidly, distances become more difficult to assess, and so on (Liu & Yuan, 2018).

e. *Detecting Challenging Anomalies in a Crowded Environment*: Existing video analysis algorithms perform poorly when the video contains a busy environment or a complex event, such as a terrorist attack, a suicide bomber at a public protest, or a theft in a crowd. As a result, dealing with these complicated settings always results in lower accuracy when detecting usual or unusual behavior in video footage (Guo & Lai, 2014; Liu & Yuan, 2018).

f. *Visual Appeal and Semantic Coverage*: Despite the occurrence of artifacts (rapid shifting of shots or frames) in a video sequence may at times distract from its semantic nature and smoothness. As a result, video summarization should adhere to two criteria: Visual appearance as well as semantic coverage (Avellino et al., 2021; Tiwari & Bhatnagar, 2021).

g. *Misinterpretation of Human Behavior*: The algorithm frequently misinterprets human actions in video sequences; for instance, jogging can be misconstrued as fast running, alongside the model fails to differentiate between boxing and punching (Ahmad et al., 2019; Zare et al., 2020; Zhao et al., 2019).

h. *The Existing Model Has Limited Accuracy and Efficiency*: DL-based models require a large amount of data to recognize objects, but as the volume of hidden layers in the framework increases, so does the complexity and execution time. As a consequence, the model's accuracy and effectiveness deteriorate (Muhammad et al., 2020).

i. *Limited Dataset*: A huge amount of dataset is required for the deployment of robust deep learning models such as CNN, RNN, and LSTM (Rouast & Adam, 2020).

j. *The Utilization of Deep Sequence Models such as RNN and LSTM is Limited*: According to the available literature, sequence learning models for human-action-based video analysis have received little attention in this area. The techniques known as LSTM (long short-term memory networks) and RNN are rarely employed in detection methods (Jalal et al., 2014).

12.5 CONCLUSIONS

The computer vision process involves several processes, including image capture and processing, analysis, decision-making, and taking the necessary action. A digital camera or CCTV is always used as part of computer vision software or applications to take the image. Therefore, it first takes a picture and saves it as a digital file and then preprocess this image to take the required action. Object and activity identification, image segmentation and labeling, video analysis, and summarization are some of the different computer vision techniques used for video analysis. A common technique for providing a brief summary of a lengthy video is video summarization. It can be either handcrafted-based feature techniques (using feature descriptors) or deep learning (i.e., DL-based technique). This study investigates cutting-edge (SOTA) computer vision algorithms for video analysis, ranging from classical to data-driven approaches. Additionally, based on the conventional deep method, we presented a taxonomy for the classification of computer vision algorithms. Using benchmark datasets and performance metrics, we also give an analysis of evaluation processes for different approaches. According to this study, the majority of the research has been focused on activity or event detection algorithms, with minimal contribution toward the summarization and captioning research field. Furthermore, for each subcategory, we identify and outline several open research issues that should be further explored by the research community in the field of computer vision.

REFERENCES

Aggarwal, J. K., & Ryoo, M. S. (2011). Human activity analysis: A review. *ACM Computing Surveys*, *43*(3). https://doi.org/10.1145/1922649.1922653

Ahmad, Z., Illanko, K., Khan, N., & Androutsos, D. (2019). Human action recognition using convolutional neural network and depth sensor data. *ACM International Conference Proceeding Series*, 1–3. https://doi.org/10.1145/3355402.3355419

Aldahoul, N., Karim, H. A., Sabri, A. Q. M., Tan, M. J. T., Momo, M. A., & Fermin, J. L. (2022). A comparison between various human detectors and CNN-based feature extractors for human activity recognition via aerial captured video sequences. *IEEE Access, 10*, 63532–63553. https://doi.org/10.1109/ACCESS.2022.3182315

Ali, J. J., Shati, N. M., & Gaata, M. T. (2020). Abnormal activity detection in surveillance video scenes. *Telkomnika (Telecommunication Computing Electronics and Control), 18*(5), 2447–2453. https://doi.org/10.12928/TELKOMNIKA.V18I5.16634

Avellino, I., Nozari, S., Canlorbe, G., & Jansen, Y. (2021). Surgical video summarization: Multifarious uses, summarization process and ad-hoc coordination. *Proceedings of the ACM on Human-Computer Interaction, 4*(4), 1–23. https://hal.archives-ouvertes.fr/hal-03160860%0Ahttps://hal.archives-ouvertes.fr/hal-03160860/document

Beddiar, D. R., Nini, B., Sabokrou, M., & Hadid, A. (2020). Vision-based human activity recognition: A survey. *Multimedia Tools and Applications, 79*(41–42), 30509–30555. https://doi.org/10.1007/s11042-020-09004-3

Beghdadi, A., Asim, M., Almaadeed, N., & Qureshi, M. A. (2018). Towards the design of smart video-surveillance system. *NASA/ESA Conference on Adaptive Hardware and Systems (AHS)*, 162–167. https://doi.org/978-1-5386-7753-7

Chang, C. W., Chang, C. Y., & Lin, Y. Y. (2022). A hybrid CNN and LSTM-based deep learning model for abnormal behavior detection. *Multimedia Tools and Applications, 81*(9), 11825–11843. https://doi.org/10.1007/s11042-021-11887-9

Chaquet, J. M., Carmona, E. J., & Fernández-Caballero, A. (2013). A survey of video datasets for human action and activity recognition. *Computer Vision and Image Understanding, 117*(6), 633–659. https://doi.org/10.1016/j.cviu.2013.01.013

Choroś, K. (2014). Categorization of sports video shots and scenes in tv sports news based on ball detection. *Lecture Notes in Computer Science (Including Subseries Lecture Notes in Artificial Intelligence and Lecture Notes in Bioinformatics), 8397*(PART 1), 591–600. https://doi.org/10.1007/978-3-319-05476-6_60

Del Molino, A. G., Tan, C., Lim, J. H., & Tan, A. H. (2017). Summarization of egocentric videos: A comprehensive survey. *IEEE Transactions on Human-Machine Systems, 47*(1), 65–76. https://doi.org/10.1109/THMS.2016.2623480

Gandapur, M. Q. (2022). E2E-VSDL: End-to-end video surveillance-based deep learning model to detect and prevent criminal activities. *Image and Vision Computing, 123*, 104467. https://doi.org/10.1016/j.imavis.2022.104467

Gowsikhaa, D., Abirami, S., & Baskaran, R. (2014). Automated human behavior analysis from surveillance videos: A survey. *Artificial Intelligence Review, 42*(4), 747–765. https://doi.org/10.1007/s10462-012-9341-3

Guo, G., & Lai, A. (2014). A survey on still image based human action recognition. *Pattern Recognition, 47*(10), 3343–3361. https://doi.org/10.1016/j.patcog.2014.04.018

Hosseini, A., Hashemzadeh, M., & Farajzadeh, N. (2022). UFS-net : A unified flame and smoke detection method for early detection of fire in video surveillance applications using CNNs. *Journal of Computational Science, 61*(February), 101638. https://doi.org/10.1016/j.jocs.2022.101638

Hussain, N., Khan, M. A., Sharif, M., & Khan, S. A. (2020). *A deep neural network and classical features based scheme for objects recognition : an application for machine inspection. Cv.*

Hussain, Z., Sheng, M., & Zhang, W. E. (2019). *Different Approaches for Human Activity Recognition: A Survey.* 1–28. https://doi.org/10.1016/j.jnca.2020.102738

Hussein, F., & Piccardi, M. (2017). V-Jaune. *ACM Transactions on Multimedia Computing, Communications, and Applications, 13*(2), 1–19. https://doi.org/10.1145/3063532

Intel. (2020). *Robotics in Healthcare to Improve Patient Outcomes.* https://www.intel.com/content/www/us/en/healthcare-it/robotics-in-healthcare.html

Jalal, A., Kamal, S., & Kim, D. (2014). A depth video sensor-based life-logging human activity recognition system for elderly care in smart indoor environments. *Sensors (Switzerland), 14*(7), 11735–11759. https://doi.org/10.3390/s140711735

Jobanputra, C., Bavishi, J., & Doshi, N. (2019). Human activity recognition: A survey. *Procedia Computer Science, 155*(January 2019), 698–703. https://doi.org/10.1016/j.procs.2019.08.100

Jyotsna, C., & Amudha, J. (2020). *Detection from Surveillance Video. Icimia,* 335–339.

Khan, A., Khan, M. A., Javed, M. Y., Alhaisoni, M., Tariq, U., Kadry, S., Choi, J. I., & Nam, Y. (2022). Human gait recognition using deep learning and improved ant colony optimization. *Computers, Materials and Continua, 70*(2), 2113–2130. https://doi.org/10.32604/cmc.2022.018270

Khan, S., Khan, M. A., Alhaisoni, M., Tariq, U., Yong, H. S., Armghan, A., & Alenezi, F. (2021). Human action recognition: A paradigm of best deep learning features selection and serial based extended fusion. *Sensors, 21*(23). https://doi.org/10.3390/s21237941

Koutras, P., Zlatinsi, A., & Maragos, P. (2018). Exploring CNN-Based Architectures for Multimodal Salient Event Detection in Videos. *2018 IEEE 13th Image, Video, and Multidimensional Signal Processing Workshop, IVMSP 2018 - Proceedings,* 1–5. https://doi.org/10.1109/IVMSPW.2018.8448977

Li, Y., Zhai, Q., Ding, S., Yang, F., Li, G., & Zheng, Y. F. (2019). Efficient health-related abnormal behavior detection with visual and inertial sensor integration. *Pattern Analysis and Applications, 22*(2), 601–614. https://doi.org/10.1007/s10044-017-0660-5

Liu, M., & Yuan, J. (n.d.). *Recognizing Human Actions as the Evolution of Pose Estimation Maps.*

Liu, M., & Yuan, J. (2018). Recognizing Human Actions as the Evolution of Pose Estimation Maps. *Proceedings of the IEEE Computer Society Conference on Computer Vision and Pattern Recognition,* 1159–1168. https://doi.org/10.1109/CVPR.2018.00127

Luna, E., Miguel, J., Ortego, S., & Martínez, D., J. M. (2018). Abandoned object detection in video-surveillance: Survey and comparison. *Sensors (Switzerland), 18*(12). https://doi.org/10.3390/s18124290

Mehmood, A., Khan, M. A., Tariq, U., Jeong, C. W., Nam, Y., Mostafa, R. R., & ElZeiny, A. (2021). Human gait recognition: A deep learning and best feature selection framework. *Computers, Materials and Continua, 70*(1), 343–360. https://doi.org/10.32604/cmc.2022.019250

Mlik, N., Barhoumi, W., & Zagrouba, E. (2014). *Object-based event detection for the extraction of video key-frames. January 2012.*

Muhammad, K., Ahmad, J., Lv, Z., Bellavista, P., Yang, P., & Baik, S. W. (2019). Efficient deep CNN-based fire detection and localization in video surveillance applications. *IEEE Transactions on Systems, Man, and Cybernetics: Systems, 49*(7), 1419–1434. https://doi.org/10.1109/TSMC.2018.2830099

Muhammad, K., Ahmad, J., Mehmood, I., Rho, S., & Baik, S. W. (2018). Convolutional neural networks based fire detection in surveillance videos. *IEEE Access, 6*(March), 18174–18183. https://doi.org/10.1109/ACCESS.2018.2812835

Muhammad, K., Hussain, T., & Baik, S. W. (2020). Efficient CNN based summarization of surveillance videos for resource-constrained devices. *Pattern Recognition Letters, 130,* 370–375. https://doi.org/10.1016/j.patrec.2018.08.003

Mumtaz, A., Sargano, A. B., & Habib, Z. (2018a). Violence detection in surveillance videos with deep network using transfer learning. *Proceedings - 2018 2nd European Conference on Electrical Engineering and Computer Science, EECS 2018,* 558–563. https://doi.org/10.1109/EECS.2018.00109

Mumtaz, A., Sargano, A. B., & Habib, Z. (2018b). Violence detection in surveillance videos with deep network using transfer learning. *Proceedings - 2018 2nd European Conference on Electrical Engineering and Computer Science, EECS 2018,* 558–563. https://doi.org/10.1109/EECS.2018.00109

Münzer, B., Schoeffmann, K., & Böszörmenyi, L. (2018). Content-based processing and analysis of endoscopic images and videos: A survey. *Multimedia Tools and Applications*, *77*(1), 1323–1362. https://doi.org/10.1007/s11042-016-4219-z

Raghunandan, A., Mohana, Raghav, P., & Aradhya, H. V. R. (2018). Object Detection Algorithms for Video Surveillance Applications. *Proceedings of the 2018 IEEE International Conference on Communication and Signal Processing, ICCSP 2018*, 563–568. https://doi.org/10.1109/ICCSP.2018.8524461

Rouast, P. V., & Adam, M. T. P. (2020). Learning deep representations for video-based intake gesture detection. *IEEE Journal of Biomedical and Health Informatics*, *24*(6), 1727–1737. https://doi.org/10.1109/JBHI.2019.2942845

Ruchika, L., Purwar, R. K., Verma, S., & Jain, A. (2021). Crowd abnormality detection in video sequences using supervised convolutional neural network. *Multimedia Tools and Applications*, *0123456789*. https://doi.org/10.1007/s11042-021-11781-4

Sabha, A., & Selwal, A. (2021). HAVS: Human action-based video summarization, Taxonomy, Challenges, and Future Perspectives. *Proceedings of the 2021 IEEE International Conference on Innovative Computing, Intelligent Communication and Smart Electrical Systems, ICSES 2021*, 1–9. https://doi.org/10.1109/ICSES52305.2021.9633804

Sabha, A., & Selwal, A. (2023a). CoSumNet: A video summarization-based framework for COVID-19 monitoring in crowded scenes. *Artificial Intelligence In Medicine*, 107386. https://doi.org/10.1016/j.artmed.2023.102544

Sabha, A., & Selwal, A. (2023b). Domain adaptation assisted automatic real-time human-based video summarization. *Engineering Applications of Artificial Intelligence*, *124*(April), 106584. https://doi.org/10.1016/j.engappai.2023.106584

Saeed, A., Ozcelebi, T., & Lukkien, J. (2019). Multi-task self-supervised learning for human activity detection. *ArXiv*, *3*(2). https://doi.org/10.1145/3328932

Sahu, A., & Chowdhury, A. S. (2020). Multiscale summarization and action ranking in egocentric videos. *Pattern Recognition Letters*, *133*, 256–263. https://doi.org/10.1016/j.patrec.2020.02.029

Sanal Kumar, K. P., & Bhavani, R. (2019). Human activity recognition in egocentric video using PNN, SVM, kNN and SVM+kNN classifiers. *Cluster Computing*, *22*(s5), 10577–10586. https://doi.org/10.1007/s10586-017-1131-x

Sharma, D., & Selwal, A. (2021). On data-driven approaches for presentation attack detection in Iris recognition systems. In: Singh, P.K., Singh, Y., Kolekar, M.H., Kar, A.K., Chhabra, J.K., Sen, A. (eds) *Recent Innovations in Computing. ICRIC 2020. Lecture Notes in Electrical Engineering*, vol 701. Springer, Singapore. https://doi.org/10.1007/978-981-15-8297-4_38

Sharma, D., & Selwal, A. (2022). An intelligent approach for fingerprint presentation attack detection using ensemble learning with improved local image features. *Multimedia Tools and Applications* **81**, 22129–22161 (2022). https://doi.org/10.1007/s11042-021-11254-8

Sharma, D., & Selwal, A. (2023a). A survey on face presentation attack detection mechanisms: Hitherto and future perspectives. *Multimedia Systems* **29**, 1527–1577 (2023). https://doi.org/10.1007/s00530-023-01070-5

Sharma, D., & Selwal, A. (2023b). SFincBuster: Spoofed fingerprint buster via incremental learning using leverage bagging classifier, *Image and Vision Computing*, *135*, 104713, ISSN 0262-8856, https://doi.org/10.1016/j.imavis.2023.104713.

Singh, R., Sonawane, A., & Srivastava, R. (2020). Recent evolution of modern datasets for human activity recognition: A deep survey. *Multimedia Systems*, *26*(2), 83–106. https://doi.org/10.1007/s00530-019-00635-7

Song, X., Sun, L., Lei, J., Tao, D., Yuan, G., & Song, M. (2016). Event-based large scale surveillance video summarization. *Neurocomputing*, *187*, 66–74. https://doi.org/10.1016/j.neucom.2015.07.131

Specht, D. F. (1990). Probabilistic neural networks. *Neural Networks*, *3*(1), 109–118. https://doi.org/10.1016/0893-6080(90)90049-Q

Sreenu, G., & Saleem Durai, M. A. (2019). Intelligent video surveillance: A review through deep learning techniques for crowd analysis. *Journal of Big Data*, *6*(1), 1–27. https://doi.org/10.1186/s40537-019-0212-5

Tabish, M., Tanooli, Z. R., & Shaheen, M.. (2021). Activity recognition framework in sports videos. *Multimedia Tools and Applications*. https://doi.org/10.1007/s11042-021-10519-6

Tian, Z., Xue, J., Lan, X., Li, C., & Zheng, N. (2011). Key object-based static video summarization. *MM'11 - Proceedings of the 2011 ACM Multimedia Conference and Co-Located Workshops*, 1301–1304. https://doi.org/10.1145/2072298.2071999

Tian, Z., Xue, J., Lan, X., Li, C., & Zheng, N. (2014). Object segmentation and key-pose based summarization for motion video. *Multimedia Tools and Applications*, *72*(2), 1773–1802. https://doi.org/10.1007/s11042-013-1488-7

Tiwari, V., & Bhatnagar, C. (2021). A survey of recent work on video summarization: Approaches and techniques. *Multimedia Tools and Applications*, *80*(18), 27187–27221. https://doi.org/10.1007/s11042-021-10977-y

Vrigkas, M., Nikou, C., & Kakadiaris, I. A. (2015). A review of human activity recognition methods. *Frontiers Robotics AI*, *2*(NOV), 1–28. https://doi.org/10.3389/frobt.2015.00028

Wang, T., Chen, J., & Snoussi, H. (2013). Online detection of abnormal events in video streams. *Journal of Electrical and Computer Engineering*, *2013*, 1–12. https://doi.org/10.1155/2013/837275

Wang, X., & Gupta, A. (2018). Videos as space-time region graphs. *Lecture Notes in Computer Science (Including Subseries Lecture Notes in Artificial Intelligence and Lecture Notes in Bioinformatics)*, *11209 LNCS*, 413–431. https://doi.org/10.1007/978-3-030-01228-1_25

Wei, L., & Shah, S. K. (2017). Human activity recognition using deep neural network with contextual information. *VISIGRAPP 2017 - Proceedings of the 12th International Joint Conference on Computer Vision, Imaging and Computer Graphics Theory and Applications*, *5*(Visigrapp), 34–43. https://doi.org/10.5220/0006099500340043

Xu, J., Sun, Z., & Ma, C. (2021). Crowd aware summarization of surveillance videos by deep reinforcement learning. *Multimedia Tools and Applications*, *80*(4), 6121–6141. https://doi.org/10.1007/s11042-020-09888-1

Xu, L., Yan, S., Chen, X., & Wang, P. (2019). Motion recognition algorithm based on deep edge-aware pyramid pooling network in human-computer interaction. *IEEE Access*, *7*, 163806–163813. https://doi.org/10.1109/ACCESS.2019.2952432

Zand, M., Etemad, A., & Greenspan, M. (2022). Oriented bounding boxes for small and freely rotated objects. *IEEE Transactions on Geoscience and Remote Sensing*, *60*, 1–15. https://doi.org/10.1109/TGRS.2021.3076050

Zare, A., Abrishami Moghaddam, H., & Sharifi, A. (2020). Video spatiotemporal mapping for human action recognition by convolutional neural network. *Pattern Analysis and Applications*, *23*(1), 265–279. https://doi.org/10.1007/s10044-019-00788-1

Zaynab, E., & Youness Tabii, A. B. (2015). Video summarization: Techniques and applications. *International Journal of Computer and Information Engineering*, *9*(4), 928–933. https://waset.org/publications/10000964/video-summarization-techniques-and-applications

Zhao, B., Li, X., & Lu, X. (2018). HSA-RNN: Hierarchical Structure-Adaptive RNN for Video Summarization. *Proceedings of the IEEE Computer Society Conference on Computer Vision and Pattern Recognition*, 7405–7414. https://doi.org/10.1109/CVPR.2018.00773

Zhao, R., Xu, W., Su, H., & Ji, Q. (2019). Bayesian hierarchical dynamic model for human action recognition. *Proceedings of the IEEE Computer Society Conference on Computer Vision and Pattern Recognition*, *2019-June*, 7725–7734. https://doi.org/10.1109/CVPR.2019.00792

13 An Efficient and Robust Iris Spoof Detection Pipeline via Optimized Deep Features

Zeenat Zahra, Arvind Selwal, and Deepika Sharma

13.1 INTRODUCTION

Biometric-based recognition systems are being tremendously utilized for many critical applications, such as law enforcement, healthcare, cell-phone authentication, person's identification, border control, and commercial products. Dominantly, iris recognition systems are being utilized for this purpose due to their higher accuracy with user's convenience. A recent report [1] indicates that the iris market is anticipated to increase from USD 2.3 billion in 2019 to USD 4.3 billion by 2024, with a CAGR of 13.2% over the course of the projected year. The key driving factor influencing market growth is how frequently government organizations utilize iris recognition technology for identity verification. The increasing use of iris recognition technology in the consumer electronics sector and the strong demand for iris scanners for access control applications are two additional key factors that are favourably impacting the growth of the iris recognition industry. Even though these systems provide enhanced security to a range of computer applications, they are nevertheless subject to several security-threatening assaults. Among the eight vulnerable attack points identified by Jain et al. [2], the presentation or spoof assaults are considered the most widely and easier attempted at the sensor level. The sensing module of an iris biometric authentication system is primarily compromised when a forged modality is presented utilizing a number of artefacts, including artificial eyes, textured contact lenses, paper printouts of the iris, and more [3–5].

With the emergence of data-driven approaches (handcrafted or automated classifiers), counter measuring these spoof attacks has become a comparatively easier and more accurate task of computer vision. The main focus of this work is to design an efficient anti-spoofing mechanism that makes the counterfeit class difficult to surpass the model. The technique is efficient mainly because of the fact that pre-trained model is employed to extract the deep level features from an iris image. We have proposed a novel DeFusNet model based on a score level fusion of features from fine-tuned models, namely VGG-19 and ResNet-50. The principal component analysis (PCA) algorithm is used to select optimal parameters after feature set concatenation. Afterwards, we evaluated the proposed DeFusNet on benchmark datasets: Notre

DOI: 10.1201/9781032614663-13

Dame 2017 and NDCLD-15. We have conducted several experiments to investigate the effectiveness of the proposed scheme. To alleviate spoof attacks, an iris spoof detection network (DeFusNet) is incorporated with the identification system that serves as a check point.

Main contributions of the work are summarized as follows:

i. We proposed a novel technique for iris anti-spoofing via fusion of deep level features from fine-tuned pre-trained models.
ii. The proposed technique used the concept of transfer learning for efficient modelling.
iii. Our algorithm demonstrates excellent performance in an experimental setup.

The remainder of the article is organized as follows: Section 13.2 illustrates the framework for iris anti-spoofing. However, Section 13.3 discusses the proposed training and testing algorithms. Section 13.4 discusses the result and discussion, and finally, conclusion is presented in Section 13.5.

13.2 PROPOSED DEFUSNET MODEL FOR IRIS ANTI-SPOOFING

This section presents DeFusNet and provides an overview of the proposed framework for iris vitality detection. The framework will incorporate all essential ideas required for spoof detection, including dataset selection, augmentation techniques, feature extraction, and classification. The recommended picture training and testing algorithms are also covered in Section 13.4.3.

13.2.1 DeFusNet Framework

In Figure 13.1, the suggested DeFusNet method is depicted. The phases of training and testing are two possible divisions. The following steps make up the framework are shown in Figure 13.1.

Initially, the iris images are pre-processed by applying a set of elementary operations, such as resizing, image quality enhancement, image normalization, data augmentation, and label encoding. Thereafter, two pre-trained models, such as VGG-19 [6] and ResNet-50 [7], are fine-tuned by discarding the classification header. The pre-processed images are fed to the pre-trained model, and two distinct feature vectors (i.e., fv_1, fv_2) are extracted, respectively, from two pre-learned models. These feature vectors are concatenated to yield a combined set, namely fv. As the dimensionality of the resultant feature vector is larger and some features may be redundant, feature selection techniques need to be applied. One of the reasons for selecting the pre-trained model for our DeFusNet iris spoof detector model is its robustness and ability to tackle inconsistencies in the images. Initially, VGG-19 network is used, and the features are extracted and stored in an empty list such as fv_1 [8–12] (Figure 13.2).

Likewise, another model, i.e., ResNet-50 is utilized and features are extracted by discarding the classification layers. The features obtained from ResNet-50 model are stored in another list named fv_2 (Figure 13.3).

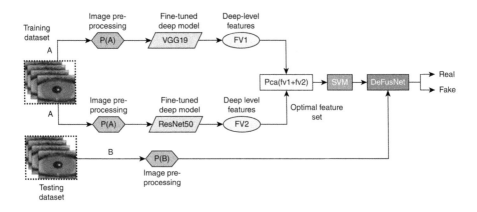

FIGURE 13.1   Framework of the proposed DeFusNet technique.

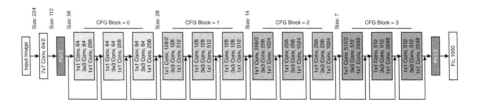

FIGURE 13.2   An illustration of the fine-tuned ResNet-50 model.

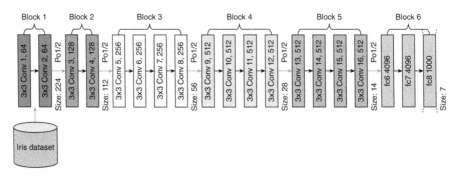

FIGURE 13.3   An illustration of fine-tuned VGG-19 model.

13.2.2   Feature Level Fusion

In our proposed approach, we use concatenation operation to merge the deep level features extracted from iris images. In this manner, the feature sets become very large, resulting in millions of features that are computationally inefficient. Hence, a dimensionality reduction approach is needed to select only highly significant features from the iris images. Therefore, we apply a PCA to select highly significant features from the combined feature set. Suppose 'n' is the dimensionality of the

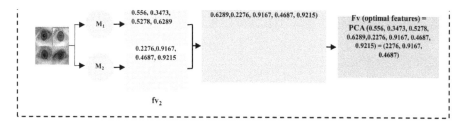

FIGURE 13.4   An example of proposed feature level fusion in DeFusNet for iris anti-spoofing.

feature set extracted from the VGG-19 model and 'm' is the size of the feature set extracted from the fine-tuned ResNet-50 model. Hence, the total size of the concatenated feature set is of the order of 'n+m,' which is of the order of ~ million features. Therefore, the PCA can help us choose an optimal feature set where all the features are highly discriminative.

The feature level fusion of our proposed approach for iris liveness detection is depicted in Figure 13.4. The input iris images are subjected to selected pre-trained models M_1 and M_2, where two feature vectors fv_1 and fv_2 are extracted, respectively, for each image in the dataset. The feature level fusion results in simply concatenating both the extracted feature vectors to build a feature vector fv. Thereafter, the optimal features are selected by applying a potent PCA algorithm to generate fv (optimal features). Then, we learn a linear support vector machine (SVM) based on the optimal features extracted from robust deep level models.

13.3   PROPOSED TRAINING AND TESTING ALGORITHMS

The process of training and evaluating algorithms is presented in this section. Any model must go through a critical training and testing phase, as we all know, and how those phases are carried out will affect how well the model performs.

13.3.1   TRAINING ALGORITHM

Figure 13.5 shows a training algorithm for learning a DefusNet model. The training dataset, which consists of iris images of size 't,' is initially collected from the anti-spoofing collection 'Dt.' This dataset is subjected to a series of pre-processing techniques in order to improve and get these collected samples ready for further processing.

Algorithm 13.1: To build a DeFusNet model using pre-trained models.

Input: D_t of iris images (Live and Fake)
Output: DeFusNet
1:   Begin
2:   Let there are t= $|D_t|$ number of training images
3:   for i= 1 to t do

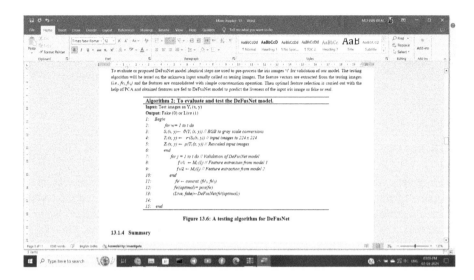

FIGURE 13.5   A depiction training algorithm for our proposed DefusNet for iris liveness detection.

4:              $S_i(x, y) \leftarrow \vartheta(X_i(x, y))$ // RGB to grey scale conversions
5:              $T_i(x, y) \leftarrow r(S_i(x, y))$ //input pictures to 224 × 224 in size
6:              $G_i(x, y) \leftarrow \partial(T_i(x, y))$ // Data augmentation
7:              $Z_i(x, y) \leftarrow \mu(G_i(x, y))$// Rescaled input images
8:      end
9:              for j = 1 to 2 do // Finetuning the models M_j
10:                 $Q \leftarrow (M_j - d)$ // Discard the output layer
11:                 $Q \leftarrow f(Q)$ // Freeze the non-trainable layers
12:                 $Q \leftarrow (Q + n)$ // augment output header layer with 2 neurons
13:           end
14:             for k = 1 to i do // extract feature vectors fv_1, fv_2 from M_1, M_2
15:      for image I belongs to database D_k
16:             Extract fv^k_1 from M_1 using D_k s.t $M_1 \leftarrow I(D_k)$
17:             Pick all the instances of database D_j
18:             Extract fv^k_2 from M_2 using D_k s.t $M_2 \leftarrow V(D_k)$
19:                end
20:             $fv^k \leftarrow concat(fv^k_1, fv^k_2)$
                $fv(optimal) = pca(fv^k)$
21:         DeFusNet $\leftarrow$ svm(fv(optimal)) // training and hyper tuning DeFusNet
22:   end

To simplify the complexity of the computation, RGB is initially converted to greyscale using the 'ϑ'operator. Then, photos are downsized by 'r' to 224×224 in order to achieve homogeneity in our model. Additional augmentation processes

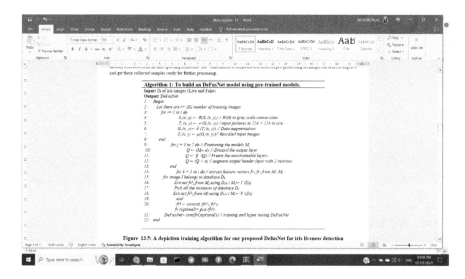

FIGURE 13.6 A testing algorithm for DeFusNet.

'∂' are carried out to fictitiously increase the volume of data. Images eventually get rescaled 'μ' to create the best comparability between data collection methods and texture instances. After fine-tuning both models following image pre-processing, the dense 'd' layer is removed and a new 'n' output layer is included in the model 'Q.' The refined models M_1 and M_2 are then trained on all of the occurrences in the database 'Dk.' The combined model output is represented as 'fvk.' DeFusNet is finally constructed as 'svm (fv(optimal))' by hyper-tuning with ideal parameters.

13.3.2 TESTING ALGORITHM

To evaluate or propose the DeFusNet model, identical steps are used to pre-process the iris images 't' for validation of our model. The testing algorithm will be tested on the unknown input, usually called testing images as shown in Figure 13.6. The feature vectors are extracted from the testing images (i.e., fv_1, fv_2), and the features are consolidated with simple concatenation operation. Then optimal feature selection is carried out with the help of PCA, and obtained features are fed to the DeFusNet model to predict the liveness of the input iris image as fake or real.

Algorithm 13.2: To evaluate and test the DeFusNet model.

Input: Test images as Y_t (x, y)
Output: Fake (0) or Live (1)
1:   Begin
2:   for w= 1 to t do
3: S_i (x, y)← $\vartheta(Y_i$ (x, y)) // RGB to grey scale conversions
4: T_i (x, y) ← $r(S_i$ (x, y)) // input images to 224 x 224

5:          $Z_i(x, y) \leftarrow \mu(T_i(x, y))$ // Rescaled input images
6:          end
7:              for j = 1 to t do // Validation of DeFusNet model
8:                  $fv1 \leftarrow M_1(I_j)$ // Feature extraction from model 1
9:                  $fv2 \leftarrow M_2(I_j)$ // Feature extraction from model 2
10:         end
11:             $fv^j \leftarrow concat(fv^j_1, fv^j_2)$
12:             $fv^j(optimal) = pca(fv^j)$
13:             $(Live, fake) \leftarrow DeFusNet(fv^j(optimal))$
14:
15:     end

13.4   RESULTS AND DISCUSSIONS

This section presents the results of our model and suggested algorithms. By putting the methods into practice, these results were attained. Due to the limits of GPU servers, we decided to do the aforementioned operation using Google Colab. A comparison of our findings with SOTA image IVD is also provided. The entire setup for the experiment is explained aside from that.

13.4.1   EXPERIMENTAL ANALYSIS

In this part, we evaluate the potency of our strategy as a spoof identification tool. We first give a quick rundown of the assessment datasets and performance methods we utilized as benchmarks for judging performance. DeFusNet is tested using the Notre Dame-17 and Notre Dame-15 iris datasets after it has been adjusted. In order to assess the technique's capacity for generalization, the model is also examined in cross-dataset scenarios. The success rate of the DeFusNet model and the associated SOTA IVD techniques are then contrasted.

13.4.2   EVALUATION DATASETS

Three benchmark iris anti-spoofing datasets, LivDet 2017 Notre Dame [13], IIITD-WVU [13] and LivDet 2015 NDCLD [14], are used for evaluation purposes. Table 13.1 provides a summary of the information in these datasets. In total, 4800 samples were used for Notre Dame 2017: 1200 training iris images (600 real, 600 fake), 1800 test photos (900 real, 900 false), and 1800 unidentified test samples (900 real, 900 fake). Only contact lenses are included in fake samples. However, LivDet 2015 NDCLD contains counterfeit samples of just textured contact lenses and 4068 sample iris pictures obtained with IrisGuardAD100 and IrisAccessLG400.

Due to the high resource requirements for training huge datasets in deep learning models, such as GPU servers and large RAM. However, assessing the model's performance on such a short dataset is insufficient because deep learning models need a million data points in order to perform better. As a result, we have used data augmentation techniques to expand our small subset of dataset in order to get around the

TABLE 13.1

An Outline of LivDet 2017 Notre Dame and LivDet 2015 NDCLD Datasets

S. No.	Dataset	Wavelength	Image Size	Sensors Used	Live	Fake	Types of Fakes
1	LivDet 2017 Notre Dame	NIR	640×480	IrisGuardAD100 and IrisAccessLG4000	2400	2400	CL
2	LivDet 2015 NDCLD	NIR	640×480	IrisGuardAD100 and IrisAccessLG400	–	4068	TCL
3	IIITD-WVU	NIR	640×480	IriShield MK2120U	2250	4000	Print, TCL

issue of a small dataset. We have used scaling, horizontal flip, rotation, and shearing as data augmentation approaches.

13.4.3 PERFORMANCE PROTOCOLS

We have chosen the most efficient and frequently used evaluation methodologies in order to assess performance. We utilize the training photos from both datasets to train the DeFusNet, and testing examples are selected across an extensive variety of domains to evaluate performance. APCER, BPCER, ACER, ACA, and ROC are five common performance indicators used to evaluate models. Table 13.2 covers each protocol's specific description in great depth.

13.4.4 EXPERIMENTAL RESULTS

To evaluate the effectiveness of our proposed DeFusNet, we performed several experiments. The results for the proposed model evaluated under different scenarios are reported in the succeeding sub-sections.

13.4.4.1 Experiment 1: Hyper-Parameter Tuning

The performance of the overall model is highly impacted when evaluated under different parameter settings. These parameters are explicitly defined and may control the overall learning process before the application of a classification algorithm to a dataset. The DeFusNet is evaluated for different set of parameters, such as kernel function, c value, degree, and gamma, and the results are listed in Table 13.3. The following are the hyper-parameters that are changed with different settings: The c value is a regularization parameter, with regularization intensity inversely proportional to the regularization strength. The kernel function turns the training dataset into higher dimensions so that it can be separated linearly. The radial basis function, abbreviated rbf, is the default kernel function for the Python implementation

TABLE 13.2

A Summary of Performance Metrics Used for the Evaluation of DeFusNet

S. No	Acronym	Metrics Name	Mathematical Expression	Definition
1	APCER	Attack presentation classification error rate	$APCER = \dfrac{FP}{TN + FP}$	Ratio of fake samples identified as real with total samples using same presentation attack instrument (PAI) samples.
2	BPCER	Bonafide presentation classification error rate	$BPCER = \dfrac{FN}{TP + FN}$	Ratio of genuine presentations that are incorrectly classified with the total number of genuine presentations.
3	ACA	Average classification accuracy	$ACA = \dfrac{TP + TN}{N}$	It represents the percentage of correctly classified instances out of the total instances in a dataset.
4	ACER	Average classification error rate	$ACER = \dfrac{APCER + BPCER}{2}$	It is the average of APCER and BPCER for pre-defined threshold.
5	ROC	Receiver operating characteristic		It is a graphical representation of the performance of a binary classification model, which shows the trade-off between the true positive rate (TPR) and the false positive rate (FPR) at various classification thresholds.

TABLE 13.3

Performance Evaluation of DeFusNet at Various Parameter Settings

S. No.	Hyper-Parameters	Search Space	Parameter Setting	Model Performance (%)	Selected Value
1	c value	[1.0, 10, 100, 1000]	0.1	96.25	100
			10	98.95	
			100	**99.33**	
			1000	98.89	
2	Kernel	[linear, rbf, polynomial]	Linear	99.44	rbf
			Rbf	**99.82**	
			Polynomial	98.67	
3	Degree	[1, 2, 3]	1	99.39	2
			2	**99.50**	
			3	99.06	
4	Gamma	[auto, scale]	Auto	97.21	auto
			scale	96.10	

of the support vector classifier. The degree represents the degree of the polynomial employed by a polynomial kernel. Finally, the gamma is a coefficient for RBF, polynomial, and sigmoid kernels that adjusts the influence of a single training sample.

Table 13.3 clearly reveals that the DeFusNet results in an ACA=99.33% for c value=100, whereas least accuracy is obtained for a c value of 0.1. The kernel function with rbf resulted in 99.82% accuracy. When the model is evaluated with polynomial function, the degree of 2 provides the highest accuracy of 99.50%. Finally, the model resulted best with the gamma value of auto.

13.4.4.2 Experiment 2: Performance Evaluation on Notre Dame 2017

To detect the efficacy of the proposed DeFusNet, the model is evaluated on Notre Dame LivDet 2017 iris dataset, and the results are depicted in Table 13.4. Different pre-trained models are validated individually on the Notre Dame dataset. Among four pre-learned models, the highest accuracy of 97.21% is obtained with VGG-19 Network. The highest ACER=9.10% is resulted when the model uses Inception Net architecture for iris anti-spoofing. The proposed model results in outstanding performance with ACA=99.43%, whereas score level fusion also results in improved accuracy and a lower ACER of 2.23%.

13.4.4.3 Experiment 3: Performance Evaluation on IIITD-WVU 2017

The proposed model is evaluated on IITD-WVU dataset, and results are reported in Table 13.5. The DeFusNet results in an ACA=99.92% with a least ACER of 0.98%. The results show that highest ACER=8.19% is obtained when live and spoof iris image classification is performed with MobileNet model. In the case of score level fusion, an ACA of 98.99% is attained, which shows the efficiency of VGG-19 and ResNet-50 networks for iris anti-spoofing.

13.4.4.4 Experiment 4: Cross-dataset Evaluation of DeFusNet

The proposed model is evaluated under cross-dataset scenario to detect the generalization capability and results are listed in Table 13.5. In this case, the model is trained on one dataset and validated with the images from the other anti-spoofing dataset. Table 13.5 clearly reveals that the highest classification accuracy of 98.29% is obtained when DeFusNet is trained on IIITD-WVU dataset and evaluated on

---

TABLE 13.4

Evaluation of Different Pre-Trained Models on Notre Dame 2017 Dataset

S. No	Model	ACA (%)	ACER (%)
1	VGG-19	97.21	4,22
2	ResNet-50	94.56	9.01
3	InceptionNet	92.11	9.10
4	MobileNet	93.78	7.22
5	Score level fusion (VGG-19+ResNet-50+SVM)	98.21	2.23
6	DeFusNet (VGG-19+ResNet-50+SVM)	**99.43**	1.01

TABLE 13.5

Evaluation of Different Pre-Trained Models on Notre Dame 2017 Dataset

S. No	Model	ACA (%)	ACER (%)
1	VGG-19	98.33	2.11
2	ResNet-50	96.76	5.01
3	InceptionNet	93.11	7.19
4	MobileNet	92.93	8.19
5	Score level fusion (VGG-19+ResNet-50+SVM)	98.99	2.45
6	DeFusNet (VGG-19+ResNet-50+SVM)	**99.92**	0.98

NDCLD-15 dataset. Similarly, it performs well with APCER=2.1 @BPCER=1.10 when trained on Notre Dame 2017 and validated with NDCLD-15 dataset. It performs well when trained with samples of IITD-WVU dataset and tested on the Notre Dame or NDCLD-15 dataset, which may be due to the large number of training images in IITD-WVU dataset as compared to the other two.

13.4.4.5　Experiment 5: Comparison with SOTA Iris Anti-Spoofing Techniques

To further validate the performance of proposed DeFusNet, the model is compared with six different SOTA iris anti-spoofing approaches evaluated on Notre Dame and IITD-WVU datasets, and results are depicted in Tables 13.6 and 13.7, respectively, with ACA performance metrics.

Table 13.8 clearly shows that the DeFusNet model outperforms the SOTA iris PAD techniques with overall ACER=1.01%. The highest ACER=8.89% is shown by SpoofNet model.

Similarly, in the case of IIITD-WVU dataset, the least ACER=0.98% is shown by our proposed DeFusNet model, which shows the robustness of overall iris PAD approach as compared to other SOTA techniques. Figure 13.7 shows the comparison of DeFusNet model with other SOTA similar approaches implemented on Notre Dame and IIITD-WVU datasets.

TABLE 13.6

Cross-Dataset Performance of DeFusNet

S. No	Training Dataset	Testing Dataset	APCER (%)	BPCER (%)	ACER (%)	ACA (%)
1	Notre Dame-17	IIITD-WVU	1.23	3.67	2.45	97.23
2	Notre Dame-17	NDCLD-15	2.21	1.10	1.65	98.01
3	IIITD-WVU	Notre Dame-17	3.11	2.01	2.56	97.11
4	IIITD-WVU	NDCLD-15	1.21	1.24	1.22	98.29
5	NDCLD-15	Notre Dame-17	3.37	2.84	3.10	96.17
6	NDCLD-15	IIITD-WVU	3.43	3.29	3.36	95.23

TABLE 13.7

A Comparison of DeFusNet with Related Approaches Evaluated on Notre Dame 2017

S. No	Technique	ACER (%)
1	LivDet iris 2017 winner [15]	4.03
2	MSA [16]	6.23
3	SpoofNet	9.49
4	MobileNet fusion	8.89
5	A-PBS	3.94
6	PBS	4.97
7	Proposed DeFusNet	1.01

TABLE 13.8

A Comparison of DeFusNet with Related Approaches Evaluated on IIITD-WVU2017

S. No	Technique	ACER (%)
1	LivDet iris 2017 winner [5]	16.70
2	MSA	11.13
3	SpoofNet	18.62
4	MobileNet fusion	15.09
5	A-PBS	6.90
6	PBS	7.01
7	Proposed DeFusNet	0.98

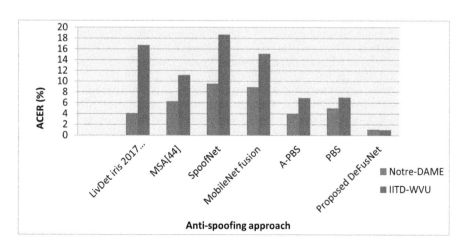

FIGURE 13.7 Performance of DeFusNet and other iris SOTA anti-spoofing approaches.

13.5 CONCLUSIONS AND FUTURE SCOPE

This work offers a thorough analysis of DL-based iris anti-spoofing methods. Many studies have been conducted in this fascinating area of iris authentication system vulnerability detection [17–19]. Our survey unequivocally demonstrates that, for iris authentication reasons, the paradigm has evolved from modern, customized based on feature solutions to current DL-based systems since the year 2017. Although there are many advantages that the DL approaches have over their handcrafted-based cousin, there are still a lot of problems that the field of research needs to address. We had presented a new DNeFusNet framework that was based on combining the forecasts from two effective fine-tuned models in order to address some of the major problems. ResNet-50 and VGG-19 were used to achieve weighted fusion at the feature level. Using the iris anti-spoofing datasets from Notre Dame 2017 and NDCLD 2015, we proved the model's feasibility. Our weighted score level fusion technique's competitive accuracy is demonstrated by contrasting the results with those of the SOTA algorithms. However, our weighted feature level fusion strategy aids in enhancing the model's classification accuracy on the selected iris datasets. We wish to test the given method with different datasets, including LivDet-iris 2020. A future study will also focus on assessing the model's efficiency in cross-sensor and cross-material settings. Additionally, the effectiveness of additional biometric modalities, such as fingerprint, face, palm print, and others, might be assessed.

REFERENCES

1. Z. Rui and Z. Yan, "A Survey on Biometric Authentication : Towards Secure and PrivacyPreserving," IEEE Access, vol. PP, no. c, p. 1, 2018. doi: 10.1109/ACCESS.2018.2889996.
2. A. Jain, R. Bolle, and S. Pankanti, *Introduction to Biometrics* (pp. 1–41). Springer US.
3. S. Sumner, "Biometrics and The Future," Syngress, vol. 2, pp. 183–198, 2016.
4. W. Yang, S. Wang, J. Hu, G. Zheng, and C. Valli, "SS symmetry Security and Accuracy of Fingerprint-Based Biometrics : A Review," *Symmetry*, *11*(2), 141, 2019. doi: 10.3390/sym11020141.
5. M. Adámek, M. Matýsek and P. Neumann, "Security of Biometric Systems," Procedia Eng., vol. 100, pp. 169–176, 2015. doi: 10.1016/j.proeng.2015.01.355.
6. J. A. Gliner, G. A. Morgan, N. L. Leech, J. A. Gliner and G. A. Morgan, "Measurement Reliability and Validity," Res. Methods Appl. Settings, pp. 319–338, 2021.
7. K. He, X. Zhang, S. Ren and J. Sun, "Deep Residual Learning for Image Recognition," Proc. IEEE Comput. Soc. Conf. Comput. Vis. Pattern Recognit., vol. 2016-Decem, pp. 770–778, 2016. doi: 10.1109/CVPR.2016.90.
8. A. K. Jain and A. Ross, Handbook of Biometrics, A. K. Jain, P. Flynn and A. A. Ross, Eds. Springer London, 2008, pp. 1–22.
9. A. K. Jain, A. Ross and S. Prabhakar, "An Introduction to Biometric Recognition," IEEE Trans. Circuits Syst. Video Technol., vol. 14, no. 1, pp. 4–20, 2004. doi: 10.1109/TCSVT.2003.818349.
10. D. Sharma and A. Selwal, "FinPAD: State-of-the-Art of Fingerprint Presentation Attack Detection Mechanisms, Taxonomy and Future Perspectives," Pattern Recognit. Lett., vol. 152, no. 1, pp. 225–252, 2021.

11. D. Sharma and A. Selwal, "A Survey on Face Presentation Attack Detection Mechanisms: Hitherto and Future Perspectives," Multimedia Syst., vol. 29, no. 3, pp. 1527–1577, 2023.: 10.1007/s00530-023-01070-5.

12. A. K. Jain and A. Kumar, "Biometrics of Next Generation : An Overview," *Second Generation Biometrics*, *12*(1), 2–3. 2010.

13. D. Yambay *et al.*, "LivDet Iris 2017 – Iris Liveness Detection Competition 2017," IEEE Int. Jt. Conf. Biometrics, IJCB 2017, vol. 2018-Janua, pp. 733–741, 2018. doi: 10.1109/BTAS.2017.8272763.

14. J. S. Doyle and K. W. Bowyer, "Robust Detection of Textured Contact Lenses in Iris Recognition Using BSIF," IEEE Access, vol. 3, pp. 1672–1683, 2015. doi: 10.1109/ACCESS.2015.2477470.

15. D. Yambay *et al.* (2017, October). LivDet iris 2017—Iris liveness detection competition 2017. In *2017 IEEE International Joint Conference on Biometrics (IJCB)* (pp. 733–741). IEEE.

16. M. Fang, N. Damer, F. Boutros, F. Kirchbuchner and A. Kuijper, "Cross-Database and Cross-Attack Iris Presentation Attack Detection Using Micro Stripes Analyses," Image Vis. Comput., vol. 105, p. 104057, 2021. doi: 10.1016/j.imavis.2020.104057.

17. D. Sharma and A. Selwal (2021). On Data-Driven Approaches for Presentation Attack Detection in Iris Recognition Systems. In: P. K. Singh, Y. Singh, M. H. Kolekar, A. K. Kar, J. K. Chhabra, A. Sen, Eds., Recent Innovations in Computing. ICRIC 2020. Lecture Notes in Electrical Engineering, vol 701. Springer, Singapore. https://doi.org/10.1007/978-981-15-8297-4_38.

18. D. Sharma and A. Selwal, SFincBuster: Spoofed Fingerprint Buster via Incremental Learning Using Leverage Bagging Classifier, Image Vis. Comput., vol. 135, 2023. https://doi.org/10.1016/j.imavis.2023.104713.

19. D. Sharma and A Selwal. A Survey on Face Presentation Attack Detection Mechanisms: Hitherto and Future Perspectives. Multimedia Syst. vol. 29, pp. 1527–1577, 2023. https://doi.org/10.1007/s00530-023-01070-5

14 Advancements in Computer Vision for Biometrics Enhancing Security and Identification

Vivek Upadhyaya

14.1 INTRODUCTION

Biometrics is the study of the physical and behavioral traits that make each person unique, such as fingerprints, iris patterns, face features, voice, and even things like the way a person walks or types. People's identities can be established and confirmed by using these intrinsic identifiers. They are an important part of current security and identification systems. Biometrics are more accurate and secure than traditional methods like passwords or ID cards because they are hard to fake or copy. As technology has changed, so has the field of biometrics. Computer vision methods are now used to capture, analyze, and interpret biometric data, making security and identification processes more reliable and efficient.

You can't say enough about how important biometrics are for security and recognition. Since digital transactions, online services, and private information are becoming more common, the need for strong identity verification has grown by a factor of ten. Biometric systems make it easy and safe to confirm a person's identity. This makes it less likely that someone will get in without permission, steal someone's name, or commit fraud. In areas like law enforcement, border control, and financial services, accurate identification through biometrics helps avoid and solve crimes, keep borders safe, and keep financial transactions safe. Biometrics also makes life easier for people because they don't have to remember multiple passwords or carry around physical ID papers.

Zhang et al. (2022) describe that using biometrics in security and recognition systems can improve accuracy, speed, and the user experience, among other things. Biometric data is also a strong defense against identity theft or unauthorized entry because it is unique to each person. As technology improves and computer vision methods make it easier to collect and analyze biometric data, the number of ways biometrics could be used to protect our digital and physical lives keeps growing. To find a good mix between security, convenience, and people's rights, it is important to use the power of biometrics while taking into account privacy concerns and ethical issues. In the next part, we'll talk about computer vision and what role it plays in biometric systems.

 DOI: 10.1201/9781032614663-14

The chapter commences with an initial section that provides an introduction, elucidating the importance of biometrics in augmenting security and identity. This part emphasizes the difficulties and constraints associated with conventional biometric systems and establishes the foundation for the breakthroughs explored in the next sections. Subsequently, the chapter explores the core principles of computer vision, providing a comprehensive explanation of the essential concepts and methodologies that serve as the foundation for the progress in biometric applications. This part serves to facilitate the comprehension of the technical underpinnings of the topic, especially for readers with limited prior expertise.

The primary focus of this chapter centers around an in-depth examination of the latest breakthroughs in computer vision as applied to biometric systems. The content is partitioned into multiple subsections, with each portion dedicated to examining a distinct facet of the technology. The subjects that may be addressed encompass facial recognition, iris recognition, fingerprint analysis, and gait recognition, among various others. The chapter offers a comprehensive analysis of recent advancements in several biometric modalities, including deep-learning-based techniques, multi-modal biometrics, and resilience against adversarial attacks. Furthermore, this study includes the presentation of real-world applications and case studies in order to demonstrate the practical significance of these improvements. The chapter concludes by providing a concise overview of the main points discussed and exploring the potential future avenues and obstacles in the domain of computer vision for biometrics. This comprehensive analysis equips readers with a thorough comprehension of the topic and its significance in augmenting security and identification systems.

14.2   FUNDAMENTALS OF BIOMETRICS AND COMPUTER VISION

Fundamentals of Biometrics and Computer Vision are about how to use advanced technologies to get information from visual data, analyze it, and figure out what it means for different uses. Biometrics is the study of people's unique physical and behavioral traits, like fingerprints, face features, and iris patterns, that can be used to identify them with a high degree of accuracy. The goal of computer vision is to give machines the ability to understand and analyze visual information from the real world. This is done by doing things like finding objects, dividing up images, and tracking motion. Together, these fields use advanced algorithms, machine learning, and image processing methods to improve security, authentication, surveillance, medical diagnostics, and many other areas by using the power of visual data analysis and pattern recognition. In this section, we will elaborate on different types of biometric modalities and introduction to computer vision.

14.2.1   Explanation of Biometric Modalities (e.g., Fingerprint, Iris, Face, Voice, etc.)

Modern security and recognition systems are based on biometric modalities, which include a wide range of physical and behavioral traits that are unique to each person. Fingerprint biometrics is one of the most well-known methods. It uses the unique patterns of ridges, valleys, and small details on the fingers to identify people. Fingerprint

TABLE 14.1
Different Biometric Modalities with Key Features

Biometric Modality	Physical Attribute	Unique Patterns	Non-Intrusiveness	Applicability Range	Spoofing Vulnerability
Fingerprint	Fingers	High	High	Wide	Moderate
Iris	Eye	Very High	Moderate	Wide	Low
Face	Facial Features	Moderate	High	Wide	Moderate
Voice	Voice	Moderate	Moderate	Limited	Low
Palmprint	Palm	High	Moderate	Limited	Moderate

recognition systems use special sensors to pick up these patterns and algorithms to compare and match them against a database. This is a quick and reliable way to check someone's identity which is described by Uwaechia and Ramli (2021) in their work. Table 14.1 represents different biometric modalities with key features.

14.2.2 INTRODUCTION TO COMPUTER VISION TECHNIQUES (IMAGE PROCESSING, FEATURE EXTRACTION, PATTERN RECOGNITION)

Mahadevkar et al. (2022) represented computer vision techniques effectively in their work. They explained that computer vision techniques are a big step forward for artificial intelligence because they let computers understand and make sense of visual data from the real world. This amazing piece of technology is built on three main pillars: processing of images, extracting features, and recognizing patterns. Together, these methods give computers the ability to break apart images, pick out important details, and recognize complex patterns. This lays the groundwork for a wide range of applications in fields like healthcare, automotive, surveillance, and entertainment.

In Table 14.2, various computer vision techniques are mentioned with various characteristics.

TABLE 14.2
Various Computer Vision Techniques

Computer Vision Technique	Definition	Purpose	Application	Input Data	Output Data
Image Processing	Manipulating and enhancing images to improve their quality or extract information.	Enhance visibility, remove noise, adjust colors, and more.	Medical imaging, satellite imagery, photography.	Raw or preprocessed images.	Processed images with improved quality or extracted information.

(Continued)

TABLE 14.2 (*Continued*)
Various Computer Vision Techniques

Computer Vision Technique	Definition	Purpose	Application	Input Data	Output Data
Feature Extraction	Identifying and extracting specific attributes or patterns from images.	Reduce dimensionality, highlight relevant information.	Object recognition, facial analysis, image classification.	Images or image patches.	Extracted features, often represented as vectors.
Pattern Recognition	Identifying regularities or patterns within images using statistical or machine learning methods.	Identify known patterns, classify objects, or detect anomalies.	Handwriting recognition, object classification, medical diagnosis.	Image data with labeled patterns.	Classification labels or anomaly indicators.
Object Detection	Locating and identifying instances of specific objects within an image.	Locate objects and provide their spatial coordinates.	Autonomous vehicles, surveillance, robotics.	Images with potential objects of interest.	Detected object bounding boxes and labels.

14.3 TRADITIONAL BIOMETRIC SYSTEMS

Traditional biometric identification methods have been a key part of security and identification systems for decades, helping to control access, authenticate people, and make sure they are who they say they are. These methods use physical or behavioral traits that are unique to each person. This makes it possible to tell one person from another in a unique way. Even though these methods have worked well in some situations, they have some flaws and problems that have led to the development of more advanced fingerprint methods. Traditional biometric system is well explained by Feng (2018), Chiou (2013), and Ogbanufe and Kim (2018).

Various limitations and challenges faced by traditional methods are mentioned in Table 14.3.

Computer vision and its role in the biometrics system are discussed in the next section.

14.4 ROLE OF COMPUTER VISION IN BIOMETRICS

Biometrics relies on computer vision to automatically extract and analyze unique physical and behavioral attributes from photos and videos. Face recognition, fingerprint matching, and iris scanning improve security and user verification

TABLE 14.3

Limitations and Challenges Faced by Traditional Methods

Challenges	Description
Accuracy	Traditional methods often struggle with achieving high accuracy, especially in complex and real-world scenarios.
Variability	Variability in lighting, pose, and environmental conditions can lead to reduced performance of traditional biometric systems.
Non-Cooperative Subjects	Traditional methods are less effective when dealing with non-cooperative subjects who may not adhere to proper positioning or capture conditions.
Template Security	Storing biometric templates in databases poses security risks due to potential breaches and unauthorized access.
Spoofing Attacks	Traditional methods are susceptible to various spoofing attacks, such as presenting fake biometric samples to deceive the system.
Processing Speed	Real-time processing and response requirements may not be met by traditional algorithms, especially as data volumes increase.
Scalability	Traditional methods might struggle to scale effectively to handle large databases or rapidly growing user bases.
Interoperability	Lack of standardization can lead to compatibility issues between different biometric systems and technologies.
Privacy Concerns	Collecting and storing biometric data raise privacy concerns and regulatory challenges related to data protection.
Hardware Dependence	Some traditional methods may rely on specific hardware configurations, limiting their deployment on diverse platforms.
Multi-modal Integration	Integrating multiple biometric traits using traditional methods can be complex and may result in reduced system efficiency.
User Acceptance	The user experience might be negatively impacted by invasive or uncomfortable traditional biometric capture methods.
Adaptability	Traditional systems may struggle to adapt to dynamic environments and evolving user needs without significant modifications.
Complexity	Traditional methods might involve complex feature engineering and rule-based decision-making, leading to maintenance challenges.

in numerous applications. Computer Vision's capacity to process and interpret visual data improves biometric systems' reliability and efficiency.

14.4.1 How Computer Vision Enhances Biometric Systems

Computer vision is a key part of making fingerprint systems work better. It uses advanced methods for analyzing what you see. One of the best things about computer vision is that it can pull out complicated and unique features from biometric data like fingerprints, face features, or iris patterns. Traditional methods have trouble with differences in lighting, pose, and facial expression, but computer vision algorithms can handle these problems well, making sure accurate feature extraction even in settings that are different and hard. Computer vision models can learn hierarchical representations of biometric traits with the help of deep learning designs like convolutional neural networks (CNNs). This lets them see patterns that were hard to notice before and hard to remember. This function improves the accuracy of biometric identification and authentication (Daas et al., 2020; Neto et al., 2022; Pejas & Piegat, 2006).

14.4.2   Overview of Image Acquisition, Preprocessing, and Enhancement Techniques

Computer vision has come a long way, and this has led to big changes in how images are taken, processed, and improved. The goal of these methods is to make biometric applications safer and easier to recognize. Here's a quick summary of these ways:

14.4.2.1   Image Acquisition

In biometric devices, the first step is to get an image. Here, good photos of biological traits are taken so that they can be used later. Computer vision has given us many new ways to make security and identification better (Dvorák et al., 2021).

  a. *3D Imaging*: Depth sensors and 3D cameras enable the acquisition of three-dimensional information, allowing for more accurate and robust capture of facial features or hand shapes. This mitigates challenges posed by variations in pose and lighting.
  b. *Multi-Spectral Imaging*: Capturing biometric traits in multiple spectra (such as visible, near-infrared, or thermal) provides additional information and enhances feature discrimination, making the system more resistant to spoofing attacks.
  c. *Contactless Capture*: Computer vision enables touchless biometric capture, reducing hygiene concerns and enabling more convenient and user-friendly identification processes.

14.4.2.2   Preprocessing

Before further research, the goal of preprocessing is to improve the quality and reliability of biometric data (Bharathi & Sudhakar, 2019; Bychkov et al., 2019). Computer vision has made a number of improvements in this field:

  a. *Normalization*: Techniques such as histogram equalization and contrast enhancement improve the visibility of features by reducing lighting and contrast variations, thus enhancing the discriminative power of biometric data.
  b. *Noise Reduction*: Advanced denoising algorithms, often based on deep learning, can remove sensor noise or artifacts, resulting in cleaner and more accurate biometric data.
  c. *Pose Correction*: Computer vision algorithms can detect and correct facial or body pose variations, aligning the captured image with a standardized template for more accurate matching.
  d. *Super-Resolution*: Super-resolution techniques enhance image resolution and detail, aiding in finer feature extraction and improving the overall accuracy of biometric identification.

14.4.2.3   Enhancement

Enhancement methods focus on making biometric data look better and make it easier to tell them apart (Iqbal et al., 2016; Prasad & Aithal, 2017). Improvements in computer vision have led to the following changes:

a. *Feature Extraction*: Deep-learning-based feature extraction methods automatically learn and extract relevant features from raw biometric data, improving accuracy and robustness.
b. *Augmentation*: Data augmentation techniques generate synthetic variations of biometric images, augmenting the training dataset and enhancing the model's ability to generalize to diverse scenarios.
c. *Fusion of Modalities*: Computer vision enables the fusion of multiple biometric modalities (e.g., fingerprint, face, voice) for more reliable and secure identification by leveraging complementary information.
d. *Dynamic Trait Analysis*: Behavioral biometrics, such as gait or typing patterns, are analyzed using computer vision to enhance continuous authentication and security.

In a nutshell, the progressions that have been made in computer vision have fundamentally altered the methods of picture acquisition, preprocessing, and augmentation that are used in the field of biometrics for the purposes of security and identification. These developments make biometric systems more accurate, resilient, and secure, which in turn makes them more effective tools for authenticating persons and increasing overall security in a variety of applications.

14.5   ADVANCEMENTS IN BIOMETRIC DATA ACQUISITION

Identity verification and security systems have entered a new era marked by increased precision, dependability, and user-friendliness as a direct result of technological advancements in biometric data collecting. Inconsistent lighting, position fluctuations, and restricted sensor capabilities were typical problems that were encountered while using traditional approaches. Nevertheless, a major evolution can be seen in the process of acquiring biometric data as a result of the introduction of cutting-edge technologies (Devaraj & Modi, 2022).

14.5.1   INTRODUCTION TO 3D IMAGING AND DEPTH SENSING FOR IMPROVED BIOMETRIC DATA COLLECTION

In the field of biometrics, 3D imaging and depth sensing have emerged as transformational technologies, revolutionizing the way biometric data may be collected and utilized for improved security and identification. The traditional approaches of data gathering frequently struggled with the difficulties presented by varying lighting conditions, changes in position, and possible attempts to fake the results. The combination of 3D imaging and depth sensing techniques, on the other hand, has opened up new opportunities for overcoming these constraints and providing biometric data that is more precise, dependable, and resilient (Chen et al., 2018).

The act of capturing the three-dimensional structure of objects or situations is referred to as 3D imaging. Imaging in 3D provides depth information in addition to the more conventional 2D photographs. Utilizing this technology, researchers have been able to record the complex geometry and curves of biometric features such as faces, hands, and even body motions. Imaging in 3D allows for a more thorough depiction of the biometric traits since it incorporates depth perception. This enables systems to better discern between real individuals and fraudulent attempts to impersonate them.

14.5.2 Use of Multi-Modal Data (combining Different Biometric Sources) for Enhanced Accuracy

Utilizing multi-modal data, which entails merging information obtained from a variety of biometric sources, can in fact result in improved accuracy and security across a variety of use cases (Tiwari, 2021). This strategy takes advantage of the benefits offered by a number of different biometric technologies, which allows it to circumvent some constraints and deliver an authentication or identification procedure that is more robust and dependable. The following is a list of applications that can make use of multi-modal data to improve accuracy:

a. *Improved Recognition Accuracy*: Combining multiple biometric sources such as fingerprints, facial features, iris patterns, voiceprints, and even behavioral traits like gait analysis can significantly enhance accuracy. By integrating the strengths of each biometric modality, the system can overcome individual limitations and provide a more comprehensive and accurate identification.

b. *Enhanced Security*: Multi-modal systems are inherently more secure as they require an attacker to successfully bypass multiple layers of authentication. This makes it much more challenging for unauthorized individuals to gain access to sensitive systems or data.

c. *Reduced False Positives and Negatives*: Each biometric modality has its own strengths and weaknesses. By combining different sources, the system can mitigate the weaknesses of one modality with the strengths of another, resulting in a reduction in both false positive (accepting unauthorized individuals) and false negative (rejecting authorized individuals) rates.

d. *Anti-Spoofing Measures*: Multi-modal systems can incorporate anti-spoofing techniques that can detect and prevent various types of attacks such as using photos, masks, or voice recordings to impersonate legitimate users. These techniques can analyze different biometric sources to ensure the presented data is from a live, authentic source.

e. *Challenging Environmental Conditions*: In real-world scenarios, lighting conditions, noise, and other environmental factors can affect the accuracy of a single biometric modality. By combining multiple sources, the system can adapt to these conditions more effectively and maintain accuracy.

f. *User Convenience*: Some users may find it easier or more comfortable to provide certain types of biometric data over others. For instance, a user might prefer facial recognition over fingerprint scanning. Offering multiple options can improve user experience while maintaining security.

g. *Redundancy and Fault Tolerance*: Multi-modal systems can be designed with redundancy in mind. If one biometric modality fails due to various reasons (e.g., injury affecting fingerprint, hoarseness affecting voice), the system can still authenticate using other available modalities.

h. *Personalization and Adaptability*: Multi-modal systems can be designed to learn and adapt to changes in a user's biometric data over time. For instance, as a person ages, their facial features might change. The system can incorporate new data to ensure continued accurate authentication.

i. *Versatility across Applications*: Different biometric modalities might be more suitable for different scenarios. For example, fingerprints might be preferred in access control systems, while voice recognition might be more practical for phone-based authentication. A multi-modal system can cater to a wider range of applications.

The incorporation of a number of distinct biometric data sources into a multi-modal authentication and identification system provides a potent answer to the problem of how to improve authentication and identification processes without sacrificing accuracy, safety, or usability. However, it is essential to point out that the implementation of such systems necessitates careful consideration of problems regarding privacy, the storage of data, the requirements for processing, and ethical considerations surrounding the use of biometric data. In the following part, the application of deep learning in biometrics will be the primary focus of our attention.

14.6   DEEP LEARNING IN BIOMETRICS

Deep learning has a wide range of applications in the field of biometrics, which has led to a dramatic improvement in the precision and safety of a variety of identification and authentication methods. CNNs have shown extraordinary skill in extracting detailed facial traits, which enables perfect matching even across various angles and lighting conditions. One of the most important applications lies in facial identification. CNNs have shown this proficiency in facial recognition. These networks acquire hierarchical representations of a person's facial characteristics, which enables robust identification for the purposes of access control, surveillance, and user authentication (Almabdy & Elrefaei, 2021; Dhiman et al., 2021; López, 2019).

14.6.1   EXPLANATION OF CONVOLUTIONAL NEURAL NETWORKS (CNNS) AND THEIR APPLICATIONS IN BIOMETRICS

CNNs, have recently emerged as a game-changing technology in the field of biometrics, redefining the landscape of technologies used for identification and authentication. One of the most important applications is face recognition, which is where CNNs really shine because of how well they can extract complex facial features.

CNNs are taught to recognize high-level characteristics like as eyes, noses, and contours by using cascading layers of convolutional and pooling processes. This enables CNNs to conduct accurate and robust facial matching despite being subjected to a wide variety of environmental factors. This functionality is useful for public monitoring, user access controls, and security system design (Jin, 2022). Table 14.4 demonstrates the differences between standard biometric systems and biometric systems based on CNNs.

The fact that CNN-based biometric systems offer major benefits in terms of accuracy and adaptability should not be overlooked; nonetheless, it is crucial to highlight that these systems also come with obstacles, such as the requirement for a large amount of labeled data, the requirement for processing resources, and the possibility of biases. The decision between classical and CNN-based systems is determined by a number of considerations, including the complexity of the application, the resources that are available, and the level of performance that is sought.

TABLE 14.4
Convolutional Neural Network (CNN)-Based Biometric Systems

Aspect	Traditional Biometric Systems	CNN-based Biometric Systems
Data Representation	Typically rely on handcrafted features	Learn features automatically from data
Feature Extraction	Features are manually designed	Hierarchical feature learning through CNNs
Adaptability to Variations	Limited adaptability to variations	Better adaptability to varying conditions
Accuracy	Limited accuracy in complex scenarios	Improved accuracy, especially in complex cases
Handling Unstructured Data	May struggle with raw or noisy data	Can process raw data effectively
Robustness to Noise and Variability	Vulnerable to noise and variations	Better handling of noise and variability
Scalability	May require manual adjustment for scale	Can scale with large datasets and tasks
Training Time	Relatively shorter training times	Longer training times for complex models
Interpretability	Features may lack interpretability	May lack human-interpretable features
Anti-Spoofing	May lack robust anti-spoofing mechanisms	Can incorporate anti-spoofing with learning
Multi-Modal Fusion	Limited capability for fusion	Enhanced fusion of multiple modalities
Adaptation to New Data	Requires manual adjustment for new data	Can adapt to new data with retraining

14.6.2   Case Studies of Deep-Learning-Based Biometric Recognition Systems

A new era of precision and safety in a variety of applications has been ushered in with the help of biometric identification systems that are powered by deep learning. One particularly interesting example can be found in the field of facial recognition. In this application, deep neural networks are able to automatically learn and extract detailed facial traits, which enables accurate identification in a wide variety of settings, including lighting, positions, and expressions. There are uses for this in areas such as law enforcement, access control, and user authentication; nevertheless, it also presents privacy concerns due to the possibility of data misuse and monitoring.

Certainly, the following are a few case studies that illustrate the implementation of biometric recognition systems that are based on deep learning in real-world scenarios.

14.6.2.1   Clearview AI – Face Recognition for Law Enforcement

This contentious firm, Clearview AI (Rezende, 2020), is responsible for the creation of a facial recognition system that is driven by deep learning. For the purpose of identifying persons, the system compiles a big database using photographs scraped from various social media networks. Concerns regarding invasions of privacy and the technology's potential for abuse have been voiced despite the fact that law enforcement agencies have utilized the technology for investigations. The deep learning algorithms of the system give it the ability to match faces across a massive amount of data, which is helpful for both criminal investigations and cases involving missing individuals.

14.6.2.2   Apple Face ID – Facial Recognition for Smartphone Security

Deep learning has been successfully applied to biometrics for user identification in a number of ways, including Apple's Face ID (AbdElaziz, 2021). A complex neural network is used by the system to generate a mathematical representation of the user's face. Authenticating the user and safely unlocking the device are both accomplished with the help of this model. Deep learning enables the system to handle fluctuations in lighting, facial expressions, and changes in appearance over time. This enables the system to offer a biometric identification mechanism that is both convenient and secure for use on smartphones.

14.6.2.3   Nuance Communications – Voice Biometrics for Financial Services

Nuance Communications has created a speech biometrics solution that is based on deep learning and is used in the financial services industry (Kuznetsov et al., 2021). When a user is speaking over the phone with a customer care representative, the system will authenticate the user's identification by analyzing the distinctive qualities of the user's speech. Voice samples are fed into deep learning models, which then analyze the data to identify intricacies in speech patterns that are difficult to imitate. This technology boosts safety by prohibiting unauthorized users from accessing their account information.

14.6.2.4 MorphoWave Compact by IDEMIA – Contactless Fingerprint Identification

The IDEMIA MorphoWave Compact is a contactless fingerprint identification device that is powered by deep learning (Attrish et al., 2021). It functions without the need for physical contact. Multiple cameras are used to take three-dimensional pictures of the user's fingers, which are then analyzed by artificial neural networks. Applications like access control and time monitoring benefit from the system's capacity to acquire high-quality fingerprint photos despite the fact that the fingerprints being captured may be in a variety of orientations or have varying degrees of skin condition.

14.6.2.5 Hyundai's Biometric Car Entry System

Fingerprint recognition is the basis of a new biometric system that has been created by Hyundai and is powered by deep learning (SriAnusha et al., 2019). The technology enables drivers to unlock their automobiles and start them. The technology reads fingerprint data and processes it with the assistance of deep neural networks to ensure that entry into the car is both safe and uncomplicated. This technology not only makes things more convenient for the driver, but it also provides an additional degree of protection against unauthorized entry.

These case studies illustrate the many applications of biometric identification systems based on deep learning across a variety of industries, including law enforcement, smartphone security, financial services, and automobiles. Although these technologies present a number of opportunities for improvement, there are also ethical and privacy issues that must be properly addressed prior to their implementation. In the section that has been forwarded, the biometric modality of facial recognition, which is a very effective method, is explained.

14.7 FACIAL RECOGNITION: FROM 2D TO 3D

The original 2D applications of facial recognition technology have given way to more recent advancements that take into account the three-dimensionality of the human face. The first generation of face recognition systems relied solely on two-dimensional images that were acquired by cameras (Jingwen, 2011). This caused a number of difficulties in terms of accuracy and dependability when dealing with a variety of factors, including differences in lighting, angles, and facial expressions. However, recent developments in technology have allowed for the development of 3D facial recognition, which provides a method that is both more reliable and extensive when it comes to recognizing persons.

Table 14.5 is a table of comparisons illustrating the development of facial recognition from 2D to 3D approaches.

The advantages and disadvantages of utilizing 3D facial data for the purpose of identification are outlined in Table 14.6.

Facial data in 3D offers the promise of greatly improving identification accuracy and resilience in a variety of contexts, but it also comes with its own set of obstacles, such as sensor limitations, processing complexity, and privacy concerns. However, it also holds the promise of significantly improving identification accuracy and robustness. The appropriateness of using 3D facial data for certain applications is determined by how well these advantages and disadvantages are weighed against one another.

TABLE 14.5

Comparison Table Highlighting the Evolution of Facial Recognition from 2D to 3D Techniques

Aspect	2D Facial Recognition	3D Facial Recognition
Data Representation	Relies on flat 2D images	Captures depth and spatial information
Handling Variations	Limited tolerance for variations	Robust to variations in lighting and angles
Lighting Sensitivity	Sensitive to changes in lighting	Less affected by variations in lighting
Angle Sensitivity	Sensitive to varying angles	Handles variations in pose and angle better
Facial Expression	Vulnerable to expression changes	More robust to facial expression variations
Spoofing Detection	Prone to spoofing with 2D images	More resistant to spoofing attempts
Accuracy	Limited accuracy in challenging conditions	Improved accuracy in diverse scenarios
Depth Information	No depth information	Captures depth details for better accuracy
Real-time Performance	Faster processing of 2D images	May require more processing for depth data
Applications	Basic identification and authentication	Enhanced security in various applications
Security and Privacy	More susceptible to spoofing	Better protection against impersonation
Emerging Use Cases	Access control, basic authentication	High-security access, healthcare diagnostics

TABLE 14.6

Benefits and Challenges of Using 3D Facial Data for Identification

Aspect	Benefits of 3D Facial Data	Challenges of 3D Facial Data
Accuracy	Captures depth and spatial information for precise identification	May require advanced sensors for accurate depth mapping
Variation Handling	Robust to variations in lighting, angles, and expressions	Processing complexity increases with 3D data
Angle Tolerance	Handles variations in pose and angle better	Sensor positioning affects angle accuracy
Spoofing Resistance	More resistant to spoofing attempts using 2D images	Certain 3D masks or models can bypass detection
Security	Enhances security against impersonation attempts	Privacy concerns due to capturing detailed facial structure
Usability	Improved performance in challenging scenarios	Potential for higher computational requirements
Expression Robustness	Better recognition under varying expressions	Ensuring consistent recognition under all expressions
Realism	Captures more realistic facial features	Sensor limitations can impact realism
Medical Applications	Potential for medical diagnostics and analysis	Requires integration with medical technology
Complex Environments	Performs well in low-light or noisy conditions	Environmental factors can affect depth accuracy

14.8 IRIS RECOGNITION AND EYE TRACKING

Iris recognition and eye tracking are two independent technologies that can be utilized for a variety of purposes, each of which makes use of the distinctive characteristics of the human eye. Iris recognition is a form of biometric identification that includes photographing and analyzing the complicated patterns that are present in the colored region of the eye (the iris). These patterns are unique to each person. This technology provides an exceptionally high level of accuracy as well as security because iris characteristics do not change over the course of a person's life and are difficult to imitate. Iris recognition has found use in a variety of contexts, including secure access control, immigration checkpoints, and national identification systems. Iris recognition systems are able to verify persons fast and accurately because of the application of sophisticated image processing techniques and pattern recognition algorithms. This not only improves security but also makes the authentication process more user-friendly (Némesin & Derrode, 2016).

14.8.1 ADVANCEMENTS IN IRIS RECOGNITION TECHNOLOGY

Iris recognition technology has seen significant advancements in recent years, which have resulted in significant gains in terms of accuracy, speed, and the breadth of industries in which it may be applied (Farouk et al., 2022; Malgheet et al., 2021). The following are some noteworthy recent events:

a. *High-Resolution Imaging*: Modern iris recognition systems utilize high-resolution cameras and sophisticated imaging techniques to capture detailed iris patterns. This enables the extraction of finer features and enhances the accuracy of identification, even in challenging conditions.

b. *Multi-Spectral Imaging*: Multi-spectral imaging captures iris data across different wavelengths, allowing systems to overcome issues caused by lighting variations, contact lenses, or certain eye conditions. This advancement has made iris recognition more robust and reliable.

c. *Template Compression and Encryption*: Advancements in compression and encryption algorithms have made it possible to store and transmit iris templates in a more secure and efficient manner. This ensures privacy and reduces storage requirements while maintaining accuracy.

d. *Anti-Spoofing Mechanisms*: Iris recognition systems now incorporate anti-spoofing measures to detect presentation attacks using fake iris images or printed photographs. Advanced algorithms analyze pupil dynamics, specular reflections, and texture variations to differentiate real irises from fake ones.

e. *Mobile Integration*: Iris recognition is making its way into mobile devices, enabling secure authentication for smartphones and tablets. Miniaturized cameras and optimized algorithms allow for rapid iris capture and authentication on the go.

f. *Cross-Database Matching*: Deep learning techniques have improved the ability of iris recognition systems to match irises across different databases and conditions, enhancing interoperability and accuracy.

g. *Real-Time Processing*: Advanced hardware and software optimizations have enabled real-time iris recognition, making it suitable for applications requiring quick authentication, such as access control and border crossings.

h. *Enhanced User Experience*: User-centric designs focus on making iris recognition more user-friendly. Systems are becoming more tolerant of slight eye movements and varying gaze directions, leading to smoother and quicker authentication processes.

i. *Healthcare and Medical Applications*: Iris recognition is finding applications in healthcare, where it can be used for patient identification, medical record management, and improving the accuracy of diagnoses based on biometric data.

j. *Diverse Applications*: Beyond security, iris recognition is being adopted in various fields including banking, healthcare, and transportation. It is used for attendance tracking, securing financial transactions, and ensuring compliance in regulated industries.

Overall, advancements in iris recognition technology have expanded its utility, making it a robust and secure biometric identification method applicable across a wide range of industries and scenarios.

14.8.2 UTILIZING EYE TRACKING FOR AUTHENTICATION AND IDENTIFICATION PURPOSES

Although eye tracking is normally not utilized as a stand-alone approach for authentication and identification reasons due to its limitations in terms of uniqueness and security, it is nevertheless able to play a supportive role in boosting these processes when paired with other biometric or contextual information (Yin et al., 2022). This is because eye tracking is limited in its ability to distinguish individuals from one another. Authentication and identification can be accomplished with the use of eye tracking in the following ways:

a. *Multi-Factor Authentication (MFA)*: Eye tracking can be integrated as an additional factor in a MFA system. When combined with other biometric methods like fingerprint, facial recognition, or iris scanning, eye tracking can contribute to a more comprehensive and secure authentication process. For instance, a system might require the user to follow a specific pattern with their eye movements after successfully providing their fingerprint or face.

b. *Continuous Authentication*: Eye tracking can be used for continuous authentication, where a user's identity is verified continuously over time as they interact with a device or application. By monitoring a user's gaze patterns and eye movements, the system can ensure that the authenticated user remains present and engaged, reducing the risk of unauthorized access if the user steps away.

c. *Adaptive Interfaces*: Eye tracking can be used to adapt interfaces and user experiences based on a person's gaze patterns. If a user's gaze deviates from the expected pattern or focus, it could trigger additional authentication steps to ensure the user's identity and prevent unauthorized access.

d. *Behavioral Biometrics*: Eye movement patterns can be considered behavioral biometrics, which is a dynamic characteristic unique to each individual. While not as strong as static biometrics like fingerprints or iris patterns, combining behavioral biometrics with other factors can enhance the overall security of authentication systems.

e. *Health Monitoring and Identification*: Eye tracking can also be used in medical contexts to monitor a person's eye movements and gaze patterns for identification or health monitoring purposes. This could be used to verify the presence of specific individuals in a healthcare facility or to monitor patients with certain conditions.

Voice recognition and speaker verification are cutting-edge biometrics technologies that identify people by voice. Voice recognition recognizes what a user says, but speaker verification verifies their identification by examining their voice patterns. A detailed description is mentioned below.

14.9   VOICE RECOGNITION AND SPEAKER VERIFICATION

Voice recognition and speaker verification are two technologies that are closely related to one another. These technologies both utilize the distinctive vocal features of persons for the goals of identification and authentication. Speech recognition requires conducting a study of an individual's speech in order to determine who is speaking, whereas speaker verification focuses on establishing the individual's identity by validating their identity as the speaker in question. Both methods have potential uses in areas like as user authentication, data security, and a variety of business sectors.

Voice recognition makes use of several machine learning approaches, such as deep learning, to record and analyze the vocal patterns, pitch, tone, and speech features that are individual to each person (Tirumala et al., 2017). This technology has a number of applications, including voice assistants, call centers, and speech-controlled devices. In these contexts, it provides personalized interactions and replies that are tailored depending on the recognized voices of the users. Voice recognition systems are able to differentiate between the various speakers and assign them to particular user profiles, which improves the user experience and makes the system more convenient.

14.9.1   Role of Computer Vision in Voice Recognition
and Speaker Verification

Computer vision is a key part of voice recognition and speaker verification because it makes these technologies more accurate, reliable, and safe (Bai & Zhang, 2021).

Even though computer vision is most often used to process visual data, combining it with technologies that deal with voices has several advantages:

a. *Data Preprocessing*: Using computer vision, audio data can be preprocessed before it is fed into models for voice recognition or speaker proof. This includes getting rid of background noise, setting the volume levels to the same level, and separating the spoken words. Video recordings can also help line up audio parts with the lip movements that go with them for better accuracy.

b. *Lip Reading and Visual Cues*: Computer vision can supplement voice recognition by analyzing the motions of speakers' lips and facial expressions. Even though it is not a foolproof method, lip reading techniques can provide additional information to improve the recognition of spoken words. This is especially helpful in noisy locations or in situations when the quality of the audio is not ideal.

c. *Multi-Modal Fusion*: Voice recognition and speaker verification systems might potentially achieve higher levels of accuracy when visual data is combined with audio data. Multi-modal fusion techniques improve the overall accuracy of identity verification by combining the aural features recovered from voice recordings with the visual features collected from lip movements, facial expressions, or even hand gestures. These techniques combine the audio features extracted from voice recordings.

d. *Anti-Spoofing Measures*: The fight against speaker spoofing can benefit from the use of computer vision's anti-spoofing capabilities. The technology is able to determine whether a real person is present during voice recording by analyzing visual indicators such as eye blinking, head motions, and skin texture. This thwarts any attempts to impersonate the recording using a pre-recorded voice or a synthetic one.

e. *User Authentication and Verification*: During the speech verification process, computer vision can be used to assist in establishing the credibility of a speaker. The system can guarantee that the claimed speaker matches the visual identification by capturing the speaker's face using cameras or other imaging equipment. This provides an additional degree of protection for the verification process.

f. *Behavioral Analysis*: The use of computer vision makes it possible to do behavioral analysis by watching a person's posture and how they move their hands while they are talking. This information can be utilized to construct more in-depth voice profiles for speaker verification, which will ultimately result in an increase in both the system's precision and its level of safety.

g. *Enhanced User Experience*: Computer vision has the potential to provide users of voice-controlled apps with visual feedback or cues to help guide them through interactions. This can be especially helpful for people who have hearing impairments, which helps to ensure that everyone has access to a more inclusive and user-friendly experience.

The use of computer vision into voice recognition and speaker verification systems highlights the strength of multi-modal techniques in biometrics, which ultimately results in better accuracy, resilience, and overall efficacy of these technologies.

14.9.2 INTEGRATION OF LIP MOVEMENT ANALYSIS WITH VOICE RECOGNITION FOR IMPROVED SECURITY

In voice-based authentication and identification systems, the integration of lip movement analysis with voice recognition has the potential to dramatically improve both the security of the system as well as the accuracy of its results (Ezz et al., 2020; Li et al., 2023). These systems are able to offer increased verification capabilities and mitigate potential vulnerabilities because of the way in which they combine the audio information from spoken words with the visual clues acquired from lip movements. The following description will explain how this integration works as well as its benefits:

a. *Multi-modal Fusion*: Processing both audio and visual data simultaneously is required for integrating lip movement analysis with voice recognition. While a person is speaking, computer vision algorithms monitor and analyze how their lips, mouth, and facial expressions move in response to what they are hearing. Next, the audio elements that were extracted from the spoken recording are combined with these visual signals to create a new composite. The combination of these modalities allows the system to acquire a more complete representation of the speaker's identity, which results in an increase in the degree to which authentication is successful.

b. *Enhanced Security*: The purpose of lip movement analysis is to ensure that the uttered words and the movements of the speaker's lips are in sync with one another. This provides an additional layer of security. This helps protect against playback attacks, which are an impersonation technique in which pre-recorded audio is employed. The resilience of the system can be increased against these kinds of spoofing attempts if it is confirmed that there is a real-time correlation between audio and visual inputs.

c. *Robustness in Noisy Environments*: Analysis of lip movement can provide useful supplemental information in situations where audio quality is degraded, such as busy surroundings or conversations with background noise. Because visual cues are less susceptible to being influenced by ambient noise, the system is more dependable in circumstances in which relying just on auditory could lead to errors.

d. *Reduced Vulnerability to Replay Attacks*: In order to mislead voice recognition systems, replay assaults entail playing back previously recorded audio. The study of lip motions makes such attacks significantly more difficult because the visual indications from the movements of the lips would not match the pre-recorded audio, which would hinder a successful impersonation.

e. *Inclusive User Experience*: Integration of lip movement analysis can also improve the user experience, particularly for people whose speech is impaired. The visual component contributes an additional dimension to the authentication process, making it possible to accommodate a greater variety of users without compromising data safety.

f. *Complex Impostor Attacks Prevention*: The combination of lip movement analysis and speech recognition allows for more accurate detection of complex attacks that utilize a voice that has been digitally fabricated to a high standard. Attempts at advanced impersonation can be foiled by the system's ability to detect inconsistencies between the movements of the lips and the audio that is being generated.

Using many modalities, such as incorporating lip movement analysis into speech recognition systems, is one example of how dramatically improving security, accuracy, and resistance against a variety of forms of attack can be achieved by leveraging multiple modalities. However, it is essential to recognize the various obstacles that may arise, such as variances in lip movement as a result of differences in speech patterns, facial emotions, or dialects. These are the kinds of considerations that a well-built system needs to give attention to in order to provide users with both safety and ease of use. Different parts of Behavioral Biometrics and Gait Analysis, which examine walking patterns and other behavioral features to identify identity, are provided below.

14.10   BEHAVIORAL BIOMETRICS AND GAIT ANALYSIS

Behavioral biometrics and gait analysis are two cutting-edge sub-disciplines within the field of biometric identification. These sub-disciplines concentrate on the distinctive behavioral patterns and movements that individuals display (Delgado-Santos et al., 2023; Singh et al., 2021). Behavioral biometrics investigate the dynamic features of human behavior, as opposed to traditional biometrics such as fingerprints or iris patterns, which are anatomically fixed and unchanging. As a result, they offer new dimensions for the verification and validation of identities.

14.10.1   USE OF COMPUTER VISION TO ANALYZE BEHAVIORAL BIOMETRICS (TYPING RHYTHM, GAIT, ETC.)

Computer vision is an essential component in the process of analyzing behavioral biometrics like typing rhythm and gait. This is accomplished by processing visual data in order to extract patterns and characteristics that are specific to the behavior of each individual. The following is an example of how computer vision can be utilized for this purpose:

14.10.1.1   Typing Rhythm Analysis

The way humans type on keyboards or interact with touchscreens can be captured and analyzed using computer vision (Boychuk et al., 2020). This can be done on both desktop and mobile devices. Computer vision algorithms are able to construct a dynamic typing profile for each individual user by monitoring the user's finger movements, keystrokes, and the intervals of time between each of these events. This behavioral biometric takes into consideration things like typing speed, the length of each key press, and the amount of time between each key press. The application of computer vision techniques allows for the processing of recorded video or photos of a user typing, which then allows for the extraction of essential elements that reflect the individual's unique typing rhythm. It is possible to train deep learning models to recognize patterns in these features and differentiate across users based on those patterns. Using this method allows for continuous and passive authentication of users whenever they interact with gadgets.

14.10.1.2   Gait Analysis

Gait analysis is the process of collecting and analyzing an individual's walking patterns. Computer vision is an integral component of gait analysis (Saboor et al., 2020). Computer vision algorithms are then used to interpret this visual data after cameras and sensors have been utilized to record a person's movements as they walk using the person as a subject. These algorithms are able to extract gait-related data that are unique to each individual by tracking joint angles, limb movements, and body posture. The combination of these characteristics produces a gait signature that can be utilized for identification purposes. In order to compensate for differences in clothing, lighting, and camera angles, computer vision helps in the process of segmenting and monitoring essential body parts. The utilization of deep learning models improves the precision of gait analysis by discovering intricate patterns from the available visual data. This results in trustworthy identification from a greater distance.

In either scenario, the extraction of relevant information from visual data relating to behavioral biometrics is impossible without the use of computer vision. These technologies provide ways of authentication that are both continuous and unobtrusive, so enhancing security without negatively impacting the user experience. Nevertheless, in order to achieve accurate and dependable results, it is necessary to handle issues such as fluctuations in the settings, the lighting, and the camera angles.

14.10.2   ENHANCING SECURITY THROUGH CONTINUOUS AUTHENTICATION BASED ON BEHAVIORAL PATTERNS

This approach to identity verification takes a proactive and dynamic stance toward the verification process (Baig et al., 2023). This method enables continual verification beyond the initial phase of logging in by continuously monitoring and analyzing the behavioral patterns of an individual. These patterns can include the rhythm of typing, the motions of the mouse, or the interaction with a device. When users interact with devices or systems, machine learning algorithms detect deviations from known behavioral baselines. If abnormalities are found, these algorithms can trigger alarms or additional authentication processes. This preventative method provides an additional layer of defense against unauthorized access since it enables a speedy response to suspicious activity or efforts at impersonation, thereby halting possible security breaches before they can become more serious. In addition, continuous authentication based on behavioral patterns reduces the dependency on static credentials such as passwords, so providing a smooth and hassle-free user experience while yet upholding stringent security standards.

Continuous authentication based on behavioral patterns comprises a wide range of different methods, each of which uses distinctive behavioral characteristics for the purpose of continual identity verification. The following are some examples of significant types:

a. *Keystroke Dynamics*: This type involves analyzing the rhythm, speed, and patterns of a user's typing on a keyboard. Algorithms monitor the timing between keystrokes and the pressure applied, creating a dynamic typing profile. Deviations from the established pattern trigger alerts or authentication prompts.

b. *Mouse Movement Analysis*: Tracking the way a user moves and interacts with a mouse or touchpad can provide valuable behavioral insights. Mouse movement analysis considers factors like speed, acceleration, and navigation patterns to create a personalized mouse usage profile.

c. *Touchscreen Interaction*: Similar to mouse movement, this type focuses on how users interact with touchscreens. It considers factors like touch pressure, finger movement speed, and gesture patterns to establish a unique touchscreen interaction signature.

d. *Device Orientation*: Behavioral patterns related to how users hold or interact with their devices can also be used for continuous authentication. Sensors like accelerometers and gyroscopes capture orientation changes, enabling the system to recognize the device holder based on their specific movements.

e. *Gesture Recognition*: Users' gesture patterns, such as swipes, pinches, and taps, can be captured and analyzed for continuous authentication. The timing and sequence of these gestures contribute to a personalized behavioral profile.

f. *Voice Characteristics*: Analyzing the unique characteristics of an individual's voice beyond simple speech recognition, such as changes in pitch, tone, and speaking rate, provides another avenue for continuous authentication.

g. *Biometric Recognition Fusion*: This approach combines various behavioral biometric traits, such as keystroke dynamics, mouse movement, and voice characteristics, into a unified authentication system. By analyzing multiple behavioral patterns simultaneously, the system becomes more robust and resistant to spoofing attempts.

h. *Walking Behavior*: Gait analysis, which examines how individuals walk, can be used for continuous authentication. Cameras and sensors track walking patterns and deviations, comparing them to established baselines for identification.

Continuous authentication methods that are based on behavioral patterns offer real-time verification, adaptability to changes in user behavior, and less reliance on static credentials. These factors all contribute to an improved user experience and increased level of security.

In the next part, we'll talk about ways to stop spoofing.

14.11   ANTI-SPOOFING TECHNIQUES

Anti-spoofing techniques are approaches that are aimed to combat fraudulent attempts to fool biometric authentication systems by employing bogus or modified biometric data (Hajare & Ambhaikar, 2023). These techniques are also known as "anti-spoofing methods." These methods involve the utilization of a variety of different methodologies in order to identify and prevent spoofing assaults. Some examples of these attacks include the creation of bogus fingerprints, pictures, or voice recordings in order to gain unauthorized access. Common anti-spoofing measures include liveness detection, which evaluates the vitality of the presented biometric trait through dynamic features such as movement or blood flow; texture analysis, which differentiates between real and fake textures, and the integration of multimodal biometrics, which combines different traits to ensure a higher level of security. Biometric systems can considerably improve their robustness and reliability against increasingly complex spoofing assaults if these strategies are implemented. Various spoofing attacks are mentioned in Table 14.7.

TABLE 14.7
Various Spoofing Attacks in Biometrics

Spoofing Attack	Description	Countermeasures
Fake Fingerprint	Presentation of a fabricated fingerprint impression	Liveness detection, texture analysis
Photo/Video Attack	Use of a printed photo or video of the genuine user	Liveness detection, 3D depth sensing
Voice Replay Attack	Playback of pre-recorded voice samples	Random challenge-response, voiceprint analysis
3D Mask Attack	Presentation of a lifelike 3D mask of the user's face	Liveness detection, depth sensing, thermal imaging
Silicon Mold Attack	Use of a mold to create a fake biometric impression	Texture analysis, multi-modal fusion
Voice Synthesis Attack	Generation of synthetic voice resembling the user	Voiceprint analysis, dynamic speech analysis
Palmprint Forgery	Presentation of a fake palmprint impression	Liveness detection, multi-modal biometrics
Iris Image Forgery	Submission of manipulated iris images	Liveness detection, multi-spectral imaging
Signature Forgery	Reproduction of a fake signature	Dynamic signature analysis, behavioral biometrics
Eye Image Forgery	Use of printed eye images or contact lenses	Liveness detection, pupil dynamics analysis

Implementing reliable countermeasures (Marshalko & Nikiforova, 2019), such as liveness detection, multi-modal fusion, and behavior analysis, is absolutely necessary in order to protect biometric systems against the numerous spoofing assaults that are now in use.

14.11.1 ADVANCED COMPUTER-VISION-BASED ANTI-SPOOFING TECHNIQUES

Advanced computer-vision-based anti-spoofing techniques leverage sophisticated algorithms and technologies to enhance the security and reliability of biometric systems. Here are some notable methods (Elloumi et al., 2020; Saha et al., 2020):

a. *Liveness Detection Using Depth Sensing*: Cameras with depth sensing capabilities, such as time-of-flight or structured light cameras, are able to record data in three dimensions regarding the biometric characteristic being viewed. This makes it easier to differentiate between real human features and the flat, printed pictures or masks that are often employed in attempts to fool people. Liveness detection based on depth provides extra depth indicators that are difficult to mimic in 2D faking materials.

b. *Texture Analysis*: Advanced algorithms for analyzing textures are able to distinguish between biologically authentic textures and artificially manufactured ones. These algorithms are able to discover anomalies that are characteristic of false materials or images by conducting an analysis of features such as the surface roughness, micropatterns, and specular reflections.

c. *Thermal Imaging*: Thermal imaging cameras are able to discern between actual skin and artificial materials because they record the heat that is released by living tissues. Using this method, temperature discrepancies and shifts brought on by changes in blood circulation can be uncovered, both of which are missing in artificial materials.

d. *Dynamic Analysis*: Analyzing dynamic characteristics of biometric traits, such as facial expressions or eye movements, is an effective method for distinguishing between genuine users and spoofing materials that are static in nature. Learning machines are able to pick up on even the minutest differences in dynamic behaviors, which are notoriously difficult to simulate.

e. *Pupil Dynamics Analysis*: Movements of the pupil, such as dilatation and constriction, are examples of dynamic cues that can be used for liveness identification. Computer vision algorithms are able to discern whether or not a spoofing attempt is being made by following these changes and determining whether or not a real eye is there.

f. *Challenge-Response Systems*: During the authentication procedure, these systems direct users to carry out particular actions such as blinking, smiling, or nodding. Other actions may also be required. These answers are tracked and analyzed by computer vision algorithms in order to validate the user's liveness and authenticity.

g. *Multi-Spectral Imaging*: When capturing biometric features, using light with many wavelengths at the same time uncovers secret information that is difficult for impostors to recreate. The subsurface characteristics, skin qualities, and blood flow patterns can all be better understood with the use of multi-spectral imaging.

h. *AI and Deep Learning*: Deep learning algorithms have the ability to understand intricate patterns and variances, which enables them to effectively differentiate between authentic and fabricated biometric data. In order to achieve higher levels of accuracy, neural networks can be trained using a wide variety of spoofing attempts as their input.

i. *Fusion of Modalities*: The effectiveness of the system to detect efforts at spoofing can be improved by combining information from a number of different sensors or modalities, such as depth, color, and thermal data. A more complete picture of the presented biometric characteristic can be obtained through the use of multi-modal fusion.

These cutting-edge anti-spoofing techniques, which are based on computer vision, provide a multi-pronged strategy for preventing unauthorized access to biometric systems as well as fraudulent activities in those systems. The integration of these components improves the reliability and safety of these systems in all of their respective applications. A comparative analysis for computer vision based anti-spoofing techniques is mentioned in Table 14.8 below.

TABLE 14.8
Advanced Computer-Vision-Based Anti-Spoofing Techniques Comparative Analysis

Technique	Advantages	Challenges	Applications
Depth Sensing	Effective against 2D spoofing materials	Hardware requirements	Face recognition, iris recognition
Texture Analysis	Robust against various spoofing materials	Complex algorithm development	Face recognition, fingerprint recognition
Thermal Imaging	Detects temperature differences	Specialized hardware	Face recognition, vein recognition
Dynamic Analysis	Captures behavioral nuances	Requires sufficient training data	Face recognition, voice recognition
Pupil Dynamics	Natural and non-intrusive	Sensitivity to lighting conditions	Eye tracking, face recognition
Challenge-Response	Requires user engagement and participation	User resistance	Face recognition, voice recognition
Multi-Spectral Imaging	Reveals hidden features	Specialized hardware	Fingerprint recognition, vein recognition
AI and Deep Learning	Learns complex patterns	Data requirements, potential adversarial attacks	Various biometric recognition systems
Multi-Modal Fusion	Enhanced detection through combined cues	Increased complexity	Multi-modal biometric systems

14.12 PRIVACY AND ETHICAL CONSIDERATIONS

It is vital to address the critical privacy and ethical problems that occur as a result of developments in computer vision that continue to strengthen identification through biometrics. These advancements continue to improve security (Baichoo et al., 2018; Deliversky & Deliverska, 2018; Laas-Mikko et al., 2022). Concerns regarding individual privacy and the possibility of widespread surveillance are brought up in light of the proliferation of biometric technologies like facial recognition and behavioral analysis. The gathering and storage of biometric information carries with it the possibility of data breaches and unauthorized access, which could result in the disclosure of extremely sensitive personal data. It is absolutely necessary to find a happy medium between increased security and the protection of people's rights to personal privacy. For the purpose of protecting sensitive biometric information, it is absolutely necessary to implement data usage regulations that are transparent, unambiguous permission methods, and strong data encryption practices. In addition, mitigating the risks connected with the unauthorized use of data can be accomplished by installing stringent access restrictions and limiting the amount of biometric data that is retained.

As biometric technology becomes increasingly incorporated into our everyday lives, there is a corresponding increase in the importance of ethical considerations. For example, facial recognition could unwittingly reinforce biases and lead to discriminatory outcomes, particularly if the training data used for these systems is not diverse and representative. This could have a particularly negative impact on those who are already marginalized. It is vital to create algorithms in a transparent manner, conduct regular audits, and maintain continuing efforts to mitigate bias in order to guarantee fairness and eliminate algorithmic discrimination. In addition, the possibility of ubiquitous surveillance might restrict individuals' personal liberties and have a restraining influence on public behavior. This can have a chilling effect. As these technologies continue to advance, governments, technologists, and society as a whole need to engage in ongoing debates in order to build comprehensive regulatory frameworks that prioritize security without compromising individual privacy, civil rights, and societal values.

14.12.1 CONCERNS RELATED TO BIOMETRIC DATA PRIVACY AND SECURITY

The singularity of biometric information, which is highly personally identifiable and cannot be replicated, gives rise to issues over the privacy and security of biometric data. The following are some major concerns (Jiang et al., 2017):

a. *Data Breaches*: Because compromised biometric characteristics are extremely impossible to change, data breaches involving biometric information can have serious repercussions. It is possible to commit identity theft or get unauthorized access to sensitive systems by using stolen biometric data such as fingerprints, facial scans, or other types of biometric data.

b. *Unconsented Data Usage*: Individuals' rights to maintain control over their personal information may be violated if biometric data are collected and used without prior informed consent that is both specific and unambiguous. The loss of trust in organizations that handle biometric data can be attributed to a lack of clarity over how those data will be handled.

c. *Biometric Template Storage*: It's not a good idea to store biometric templates, which are mathematical representations of biometric data, on databases since these templates could be stolen, reverse-engineered, or utilized to gain unauthorized access. Techniques such as hashing and encryption are required in order to safeguard these templates.

d. *Spoofing and Impersonation*: The dependability of biometric systems can be compromised by the use of sophisticated spoofing techniques, such as the creation of phony fingerprints, voice recordings, or 3D masks. It is crucial to ensure that adequate anti-spoofing procedures are in place.

e. *Transferability of Biometric Data*: Biometric characteristics, in contrast to passwords, are not kept in secret and can be obtained from an individual even without their knowledge or consent. This raises issues regarding the transferability of biometric data, which means that data collected in one context could potentially be utilized in another context without authorization.

f. *Biometric Databases*: Centralized biometric databases store a variety of sensitive information, making them an enticing target for attackers because of this information. It is a big problem to prevent these databases from being broken into or accessed by unauthorized parties.

g. *Algorithmic Bias*: The use of biased data in the training of biometric systems may provide discriminatory results, which may disproportionately affect members of underrepresented groups. It is vital to address biases introduced by algorithmic decision-making in order to prevent unjust effects.

h. *Surveillance and Privacy*: Concerns regarding mass surveillance and the loss of individual privacy in public places have been brought to light as a result of the widespread deployment of biometric technology like facial recognition.

i. *Legal and Regulatory Gaps*: The legislative structures that govern the protection of biometric data might be very different from one country to the next. Problems might arise while attempting to ensure that data privacy and security practices are consistent due to inconsistent regulations.

j. *Biometric Data Aggregation*: It is possible to compile detailed profiles of individuals using biometric data that has been obtained from a variety of sources; this raises additional problems and hazards about individuals' privacy.

In order to address these concerns, a mix of technological safeguards, clear legislation, practices that promote informed consent, and ethical considerations will need to be implemented. This will ensure that the advantages of biometric technology are balanced with the preservation of individuals' privacy and security.

14.12.2 ETHICAL CONSIDERATIONS IN THE USE OF COMPUTER VISION FOR BIOMETRIC IDENTIFICATION

Biometric identification requires a comprehensive ethical framework to protect the fundamental rights of individuals and guarantee the responsible application of this technology. Individuals have the right to be completely informed about the collection, storage, and use of their biometric data, and obtaining informed consent is a requirement that cannot be waived. In addition, biometric data must be protected from intrusions and unauthorized access with stringent data security measures, such as encryption and access controls(Martinez-Martin et al., 2021).

Second, algorithmic bias is a significant cause for concern. Biometric systems can perpetuate the biases prevalent in their training data, which can result in discrimination. Ensuring equity across demographic groups requires the selection and preparation of diverse training datasets, as well as ongoing monitoring and mitigation of bias. Transparency regarding the limitations of the technology is crucial, particularly with regard to accuracy and the possibility of misidentification, which can have severe consequences such as unlawful arrests or denials of access.

14.13   REAL-WORLD APPLICATIONS

Showcase of real-world applications that leverage advanced computer vision for biometrics to enhance security and identification across various domains:

a. *Airport Security and Border Control*: Advanced computer-vision-based biometric systems are widely used in airport security and border control for efficient and secure passenger verification. Facial recognition technology is employed to match travelers' faces against their passport photos, expediting the boarding process and enhancing security by identifying potential threats or individuals using forged documents.

b. *Financial Services*: In the financial sector, computer-vision-based biometrics are employed to strengthen authentication in digital banking applications. Voice recognition and facial recognition technologies are used to verify users' identities during transactions, reducing the risk of unauthorized access and fraud.

c. *Healthcare Access Management*: Computer vision is utilized in healthcare facilities to enhance patient identification and access management. Iris recognition technology ensures accurate patient identification, preventing medical errors and enhancing patient safety by ensuring that the right treatment is administered to the right person.

d. *Retail and Customer Experience*: Retailers leverage computer-vision-based biometric systems to enhance customer experience. Facial recognition technology is used to identify loyal customers and personalize shopping experiences based on their previous interactions and preferences, improving customer satisfaction and loyalty.

e. *Smartphones and Mobile Devices*: Advanced computer-vision-based biometrics play a crucial role in smartphone security. Facial recognition and fingerprint recognition technologies enable users to unlock their devices and authorize transactions securely, providing a seamless and convenient user experience while safeguarding personal data.

f. *Automotive Security*: Computer vision is used in the automotive industry for driver identification and access control. Facial recognition and voice recognition technologies enable personalized driver profiles, ensuring that only authorized individuals can operate the vehicle and access its features.

g. *Workplace Security*: Biometric identification systems based on computer vision are employed in workplaces to enhance access control and security. Employees' faces or iris patterns are captured by cameras at entry points, ensuring that only authorized personnel can enter restricted areas.

h. *Law Enforcement and Surveillance*: Computer-vision-based biometric systems are utilized by law enforcement agencies for criminal identification and surveillance. Facial recognition technology assists in identifying suspects from surveillance footage, aiding investigations, and improving public safety.

i. *Education*: Educational institutions use computer-vision-based biometrics for attendance tracking and security. Facial recognition systems automatically mark student attendance, reducing administrative burdens and enhancing campus security.

j. *Social Services*: Computer-vision-based biometrics are applied in social services for identifying beneficiaries and preventing fraudulent claims. Fingerprint recognition technology ensures the accurate distribution of benefits and services to eligible individuals.

k. *Hospitality and Access Management*: Hotels and resorts implement computer-vision-based biometrics for guest identification and access control. Facial recognition technology enables seamless check-in processes and ensures that only authorized guests can access their rooms and amenities.

l. *Sports and Entertainment*: Computer-vision-based biometric systems are utilized in sports arenas and entertainment venues to enhance fan experiences. Facial recognition technology allows quick and secure entry for ticket holders, minimizing lines and improving event security.

These real-world applications demonstrate how advanced computer vision for biometrics is transforming various industries, enhancing security, improving identification accuracy, and providing seamless user experiences. However, it's crucial to approach these applications with ethical considerations to ensure privacy, fairness, and responsible use of biometric data.

14.14   FUTURE DIRECTIONS AND CHALLENGES

Deep learning for facial recognition and other biometric modalities, the fusion of multiple biometric traits for robust authentication, and privacy-preserving methods to address data protection and ethical concerns are emerging computer vision and biometric trends. Additionally, biometrics and computer vision are being adopted in healthcare, retail, and smart cities, demonstrating a rising role in defining technology.

14.14.1 Emerging Trends in Computer Vision and Biometrics

A table representing emerging trends in computer vision and biometrics is mentioned in Table 14.9 below.

TABLE 14.9

Emerging Trends in Computer Vision and Biometrics

Trend	Description	Impact and Benefits	Applications
Deep Learning and Neural Networks	Continued advancements in deep learning techniques	Improved accuracy, robustness in biometric recognition	Face recognition, fingerprint identification
Generative Adversarial Networks	Use of GANs to generate synthetic biometric data	Augmenting datasets, improving system resilience	Data augmentation, anti-spoofing training
Multi-Modal Biometrics	Integration of multiple biometric traits	Higher accuracy, adaptable systems for diverse scenarios	Multi-factor authentication, security systems
Continuous Authentication	Real-time verification through behavioral patterns	Enhanced security through ongoing user verification	User authentication, access control
Privacy-Preserving Biometrics	Techniques for verification without revealing raw data	Protecting sensitive information while enabling access	Healthcare records, secure authentication
Explainable AI	Methods to provide insights into AI decision-making	Enhancing transparency, building user trust	Audit trails, compliance monitoring
Edge Computing	Processing biometric data on edge devices	Reduced latency, enhanced privacy, resource efficiency	IoT devices, remote authentication
Anti-Spoofing Advancements	Advancements in techniques to counter spoofing	Improved protection against increasingly sophisticated attacks	Secure access, face recognition
Ethical AI	Focus on fairness, transparency, and responsible AI	Minimizing biases, building public trust in biometric systems	Identity verification, law enforcement
User-Centric Design	Prioritizing usability and user experience	Enhanced accessibility and comfort for various demographics	Mobile authentication, customer services
3D Biometrics	Use of 3D data for more accurate and secure recognition	Reduced susceptibility to spoofing attacks, enhanced accuracy	Facial recognition, access control
Behavioral Biometrics	Analyzing behavioral patterns for identification	Continuous authentication, improved security	Typing rhythm analysis, voice recognition

(Continued)

TABLE 14.9 (*Continued*)
Emerging Trends in Computer Vision and Biometrics

Trend	Description	Impact and Benefits	Applications
Wearable Biometrics	Integration of biometric sensors in wearable devices	Seamless and unobtrusive user authentication	Fitness tracking, healthcare access
Contactless Solutions	Minimizing physical contact through biometric tech	Improved hygiene, faster authentication	Public transportation, access control
AI-Enhanced Surveillance	Using AI for enhanced video analytics	Improved threat detection, efficient monitoring	Public safety, security systems
Secure Remote Identity Verification	Biometric solutions for remote verification	Secure online services and transactions	Remote authentication, digital banking

14.14.2 Anticipated Challenges and Potential Solutions for Widespread Adoption

To successfully integrate advanced computer-vision-based biometrics across multiple businesses, certain projected challenges must be overcome. Data leaks and privacy intrusions are major issues. Collection and storage of sensitive biometric data might raise concerns about unauthorized access, data abuse, and enhanced monitoring. Strong data security laws and robust encryption are needed to solve this challenge. These will protect biometric data and control access. Implementing privacy-by-design principles and providing tools to help consumers govern their data are two more methods to boost technological trust.

Removal of algorithmic biases that can unfairly affect underrepresented groups is another challenge. Biometric systems may unintentionally reinforce societal prejudices in training data, resulting in biased results. To solve this issue, diverse and representative training datasets and continuous bias evaluation and mitigation should be used while developing the system. Transparent algorithms and audits can potentially reveal and rectify biases. Education and public awareness are also needed to ensure that potential users understand the pros and cons of computer vision-based biometric systems, which will encourage ethical use. By solving the obstacles, ethical considerations, strong technical capabilities, and social obligations can be achieved to enable broad adoption of computer-vision-based biometrics.

14.15 CONCLUSION

In conclusion, the convergence of computer vision and biometrics is transforming the landscape of security, identification, and user experience across a wide variety of businesses. This phenomenon is occurring in a number of different contexts. The progress of biometric systems is being driven by recent developments in deep learning, multi-modal fusion, and strategies that protect users' privacy. These breakthroughs are improving the systems' adaptability, accuracy, and security. Nevertheless, as we go forward into this age of innovation, it is essential that we navigate the ethical problems related to the privacy of biometric data, algorithmic prejudice, and monitoring. The deployment of these technologies in a responsible manner and maintaining open lines of communication are necessities if we are to reap the benefits of these innovations while still upholding individual and community norms and standards.

The road to widespread acceptance of computer-vision-based biometrics will not be an easy one and will be fraught with obstacles. These challenges call for in-depth problem solving, whether it be to protect against data breaches, correct algorithmic biases, or find the optimal balance between security and privacy. We are able to cultivate an atmosphere of trust and accountability in our community by putting in place stringent data protection procedures, encouraging diversity in training datasets, and raising awareness among the general public. Collaboration among stakeholders, such as technologists, policymakers, and society, will play a pivotal role in shaping a future where cutting-edge security is seamlessly integrated with ethical considerations, ensuring a harmonious coexistence between technological progress and human values. As emerging trends continue to unfold, they will be driven by the fusion of computer vision and biometrics.

REFERENCES

AbdElaziz, A. A. (2021). A survey of smartphone-based face recognition systems for security purposes. *Kafrelsheikh Journal of Information Sciences, 2*(1), 1–7.

Almabdy, S.M., Elrefaei, L.A. (2021). *An Overview of Deep Learning Techniques for Biometric Systems. In: Hassanien, A., Bhatnagar, R., Darwish, A. (eds) Artificial Intelligence for Sustainable Development: Theory, Practice and Future Applications.* Studies in Computational Intelligence, vol 912. Springer, Cham. https://doi.org/10.1007/978-3-030-51920-9_8

Attrish, A., Bharat, N., Anand, V., & Kanhangad, V. (2021). A contactless fingerprint recognition system. *arXiv preprint arXiv:2108.09048.*

Baichoo, S., Khan, M. H. M., Bissessur, P., Pavaday, N., Boodoo-Jahangeer, N., & Purmah, N. R. (2018). Legal and ethical considerations of biometric identity card: Case for Mauritius. *Computer Law & Security Review, 34*(6), 1333–1341.

Baig, A. F., Eskeland, S., & Yang, B. (2023). Privacy-preserving continuous authentication using behavioral biometrics. *International Journal of Information Security, 22*, 1–15.

Bai, Z., & Zhang, X. L. (2021). Speaker recognition based on deep learning: An overview. *Neural Networks, 140*, 65–99.

Bharathi, S., & Sudhakar, R. (2019). Biometric recognition using finger and palm vein images. *Soft Computing, 23*(6), 1843–1855.

Boychuk, E., Lagutina, K., Vorontsova, I., Mishenkina, E., & Belyayeva, O. (2020). Evaluating the performance of a new text rhythm analysis tool. *English Studies at NBU, 6*(2), 217–232.

Bychkov, O., Merkulova, K., & Zhabska, Y. (2019, December). Software Application for Biometrical Person's Identification by Portrait Photograph Based on Wavelet Transform. In 2019 IEEE International Conference on Advanced Trends in Information Theory (ATIT) (pp. 253–256).

Chen, N., Zuo, C., Lam, E. Y., & Lee, B. (2018). 3D imaging based on depth measurement technologies. *Sensors, 18*(11), 3711.

Chiou, S. Y. (2013). Secure method for biometric-based recognition with integrated crypto-graphic functions. *BioMed Research International, 2013.*

Daas, S., Yahi, A., Bakir, T., Sedhane, M., Boughazi, M., & Bourennane, E. B. (2020). Multimodal biometric recognition systems using deep learning based on the finger vein and finger knuckle print fusion. *IET Image Processing, 14*(15), 3859–3868.

Delgado-Santos, P., Tolosana, R., Guest, R., Deravi, F., & Vera-Rodriguez, R. (2023). Exploring transformers for behavioural biometrics: A case study in gait recognition. *Pattern Recognition, 143,* 109798.

Deliversky, J., & Deliverska, M. (2018). Ethical and legal considerations in biometric data usage—Bulgarian Perspective. *Frontiers in Public Health, 6,* 25.

Devaraj, L., & Modi, K. (2022). Advancements in Biometric Technology with Artificial Intelligence. *arXiv preprint arXiv:2212.13187.*

Dhiman, A., Gupta, K., & Sharma, D. K. (2021). An introduction to deep learning applications in biometric recognition. In *Trends in Deep Learning Methodologies* (pp. 1–36); Academic Press, Elsevier, London.

Dvořák, M., Kanich, O., & Drahanský, M. (2021). Scalable imaging device using line scan camera for use in biometric recognition and medical imaging. *In BIODEVICES, 1,* 160–168.

Elloumi, W., Chetouani, A., Charrada, T. B., & Fourati, E. (2020). Anti-spoofing in face recognition: Deep learning and image quality assessment-based approaches. In *Deep Biometrics,* 51–69; Springer, Cham.

Ezz, M., Mostafa, A. M., & Nasr, A. A. (2020). A silent password recognition framework based on lip analysis. *IEEE Access, 8,* 55354–55371.

Farouk, R. H., Mohsen, H., & El-Latif, Y. M. A. (2022). A proposed biometric technique for improving Iris recognition. *International Journal of Computational Intelligence Systems, 15*(1), 79.

Feng, Z. (2018, July). Biometric identification technology and development trend of physiological characteristics. In Journal of Physics: Conference Series (Vol. 1060, No. 1, p. 012047). IOP Publishing.

Hajare, H. R., & Ambhaikar, A. (2023, April). Face Anti-Spoofing Techniques and Challenges: A short survey. In *2023 11th International Conference on Emerging Trends in Engineering & Technology-Signal and Information Processing (ICETET-SIP)* (pp. 1–6). IEEE.

Iqbal, K., Odetayo, M., James, A., Iqbal, R., Kumar, N., & Barma, S. (2016). An efficient image retrieval scheme for colour enhancement of embedded and distributed surveillance images. *Neurocomputing, 174,* 413–430.

Jiang, R., Al-Maadeed, S., Bouridane, A., Crookes, D., & Beghdadi, A. (2017). *Biometric Security and Privacy.* Springer International Publishing AG.

Jin, J. (2022). Convolutional Neural Networks for Biometrics Applications. In *SHS Web of Conferences* (Vol. 144, p. 03013). EDP Sciences.

Jingwen, Y. (2011). Face recognition: From 2D to 3D. *Computer Engineering and Applications.*

Kuznetsov, A. Y., Murtazin, R. A., Garipov, I. M., Fedorov, E. A., Kholodenina, A. V., & Vorobeva, A. A. (2021). Methods of countering speech synthesis attacks on voice biometric systems in banking. *Научно-технический вестник информационных технологий, механики и оптики, 21*(1), 109–117.

Laas-Mikko, K., Kalvet, T., Derevski, R., & Tiits, M. (2022). Promises, social, and ethical challenges with biometrics in remote identity onboarding. In *Handbook of Digital Face Manipulation and Detection: From DeepFakes to Morphing Attacks* (pp. 437–462). Cham: Springer International Publishing.

Li, D., Gao, Y., Zhu, C., Wang, Q., & Wang, R. (2023). Improving speech recognition performance in noisy environments by enhancing lip Reading accuracy. *Sensors, 23*(4), 2053.

López, A. B. (2019). Deep learning in biometrics: A survey. *ADCAIJ: Advances in Distributed Computing and Artificial Intelligence Journal, 8*(4), 19–32.

Mahadevkar, S. V., Khemani, B., Patil, S., Kotecha, K., Vora, D., Abraham, A., & Gabralla, L. A. (2022). A review on machine learning styles in computer vision-techniques and future directions. *IEEE Access*, *10*, 107293–107329.

Malgheet, J. R., Manshor, N. B., Affendey, L. S., & Abdul Halin, A. B. (2021). Iris recognition development techniques: A comprehensive review. *Complexity*, *2021*, 1–32.

Marshalko, G. B., & Nikiforova, L. O. (2019). Spoofing attack on eigenfaces-based biometric identification system. *Automatic Control and Computer Sciences*, *53*, 980–986.

Martinez-Martin, N., Luo, Z., Kaushal, A., Adeli, E., Haque, A., Kelly, S. S., & Milstein, A. (2021). Ethical issues in using ambient intelligence in health-care settings. *The Lancet Digital Health*, *3*(2), e115–e123.

Némesin, V., & Derrode, S. (2016). Quality-driven and real-time iris recognition from close-up eye videos. *Signal, Image and Video Processing*, *10*, 153–160.

Neto, P. C., Gonçalves, T., Pinto, J. R., Silva, W., Sequeira, A. F., Ross, A., & Cardoso, J. S. (2022). Explainable biometrics in the age of deep learning. arXiv preprint arXiv:2208.09500.

Ogbanufe, O., & Kim, D. J. (2018). Comparing fingerprint-based biometrics authentication versus traditional authentication methods for e-payment. *Decision Support Systems*, *106*, 1–14.

Pejas, J., & Piegat, A. (Eds.). (2006). *Enhanced Methods in Computer Security, Biometric and Artificial Intelligence Systems*. Springer Science & Business Media.

Prasad, K. K., & Aithal, P. S. (2017). A conceptual study on image enhancement techniques for fingerprint images. *International Journal of Applied Engineering and Management Letters (IJAEML)*, *1*(1), 63–72.

Rezende, I. N. (2020). Facial recognition in police hands: Assessing the 'Clearview case' from a European perspective. *New Journal of European Criminal Law*, *11*(3), 375–389.

Saboor, A., Kask, T., Kuusik, A., Alam, M. M., Le Moullec, Y., Niazi, I. K., … & Ahmad, R. (2020). Latest research trends in gait analysis using wearable sensors and machine learning: A systematic review. *Ieee Access*, *8*, 167830–167864.

Saha, S., Xu, W., Kanakis, M., Georgoulis, S., Chen, Y., Paudel, D. P., & Van Gool, L. (2020). Domain agnostic feature learning for image and video based face anti-spoofing. In *Proceedings of the IEEE/CVF Conference on Computer Vision and Pattern Recognition Workshops* (pp. 802–803).

Singh, J. P., Jain, S., Arora, S., & Singh, U. P. (2021). A survey of behavioral biometric gait recognition: Current success and future perspectives. *Archives of Computational Methods in Engineering*, *28*, 107–148.

SriAnusha, K., Saddamhussain, S. K., & Kumar, K. P. (2019, March). Biometric car security and monitoring system using IOT. In *2019 International Conference on Vision Towards Emerging Trends in Communication and Networking (ViTECoN)* (pp. 1–7). IEEE.

Tirumala, S. S., Shahamiri, S. R., Garhwal, A. S., & Wang, R. (2017). Speaker identification features extraction methods: A systematic review. *Expert Systems With Applications*, *90*, 250–271.

Tiwari, M. (2021). Enhancing the accuracy of multimodal biometric systems. *Turkish Journal of Computer and Mathematics Education (TURCOMAT)*, *12*(3), 5142–5149.

Uwaechia, A. N., & Ramli, D. A. (2021). A comprehensive survey on ECG signals as new biometric modality for human authentication: Recent advances and future challenges. *IEEE Access*, *9*, 97760–97802.

Yin, J., Sun, J., Li, J., & Liu, K. (2022). An effective gaze-based authentication method with the spatiotemporal feature of eye movement. *Sensors*, *22*(8), 3002.

Zhang, M., Xiao, Y., Xiong, F., Li, S., Cao, Z., Fang, Z., & Zhou, J. T. (2022). Person re-identification with hierarchical discriminative spatial aggregation. *IEEE Transactions on Information Forensics and Security*, *17*, 516–530.

15 Digital Forensics and Its Applications

*Gulshan Goyal, Ankita Sharma,
Kashishpreet Kaur, and Shivam Kumar*

15.1 INTRODUCTION

Digital forensics is a specialized area of forensic science that has become increasingly important in the modern world, where digital devices and online interactions are a part of everyday life [1]. The field of digital forensics focuses on digital devices and cybercrime and involves analysing, interpreting, and documenting digital evidence extracted from various digital sources. This is done with the aim of aiding in the reconstruction of events determined to be of a criminal nature or assisting in predicting unauthorized actions that are proven to disrupt planned operations [2]. The process of digital forensics can be broadly divided into the following steps [3]:

1. Identification
2. Preservation
3. Analysis
4. Documentation
5. Presentation

These steps are described as given below and summarized in Table 15.1.

1. *Identification*: The first stage is to identify potential sources of evidence. The identification process involves accessing available evidence, determining its storage location, and understanding the format in which it is stored. Storage media can include PDAs and personal computers.
2. *Extraction*: The next stage is the extraction of evidence, which can be a complex process due to the need to recover deleted or hidden files and crack encryption codes. The extracted data is then interpreted and organized into a format that can be understood and used in legal proceedings.
3. *Preservation*: In this stage, data is protected and secured. It involves restricting access to the digital device to prevent any tampering with digital evidence.
4. *Analysis*: During the analysis, investigative agents reconstruct data fragments and derive conclusions from the gathered evidence. This process often requires multiple rounds of analysis to substantiate a particular theory of the crime.
5. *Documentation*: It is essential to generate a comprehensive record of all observable data. This record aids in reconstructing and subsequently

DOI: 10.1201/9781032614663-15

TABLE 15.1
Processes in Digital Forensics [3]

Step	Description
Identification	• Identify purpose of investigation
	• Identification of the required resources
Extraction	• Data is extracted and organized into understandable format
Preservation	• Data is secured and isolated
Analysis	• Processing of data
	• Interpretation of the result which is analysed
Documentation	• Photographing for the documentation of crime scene
Presentation	• Process of concluding the data gathered from all the facts

reviewing the crime scene. This step encompasses meticulous documentation, photography, and mapping of the crime.

6. *Presentation*: In the final stage, the process involves summarizing and explaining the conclusions reached [4]. The aim is to represent this information in simple terms, avoiding technical jargon, and referring to specific details.

In the digital era, where technology has permeated every aspect of our lives, this field has emerged as a critical discipline in the pursuit of justice and security. This comprehensive exploration of digital forensics delves into its principles, techniques, challenges, applications, and future directions, offering a panoramic view of this dynamic field. The significant importance of digital forensics can be easily understood with points described below:

1. The applications of digital forensics are diverse. In law enforcement and criminal justice, digital forensics aids in the investigation of a wide range of crimes, providing crucial evidence that can identify suspects, establish timelines, and uncover motives.
2. Digital evidence can be found on a variety of devices, including computers, smartphones, tablets, hard drives, CDs, DVDs, flash drives, cloud storage, and even in emails or social media accounts. This evidence can be used in a wide range of legal scenarios, including criminal prosecutions, civil disputes, insurance claims, and corporate investigations [5].
3. The importance of digital forensics has grown with the rise in cybercrime, including identity theft, hacking, online fraud, and cyberstalking. Law enforcement agencies around the world now have specialized digital forensics units to handle these types of crimes.

15.1.1 Motivation behind Study

The motivation behind writing this study stems from a genuine curiosity and passion for the field of digital forensics. Recognizing the critical role it plays in today's interconnected world. We were intrigued by the complex challenges it addresses, from investigating cybercrimes to safeguarding sensitive digital information. Through

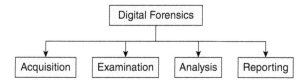

FIGURE 15.1 Different techniques used in digital forensics [6].

this study, we aimed to contribute to the knowledge base of digital forensics, hoping that the insights and findings may help bolster our defences against digital threats and enhance our understanding of this vital discipline.

15.2 DIGITAL FORENSICS TECHNIQUES

Digital forensics involves a wide range of techniques that can be used to identify, preserve, extract, interpret, and document digital evidence. These techniques can be broadly categorized into the following four areas, as shown in Figure 15.1 [6]:

1. Acquisition Techniques
2. Examination Techniques
3. Analysis Techniques
4. Reporting Techniques

These techniques are described as given below.

15.2.1 ACQUISITION TECHNIQUES

The data acquisition aspect in digital forensics involves the identification, preservation, and collection of digital evidence that will be analysed in subsequent stages. The diagram illustrates two main types of data that can be acquired: Live Data and Preserved Data as shown in Figure 15.2 [6].

a. *Live data acquisition*: Live data refers to data that is active and currently in use by the system. This includes data stored in random access memory (RAM), network traffic, and other volatile data. This involves gathering data from a running or active system, such as a computer or a mobile

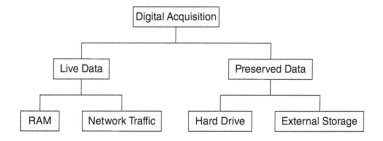

FIGURE 15.2 Digital acquisition and its types [6].

device. It's important to minimize disruption to the system while collecting volatile data like running processes and network connections. Capturing the contents of a system's RAM is crucial, as it can contain active processes, encryption keys, passwords, and other volatile data that would be lost once the system is powered down. Analysing RAM data can provide insights into currently running applications, open files, and system state. Capturing network traffic helps in understanding communication patterns, identifying potential security breaches, and analysing interactions between the system and external entities [6]. This includes capturing packets from network interfaces to analyse protocols, ports, source and destination IP addresses, and the content of data being transmitted.

b. *Preserved data acquisition*: Preserved data also refers to data that's stored and preserved on digital media. This method involves copying data from a storage device, preserving its integrity, and ensuring it remains unchanged during the acquisition process. This involves creating a bit-by-bit copy (forensic image) of the entire contents of a hard drive. It captures both used and unused sectors, including the file system, deleted files, and metadata. Hard drive imaging helps preserve the integrity of the original data and allows for analysis without modifying the source drive. Similar to hard drives, external storage devices like external hard drives, USB drives, and memory cards can also be imaged to preserve their contents. This includes capturing files, folder structures, and metadata present on these devices.

The acquisition of both live and preserved data is guided by the principle of preserving the original state of the data. This is often achieved through the use of write-blocking devices and software, which prevent any modifications to the original data source. The acquired data is then hashed to create a unique digital fingerprint, which can be used to verify the integrity of the data throughout the forensic process.

15.2.2 EXAMINATION TECHNIQUES

The examination stage involves extracting and recovering data from the acquired digital evidence. This can be a complex process due to the need to recover deleted or hidden files, crack encryption codes, and interpret raw data. The examination techniques are shown in Figure 15.3.

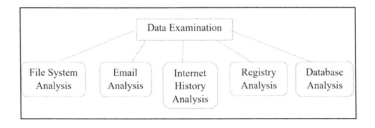

FIGURE 15.3 Data examination techniques [6].

The examination stage involves extracting and recovering data from the acquired digital evidence. This can be a complex process due to the need to recover deleted or hidden files, crack encryption codes, and interpret raw data.

One of the primary techniques employed during the examination stage is **file carving**. This technique revolves around the meticulous search and recovery of files based on their content attributes, rather than relying solely on file system metadata. File carving proves invaluable when attempting to retrieve deleted files or salvaging information from compromised, damaged, or formatted storage media. By recognizing specific file signatures or headers, digital forensics experts can reconstruct files that may have been intentionally deleted or made inaccessible due to corruption. **Email analysis** involves analysing email messages and attachments to extract relevant information such as sender, recipient, timestamps, and content. It's crucial for understanding communication patterns and potential evidence. **Internet history analysis** involves examining web browsing history, cookies, and cached data to reconstruct a user's online activities. This can reveal visited websites, online searches, and user behaviour.

In the process of **registry analysis**, the windows registry contains the configuration settings and required information about software, hardware, and user activities. Analysing the registry can offer insights into system changes, user actions, and installed software. Analysing databases involves examining structured data stored in databases like SQL or NoSQL. This can uncover patterns, relationships, and potential evidence in various types of investigations.

In parallel, the technique of keyword searching emerges as another crucial component of the examination process. This approach involves combing through the digital evidence for specific words or phrases that hold relevance to the ongoing investigation. To facilitate this process, an array of specialized tools can be employed, including powerful utilities like dtSearch or X-Ways Forensics. By pinpointing specific keywords or phrases, investigators can uncover relevant information buried within the digital landscape, shedding light on potential leads, motives, or connection.

15.2.3 ANALYSIS TECHNIQUES

The analysis stage involves interpreting the extracted data and drawing conclusions based on it. This can involve a range of techniques, as shown in Figure 15.4, which depends on the nature of the case and the type of digital evidence.

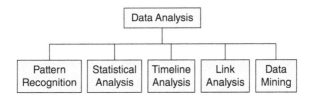

FIGURE 15.4 Different techniques used for analysis.

The primary technique employed during the analysis stage is called **timeline analysis**, which entails the creation of a chronological sequence of events grounded in the timestamps associated with the digital evidence [5]. This can help to establish when certain events occurred and how they are related.

Another important technique is methodology is **link analysis**, encompassing the identification of interconnections among diverse fragments of digital evidence. This can help establish connections between different individuals, devices, or events. Furthermore, link analysis stands as another pivotal technique employed during the analysis stage. This method centres on the identification and exploration of interrelationships existing between various fragments of digital evidence. By scrutinizing connections between disparate elements—be it individuals, devices, or incidents—investigators can map out intricate networks of associations. Link analysis not only helps to uncover connections that might otherwise remain concealed but also provides a holistic view of the broader context in which the events unfolded.

Pattern recognition serves as a complementary technique, contributing to the discernment of recurring trends or behaviours within the digital evidence. This method involves the identification of consistent patterns in data, shedding light on potentially significant behaviours, trends, or anomalies that might hold pivotal significance within the investigation.

Statistical methods are employed to analyse data distributions, frequencies, and correlations. This can provide insights into trends, irregularities, or parts that might not be immediately obvious.

Data mining techniques involve searching for patterns, trends, and correlations within large datasets. This can uncover insights that might not be apparent through manual examination, helping to identify relevant information for investigations.

15.2.4 REPORTING TECHNIQUES

The reporting phase encompasses the documentation of the forensic process, culminating in the presentation of the findings through a clear and concise manner. This can involve creating a written report, presenting the findings in court, or providing expert testimony. The reporting techniques are shown in Figure 15.5.

In the process of **expert witness testimony** in legal cases, digital forensic experts generally provide testimony in court. They explain their findings, methodologies, and the significance of their analysis to help judges and juries understand the technical aspects of the case.

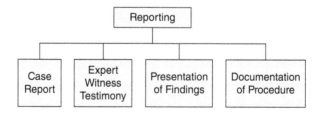

FIGURE 15.5   Reporting techniques [6].

A comprehensive written **case report** detailing the findings, methods used, and conclusions drawn from the digital forensic analysis. This report is an essential document for documenting the investigation process and the evidence discovered. **Presenting findings** to stakeholders, law enforcement, or legal professionals is important. This might involve creating visual presentations that convey the key points, evidence, and conclusions in a clear and understandable manner.

Another important technique is chain of **custody documentation**, which involves documenting every step of the process of digital forensics to demonstrate that the proof has been handled. Detailed documentation of the procedures followed during the investigation is crucial for transparency, repeatability, and quality assurance. This documentation outlines the steps taken, tools used, and any deviations encountered during the analysis.

15.3   TOOLS USED IN DIGITAL FORENSICS

Various tools used in digital forensics are described as given below:

1. *Forensic software tools*: This category includes highly specialized software designed to carefully examine and extract data from digital devices and complex network structures. These tools play a key role in digital forensics by facilitating comprehensive analysis of potentially critical information. Prominent examples of such software include EnCase, which boasts sophisticated data retrieval and analysis capabilities [7]. FTK (Forensic Toolkit), known for its robust data processing and visualization capabilities; and X-Ways Forensics, known for its expertise in conducting in-depth examinations of digital artefacts.

2. *Forensic imaging tools*: This process is the cornerstone of digital forensics and involves the methodical creation of an exact replica of a digital device or network. This replication, often referred to as disc cloning or disc imaging, involves carefully duplicating every single bit of data located on the target device. The process can be performed by both hardware and software means, ensuring that the resulting image accurately mirrors the original state of the device or network, thus preserving the integrity of potential evidence [8].

3. *Forensic Analysis Software*: This category includes software tools carefully tailored to dissect and interpret the content of forensic images. These tools play a vital role in uncovering nuances in duplicate data. Notable examples include the Sleuth Kit, renowned for its comprehensive evidence-finding capabilities; Autopsy, prized for its intuitive interface and array of analytical features; and the open-source The Coroner's Toolkit (TCT), recognized for its versatile range of forensic investigation tools. These software applications enable digital forensics professionals to navigate the complex landscape of evidence, extracting relevant insights that can illuminate the context of events and contribute to informed investigative decisions [9].

15.4   DIGITAL FORENSICS ISSUES AND CHALLENGES

Digital forensics is not just about responding to crime and security breaches, however. It also plays a crucial role in preventing these incidents by identifying potential vulnerabilities and threats. For example, digital forensics techniques can be used to analyse a company's network traffic to identify any unusual patterns or activities that could indicate a potential cyberattack [10].

Despite the advancements and successes in digital forensics, practitioners often encounter several challenges that can complicate their investigations. Some of these challenges are:

1. One of the main challenges in digital forensics is the rapid pace of technological change. As new devices, software, and online services are constantly being developed, digital forensics experts need to update their skills and knowledge continually.
2. Another important challenge is the increasing use of jumbling and other protective layers that make it difficult to extract and interpret digital evidence [1].

These challenges can range from technical issues, such as encryption and anti-forensic tactics, to legal and ethical issues, such as privacy concerns and jurisdictional issues [11]. These underlying issues are described as given below:

a. *Encryption*: Encryption is a significant challenge in digital forensics. When data is encrypted, it is transformed into an unreadable format, which can only be read or processed after it has been decrypted using a decryption key. This makes the recovery of evidence from encrypted devices or files extremely difficult.

   However, researchers have developed various techniques to overcome these challenges. For instance, in the case of encrypted data, investigators can use techniques such as live memory forensics to extract encryption keys from a computer's memory (RAM). Another approach is to use cryptographic attacks, which exploit weaknesses in the encryption algorithm or its implementation, to recover the original data without the decryption key.

b. *Anti-Forensic Tactics*: Anti-forensic tactics are techniques used by criminals to hinder or mislead forensic investigations. These can include data hiding, data obfuscation, data destruction, and the use of malware to compromise forensic tools or processes [12].

   To counter these tactics, digital forensic practitioners need to stay abreast of the latest anti-forensic techniques and develop strategies to detect and overcome them. This can involve the use of advanced data recovery techniques, malware analysis, and reverse engineering.

c. *Cloud Computing*: The task of investigators to access and analyse this data grows increasingly challenging [13]. This complexity arises from multiple factors, notably the decentralized structure of cloud storage, the use of proprietary cloud storage protocols, and legal issues related to data privacy and cross-border investigations.

To tackle these challenges, researchers are developing new techniques and tools for cloud forensics. This includes techniques for remote data acquisition, analysis of cloud storage protocols, and methods for preserving and analysing volatile cloud data.

d. *Mobile Device Forensics*: Mobile devices, such as smartphones and tablets, are becoming increasingly important in digital forensics due to their widespread use and the wealth of data they contain. However, mobile device forensics presents several challenges, including the diversity of mobile operating systems, the use of encryption, and the frequent updates to mobile devices and apps [14].

To overcome these challenges, digital forensic practitioners need to use specialized tools and techniques for mobile device forensics. This includes the use of mobile device imaging tools, techniques for bypassing or cracking passcodes, and methods for analysing mobile apps and their data. Despite these challenges, in spite of these obstacles, the realm of digital forensics persists in its evolution and adjustment, giving rise to the creation of novel techniques and tools aimed at tackling these very challenges.

Despite all these issues and challenges, the domain of digital forensics continues to adapt and evolve. New methods and tools are constantly being progressed to keep up with the changing digital landscape. In addition, there is a growing emphasis on education and training in digital forensics, with many universities now offering specialized courses and degrees in this field.

15.5   DIGITAL FORENSICS APPLICATIONS

Digital forensics has a wide range of applications in various fields, from law enforcement and criminal justice to corporate security and incident response. In each of these fields, digital forensics plays a crucial role in identifying, investigating, and preventing illegal or unauthorized activities [15]. These applications are discussed in subsequent subsections, as given below.

15.5.1   CRIMINAL INVESTIGATIONS

In the field of law enforcement and criminal justice, digital forensics is used to investigate a wide range of crimes, from cybercrimes like hacking and online fraud to traditional crimes like murder and theft. Digital evidence can provide valuable information that can help identify suspects, establish timelines, and uncover motives. For example, in a murder investigation, a suspect's smartphone might contain GPS data that can place them at the scene of the crime, text messages or emails that reveal a motive, or internet search history that shows they were researching methods of murder. The role of digital forensics in law enforcement is described in more detail as follows [16]:

1. *Investigating Crimes*: Digital forensics serves as a vital tool for law enforcement agencies when investigating a wide range of criminal activities, spanning from traditional crimes to those committed in the digital realm. These

crimes can include offences like theft, fraud, drug trafficking, violent crimes, and more recently, cybercrimes.

2. *Analysing Electronic Devices*: Digital forensics involves the application of specialized techniques to extract and examine digital evidence from electronic devices like computers, tablets, smartphones, and storage media like hard drives and USB drives. These devices often contain a wealth of information, from communication records to files and browsing history [17].

3. *Detecting Cybercrimes*: In the realm of cybercrimes, digital forensics helps uncover evidence related to hacking, unauthorized access, data breaches, malware attacks, and identity theft. By analysing logs, metadata, and communication records, investigators can track the activities of cybercriminals, discern the methods used, and identify potential vulnerabilities exploited.

4. *Building Strong Cases*: Digital forensics contributes significantly to the strength of legal cases. By piecing together digital evidence, law enforcement can establish a strong foundation for prosecution. This evidence can include timestamps, geolocation data, communication records, and file histories, which collectively form a comprehensive narrative of events.

5. *Identifying Suspects*: By analysing digital traces, law enforcement agencies can trace the origin of cyberattacks or digital interactions to specific individuals or groups. This enables the identification of suspects, narrowing down potential leads, and helping to allocate resources more effectively.

6. *Establishing Timelines*: Digital forensics aids in creating accurate timelines of events related to a crime. This chronological sequence of activities can be critical in understanding how an incident unfolded and in pinpointing key moments.

7. *Reconstructing Events*: Through digital forensics, investigators can reconstruct digital events, actions, and communications leading up to and following a crime. This reconstruction not only helps build a coherent narrative for court but also provides insights into motives, planning, and collaboration among perpetrators.

8. *Supporting Prosecution*: The evidence gathered through digital forensics is admissible in court and can serve as crucial testimony to support the prosecution's case. By presenting concrete digital evidence, prosecutors can help judges and juries understand the intricacies of a case, making it more likely for justice to be served [18].

9. *Enhancing Law Enforcement Effectiveness*: The incorporation of digital forensics into law enforcement practices boosts overall efficiency. It accelerates investigations by uncovering evidence that may be hidden within complex digital systems and helps law enforcement agencies stay up-to-date with evolving criminal methodologies.

15.5.2 Intellectual Property Conflicts

In cases involving intellectual property conflicts, digital forensics assists in uncovering instances of copyright infringement, trade secret theft, and unauthorized use of proprietary information. By analysing digital records and communications, digital forensics experts can trace the origins of intellectual property violations, whether they involve unauthorized access to databases, copying of proprietary code, or other forms of unauthorized dissemination. This evidence is crucial in legal actions and settlements related to intellectual property disputes. The role of digital forensics in cases involving intellectual property conflicts is further explained in more detail as follows [19]:

1. *Copyright Infringement*: Digital forensics plays a pivotal role in identifying instances of copyright infringement where protected creative works are used without proper authorization. For example, if someone unlawfully reproduces copyrighted material, such as images, music, or written content, digital forensics can help trace the origin of the infringing content. Experts analyse digital footprints, metadata, and timestamps to establish the source of the material and the chain of distribution.

2. *Trade Secret Theft*: In cases where valuable trade secrets or proprietary information are stolen, digital forensics can help unravel the intricate details of how the theft occurred. Digital traces left behind by unauthorized access or data exfiltration can provide insights into who accessed the information, when, and how. By analysing network logs, system access records, and communication data, digital forensics experts can reconstruct the unauthorized activities that led to the trade secret theft.

3. *Unauthorized use of Proprietary Information*: Digital forensics is crucial for identifying instances where proprietary information is unlawfully used without proper authorization. This could involve using confidential business plans, designs, or product specifications without permission. Through careful analysis of digital records and communication channels, digital forensics experts can track the dissemination and usage of proprietary information, helping to establish who was involved and when the unauthorized use occurred.

4. *Uncovering Digital Traces*: When intellectual property conflicts arise, digital forensics experts dive into electronic devices and digital networks to uncover traces of unauthorized activities. These traces can include communication records, document histories, email exchanges, and even remnants of deleted files. By piecing together these digital breadcrumbs, experts can reconstruct the sequence of events and identify potential culprits.

5. *Strengthening Legal Actions*: The evidence gathered through digital forensics is crucial in legal actions related to intellectual property disputes. Courts require concrete evidence to establish claims of infringement, theft, or unauthorized use. Digital evidence can provide a clear trail that demonstrates the origin of the infringement, the method of dissemination, and the parties involved. This evidence significantly strengthens legal arguments and supports settlements [20].

6. *Data Manipulation Analysis*: In some cases, intellectual property conflicts involve allegations of data manipulation, where digital information has been altered to misrepresent facts. Digital forensics can ascertain whether data has been tampered with, altered, or fabricated. This analysis ensures that evidence presented is accurate and reliable in legal proceedings.

15.5.3 COMMERCIAL SECURITY

Organizations leverage digital forensics to enhance their security measures and protect sensitive information. Digital forensics aids in identifying security breaches, analysing the extent of data breaches, and tracing the paths attackers took within a network. This enables organizations to strengthen their cybersecurity measures, prevent future attacks, and ensure compliance with data protection regulations. By dissecting attack vectors and patterns, digital forensics helps organizations fortify their infrastructure against cyber threats. The role of digital forensics in the context of commercial security is described in more detail as follows [3]:

1. *Enhancing Security Measures*: Digital forensics is a valuable tool for organizations aiming to bolster their cybersecurity defences. By leveraging digital forensics techniques, organizations can proactively identify vulnerabilities and potential security gaps within their systems and networks.

2. *Detecting Security Breaches*: One of the key functions of digital forensics in commercial security is the detection of security breaches. When a security breach occurs, digital forensics experts investigate the incident to understand the scope of the breach, the methods used by the attackers, and the extent of the compromise. This proactive approach helps organizations respond swiftly and effectively to minimize damage.

3. *Analysing Data Breaches*: In the event of a data breach, digital forensics experts analyse the compromised data to determine what specific information has been exposed. This is crucial for assessing the potential impact on individuals, sensitive data, and business operations. Understanding the type of data compromised helps organizations take appropriate measures to mitigate risks [21].

4. *Tracing Attack Paths*: Digital forensics aids in tracing the paths attackers took within an organization's network. This involves retracing the steps of the cybercriminals to understand how they gained unauthorized access, moved laterally within the network, and exfiltrated data. This information helps organizations close the security gaps that were exploited and prevent similar attacks in the future.

5. *Strengthening Future Defences*: After a security incident, digital forensics insights can guide organizations in fortifying their cybersecurity defences. By understanding the techniques and vulnerabilities exploited by attackers, organizations can implement targeted security improvements, such as patching vulnerabilities, enhancing access controls, and deploying intrusion detection systems.

6. *Ensuring Compliance*: Organizations are often subject to various data protection regulations, such as GDPR, HIPAA, or industry-specific standards. Digital forensics assists in ensuring compliance by providing a means to track and demonstrate how data breaches occurred, how they were mitigated, and what steps were taken to prevent future breaches. This documentation is crucial in meeting legal and regulatory requirements.

7. *Dissecting Attack Vectors and Patterns*: Digital forensics experts analyse attack vectors and patterns to identify trends in cyberattacks. This proactive analysis helps organizations stay ahead of emerging threats and adapt their security strategies accordingly. By understanding the evolving tactics of cybercriminals, organizations can better anticipate and defend against new attack methods.

8. *Incident Response Planning*: Digital forensics plays a central role in incident response planning. Organizations create detailed response plans that outline how to effectively respond to security incidents. Digital forensics insights help organizations define the appropriate actions to take during an incident, from containing the breach to recovering compromised systems and data [22].

15.5.4 LEGAL SYSTEM

Digital forensics plays an integral role in the legal system by providing evidence that can be presented in court to support legal claims and counterclaims. This includes civil cases, where digital evidence may be used to substantiate claims related to contract disputes, liability, or cases involving digital harassment. In criminal cases, digital forensics can offer crucial evidence that links suspects to crimes, establishes motives, or uncovers hidden financial transactions. This evidence can have a significant impact on trial outcomes, influencing judges and juries. The role of Digital forensics in legal system is discussed in detail as follows [23]:

1. *Supporting Legal Claims and Counterclaims*: In the legal system, evidence holds a pivotal role in supporting legal claims and counterclaims. Digital forensics provides a way to uncover and present digital evidence that can help establish the validity of arguments presented in court. This is particularly relevant in cases where the evidence is in digital form, such as emails, documents, or electronic records.

2. *Civil Cases*: Digital forensics has a significant impact on civil cases, where individuals or organizations seek legal remedies for disputes. For instance, in contract disputes, digital evidence can reveal communication records, timestamps, and alterations in electronic documents, helping to establish the intentions and commitments of involved parties [24]. Similarly, in cases of liability claims or personal injury, digital evidence can provide insights into the circumstances surrounding an incident, contributing to the establishment of liability or innocence.

3. *Digital Harassment and Cyberbullying*: Digital forensics is crucial in cases involving digital harassment and cyberbullying. By analysing digital communications, social media interactions, and online activity, experts can determine the identity of harassers, trace the origin of threatening messages, and establish a pattern of abusive behaviour. This evidence is vital for securing restraining orders, protection orders, and legal action against perpetrators [21].

4. *Criminal Cases*: In criminal cases, digital forensics is a powerful tool for establishing guilt or innocence. Digital evidence can link suspects to

criminal activities, corroborate or challenge alibis, and provide insights into motives or premeditation. For example, in cases of cybercrimes, digital forensics experts can trace the digital footprints left by hackers or online fraudsters to identify their methods and intentions.

5. *Establishing Motive*: Digital forensics can help establish the motives behind criminal activities. By analysing digital records, communication histories, and online behaviour, experts can uncover connections between suspects and victims, shedding light on potential motives for crimes such as murder, fraud, or cyberattacks.

6. *Financial Investigations*: Hidden financial transactions can be exposed through digital forensics, contributing to both criminal and civil cases. Digital traces left by financial activities, including online transactions, email correspondence, and digital account records, can be meticulously analysed to unveil money laundering, embezzlement, or fraudulent activities.

7. *Influencing Judges and Juries*: The presentation of concrete digital evidence can have a significant impact on trial outcomes as judges and juries rely on factual evidence to make informed decisions. Digital evidence that has been meticulously analysed and presented by experts can sway their perceptions, either supporting or challenging the narratives presented by legal teams.

8. *Ensuring Fair Trials*: Digital forensics helps ensure fair trials by providing objective and unbiased evidence. This evidence is essential in preventing wrongful convictions, safeguarding individuals' rights, and maintaining the integrity of the justice system.

15.6   NEW DEVELOPMENTS IN DIGITAL FORENSICS

As technology continues to evolve, so does the field of digital forensics. Emerging technologies like machine learning, blockchain, and the Internet of Things (IoT) are creating new opportunities and challenges for digital forensic investigations. Role of these technologies is described in the following subsections.

15.6.1   MACHINE LEARNING IN DIGITAL FORENSICS

Machine learning involves the use of algorithms and methods that can learn from and make decisions or predictions based on data. In the context of digital forensics, machine learning can be used to automate the analysis of large amounts of data, helping investigators identify patterns and anomalies more quickly and accurately. For example, machine learning algorithms can be used to analyse network traffic and identify unusual patterns that could indicate a cyberattack. They can also be used to analyse text data, such as emails or social media posts, and identify suspicious or malicious content [25].

However, the use of machine learning in digital forensics also presents challenges. One of the most significant challenges is the requirement of large amounts of training data for machine learning algorithms. Another challenge is the risk of false positives, where the algorithms incorrectly identify innocent behaviour as suspicious.

15.6.2   BLOCKCHAIN FORENSICS

Blockchain is described as a distributed and decentralized digital ledger for recording transactions across many computers. It is most commonly associated with cryptocurrencies such as Bitcoin, but it is also being used in a variety of other applications, from supply chain management to voting systems. Blockchain forensics involves tracing, identifying, and analysing transactions on the blockchain to gather relevant information for investigations. This can be used to investigate crimes involving cryptocurrencies, such as money laundering or fraud. However, blockchain forensics also presents challenges.

An important challenge is the pseudonymous nature of blockchain transactions, which can make it difficult to identify the individuals involved in a transaction. Another challenge is the complexity of the blockchain technology itself, which requires a high level of technical knowledge to understand and analyse.

15.6.3   IoT FORENSICS

The term "Internet of Things" (IoT) denotes the intricate network comprising physical devices, vehicles, household appliances, and assorted items infused with electronics, software, sensors, actuators, and connectivity. This amalgamation empowers these entities to establish connections, facilitating the exchange of data. As the proliferation of internet-connected devices surges, they emerge as an escalating and noteworthy reservoir of digital evidence. IoT forensics involves the extraction and analysis of data from IoT devices. This can be used to investigate a wide range of crimes, from cyberattacks targeting IoT devices to traditional crimes where IoT devices may contain relevant evidence. However, IoT forensics also presents challenges.

One of the main challenges is the diversity of IoT devices, which can make it difficult to develop standard forensic procedures. Another challenge is the potential for data privacy issues, as IoT devices often collect sensitive personal data. Despite these issues and challenges, the field of digital forensics continues to evolve and adapt, with new tools and techniques being developed to address these emerging technologies.

15.7   CONCLUSION

Digital forensics is considered one of the most significant and challenging parts of forensic science that deals with the identification, extraction, preservation, analysis documentation, and subsequent presentation of digital evidence in legal investigations. Digital forensics is a dynamic and critically important field in current investigations. It has several uses, a huge impact, and enormous growth and development potential. The growing complexity of digital systems, as well as the rise in cyber threats, necessitates the usage of digital forensics. Various techniques and tools related to various aspects of digital forensics are described. Challenges and issues related to digital forensics are discussed. The chapter discussed various applications of digital forensics related to criminal investigations, intellectual property conflicts, commercial security, and legal system. As technology continues to advance, the field of digital forensics will need to adapt and develop improved tools and methods to address emerging challenges in digital investigations. The future of digital forensics looks bright, with new opportunities and challenges arising from emerging technologies like artificial intelligence, blockchain, and the Internet of Things (IoT). Incorporating machine learning and artificial intelligence into digital forensics can enhance the efficiency and accuracy of investigations. Future work can focus on developing AI-driven tools for evidence analysis and pattern recognition.

REFERENCES

1. Aminnezhad, A., Dehghantanha, A., & Abdullah, M. T. (2015). A survey on privacy issues in Digital Forensics. ResearchGate. https://www.researchgate.net/publication/267799382_A_Survey_on_Privacy_Issues_in_Digital_Forensics
2. Zareen, M. S., Waqar, A., & Aslam, B. (2013). Digital forensics: Latest challenges and response. In 2013 2nd National Conference on Information Assurance (NCIA) (pp. 21–29). Rawalpindi, Pakistan. doi: 10.1109/NCIA.2013.6725320.
3. Choo, K.-K. R., & Dehghantanha, A. (2017). Contemporary digital forensic investigations of cloud and Mobile applications. In Contemporary Digital Forensic Investigations of Cloud and Mobile Applications (pp. 1–6). https://doi.org/10.1016/B978-0-12-805303-4.00001-0
4. Naveen, & Naveen. (2024, January 6). What is Digital Forensics – Types, Process, and Challenges. Intellipaat. https://intellipaat.com/blog/digital-forensics
5. Yaacoub, J.-P. A., Noura, H. N., Salman, O., & Chehab, A. (2022, August). Advanced digital forensics and anti-digital forensics for IoT systems: Techniques, limitations and recommendations. Internet of Things, 19, 100544. https://doi.org/10.1016/j.iot.2022.100544
6. Kumar, G., Saha, R., Lal, C., & Conti, M. (July 2021). Internet-of-forensic (IoF): A blockchain-based digital forensics framework for IoT applications. Future Generation Computer Systems, 120, 13–25. https://doi.org/10.1016/j.future.2021.02.016.
7. Baryamereeba, V., & Tushabe, F. (2004). The Enhanced Digital Investigation Process Model. In Proceedings of Digital Forensic Research Workshop, Baltimore, MD.
8. Reith, M., Carr, C., & Gunsh, G. (2002). An examination of digital forensics models. International Journal of Digital Evidence, 1(3), 1–2.
9. Irons, A., & Lallie, H. S. (2014). Digital forensics to intelligent forensics. Future Internet, 6(3), 584–596. https://doi.org/10.3390/fi6030584.
10. Harbawi, M., & Varol, A. (2016). The role of digital forensics in combating cybercrimes. In 2016 4th International Symposium on Digital Forensic and Security (ISDFS) (pp. 138–142). Little Rock, AR, USA. doi: 10.1109/ISDFS.2016.7473532.
11. Khan, S., Gani, A., Abdul Wahab, A. W., Shiraz, M., & Ahmad, I. (2016). Network forensics: Review, taxonomy, and open challenges. Journal of Network and Computer Applications, 66, 214–235. https://doi.org/10.1016/j.jnca.2016.03.005.
12. Marturana, F., Me, G., & Tacconi, S. (2012). A Case Study on Digital Forensics in the Cloud. In 2012 International Conference on Cyber-Enabled Distributed Computing and Knowledge Discovery (pp. 111–116). Sanya, China. doi: 10.1109/CyberC.2012.26.
13. Gomez Buquerin, K. K., Corbett, C., & Hof, H.-J. (April 2021). A generalized approach to automotive forensics. Forensic Science International: Digital Investigation, 36(Supplement), 301111. https://doi.org/10.1016/j.fsidi.2021.301111
14. Raghavan, S. (March 2012). Digital forensic research: Current state of the art. CSI Transactions on ICT, 1(1). https://doi.org/10.1007/s40012-012-0008-7.

15. Jones, G. M., & Sathianesan, G. W. (2022, February 8). An insight into digital forensics: History, frameworks, types and tools. Cyber Security and Digital Forensics, 6, 105–125.

16. Adedayo, O. M. (2016). Big data and digital forensics. In 2016 IEEE International Conference on Cybercrime and Computer Forensic (ICCCF) (pp. 1–7). Vancouver, BC, Canada. doi: 10.1109/ICCCF.2016.7740422.

17. Kim, L. (2023, September 25). 2023 SANS Report: Digital Forensics | SANS Institute. https://www.sans.org/white-papers/2023-sans-report-digital-forensics/

18. Kumari, N., & Mohapatra, A. K. (2016). An insight into digital forensics branches and tools. In 2016 International Conference on Computational Techniques in Information and Communication Technologies (ICCTICT) (pp. 243–250). New Delhi, India. doi: 10.1109/ICCTICT.2016.7514586.

19. Al-Dhaqm, A., et al. (2021). Digital forensics subdomains: The state of the art and future directions. IEEE Access, 9, 152476–152502. doi: 10.1109/ACCESS.2021.3124262.

20. Nance, K., & Ryan, D. (February 2011). Legal Aspects of Digital Forensics: A Research Agenda. In Proceedings of the 44th Hawaii International Conference on System Sciences (HICSS) (pp. 1–10). doi: 10.1109/HICSS.2011.282. IEEE Xplore.

21. He, J., Wan, X., Liu, G., Huang, N., & Zhao, B. (2013). On the application of digital forensics in different scenarios. In 2013 8th International Workshop on Systematic Approaches to Digital Forensics Engineering (SADFE) (pp. 1–5). Hong Kong, China. doi: 10.1109/SADFE.2013.6911550.

22. Hou, J., Li, Y., Yu, J., & Shi, W. (2020, January). A survey on digital forensics in internet of things. IEEE Internet of Things Journal, 7(1), 1–15. doi: 10.1109/JIOT.2019.2940713

23. Amato, F., Castiglione, A., Cozzolino, G., & Narducci, F. (2020, April). A semantic-based methodology for digital forensics analysis. Journal of Parallel and Distributed Computing, 138, 172–177. https://doi.org/10.1016/j.jpdc.2019.12.017.

24. Vincze, E. A. (2016). Challenges in digital forensics. Research Articles, Volume(Issue), 183–194. https://doi.org/10.1080/15614263.2015.1128163.

25. Sadiku, M. N. O., Tembely, M., & Musa, S. M. (2017). Digital forensics. International Journal of Advanced Research in Computer Science and Software Engineering, 7(4), 274–276. https://doi.org/10.23956/ijarcsse/v7i4/01404.

16 Fingerprint Security and the Internet of Things (IoT) in the Digital Era

Neha Sharma and Pankaj Dhiman

16.1 INTRODUCTION

In our modern computerised world, authentication is becoming increasingly necessary. The technology community faces various security and privacy challenges, and advanced secure solutions are needed. Traditional authentication systems rely on tokens such as vehicle keys, cards, and passwords, which come with restrictions such as being lost, stolen, or shared. If a user shares the security token or an opponent gains access to it, they can access all of the user's sensitive information, and it can be challenging to determine which usage caused the problem. These limitations, as well as the requirement for human verification, can be overcome by using various biometric features. When designing a smart home, a security system is one of the most crucial applications to consider [1]. Biometric systems can authenticate a person based on the uniqueness of the user's bodily traits. Fingerprint identification is the most prevalent biometric attribute, yet there are numerous places where security and privacy are not sufficiently addressed. People usually install security systems in their homes to protect their families from potential threats, such as fires or hazardous gas leaks, and to keep their valuables safe from burglars and thieves. In a traditional home security system, people usually rely on keys, passwords, or security cards to unlock the door and gain entry into their home. However, these security measures are not foolproof and can be easily circumvented by attackers. Furthermore, they do not provide any record of who enters the house, leaving homeowners vulnerable to potential theft or intrusion. A human fingerprint is frequently used in human biometrics since it is unique and never changes, which is one strategy the security system can employ to address these issues [2]. To recognise numerous persons simultaneously within proximity, nevertheless, requires time. Additionally, based just on his fingerprint data, a person is difficult for a human to identify. Smart home technology is significantly enhancing the standard of daily household activities. Home IOT incorporates the typical hardware needed for private establishments. The researchers have developed authentication techniques based on behavioural biometric traits such as gesture, keystroke, and gait to protect the user's privacy since the traditional PIN and Patterns are weak and easy to crack.

The components and general operation of active authentication systems are presented in this work, along with various metrics used to assess the effectiveness of active authentication mechanisms [3]. Even though it belongs to the industrial field, home automation is closely tied to personal life. It covers various topics, including

DOI: 10.1201/9781032614663-16

media, construction, mobile communications, energy, health, security, communications, appliances, media, and MSM. This significantly accelerates the industry's total growth. Home IoTs are made up of six elements [4]. Control devices, smartphones, and operating systems comprise IoT communication protocols, typically in embedded form and wired and wireless communications. For the home IoTs to operate properly, these elements must be linked together in an organised manner [5].

16.2   APPLICATION OF IoT

The Internet of Things (IoT) is being successfully used in many different fields. IoT's potential can yet be used to create innovative new applications that benefit society. Smart things can exchange information with one another and reflect a context gathered from the environment in IoT application environments. Transportation Departments, environmental monitoring, healthcare, smart cities, industrial control, and many more areas can all benefit from the IoT's potential. This section covers several prospective application domains and discusses their drawbacks [4] (Figure 16.1).

16.2.1   SMART ENVIRONMENT

A house, plant, or office can have sensors and smart objects attached to appliances such as refrigerators, lights, and ACs to observe the surroundings. A home's lighting system can fluctuate depending on the time of day, such as how many lights are on in the evening versus how many are off in the wee hours of the morning. A fire alarm can be activated automatically whenever the temperature or smoke detector sensor senses something abnormal. Such a programme is extremely beneficial for older persons living alone at home. Some devices, such as doors in the room, lights

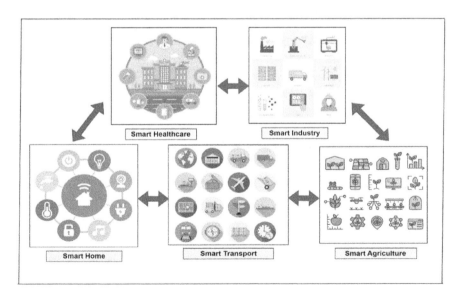

FIGURE 16.1   Using data from IoT, identify end consumers and application areas.

in the current room, and water taps/faucets in the kitchen, can be operated based on the movement of inhabitants in the house [6].

16.2.2 HEALTHCARE

Healthcare is another industry in which IoT can be utilised to follow people (such as patients and employees) or things, recognise and verify persons, and automatically gather data. Real-time tracking of people in motion is helpful when managing staff and streamlining hospital operations. Patients are protected by staff identification and verification, which also helps to prevent errors like using the wrong drug, dose, or time. Enabling automatic clinical data collection will improve the medical inventory [7].

All the sensors that measure body temperature and heart response can be attached to patients for real-time monitoring. These IoT-enabled sensors can quickly convey information to physicists after detecting an anomaly locally.

16.2.3 SMART CITIES

A smart city has emerged due to the deployment of cutting-edge communication infrastructure and unique services throughout a metropolis. Glasgow, Barcelona, and Masdar are embracing smart city technology. The IoT is being used to optimise physical infrastructure such as power grids, road networks, and parking lots. This technology is improving the standard of living for residents. By monitoring traffic flow on highways and in urban areas, vehicles can be directed to prevent congestion. Smart parking facilities are also being made available through RFID and sensor technologies, allowing drivers to identify available parking spaces in the city [8]. Data about air pollution, including the amount of carbon dioxide, can be sent to an organisation using IoT devices.

16.2.4 TRANSPORTATION AND LOGISTICS

IoT is highly utilised in autonomous vehicles and smart transportation systems for transportation and logistics. Sensors, actuators, and computing power can now be installed in trains, buses, and cars to enhance passenger monitoring and control. These devices can provide passengers, drivers, or authorities with necessary information. IoT can be used to keep track of delivery status and products in transit using RFID tags. The use of RFID and NFC in transportation, inventory management, supply chain management, and mobile ticketing presents significant business opportunities. Intel collaborates with the BMW Group and computer vision pioneer Mobileye to develop the next-generation automated driving platform [9] (Figure 16.2).

16.2.5 PERSONAL AND SOCIAL

The term "Social Internet of Things" (SIoT), coined by the author of [10], describes a society in which the objects in one's environment are capable of intelligent sensing and networking. SIoT enables people to communicate with one another and sustain social ties. By receiving and sharing real-time updates, users of Twitter and

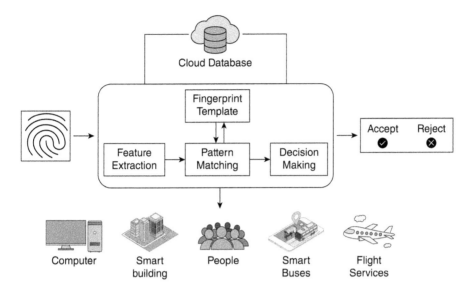

FIGURE 16.2 IoT biometric-based security system structure.

Facebook can stay in touch with friends. Existing social network privacy and protection measures may be applied to increase IoT security as shown in Figure 16.3. IoT-enabled things can be tracked and protected against theft or loss by creating applications. For instance, smart devices like laptops and smartphones automatically transmit SMS messages to their owners when they arrive at a new location or detect unauthorised access. SIoT has been utilised in a variety of products to capture user data. These facts are sent via the Internet to social networks of people and machines that can respond to problems and give help [11].

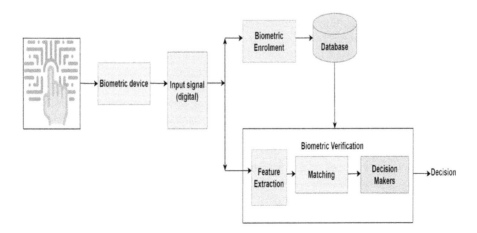

FIGURE 16.3 Scheme for a general revocable biometric system.

16.2.6 AGRICULTURE

Agriculture is a burgeoning area for IoT use, especially in developing nations like Brazil, Bangladesh, and India, where it is the primary industry [11]. Towards agricultural automation, authors in [12] proposed the AgriTech framework. Farmers can save time by using sensors to collect data on nutrients, humidity, and other aspects of agriculture. These nations' industrialisation can benefit from extra human labour. IoT can automate agriculture to optimise water, fertiliser, and insecticide use. However, because of the high initial setup costs, implementing AgriTech in developing nations is difficult. It is possible to harm field-installed sensors physically. Again, false sensor deployment could lead to unwelcome information from the farmer's field [13].

16.3 IoT SECURITY TYPES

Because of attack vulnerabilities of smart devices, IoT security is an area that concerns researchers and users. The ESS (embedded sensor systems) used in building computerisation systems, vehicles, and wearable technology provide the IoT with the most connections. Devices connected to this vast network increase the potential attack surface for hackers. IoT internetworking systems are susceptible to five attacks [14].

1. A botnet is a collection of remotely controlled systems. Criminals employ C&C servers (command-and-control) to control the system, steal personal data, exploit online banking information, and send phishing emails [15].
2. A "man-in-the-middle attack" is a theory in which an intruder or hacker shatters the data transfer link between two separate systems. The intruder stealthily sends false communications, yet the sender and the recipient think they are exchanging genuine messages. The information that is available online, including social media and mobile devices, provides a general idea of a person's identity [16].
3. Social engineering persuades someone to divulge sensitive data such as bank account information or device or email passwords. Additionally, it involves installing deceptive software that can grant access to private information. Phishing emails or redirection to websites like shopping or banking portals that appear legitimate but constantly request or persuade users to submit confidential information can be used to carry out this type of threat [17].
4. When a service that typically functions cannot be accessed, a denial-of-service (DoS) attack has taken place. A distributed denial-of-service (DDoS) attack involves multiple systems maliciously attacking a single target. This is performed through a botnet, where several devices are configured to request a service at a specific time. This attack doesn't aim to steal data or cause security breaches but to harm a company's reputation [18].

   According to the HP (Hewlett Packard) research, 70% of commonly used IoT components have significant risks. These components are weak because there is no transport encryption, the website interface is unsafe, the software is not protected, and the permission is insufficient. Each component carries, on average, roughly many potential threats to the home network. The four key categories of security needs are safe object creation and data transfer, secure user identification and authentication, secure IoT data, and secure user access to data [19].

5. Entities in groups being watched are identified via IoT biometric validation or real-time verification. The rest of the section goes into more detail about biometric security in IoT since that is the focus of this chapter. The four key categories of security needs are safe object creation and data transfer, secure user identification and authentication, secure IoT data, and secure user access to data [20].

16.4   IoT SECURITY WITH BIOMETRICS

The distinctiveness and permanence of human body traits are considered in biometric recognition [21]. Facial features, biometrics, iris, gait, hand geometry, DNA, and others are well-liked physiological characteristics used in IoT biometric security. The authentication application's requirements are typically considered while choosing a biometric.

Physiological and behavioural biometric modalities are two of the different types [22], and they are briefly described as follows.

16.4.1   Physiological

Physiological features are based on precise calculations of human body components.

16.4.1.1   Face
Face identification algorithms often consider the correlation between the positions of facial features. You can get the most recent facial recognition technologies here. The execution of a face recognition algorithm is hampered by various important characteristics like contrast, movement, cosmetic, obstruction, and postural differences [23]. The face is a widely recognised biometric that performs well in various conditions.

16.4.1.2   Fingerprint
The most popular and successful solution for IoT person authentication is fingerprint-based recognition. It has a special textural pattern resembles a person's peaks and valleys. These ridges are divided into groups utilising particular points called "minutiae." The spatial distributions are thus shown to be particular to an individual. To compare the fingerprints of two different people, these "minutiae" spots are used. Since several countries' forensic agencies used Automated Fingerprint Identification Systems (AFIS) for various purposes, this biometric has drawn more attention. In addition, numerous commercial and community applications use fingerprints for authentication [24].

16.4.1.3   Iris
It is a coloured circle that surrounds the pupil and contains a complex pattern in the eye. It has been well-known and proven fact that each individual's iris possesses

distinctive qualities. Its distinctive features include stripes, pits, and furrows, which are being reviewed as identification proof. Iris authentication is incorporated into some large-scale systems' identifying processes. Furthermore, the unavailability of earlier iris pattern databases may challenge several applications [25].

16.4.1.4 Palm Print

Palm Print is another well-liked and acknowledged biometric employed in IoT security systems. Like a fingerprint, it has characteristic ridges and flexion creases. This method is mostly used in forensics, and according to studies, 30% of palm print samples are taken from criminal cases (such as those involving knives, weapons, etc.). Minute details and wrinkles are considered for matching and identifying the desired palm print. The databases contain several palm print samples that were collected by forensics. These samples typically have poor resolutions of roughly 75 dpi. Extracting texture features for intelligent expert systems is difficult from a research perspective [26].

16.4.1.5 Hand Geometry

It is necessary to identify people based on the shape of their hands. Using low-resolution hand pattern photos, identity verification by hand geometry extracts geometrical information. The precision of hand geometry for person authentication is quite low. Since hand geometry measurement equipment is physically huge, it is not easy to integrate them into current security systems [27].

16.4.1.6 DNA (Deoxyribonucleic Acid)

Each human cell has DNA (deoxyribonucleic acid) made up of genes. This material, which is genetic and extremely stable, is used to depict physiological characteristics and identify individuals. Except for identical twins, each person's DNA is often unique. DNA patterns are created from many body components, including hair, fingernails, saliva, and blood. The matching process is carried out after forensics and law enforcement organisations create a distinctive DNA profile of a sample utilising several intermediate processes. This procedure takes a long time and costs a lot of money. As a result, developing an automated IoT security system based on DNA is complex and unsuitable for large-scale biometric deployment for public usage [28].

16.4.2 BEHAVIOURAL

Behavioural features are a type of indirect measurement of human attributes accomplished through feature extraction and machine learning. A signature, keystroke dynamics, gait, and voice are popular behavioural biometrics that will be discussed further.

16.4.2.1 Gait

The gait is the human walking pattern, which is different for everyone and defines a person. Sensors collect gait data, and statistical features are retrieved to explain a person's complicated gait dynamics [29]. Then, using these characteristics, a machine learning model is taught to recognise a person. Several factors, such as speed and walking, describe a gait pattern. Gait biometrics are typically used in healthcare applications, but they are also used in IoT biometric applications.

16.4.2.2 Signature

Another behaviour utilised in commercial transactions daily. Academics have attempted to develop a solid signature recognition model, but none have succeeded. These technologies measure the pressure-sensitive pen pad to capture distinctive traits. Real-time signing captures strokes' shape, speed, acceleration, and speed.

16.4.2.3 Voice

Speech recognition methods recognise people based on their vocalised words. The voice of a human being combines behavioural and physiological aspects. The shape and size of lips and mouth influence the physiological aspect of voice. The jaws, lips, and velum movements establish behavioural aspects that vary with age. Voice biometrics is mostly used for authentication [29].

16.4.2.4 Keystroke

It is built based on the studying typing style. These techniques present numerous challenges in demonstrating dynamic orders with high interclass variability and variable performance, primarily used for verification [30].

16.5 INTERNET OF THINGS AND BIOMETRIC SECURITY

This presents the biometric security system and its advantages in various fields.

16.5.1 BIOMETRIC SYSTEM SECURITY

Identity matching can be separated into two challenges of varying complexity: (a) authentication and (b) recognition.

The verification procedure confirms or denies a person's claim, whereas the identification procedure identifies the person. A biometrics application used in a security system is depicted in Figure 16.1.

Table 16.1 compares many types of biometrics, such as fingerprints, hand geometry, voice, retina, iris, signature, face, and so forth are all examples. Even though fingerprints have superior accuracy and ease of application than human signatures, signatures (biometric type) are more prevalent see Table 16.2. Biometric methods for IoT security and related data [31].

TABLE 16.1
Depicted the IoT Devices for the Smart Home

One-way home IoT appliances	Electricity meters, smoke detectors, gas meters, and security alarms
Two-way IoT devices for the home	Control of lights, gas, security, home appliances, and temperature in the room

---

TABLE 16.2

Comparison of Popular Biometric Technologies

Type of Biometric	Accuracy	Ease of Use	Acceptability of Users	Implementation Viewpoint	Cost
Fingerprint	⬆	(?)	⬇	⬆	(?)
Hand geometry	(?)	⬆	(?)	(?)	⬆
Voice	(?)	⬆	⬆	⬆	⬇
Retina	⬆	⬇	⬇	⬇	(?)
Iris	(?)	(?)	(?)	(?)	⬆
Handwriting	(?)	(?)	⬆	⬇	(?)
Face	⬇	⬆	⬆	(?)	⬇

High ⬆ *Low* ⬇ *N/A.*

16.5.2 BIOMETRIC SYSTEM SECURITY COMPARED TO OTHER TRADITIONAL SECURITY SYSTEMS

16.5.2.1 Accurate Information

Biometric systems are more accurate and robust than fractional (PIN/password) security systems. The user is not required to remember these credentials, and no hostile person may breach the security by copying or guessing them [32].

16.5.2.2 Simple and Secure

Biometrics is simple and secure to use. Hackers cannot obtain legitimate users' biometric information.

16.5.2.3 Accountability

A person who uses a biometric system cannot refute the action he has performed in the future. Hence, the user is accountable for his actions [33].

16.5.2.4 Scalability

From the users' perspective, biometric systems give flexibility and scalability. Users can choose higher versions of sensors and security systems depending on their needs and use their non-discriminatory properties. The possibility of biometric hash value collisions is smaller than traditional security systems.

16.5.2.5 Time-Saving

One of the benefits of this security approach over traditional methods is its faster execution speed. In a matter of seconds, a person can be validated. Furthermore, this technology can only benefit the office's growth by improving performance and lowering expenses by eliminating fraud and time waste in the verification process [34].

16.5.2.6 User-Friendly Systems

Users can quickly and easily install biometric systems on their devices, enabling efficient and reliable task performance. The systems are intuitive, require minimal training, and eliminate the need for costly password managers. With higher life expectancy and a decreased birth rate, the world faces new concerns as the population ages. Currently, there are 600 million elderly individuals worldwide, and this number is expected to double by 2025, reaching 2000 million by 2050. Therefore, it's essential to have a user-friendly system that caters to the needs of elderly individuals using IoT systems as end-users [35].

16.5.2.7 Convenience

It is now possible to eliminate the need for identification cards or secret documents when verifying one's identity. This is made possible by using various biometric scanners available in the industry. These scanners can be used for different purposes, and many organisations and companies have adopted them for security checks at entry and exit points [36].

16.5.2.8 Return on Investment

This is certainly high since humans can avoid fraud like "buddy punching," saving payroll costs, accurately calculating labour hours, and reducing management time. It is important to consider the upfront cost of implementing biometric technology. Any spelling, grammar, or punctuation errors have been corrected. Biometric systems can be extremely beneficial to industries. Rather than having to remember a password, biometric systems provide users with unique biometric information that allows them to access services following authentication. As a result, biometric technology is precious from a business standpoint [37].

16.5.3 Advantages of Using Biometric-Based Security Schemes in IoT Applications

Biometric systems can be used in various IoT applications that require human-machine interaction. Figure 16.1 depicts the various application areas that require a security system. For example, a biometric smart lock can be installed in a door to enhance security. In IoT transportation systems, the biometric system can validate the user's identification when parking a car, ensuring only authorised users can access the vehicle. Using biometric verification, traffic officers can determine whether a vehicle belongs to a driver. The end user must verify their identity when connecting IoT applications to national projects or specific areas like smart grids or defence applications. This verification process helps to increase the system's reliability, as cited in [38]. In the case of IoT healthcare systems, biometric security can play a vital role. Medical personnel must undergo biometric verification before accessing or prescribing patient data, ensuring that only authorised personnel can view and manage sensitive medical information as shown in Table 16.3. If a person

TABLE 16.3

Biometric Methods for IoT Security and Related Data

Method for IoT Security	Year of Publication	Type of Biometric Traits	Databases	Performance
Single-Modal Biometrics				
[23]	2016	Fingerprint	–	–
[24]	2016	Fingerprint	–	–
[25]	2016	Fingerprint	–	–
[26]	2018	Fingerprint	–	–
[27]	2019	Fingerprint	–	–
[28]	2019	Fingerprint	FVC2002DB3	EER = 3%
[29]	2020	Fingerprint	Private	EER = 30%
[29]	2016	Face	FERET	RA = 99.5%
[30]	2018	Face	–	–
[31]	2020	Face	–	–
[32]	2020	Face	WIDER FACE	RA = 60.7%
[33]	2016	ECG	–	–
[34]	2017	ECG	MIT-BIH	RA = 97.78%
[35]	2019	ECG	NIH PhysioBank	RA = 98.2%
[36]	2019	ECG	PTB	RA = 98.76%
[37]	2015	Voice	–	–
[38]	2020	Voice	–	–
[39]	2017	Finger-vein	MMCBNU_6000	EER = 0.36%
[40]	2019	Iris	CASIA-Iris v.3	EER = 0.22%
[41]	2019	Iris	CASIA-Iris v.4	EER = 0.20%
Multimodal Biometrics				
[42]	2016	Face and Iris	CASIA-Face v.5 CASIA-Iris v.4	RA = 99.1%
[43]	2016	Hand and Gesture	–	–
[44]	2019	Face and Voice	CSUF-SG5	Fused: EER = 8.04% Face: EER = 14.05% Voice: EER = 43.76%
[45]	2020	Finger-vein	–	–
[46]	2021	Ear and Arm Gesture	AWE HMOG	Fused: EER = 5.15% Ear: *EER* = 20.80% Arm: *EER* = 10.60%

is involved in an accident, biometric information can be used to identify him and obtain his medical history. At the moment, researchers are attempting to incorporate IoT into agricultural applications. Many third-world countries are major food grain producers, but their farmers have low literacy rates. Therefore, agricultural IoT systems must be designed to be simple to use. Biometric security technologies are particularly well-suited for this context, making biometric-based solutions highly valuable for agricultural IoT systems [39].

16.6   COMPARISON OF THE THREE MAIN AUTHENTICATION METHODS

The IoT enables items to participate in daily activities. However, controlling such items and ensuring their security in a complicated system is a complicated problem. IoT, in general, is a field where people interact with technology installed on smart devices. Four IoT elements—user, smart devices, ecosystem, and method—relate to one another and offer a comprehensive and insightful feature for IoT security. In this sense, it is necessary to maintain the privacy of human information when they engage with the intelligent technology ecosystem. Data security should also be ensured while communicating with the control processes. The objectives should be maintained, and the methods' dependability protected. The objectives should be maintained, and the methods' dependability protected. In addition, IoT security based on cognitive and systemic methodologies is moving towards more autonomy due to the increasing object autonomy to protect against various security risks. To emphasise the study challenges, we will now analyse the roles played by each actor in IoT security, including people, intelligent and smart devices, the technology environment, and processes. According to the author, the main IoT component can be divided into four nodes. The four types of fundamental nodes are the process, human, technical ecosystem, and intelligent object. The IoT security management system is represented by four scenarios on its planes: safety, security, access, and cyber security [40] (Table 16.4).

TABLE 16.4
Comparison of the Three Main Authentication Methods

Authentication Strategy	Advantages	Drawbacks
Handheld tokens (card, ID, and passport)	One can be built from the start. People can use tokens to obtain the same service in several countries, which is standard.	It is susceptible to theft. It is possible to construct a forgery or a replica. It is feasible to distribute it. A user can create many identities for himself or herself.
Knowledge-based (PIN and password):	It is simple and affordable to create. For any problem, it is simply interchangeable with a new one.	It can be guessed or broken. Long or complex passwords are difficult to remember. It can be transferred. A user may register under more than one identity.
Biometrics	It is not predictable, misplaced, forgotten, taken, or shared. It is straightforward to verify a single person with multiple identities. It provides a higher level of security than others.	Replacement is impossible for any issue, such as oily skin or fingerprints. If a person's biometric data is stolen, it is impossible to replace.

16.6.1 Requirements of Users

The following user criteria must be considered because the designed authentication strategy must be user-friendly.

1. Easy and safe password modification: The system lets users easily pick and change their passwords. In other words, after verifying the legitimacy of the cardholder, the user can change the password without assistance from any other reliable third party.
2. Single registration: To access multiple application servers, a user only must register once with the registration centre. A single registration can also lower the networks and the registration centre's operating costs.
3. Anonymity: Both business and academia are paying more and more attention to user privacy. As a result, anonymous authentication entails ensuring a user [41].

16.6.2 Revocability and Biometric Template Protection Schemes

The primary purpose is to modify the original user biometric information so that the constructed template has no negative effects and does not provide system security to recover the original [42].

An optimal method should include four characteristics:

1. *Diversity*: The same secure template should be implemented for each application.
2. *Revocability*: If a template is stolen, it is revoked or reissued.
3. *Security (non-inevitability)*: The original template is lost if the modified template is stolen.
4. *Performance*: The transformation has no adverse effects on the recognition system's performance [43].

The revocable biometric identification procedure consists of two phases: enrolment and authentication, as illustrated in (Figure 16.1). The characteristics of the user's biometric image are given to the scanner, and it transforms the image, creating a revocable biometric template using a transformation method [44].

Revocable biometric template production has gained popularity as a research subject in recent years, and several research methods have been proposed. This author [45] reviews revocable approaches separated into two levels: registration-free and registration-needed base methods. The first level was broken into two categories: ways that can be used with a specific matcher/existing matcher (Figure 16.4).

Each component of the last level is divided into two groups, including techniques that operate in the signal/feature domain. This chapter suggested categorising revocable methods into ten categories: salting methods, bio-hash methods, random projections, random permutations, bio-convolving, cancellable biometric filters, knowledge signatures, and hybrid methods [46].

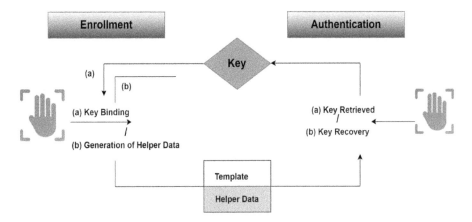

FIGURE 16.4 Scheme for a general revocable biometric system.

While the author in [47] provided a concise and well-discussed overview of various biometric techniques, a new taxonomy split these techniques into six groups. Hybrid approaches, multimodal, transformation-based, filter-based, and more categories are also given. A revocable biometric system's potential attack spots were also clearly outlined. However, BTPs were typically split into two groups: biometric cryptosystems and transformation techniques.

16.7 BIOMETRIC CRYPTOSYSTEMS

According to the basic principle, biometric and cryptographic techniques are combined to create biometric cryptosystems, which generate biometric templates based on creating cryptographic keys. Adopting biometric cryptosystems makes it possible to control cryptographic keys safely and safeguard biometric templates. Biometric cryptosystem techniques are categorised into two groups (Figure 16.2): key binding and key formation (depending on the data assistance extraction technique) [48].

In the first category, a biometric template is bound together with a cryptographic key to produce a secure sketch that makes it impossible to retrieve the information. Fuzzy commitment and fuzzy vault are two well-known examples of key-binding techniques. A direct generation of cryptographic keys using additional data and biometrics traits is used for the key generation cryptosystem [24] (Figure 16.5).

16.7.1 Approach to Feature Transformation

The common idea is that a certain function can transform that original data; the unsafe template is transformed into a new, safe one using specific transformation parameters. If the transformed template is insecure, this transformation can be retrieved and replaced. These plans can also be divided into invertible and non-invertible transforms.

The original one can be obtained using a key in the invertible transform. The most well-known method of this kind is called bio-hashing, and it is typically used

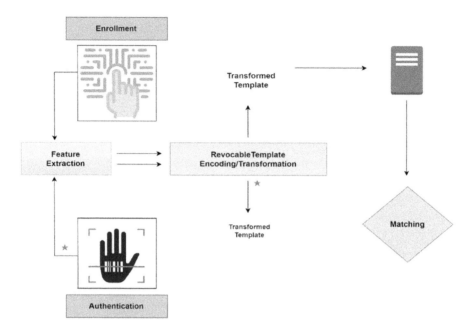

FIGURE 16.5   General strategy for key generation and binding.

as a revocable bio-code from fingerprint details by first projecting the fingerprint code onto a symmetrical basis determined through the random value. The original biometric template cannot be restored even if the key is known in a since the key is one-way, the transform cannot be reversed. This method can successfully address revocability issues [49] (Figure 16.6).

16.7.2   REVOCABLE BIOMETRICS AS AN IoT SECURITY MECHANISM

Recent years have seen a rise in the demand for low-power devices, which calls for a strong security level because it is convenient and less vulnerable to threats. Revocable biometrics has promise for the IoT. Various solutions for revocable biometric protection evolved in the literature to safeguard the confidentiality of the initial IoT systems utilising biometric templates. IoT cloud authentication using revocable biometrics for service access control as depicted in Figure 16.7.

Both biometric cryptosystems and feature transformation-based techniques will be used to present them in the next section [50].

16.8   BIOMETRIC CRYPTOSYSTEMS FOR IoT SECURITY

Several research initiatives have focused on deploying biometric cryptosystems in IoT systems. These initiatives are listed in Table 16.1, and their performance is measured by the Equal Error Rate (EER) and False Acceptance Rate (FAR). The author of [51] presented a method for implementing secret keys that can be revoked using Physically Unclonable Functions (PUFs). This method uses the SRAMs of

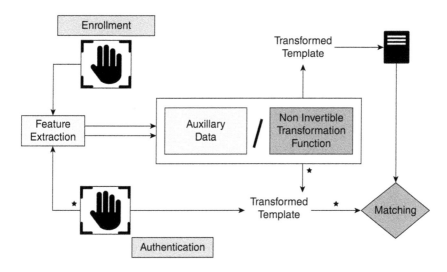

FIGURE 16.6   Scheme for general biometric feature transformation.

commercial Bluetooth Low Energy (BLE) devices. When user biometrics are sensitive, a mechanism used in the sensor node communication module encrypts them with PUFs. The suggested approach is divided into helper data generation and secret reconstruction. These stages use new PUF replies to achieve the proposed method's revocability. The approach performs well with an error equal rate (ERR) of 0.02%.

For safeguarding IoT functionality, a fuzzy commitment encryption approach worked effectively. The author [52] adopted the fuzzy commitment approach, divided into three primary phases: secure communication between things and distant systems. SRAMs used in commercial BLE devices can implement secret keys. Improvements are shown with ERR=0 performance, according to experimental results.

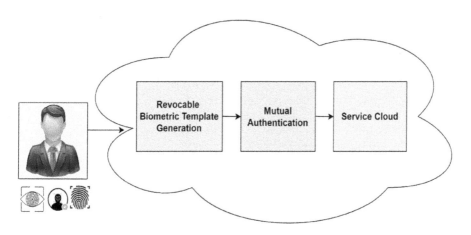

FIGURE 16.7   IoT cloud authentication using revocable biometrics for service access control.

An e-security system was created by the author in [53]. The suggested system uses methods for multiple-factor authentication using a card, PIN, and a palm print or palm vein biometric feature. Symmetric cryptography is also used. The biometric encryption employed in this study uses a random key following the extraction of the biometric attributes. The ERR and FAR for this experiment were both 0.

A biometric technique that can be cancelled based on hand gesture encoding of HDsEMG (high-density surface electromyogram) was proposed by the author [54]. When the user entered the required gesture password during the authentication process, a biometric token was created using the recorded HDsEMG signals from the right forearm muscles. Experiments have shown that HD-sEMG is highly effective in preventing attacks and increasing security and has an error rate (ERR) of only 0.003%. A biometric token was created during user authentication when the user entered the requisite gesture password while using the recorded HDsEMG signals from the right forearm muscles. Experiments demonstrated HD-sEMG's effectiveness in thwarting attacks and improving security, and they also demonstrated its effectiveness with an ERR of 0.003% (Table 16.5).

The author [55] presents a compact bio-cryptosystem for DNA encoding to protect biometric templates. They start by using a 2D_Logistic Sine Map to generate random keys, and then they convert fractional chaotic keys to useable integer forms using a hexadecimal basis. The following step involved independently confounding the images (ODD and EVEN images) with chaotic key series before merging them for encoding with random keys.

Discrete Cosine Transform (DCT) was used by the author in [56] to transform the introduced biometric before presenting a revocable biometric scheme to create a template that has been revoked. Two co-prime operators blur the original biometric. Because of this, it can be reconstructed as between the GCD of its two fuzzy versions. With EER = 0.04%, experiments demonstrate good system performance.

TABLE 16.5
An Overview of Research on Biometric Cryptosystems for IoT Security

Reference	Revocable Method	Modality	Best Performance
[35]	Physically Unclonable Functions	Fingerprint	EER=0.22
[36]	Fuzzy Commitment	Fingerprint	EER=0
[37]	Fuzzy Commitment	Fingerprint- Palm print	EER=0
		Palm vein	FAR=0
[38]	HD-sEMG-based Biometric	Hand Gesture	EER=0.003
[39]	2D logistic sine map Fingerprint	Palmprint	/
[40]	Blurring+ GCD-based method	Face	EER=0.04
		Fingerprint	
		Iris	
		Palmprint	
[41]	Double Random Phase Encoding (DRPE) and chaotic Baker map	Voice	/
		Face	

The author [57] presents a watermarking and encryption-based multimodal bio-metric verification system that is revocable and designed for IoT scenarios. Unique biometrics, voice prints, and facial photos are both used. The SVs matrix for the voice images is selected as a solid matrix to conceal the cipher text facial pic-tures, and double random phase encoding (DRPE) is employed to encrypt the face images. Watermarked pictures of a speech are finally encrypted using a chaotic Baker map.

16.8.1 Transformational Security Methods for IoT

Several research projects tackling problems with biometric-based transformation techniques are discussed in this section. Therefore, Table 16.2 summarises some significant works in this field of study.

The author [58] proposes a cancellable steganography-based approach using the iris to conceal a system for IoT network authentication that uses user-specific keys. A revoked iris template is created by applying feature quantisation, shifting on the original iris, and then transforming features based on random projections. Steganography is also employed to protect user-specific keys.

The author proposed a one-way cancellable face and fingerprint biometric approach [59]. The suggested system, which uses an FPGA approach incorporat-ing 3D chaotic maps encryption, has been proven to provide highly secure biomet-ric templates. With an EER of 1.32% and an Area under the Receiver Operating Characteristic Curve (AROC) of 99.98%, the system also displays a FAR of 1.889510-15 and a False Rejection Rate (FRR) of 2.023410-12.

In [60], a non-invertible transformation strategy is suggested. Two random vec-tors of equal length are created, and to produce the first vector, items from vector T whose indices have the same values as its entries are extracted using the first vector. Using the second vector, which accomplishes the identical task, the remaining ele-ments of v1 are obtained and produce a vector v2 with indices equal to the values of the first vector's entries. They could calculate the x and y's vectors' element-wise average from there. As shown in Table 16.6 that works that used feature transforma-tion based on biometrics for IoT security.

The author proposed a secure cloud-based IoT framework to ensure secure inter-action between people and their objects [61]. The chaos system was utilised to cre-ate the AES encryption keys for user messages, while biometric templates were encrypted using projection matrices. The experiment uses the palm print and palm vein as the two hand modalities, and the results demonstrate that the suggested approach works effectively, with a Recognition Rate (RR) of 99.895%.

In the chapters [62, 63], the authors presented a cancellable template with two components to support resource-constrained IoT applications and privacy-preserv-ing authentication systems.

First, a re-indexing approach is used to create length-flexible partial-cancellable features. Second, revocable biometric templates are produced through three opera-tions: nested difference, encoding, and bitwise XOR Boolean. Initially, they cre-ate length-flexible partial-cancellable features utilising a specially built re-indexing approach. Second, revocable biometric templates were produced by passing through

TABLE 16.6

An Overview of Works that Used Feature Transformation Based on Biometrics for IoT Security

Reference	Revocable Method	Modality Best	Performance
[42]	Random Projection + Steganography	Iris	EER=1.66
[43]	Partial DCT Transformation	Fingerprint	EER=1.32
[44]	3D Chaotic maps	Face	AROC=99.98
		Fingerprint	FAR/FRR= 1.8895×10^{-15} 2.0234×10^{-12}
[45]	Random vectors for index generation+ Element Wise Average	Fingerprint	EER=0.04
[46]	Chaos AES Key generation + Projection Matrix	Palmprint Palmvein	RR=99.895
[47]	Partial-Cancellable Feature Generation + Encoding nested-difference XOR scheme	Fingerprint	EER=2.29

three operations: the nested difference operation, the encoding operation, and the bitwise XOR Boolean operation to ensure non-inevitability [64].

16.9 CONCLUSION

Biometric technology has been used for several decades to authenticate. Biometric-based security solutions are gaining popularity as a reliable method for verifying identity in highly secure contexts. Despite its usefulness, biometric technology still faces several challenges, the most significant being high cost. The cost of biometric technology arises from various factors such as hardware maintenance, database processing power, experimental infrastructure, real-time implementation, employee training and salaries, marketing costs, exception handling, productivity loss, and system maintenance. Additionally, the rate of technology change is increasing rapidly and constantly.

The framework can be expanded by incorporating new security, privacy, and performance metrics to increase certainty and promote widespread acceptability. The database evaluation through multiple benchmarks can uncover any existing biases. Furthermore, the work can be extended to include standardization of evaluation metrics. Additionally, hyperparameter threshold settings can be defined based on the user's security and usage requirements. Moreover, future research will study sweat pores, ridge patterns, and texture information in fingerprints to enhance sensor interoperability and enable 3D touchless fingerprint capturing. We will also combine biometric data to create a secure multi-model system.

REFERENCES

1. Lobaccaro, G., Carlucci, S., & Löfström, E. (2016). A review of systems and technologies for smart homes and smart grids. Energies, 9(5), 348. https://doi.org/10.3390/en9050348.

2. Thomas, S. (1998, January). Will commercial applications for biometric-based solutions take off in 1998? Information Security Technical Report, 3(1), 86–89. https://doi.org/10.1016/s1363-4127(98)80024-1.

3. Al-Fuqaha, A., Guizani, M., Mohammadi, M., Aledhari, M., & Ayyash, M. (2015). Internet of things: A survey on enabling technologies, protocols, and applications. IEEE Communications Surveys & Tutorials, 17(4), 2347–2376. https://doi.org/10.1109/comst.2015.2444095

4. Hansen, M., Berlich, P., Camenisch, J., Clauß, S., Pfitzmann, A., & Waidner, M. (2004, January). Privacy-enhancing identity management. Information Security Technical Report, 9(1), 35–44. https://doi.org/10.1016/s1363-4127(04)00014-7

5. Attitalla, S., Chocksi, V., & B, M. (2017, April 17). IBM cloud solutions for home automation. International Journal of Computer Applications, 164(4), 15–21. https://doi.org/10.5120/ijca2017913610.

6. Tu, Y. J., Zhou, W., & Piramuthu, S. (2009, January). Identifying RFID-embedded objects in pervasive healthcare applications. Decision Support Systems, 46(2), 586–593. https://doi.org/10.1016/j.dss.2008.10.001.

7. Acampora, G., Cook, D. J., Rashidi, P., & Vasilakos, A. V. (2013, December). A survey on ambient intelligence in healthcare. Proceedings of the IEEE, 101(12), 2470–2494. https://doi.org/10.1109/jproc.2013.2262913.

8. Riazul Islam, S. M., Kwak, D., Humaun Kabir, M., Hossain, M., & Kwak, K.-S. (2015). The internet of things for health care: A comprehensive survey. IEEE Access, 3, 678–708. https://doi.org/10.1109/access.2015.2437951

9. Miorandi, D., Sicari, S., De Pellegrini, F., & Chlamtac, I. (2012, September). Internet of things: Vision, applications and research challenges. Ad Hoc Networks, 10(7), 1497–1516. https://doi.org/10.1016/j.adhoc.2012.02.016.

10. Zanella, A., Bui, N., Castellani, A., Vangelista, L., & Zorzi, M. (2014, February). Internet of things for smart cities. IEEE Internet of Things Journal, 1(1), 22–32. https://doi.org/10.1109/jiot.2014.2306328.

11. Madakam, S. (2015). Internet of things: Smart things. International Journal of Future Computer and Communication, 4(4), 250–253. https://doi.org/10.7763/ijfcc.2015.v4.395.

12. Sahmim, S., & Gharsellaoui, H. (2017). Privacy and security in internet-based computing: Cloud computing, internet of things, cloud of things: A review. Procedia Computer Science, 112, 1516–1522. https://doi.org/10.1016/j.procs.2017.08.050

13. Sharma, N., & Dhiman, P. Secure Authentication scheme for IoT enabled smart homes. (2024, March 3). in Lecture notes in Electrical Engineering, 2024, 611–624. https://doi.org/10.1007/978-981-99-8646-0_48.

14. Kharade, P., Mandalollu, L., Pooja, A., Savadatti, P., & Marali, K. (2016, November 30). Prototype implementation of IoT based autonomous vehicle on raspberry pi. Bonfring International Journal of Research in Communication Engineering, 6(Special Issue), 38–43. https://doi.org/10.9756/bijrce.8197

15. Sri Prakash, N., & Venkatram, N. (2016, May 20). Establishing efficient security scheme in home IOT devices through biometric finger print technique. Indian Journal of Science and Technology, 9(17). https://doi.org/10.17485/ijst/2016/v9i17/93039

16. Taheri, S., & Yuan, J. S. (2018, February 24). A cross-layer biometric recognition system for Mobile IoT devices. Electronics, 7(2), 26. https://doi.org/10.3390/electronics7020026

17. Yang, W., Wang, S., Zheng, G., Yang, J., & Valli, C. (2019, March). A privacy-preserving lightweight biometric system for internet of things security. IEEE Communications Magazine, 57(3), 84–89. https://doi.org/10.1109/mcom.2019.1800378

18. Golec, M., Gill, S. S., Bahsoon, R., & Rana, O. (2022, March 1). BioSec: A biometric authentication framework for secure and private communication among edge devices in IoT and industry 4.0. IEEE Consumer Electronics Magazine, 11(2), 51–56. https://doi.org/10.1109/mce.2020.3038040

19. Hossain, M. S., Muhammad, G., Rahman, S. M. M., Abdul, W., Alelaiwi, A., & Alamri, A. (2016, October). Toward end-to-end biometrics-based security for IoT infrastructure. IEEE Wireless Communications, 23(5), 44–51. https://doi.org/10.1109/mwc.2016.7721741

20. Thilagavathi, B., & Suthendran, K. (2018, January 22). Boosting based implementation of biometric authentication in IoT. Journal of Cyber Security and Mobility. https://doi.org/10.13052/2245-1439.7110

21. Gayathri, M., & Malathy, C. (2021, June 30). Fisher-yates chaotic shuffling based visual cryptography scheme for multimodal biometric authentication. Wireless Personal Communications, 127(2), 1587–1614. https://doi.org/10.1007/s11277-021-08707-6.

22. Kolhar, M., Al-Turjman, F., Alameen, A., & Abualhaj, M. M. (2020). A three layered decentralized IoT biometric architecture for city lockdown during COVID-19 outbreak. IEEE Access, 8, 163608–163617. https://doi.org/10.1109/access.2020.3021983.

23. Sharma, P., Kapoor, M., & Dhillon, N. (2016, January 5). Design of biometric authentication system using three basic human traits. International Journal of Science and Research (IJSR), 5(1), 1116–1120. https://doi.org/10.21275/v5i1.12011602.

24. Ebrahimi, S., & Bayat-Sarmadi, S. (2021, July 1). Lightweight fuzzy extractor based on LPN for device and biometric authentication in IoT. IEEE Internet of Things Journal, 8(13), 10706–10713. https://doi.org/10.1109/jiot.2021.3050555.

25. Sharma, N., & Dhiman, P. (2023, May 28). Design and Analysis of Authentication in IoT-based Smart Homes Seventh International Conference on Image Information Processing (ICIIP 2023), 3(3), 203–208. https://doi.org/10.1109/ICIIP61524.2023.10537713.

26. Barros, A., Resque, P., Almeida, J., Mota, R., Oliveira, H., Rosário, D., & Cerqueira, E. (2020, May 21). Data improvement model based on ECG biometric for user authentication and identification. Sensors, 20(10), 2920. https://doi.org/10.3390/s20102920.

27. Karimian, N., Tehranipoor, M., Woodard, D., & Forte, D. (2019). Unlock your heart: Next generation biometric in resource-constrained healthcare systems and IoT. IEEE Access, 7, 49135–49149. https://doi.org/10.1109/access.2019.2910753.

28. Matsui, K. (2017, December). Proposal and implementation of a real-time certification system for smart homes using IoT technology. Energy Procedia, 142, 2027–2034. https://doi.org/10.1016/j.egypro.2017.12.406

29. Duraibi, S., T. Sheldon, F., & Alhamdani, W. (2020, May 31). Voice biometric identity authentication model for IoT devices. International Journal of Security, Privacy and Trust Management, 9(2), 1–10. https://doi.org/10.5121/ijsptm.2020.9201.

30. Abd Elaziz, M., Ouadfel, S., Abd El-Latif, A. A., & Ali Ibrahim, R. (2022, June 22). Feature selection based on modified bio-inspired atomic orbital search using arithmetic optimization and opposite-based learning. Cognitive Computation, 14(6), 2274–2295. https://doi.org/10.1007/s12559-022-10022-6

31. S., S., & Mathew, S. (2016, December 30). Multimodal biometric authentication : Secured encryption of IRIS using fingerprint ID. International Journal on Cryptography and Information Security, 6(3/4), 39–46. https://doi.org/10.5121/ijcis.2016.6404.

32. Sahayini, T., & Manikandan, M. (2016). Enhancing the security of modern ICT systems with multimodal biometric cryptosystems and continuous user authentication. International Journal of Information and Computer Security, 8(1), 55. https://doi.org/10.1504/ijics.2016.075310

33. Grady, X., Mariofanna, M.,& Xie, M (2016). Secure Behavioral biometric authentication using leap motion sensor. 4th International Symposium on Digital Forensic and Security (ISDFS), 8(1). https://doi.org/10.21172/1.81.084.

34. Atas, M. (2017). Hand tremor based biometric recognition using leap motion device. IEEE Access, 5, 23320–23326. https://doi.org/10.1109/access.2017.2764471

35. Kusse, G., & Demissie, T. (2023, May 5). Applications of multimodal biometrics authentication for enhancing the iot security using deep learning. Ethiopian International Journal of Engineering and Technology, 1(1), 1–11. https://doi.org/10.59122/134cfc6.

36. A. Hassen, O., A. Abdulhussein, A., M. Darwish, S., Othman, Z. A., Tiun, S., & A. Lotfy, Y. (2020, October 15). Towards a secure signature scheme based on multimodal biometric technology: Application for IOT blockchain network. Symmetry, 12(10), 1699. https://doi.org/10.3390/sym12101699.

37. Cherifi, F., Amroun, K., & Omar, M. (2021, January 29). Robust multimodal biometric authentication on IoT device through ear shape and arm gesture. Multimedia Tools and Applications, 80(10), 14807–14827. https://doi.org/10.1007/s11042-021-10524-9.

38. Muro-de-la-Herran, A., Garcia-Zapirain, B., & Mendez-Zorrilla, A. (2014, February 19). Gait analysis methods: An overview of wearable and non-wearable systems, highlighting clinical applications. Sensors, 14(2), 3362–3394. https://doi.org/10.3390/s140203362.

39. Fischer, A., & Plamondon, R. (2017, April). Signature verification based on the kinematic theory of rapid human movements. IEEE Transactions on Human-Machine Systems, 47(2), 169–180. https://doi.org/10.1109/thms.2016.2634922

40. Ali, K., Liu, A. X., Wang, W., & Shahzad, M. (2017, May). Recognizing keystrokes using WiFi devices. IEEE Journal on Selected Areas in Communications, 35(5), 1175–1190. https://doi.org/10.1109/jsac.2017.2680998

41. Bhuiyan, M. N., Rahman, M. M., Billah, M. M., & Saha, D. (2021, July 1). Internet of things (IoT): A review of its enabling technologies in healthcare applications, standards protocols, security, and market opportunities. IEEE Internet of Things Journal, 8(13), 10474–10498. https://doi.org/10.1109/jiot.2021.3062630.

42. V S, S. (2019, May 31). A survey paper on fingerprint recognition and cross matching. International Journal for Research in Applied Science and Engineering Technology, 7(5), 573–575. https://doi.org/10.22214/ijraset.2019.5096

43. Calderoni, L., & Magnani, A. (2022, March). The impact of face image compression in future generation electronic identity documents. Forensic Science International: Digital Investigation, 40, 301345. https://doi.org/10.1016/j.fsidi.2022.301345.

44. Ahmed, A. A. (2019, March 10). Future effects and impacts of biometrics integrations on everyday living. Al-Mustansiriyah Journal of Science, 29(3), 139–144. https://doi.org/10.23851/mjs.v29i3.642.

45. Zhang, S., Wang, H., Huang, W., & Zhang, C. (2018, February 3). Combining modified LBP and weighted SRC for palmprint recognition. Signal, Image and Video Processing, 12(6), 1035–1042. https://doi.org/10.1007/s11760-018-1246-4.

46. Gottschlich, C. (2012, April). curved-region-based Ridge frequency estimation and curved gabor filters for fingerprint image enhancement. IEEE Transactions on Image Processing, 21(4), 2220–2227. https://doi.org/10.1109/tip.2011.2170696.

47. Xie, S., Shan, S., Chen, X., & Chen, J. (2010, May). Fusing local patterns of gabor magnitude and phase for face recognition. IEEE Transactions on Image Processing, 19(5), 1349–1361. https://doi.org/10.1109/tip.2010.2041397.

48. Madhusudhan, R., & Mittal, R. (2012). An enhanced biometrics-based remote user authentication scheme using mobile devices. International Journal of Computational Intelligence Studies, 1(4), 333. https://doi.org/10.1504/ijcistudies.2012.050360.

49. Sett, S., & Gupta, H., (2024). A Biometric Security Model for The Enhancement of Data Security. 11th International Conference on Reliability, Infocom Technologies and Optimization (Trends and Future Directions) (ICRITO),https://doi.org/10.1109/ICRITO61523.2024.10522414.

50. Maitra, T., Obaidat, M. S., Amin, R., Islam, S. H., Chaudhry, S. A., & Giri, D. (2016, December 2). A robust ElGamal-based password-authentication protocol using smart card for client-server communication. International Journal of Communication Systems, 30(11). https://doi.org/10.1002/dac.3242.

51. Sharma, N., & Dhiman, P. (2023, October 11). Lightweight privacy preserving scheme for IoT based smart home. Recent Advances in Electrical & Electronic Engineering (Formerly Recent Patents on Electrical & Electronic Engineering), 16. https://doi.org/1 0.2174/012352096526733923092806141 0.

52. Hossain, M. A., & Al Hasan, M. A. (2020, August 24). Improving cloud data security through hybrid verification techniques based on biometrics and encryption systems. International Journal of Computers and Applications, 44(5), 455–464. https://doi.org/1 0.1080/1206212x.2020.1809177.

53. Moujahdi, C., Bebis, G., Ghouzali, S., & Rziza, M. (2014, August). Fingerprint shell: Secure representation of fingerprint template. Pattern Recognition Letters, 45, 189–196. https://doi.org/10.1016/j.patrec.2014.04.001.

54. Iwai, R., & Yoshimura, H. (2011). Matching accuracy analysis of fingerprint templates generated by data processing method using the fractional Fourier transform. International Journal of Communications, Network and System Sciences, 04(01), 24–32. https://doi.org/10.4236/ijcns.2011.41003.

55. Thilakanathan, D., Chen, S., Nepal, S., & Calvo, R. (2016, April). SafeProtect: Controlled data sharing with user-defined policies in cloud-based collaborative environment. IEEE Transactions on Emerging Topics in Computing, 4(2), 301–315. https://doi.org/10.1109/tetc.2015.2502429.

56. Cui, Z., Qi, W., & Liu, Y. (2020, December 1). A fast image template matching algorithm based on normalized cross correlation. Journal of Physics: Conference Series, 1693(1), 012163. https://doi.org/10.1088/1742-6596/1693/1/012163.

57. Ganapathi, I. I., Prakash, S., Dave, I. R., Joshi, P., Ali, S. S., & Shrivastava, A. M. (2018, August 31). Ear recognition in 3D using 2D curvilinear features. IET Biometrics, 7(6), 519–529. https://doi.org/10.1049/iet-bmt.2018.5064.

58. Tulyakov, S., Farooq, F., Mansukhani, P., & Govindaraju, V. (2007, December). Symmetric hash functions for secure fingerprint biometric systems. Pattern Recognition Letters, 28(16), 2427–2436. https://doi.org/10.1016/j.patrec.2007.08.008.

59. Feng, J., & Jain, A. K. (2011, February). Fingerprint reconstruction: From minutiae to phase. IEEE Transactions on Pattern Analysis and Machine Intelligence, 33(2), 209–223. https://doi.org/10.1109/tpami.2010.77.

60. Jain, A. K., Nandakumar, K., & Nagar, A. (2008). Biometric template security. EURASIP Journal on Advances in Signal Processing, 2008(1), 579416. https://doi.org/10.1155/2008/579416.

61. Jin, Z., Hwang, J. Y., Lai, Y. L., Kim, S., & Teoh, A. B. J. (2018, February). Ranking-based locality sensitive hashing-enabled cancelable biometrics: Index-of-max hashing. IEEE Transactions on Information Forensics and Security, 13(2), 393–407. https://doi.org/10.1109/tifs.2017.2753172.

62. Cappelli, R., Ferrara, M., & Maltoni, D. (2015, June). Large-scale fingerprint identification on GPU. Information Sciences, 306, 1–20. https://doi.org/10.1016/j.ins.2015.02.016.

63. Nanni, L., & Lumini, A. (2008, November). Local binary patterns for a hybrid fingerprint matcher. Pattern Recognition, 41(11), 3461–3466. https://doi.org/10.1016/j.patcog.2008.05.013.

64. Jin, Z., Lim, M. H., Teoh, A. B. J., & Goi, B. M. (2014, June). A non-invertible randomized graph-based hamming embedding for generating cancelable fingerprint template. Pattern Recognition Letters, 42, 137–147.https://doi.org/10.1016/j.patrec.2014.02.011.

Index

Note: *Italic* and **Bold** page numbers refer to *figures* and **tables.**